Modern International Negotiation

By ARTHUR LALL

Modern

International Negotiation

PRINCIPLES AND PRACTICE

Columbia University Press

NEW YORK AND LONDON 1966

Arthur Lall, formerly Ambassador to the United Nations and Head of the Indian Delegation, is Adjunct Professor of Government at the School of International Affairs, Columbia University.

To the Memory of Dag Hammarskjöld

Foreword

THIS BOOK by Professor Arthur Lall of the School of International Affairs on the principles and practice of modern international negotiation is the fruit of the rich experience of the author as a principal participant in innumerable international conferences and vital negotiations for close to two decades since World War II. As an Indian diplomat he engaged at top level in negotiations on major issues dealt with by the United Nations as well as in other negotiations in which his country was involved.

Professor Lall describes the numerous forms of negotiation now available to governments, processes and tactics of negotiation, and the role of national interests, whether narrowly or broadly conceived.

The spectacular growth of interdependence in modern life, expressing itself in a vast increase in the number of related, combined, and common interests of nations, has in turn multiplied the tasks of negotiation. Nations no longer live alone. If they try to do so they only intensify the need for negotiations by other parties on the problems created by their effort at isolation. Fortunately, most nations do not try to escape the reality or the consequences of their growing interdependence, and as a result they participate in the endless round of conferences and negotiations necessary to the rationalization of their interdependence. The disasters of World War II and threats of nuclear annihilation have greatly broadened the institutions, the forms, and the scope of negotiation.

Traditional forms of diplomacy have not disappeared in our generation, but they operate alongside new expressions of multilateral and public diplomacy which, because of their own conspicuous character, have sometimes obscured the use of the older forms. In fact, there is no essential contradiction among the varied forms of diplomacy. On the contrary, the diplomatic efforts aiming at effective results require the utilization of both the older and the newer forms, sometimes simultaneously, sometimes consecutively, and sometimes alternately. Flexibility in the use of diplomatic methods increases the prospect of effective negotiation.

In his book Professor Lall selects for treatment many of the major issues of the last twenty years involving multilateral and bilateral methods, public diplomacy and quiet diplomacy, conference or parliamentary diplomacy, as well as combinations of these techniques.

The position that a nation may be expected to take on negotiations in a rather broad spectrum of issues is determined by its history and its contemporary status. For example, East-West and North-South tensions have affected nearly all negotiations in recent years. The relation of the two superpowers to each other and to other countries, the deep differences of the developed and the developing countries in such matters as trade and economic aid, the readjustment of the policies of metropolitan powers after the liquidation of empires, the persistence and strength of anticolonial attitudes on the part of the new nations, the understandable interest of all nations in disarmament despite the fact that relatively few have substantial military establishments—these are some of the major interests of nations that are deeply reflected in their negotiations.

Professor Lall describes how, when, and why concessions are made within the process of negotiation to achieve results, and the factors that sometimes obstruct progress. He counsels patience in negotiation, and indicates that some of the major issues confronting our generation will require many years of continuing negotiation to reach what may be regarded as satisfactory solutions.

The history of negotiation is not alone the clash, coincidences, or interplay of national interests, but involves also the individual performance of the negotiators and those behind them within the government who give them support or determine their directives. Individual performance weighs heavily in the success or failure of diplomacy. Despite its numerous frustrations, modern negotiation is filled with many illustrations of competent and statesmanlike efforts on the part of those involved.

In illustration of the many forms and processes of negotiation, Professor Lall presents a highly useful analysis of the major issues of concern to our generation. He presents the story in fascinating detail and sometimes reflects his own role in the diplomatic kaleidoscope.

The book was prepared and published as part of the research program of the Columbia University School of International Affairs.

ANDREW W. CORDIER, DEAN
SCHOOL OF INTERNATIONAL AFFAIRS

Columbia University in the City of New York
March, 1966

Preface

INTERNATIONAL situations and disputes that become actual subjects of negotiation are extremely complex. Each has a large number of facets of varied and often shifting significance, and all those facets must be given appropriate consideration.

Correspondingly intricate and complex are the attitudes of states as participants in negotiation, whether or not they are directly involved in the situation or dispute in question. In one and the same negotiation a variety of attitudes and factors may emanate from one participant, and these attitudes and factors do not always work consistently in a given direction. On the contrary, more often than not there are pulls which are so divergent that they result in movements that are almost contradictory. Consequently, when we examine the changing facets of a dispute or situation in negotiation we frequently find the attitudes of one participant emerging in differing manifestations. In the final analysis, the direction in which a particular participant will go—and will try to push the whole negotiation—will be determined by the combined effects of all its varied postures and their relative firmness.

Because of these realities of negotiation, the attitudes of a state in regard to a given situation or dispute may fall into several categories. In order to present the complex nature of the negotiating process with accuracy, it is frequently necessary in this study to take up discussion of the same issue under different headings. For example, the topic of disarmament negotiations appears in several chapters, including, among others, those titled The Primary Bases, Vital Interests, and Deterrent Forces. This is unavoidable, for to treat of an important international situation or dispute under a single heading would present not only an oversimplified but a misleading version of the many-sidedness of international negotiation.

I thank all my colleagues in the world of diplomacy for their cumulative contribution to the background of this book. Without innumerable contacts, discussions, negotiations, and much pleasant sociability with them over the years, it could never have been conceived or written.

And without direct encouragement and practical facilities to embark upon such a venture, I could not have progressed in my endeavor. These invaluable supports were supplied by Andrew W. Cordier, presently Dean of the School of International Affairs, Columbia University, and previously a colleague for many years in United Nations diplomacy. I am deeply indebted to him, and thank him also for the stimulating and distinguished Foreword he has written.

I thank, too, Steven Muller, Vice President of Cornell University, and the Cornell Center for International Studies, for making it possible for me to avail myself of the facilities provided by the School of International Affairs at Columbia.

Leo Melania and Wilder Foote, both of the United Nations Secretariat until recently, very kindly read the manuscript and made most valuble suggestions. I acknowledge also, with thanks, the intelligent and energetic help which was always available from Benon Sevan, my research assistant.

Finally, neither thanks nor acknowledgment can express my indebtedness to my wife, Betty Goetz Lall, for her encouragement and assistance.

ARTHUR LALL

New York, N. Y.
March, 1966

Contents

CHAPTER ONE

The Era of Negotiation

THE PROCEDURES and forums for modern international negotiation are numerous and varied. They are increasing in complexity year by year, and their forms and functions are evolving in adaptation to the changing needs of a rapidly expanding community of nations.

Since the end of World War II, conference diplomacy in particular has significantly widened and diversified the approaches to international negotiation. It has, for one thing, stimulated bilateral diplomacy. The fact that a party to a dispute or situation is now able to bring its cause to an international forum frequently operates to induce countries to take bilateral diplomacy much more seriously than they did before the era of continuous opportunities to resort to conference negotiation.

In former times a dispute or situation was, or could be considered, the private affair of the states involved; today there is little privacy possible in international disputes and situations. Such differences among nations have become a matter of concern to the whole world community. The result is that the disputants must either make a serious effort to resolve the issue between or among themselves, or be willing to deal with their peers at the United Nations or in other conference forums. The pressures to negotiate solutions to disputes and situations are now much more pervasive and broad-based than they were before World War II. In general, such pressures are unlikely to abate in the foreseeable future.

In this era it is almost universally agreed that where there is a conflict of interests between states, the only practicable alternative to eventual armed strife is to resort to one or another, or successively several, of the procedures or forms of negotiation. Yet it is occasionally said—perhaps as a holdover from the previous era—that even in potentially dangerous situations both negotiation and armed conflict can be avoided by the interplay of power balances. The post-World War II issue of Germany—where influence is about equally balanced between the Eastern and the Western powers—is often cited in support of this view. It is alleged that in the past few years there have been no negotiations in regard to Germany and yet there has been no armed conflict. However, a cursory examination of this argument will expose its variance with the facts.

While it is true that there has been no armed conflict in Central Europe over the German question—using that phrase to signify the absence of security and tranquillity created by the division of Germany—it is simply not true that there have been no negotiations on the issue.

On the general international level, hardly a six-month period passes in which the great powers do not make some direct or indirect effort to resolve the question. Their approaches are negotiatory in character. On the same multilateral level, a number of international negotiations which have taken place or are in train among the great powers have had to do, at least indirectly, with the German question as we have defined it. When the Eighteen-Nation Committee on Disarmament or the General Assembly of the United Nations or the NATO Council considers a proposal for the reduction of tension in Europe, such as the Rapacki Plan, the organization concerned is negotiating a facet of the German question. This is equally true when those negotiating bodies consider proposals for a nonaggression pact between the NATO and Warsaw Pact powers, or for the nonproliferation of nuclear weapons. Processes of this kind are almost constantly in progress.

On the specific level, numerous aspects of the situation have been and are being negotiated by the Germans themselves. West Berlin's Mayor Willy Brandt, in a statement of December 29, 1964, was reported to have said that the year 1963 saw the end of the acute East-West crisis in Berlin which had begun in 1958 with the Soviet ultimatum that the Western powers move out of the city. Mayor Brandt advocated a continuation of his policy of small steps toward the East German Government to deal with the situation created by the erection of the Berlin wall.[1] He undoubtedly had in mind the successful negotiations which had taken place to permit Berliners to visit each other across the wall and to increase the flow of trade and cultural exchange. Negotiations of this kind are engaged in directly between the West and East German authorities, and are constantly, even if slightly, altering the nature of the German question. Although there has been no success in negotiating the major issues, some of the small irritants have been partially smoothed away.

The German situation exemplifies the truism that negotiation is invariably an enormously difficult task. The outsider and even the informed newspaper or periodical writer often speak glibly of the failure of a negotiation. This is an unfortunate habit of thought and speech. International negotiations should not be expected to succeed in one, two, or three rounds of discussion. Most issues require years of consideration, during which time a variety of procedures have to be tried. The outcome might then be some amelioration of the situation, with increased hope for a future settlement.

Is so protracted a process worth while? The alternative in our age is conflict of a type which can well escalate into nuclear devastation. Thinking men of all nations rule out this alternative. It is important, of course, to speed up the processes of negotiation, and indeed in certain crises negotiations have progressed with remarkable speed. The 1962 Caribbean crisis was substantially resolved in a matter of months. The 1954 negotiations at Geneva on Indochina were also concluded in a few months.

The surrounding factors largely determine the speed of negotiation. If certain negotiations are extremely protracted, generally the main reason is that an awareness of impending crisis has either not developed or has not been operative long enough to produce a sense of urgency. The inconclusiveness of the disarmament talks of our era results from precisely this failure of awareness. At a party which I gave for my fellow diplomats when I was negotiating for India in 1962 and 1963 at the Geneva Conference of the Eighteen-Nation Committee on Disarmament, a senior United States official expressed this point. He said to the other eight or ten guests, among whom were several delegates of the Communist countries, "It is obvious that we must have disarmament. The question is whether we will be wise enough to get there now or after World War III. Sometimes I think we behave as though we will choose the hard way. After World War III the issues which today create such enormous difficulties will be solved in a few hours around the table."

A sense of crisis, however, is not the only motivation for negotiation. Better reasons are provided, on occasion, by far-sighted statesmanship. In 1962 it appeared that President Kennedy and Prime Minister Khrushchev were displaying that kind of statesmanship in their approaches toward disarmament. Other examples of the far-sighted management of national affairs are the negotiations that take place when nations seek to establish bilateral or multilateral trade agreements, or when they attempt to promote cooperation among themselves in economic and social matters and in cultural and scientific exchange.

However, it will be a rare conjunction of events when all the major parties to the central problems of our era direct their affairs with far-sightedness, and when the most important international conferences are held for reasons other than settling or avoiding disputes, or steering the world through dangerous situations. For that reason, and because nearly all present-day international negotiation is concerned with the alleviation of world tensions, this study and the definitions and conclusions it attempts to formulate will for the most part be directed to those aspects of negotiation which are impelled by the search for peaceful methods of settling international disputes and situations.

CHAPTER TWO

Defining International Negotiation

INTERNATIONAL NEGOTIATION is the process of consideration of an international dispute or situation by peaceful means, other than judicial or arbitral processes, with a view to promoting or reaching among the parties concerned or interested some understanding, amelioration, adjustment, or settlement of the dispute or situation.

This definition suggests the inclusion of all forms of discussion, meeting, conference, mediation, conciliation, good offices, and other direct or indirect liaison among the parties concerned. It is wider than the scope of the word as it is used in Article 33 of the United Nations Charter, which reads:

The parties to any dispute, the continuance of which is likely to endanger the maintenance of international peace and security, shall, first of all, seek a solution by negotiation, enquiry, mediation, conciliation, arbitration, judicial settlement, resort to regional agencies or arrangements, or other peaceful means of their own choice.

The Outline of Basic Provisions of a Treaty on General and Complete Disarmament in a Peaceful World, presented to the Conference of the Eighteen-Nation Committee on Disarmament on April 18, 1962 by the United States, uses similar phraseology:

Peaceful Settlement of Disputes: The parties of the Treaty would utilize all appropriate processes for the peaceful settlement of all disputes which might arise between them and any other state, whether or not a Party to the Treaty, including negotiation, inquiry, mediation, conciliation, arbitration, judicial settlement, recourse to regional agencies or arrangements, submission to the Security Council or the General Assembly of the United Nations, or other peaceful means of their choice.[1]

Every form of conscious effort for the peaceful settlement, adjustment, amelioration, or better understanding of international situations or disputes is in essence a negotiation—except, of course, recourse to a judicial organ or tribunal. Judicial settlements are different in kind from negotiated settlements. The essence of negotiation is to arrive, as nearly as possible, at agreement among the parties. This is not the case in settlements through judicial decisions. Just as under municipal law judicial proceedings, whether civil or criminal, will not necessarily end a blood feud,[2] so too in international relations recourse to judicial proceedings and judicial findings do not necessarily bring settlements. The opinions handed down by the International Court of Justice with respect to the status of South-West Africa, and the steps that are required by the Union of South Africa to comply with the terms of that status, have not resulted in any action by the Union Government. No settlement has been effected.[3]

Appropriate to this point is the United Nations Charter provision regarding compliance with decisions of the International Court of Justice. In the first paragraph of Article 94 of the Charter, "Each Member of the United Nations undertakes to comply with decisions of the International Court of Justice in any case to which it is a party." [4] The second paragraph of the same Article provides for the possibility of action, not excluding enforcement by the Security Council, should a party to a case fail to carry out its obligations under a judgment rendered by the Court. The Charter recognizes that a judgment of the International Court of Justice might fail to bring about a settlement of even a legal issue. This provision has not been put to the test because of the virtual nonexistence of important international disputes or situations on which the Court has been asked to pronounce judgment.

Since settlement by agreement or acquiescence, or a step in that direction, is the purpose of negotiation, judicial and arbitral proceedings must necessarily be excluded from our study. This omission of judicial and arbitral proceedings will not significantly narrow the consideration of international disputes and situations. Our age is not one of recourse to international judicial organs for the settlement of such issues. There is today a certain degree of disillusionment, or at any rate disappointment, regarding the capacity of international decisions of an arbitral or judicial character to affect the course of international relations, especially when issues of peace and war are involved.

The period from the 1899 Hague Convention, through the Covenant of the League of Nations, to the close of the pre-World War II era, was particularly rich in the formulation of international treaties and conventions providing for the judicial or arbitral settlement of disputes. The Covenant of the League of Nations might be seen as typifying the approach of that era. It was, moreover, the most significant of all instruments in the field of international settlement.

Not once in its twenty-six articles, or in its preamble, did the League Covenant refer to negotiation or to mediation, conciliation, or other peaceful means of the parties' choice, as does the Charter of the United Nations. Furthermore, the purposes of the League did not specifically include the practicing of tolerance and the living together of nations as "good neighbors," which are the United Nations Charter's ends. Nor was it so comprehensive as to take into consideration not only disputes among states but also international situations (as does the United Nations Charter), and it did not speak of the *adjustment* of such disputes or situations. We might note, too, in the differences of approach between the League Covenant and the United Nations Charter, that the former did not set out to make the League "a centre for harmonizing the actions of nations" (Article 1.4 of the United Nations Charter).

Virtually the entire emphasis of the Covenant was on the settlement of international disputes by arbitration or judicial processes.[5] The only alternative specifically proposed was an inquiry by the Council of the League, or, in those cases in which the dispute was not submitted to arbitration or judicial settlement, a Council effort to effect a settlement of the dispute.[6] Such disputes (namely, only those which had not been submitted to arbitration or judicial settlement) could also come before the League Assembly. There was no provision in the Covenant under which the League could try to effect settlement if arbitration or judicial process failed.

The United Nations Charter does not vest the same strong faith in judicial processes. It recognizes that disputes and other dangerous situations among sovereign states stem basically from political rather than legal causes, and that all processes of adjustment and settlement by peaceful means must be encouraged and tried.[7] Indeed, the judicial process is relegated to an unsure and secondary position. When (in accordance with Article 36 of the United Nations Charter) the Security Council decides to recommend appropriate procedures or methods of adjustment, taking into consideration any procedures for the settlement of the dispute which have already been adopted by the parties, it "should also take into consideration that legal disputes should as a general rule be referred by the parties to the International Court of Justice in accordance with the provisions of the Statute of the Court." [8] This phraseology uses the verb "should" and not "shall," and it interpolates the phrase "as a general rule," all of which reinforces the discretion of the Security Council to refrain from recommending recourse to the Court even in a legal dispute. Of course, disputes or situations which are not primarily legal—although legal issues might be involved—do not at all come within the purview of the rather uncertain reference given by this article of the Charter to the International Court.

The whole concept of the United Nations Charter, then, is to highlight nonjudicial methods of adjustment or settlement of both disputes and situations. This is both a result and a reinforcement of the fact that this is an era of negotiation (in the broadest sense of the word) of international issues, rather than an era of judicial or arbitral settlements. Whereas since World War II, no significant international dispute involving issues of war and peace has been settled by referral to the Court, negotiation has played and continues to play an active, indispensable, and major role in the preservation of world peace and in the attempts to move toward a world based on a system of international order and amity.

Negotiation, admittedly, is a difficult process, as the etymology of the word indicates. Composed of the Latin roots *neg* (not) and *otium* (ease or leisure), the word "negotiate" came into the English language in the year 1599. Almost four hundred years later, in the waning half of the twentieth century, "negotiation" is fully as ease- or leisure-denying as it was when the Romans conjoined the root words to fashion their "negotiare." [9]

Two thoughts are central to the meaning of the word as it is used today. First, a peaceful process or method is to be adopted, although no single one is prescribed. Second, the objective is agreement, compromise, or settlement. It should be observed that an agreement may be reached at one of many different levels. There may be agreed understanding of a situation and therefore a more healthy preservation of the status quo, or there may be an amelioration of the situation or dispute among those concerned; there may be agreed adjustments, or, at the optimum, an agreed solution or settlement. Similarly, a compromise can be achieved at one of various levels. The levels of compromise, and for that matter of the settlement of an issue, need not necessarily conform fully to preconceived legal or schematic norms. Settlements in international affairs follow their own patterns and laws, based on the premises of each case. In spite of similarities, each international issue tends to be sui generis.

Current dictionary definitions of "negotiation" contain numerous possibilities, all peaceful and nonjuridical, and thus generally support the wide sense in which we use the term in this study. The various nonjudicial methods of peaceful settlement in use among nations reflect these possibilities and flexibilities.

The Methods of Negotiation

In addition to negotiations proper (discussions or other forms of talks among the parties directly concerned), the Charter in Article 33 mentions (a) inquiry, (b) mediation, (c) conciliation, (d) resort to regional agencies or arrangements, or "other peaceful means of their [the parties'] own choice."

Among other peaceful means, several varieties of techniques are in use:

(e) Discussion or talk among the parties directly concerned— negotiation par excellence according to common consent and the assumptions in the United Nations Charter.

(f) Utilization of the good offices of one or more states or individuals. In the gamut of negotiations, this method stands close to mediation and conciliation.

(g) Pourparlers, which are less formal than full-fledged negotiations.

(h) Conferences of agreed states (ad hoc conferences), or utilization of existing conference mechanisms. These are methods of multilateral negotiation not necesarily restricted to the countries directly involved.

INQUIRY AND INVESTIGATION. The Charter of the United Nations uses two words, not necessarily with precisely one meaning but with one intent, for the process of the first examination of a situation or dispute. The two words are "inquiry" (Article 33) and "investigation" (Article 34). Investigation suggests the more probing process, backed by authority. Both words are used in the context of Chapter VI, which is confined to "The Pacific Settlement of Disputes" and does not include provisions for enforcement action. What is intended in the Charter is a process of peaceful exploring of the facts and nature of a dispute or situation with a view to facilitating its pacific settlement.

The parallelism of the concepts of "inquiry" and "investigation" is borne out also by the provisions of the Articles of the 1907 Hague Convention for the Pacific Settlement of International Disputes. The Convention provides that Commissions of Inquiry carry out investigations.

Article 9 reads:

> . . . the Contracting Powers deem it expedient and desirable that the parties . . . should, as far as circumstances allow, institute an International Commission of Inquiry, to facilitate a solution of these disputes by elucidating the facts by means of an impartial and conscientious investigation.

Whether these processes in fact assist in promoting amelioration or settlement of a situation or dispute can be assessed from an examination of some actual cases of investigation and inquiry.

Differences arose in 1957 and 1958 between Israel and Jordan over the Mount Scopus area, which lies near the city of Jerusalem and is surrounded by Jordanian territory. These differences led to events illustrative of the way in which both inquiry and investigation may contribute to the process of negotiation.

The Mount Scopus area had been demilitarized by a special agreement of July 7, 1948, which preceded the General Armistice Agreement of April 3, 1949 concluded between Israel and Jordan. In November 1957, the Jordanian authorities objected to the inclusion of gasoline in the fortnightly Israeli supply convoys to the Jewish area of Mount Scopus, on the grounds that the supply of this item was not consistent with the provisions of related agreements concerning convoys to Mount Scopus, and thus compromised the demilitarized nature of the area.

The machinery of the United Nations Truce Supervision Organization was available on the spot, but could not resolve the dispute. Secretary-General Dag Hammarskjöld, realizing that the situation could flare into hostilities between Israel and Jordan, which in turn could lead to general violence in the Middle East, personally "called in" on the area in one of his characteristically energetic ventures in quiet personal diplomacy. From December 1 to 7, 1957, he had talks with the Jordanian and Israeli Prime Ministers concerning Mount Scopus. He also took advantage of his visit to discuss with the Foreign Ministers of Israel and Jordan, and of Lebanon and Syria as well, certain problems connected with the authority of the United Nations Truce Supervision Organization in the area.

This inquiring around by Hammarskjöld led successively to the resumption of Israeli convoy trips to the Mount Scopus area; the appointment of a personal representative (Ambassador Francesco Urrutia of Colombia) of the Secretary-General to follow up on the discussions; and the dispatch of other United Nations missions to the area, culminating in a visit of investigation [10] by Andrew W. Cordier in June 1958 that resulted in another step toward a stable pacification of the region—the reopening of the road to the Arab village of Issawiya, which Israeli patrols had closed off for a time.

Through this series of inquiries and investigations conducted by high level United Nations personnel, the immediate "situation" was peacefully adjusted. The investigations and inquiries, involving all the parties, were in effect a round in the sporadic process of negotiation which, together with other measures such as the deployment of the Truce Supervision Organization (a continuing machinery for the implementation of the provisions of the General Armistice Agreements mainly through negotiation and adjustment), helps to preserve the still precarious peace of the Middle East.

Properly launched and conducted, observation groups, inquiries, and investigations are often appropriate deployments of the resources of diplomacy and negotiation. They can open the way to direct negotiations among the primary parties, and often (as was the case in the Mount Scopus incidents) they institute indirect exchanges which assist in the attainment of a degree of pacification.

This view is not negated by the fact that inquiries or investigations do not always achieve their purpose, any more than do other techniques of negotiation. There certainly have been unsuccessful investigations and inquiries.

One such case was the investigation which the Secretary-General of the United Nations was asked to arrange in pursuance of the fourth operative paragraph of the first resolution [11] adopted by the second Emergency Special Session of the United Nations General Assembly, which had been called to consider the Hungarian situation. The Secretary-General was to investigate the situation caused by foreign intervention in Hungary, to observe that situation directly through representatives named by him, and to report thereon to the General Assembly at the earliest moment. On November 16, 1956 the Secretary-General announced to the General Assembly that he had appointed a group of three persons, consisting of Judge Oscar Gundersen of Norway, Dr. Alberto Lleras of Colombia, and the writer, to investigate the situation in Hungary.[12] In accordance with this mandate, Oscar Gundersen, Alberto Lleras, and I studied the facts of the Hungarian situation from all the documentation obtainable in New York. We also asked the Hungarian Foreign Minister to let us visit his country, but the reply was in the negative. Events moved fast, and could be only very imperfectly observed from outside Hungary. Much less could they be investigated.

After some weeks, during which our effort to intensify our observation had failed, my colleagues and I wrote a brief report indicating what we had attempted to do, and admitting that we had not been able to carry out the investigation. However, the results of the abortive Hungarian investigation were not entirely negative, for failure to carry through the investigation and thereby to move directly toward amelioration of the situation did not rule out the likelihood that the creation and availability of investigatory machinery exercised a restraining influence on the parties involved.

MEDIATION.   Mediation is the injection of a third state or states, individual or individuals, at the request of or with the consent of the parties to an international dispute or situation, with a view to assisting in or obtaining its settlement, adjustment, or amelioration. Such efforts of states or individuals are as old as politics itself—and perhaps even older, for the idea of mediation is embedded in most early religious traditions. Mediation is a process which possesses one of the basic attributes of negotiation, namely, it is a peaceful method. The Hague Convention of 1907, which gives mediation and good offices primacy among the methods of peaceful settlement, is designated the "Convention for the Pacific Settlement of International Disputes." The pacific character of mediation will come out clearly as our study progresses, but here we might give an illustration of it.

In 1962 Ambassador Ellsworth Bunker of the United States, at the request of Secretary-General U Thant, "acted as mediator and, on the basis of certain proposals put forward by him, an agreement was concluded," [13] between Indonesia and the Netherlands on the question of West Irian (West New Guinea), which for some nine years had been a vexatious and dangerous international issue left unsettled at the time when Indonesia gained its independence in December 1949.

As this instance shows, mediation also possesses the other basic attribute of negotiation—that its goal must be the adjustment, amelioration, or resolving of the situation or dispute. The concordance of mediation with this requirement has been confirmed in Article 4 of the Hague Convention of 1907, with states, "The part of the mediator consists in reconciling the opposing claims and appeasing the feelings of resentment which may have arisen between the States at variance."

In fact, both the peaceful character of the mediator's duties and their focus upon the resolving of the situation are brought out by the Hague Convention's definition. We are, thus, justified in including mediation among the possible courses open to states in the practice of negotiation.

CONCILIATION. As a method of international diplomacy and negotiation, conciliation is the opposite of condemnation. The latter may have the effect, in international affairs as in personal relations, of hardening positions and thereby arresting the possibilities of movement toward the resolving of difficulties. Conciliation has played and continues to play a role of significance in relations among states.

An important case in point occurred in 1956, during the events following the armed attacks against Egypt in the Suez area. While completely sympathizing with Egypt and determined to do what was possible to assist her in her plight, India was not in favor of rushing headlong into a United Nations condemnation of the British, French, or Israeli actions. India counseled restraint, and welcomed the fact that there was full support for this approach from the United States delegation. Between the United States and India, with other friends, it proved possible to persuade the sorely provoked countries of the Middle East, in spite of their understandable ire, not to insist on condemnatory resolutions. The Egyptian leaders exhorted their Arab neighbors to accept the counsel of moderation. This is the background of nearly a score of resolutions adopted by the General Assembly in quick succession that avoided any condemnation of the aggressors against Egypt. Had the General Assembly adopted the seemingly more logical course of condemnation, it might well have provoked intransigence on the part of those who committed the aggression.

It was, I believe, mainly this instance, in which he himself played so distinguished and pioneering a role, that Hammarskjöld had in mind when he wrote: "If properly used, the United Nations can serve a diplomacy of reconciliation better than other instruments available to Member States." [14]

The value of conciliation as a form of current international negotiation can be seen clearly when we observe how events can develop when it is not employed. We return to the year 1956 and the Hungarian matter. The Indian delegation at the United Nations tried to work for the same restraint, the same approach of avoiding condemnation, that helped in the case of Egypt. When asked to go along with other countries in the drafting of condemnatory resolutions, it drew attention to that case. It was told, "Oh, the Russians are much worse than the British and the French. How can we treat them in the same way!"

It was difficult for the Indian Delegation to see that the attitude of conciliation should fluctuate according to the identification of the aggressor or the degree of reprehensibility of the deed. And to most Asian and African countries, the planned assault on Egypt was an even more fit subject for condemnation than the events that had occurred in Hungary. Admittedly, the Western countries were entitled to a different comparative assessment of the two situations. However, the insistence on immediate and continuing condemnation in the Hungarian case extinguished any chance that the United Nations could play a beneficial role in the interest of Hungary.

Generally speaking, and conceding imperfections in execution, much of the effort of the nonaligned countries in today's diplomacy is directed toward conciliation. This activity involves deliberation, discussion, and the sifting of alternatives so as to find, for the particular issue or situation concerned, the most feasible approach to peaceful adjustment or settlement.

There have also been moves within the United Nations to create channels of conciliation on a formal basis. Part B of a comprehensive resolution adopted during the Third Session of the General Assembly,[15] recommended to the Security Council that as an integral part of its procedures for the pacific settlement of disputes it should attempt to get the parties to agree that one of the members of the Security Council should act as rapporteur or conciliator to assist the process of settlement. In this connection, the resolution of the Assembly drew on the League of Nations' experience, stating the following in its consideranda:

Noting the experience of the League of Nations, which it has caused to be studied, whereby cases were presented to the Council of the League of Nations by a rapporteur who had the functions of a conciliator, and that this practice allowed private conversations among the parties and the rapporteur and avoided the crystallization of views that tends to result from taking a stated public position.

This was a laudable effort, but the resolution has remained a dead letter. It has failed because it attempted to make too formal and automatic a procedure which essentially calls for a quieter tone and a degree of negotiating subtlety which so resolute an arrangement tends to stifle. Moreover, the reference to the League practice was inept. It overlooked—as was understandable in the first few years of the existence of the United Nations—that the whole concept of action through the League was more rigidly formalistic than the much more flexible approaches provided in the Charter of the United Nations.

Similarly, the panel of persons nominated by member states—in terms of Part D of the resolution—has remained a paper exercise. Few states bother to make nominations, and the panel is not used. The selection of persons by the Secretary-General and by the organs of the United Nations to perform negotiatory functions under the terms of the resolutions of the General Assembly or other bodies has not been made through this panel. Here again, the approach was too abstract and formalistic. The essence of conciliation is that it should be employed at the right time, with diplomatic skill, and on those issues for which the offer of a soothing poultice might be acceptable.

It is not only at the United Nations that we come across conciliation as a vehicle of negotiation. There is, for example, the General Convention of Inter-American Conciliation, signed in Washington on January 5, 1929. [16] Its thirteen articles set out a process of inquiry and conciliation.

RESORT TO REGIONAL AGENCIES OR ARRANGEMENTS. The most active regional arrangements for the settlement of disputes and situations are those in the Western Hemisphere, which began in the latter half of the nineteenth century and crystallized shortly after the creation of the United Nations in the Inter-American Treaty of Reciprocal Assistance, 1947 (commonly known as the Rio Treaty), the Charter of the Organization of American States adopted at Bogota in 1948, and the American Treaty of Pacific Settlement, 1948 (the Pact of Bogota).

(The arrangements created by the aforementioned international agreements, when they come fully into force, extinguish the procedures of the Convention of Inter-American Conciliation, 1929, together with those in the Additional Protocol (1933) to the Convention—the effect of the latter being to permit the constitution of commissions of inquiry and conciliation in advance of the actual disputes.)

The peaceful procedures prescribed in Article 21 of the Charter of the OAS are practically identical with those contained in Article 33 of the United Nations Charter. In other words, they are procedures which are characterizable as types of negotiation. The same is true of the procedures prescribed in the American Treaty of Pacific Settlement, 1948.

The articles of the Inter-American Treaty of Reciprocal Assistance (the Treaty of Rio of 1947), read with those of the American Treaty of Pacific Settlement, are, in some respects, more activist than Chapter VI of the United Nations Charter providing for the pacific settlement of disputes. However, the American States are fully aware of, and have subscribed to, the interdiction contained in Article 53 of the United Nations Charter on enforcement action by regional agencies or regional arrangements without authorization of the Security Council of the United Nations. Therefore, it is correct to conclude that under the regional arrangements for the American States we are, in effect, largely left with peaceful processes on the lines of those specifically catalogued in Article 33 of the United Nations Charter. Apart from arbitration and judicial settlement, these are processes of negotiation.

Under the terms of Chapter VI of the United Nations Charter, regional arrangements and agencies are listed among those procedures which the parties to a dispute shall "first of all" [17] seek to utilize. If the parties fail to settle the dispute by these first priority methods, "they shall refer it to the Security Council." [18] The Council will then make a finding as to whether the continuance of the dispute is in fact likely to endanger the maintenance of international peace and security. If the finding is in the affirmative, the Security Council will recommend appropriate procedures or methods of adjustment or settlement. [19]

The recourse to regional arrangements or agencies, unless it resolves the dispute, may be a prelude to the application of those further peaceful processes by the Security Council which, for the most part, are processes of negotiation. This is not an overlapping or duplication. It is based on the sound view that a family quarrel sometimes cannot be solved within the family and must be taken to a wider and more detached forum.

DISCUSSIONS AMONG THE PARTIES DIRECTLY CONCERNED. Earlier in this chapter we listed four peaceful methods of settlement or adjustment of disputes and situations among nations, other than those mentioned in Article 33 of the United Nations Charter. The first of these is direct discussion among the parties concerned. Direct peaceful exchanges among the parties to a dispute or situation, with a view to settlement or adjustment, is the very essence of negotiation. It is to this form of activity that the United Nations Charter directs attention when it uses the word "negotiation" in Article 33.

Those who have spent years in the general field of international negotiation would, I believe, agree that for a large proportion of disputes or situations between states the most productive form of negotiation is direct discussion among the parties concerned. Two recent examples may be cited.

One is provided by the unusual form of chairmanship at the Conference of the Eighteen-Nation Committee on Disarmament.[20] Although the Committee is not too large to be a forum for intensive negotiations, and although peripheral to such conferences there are many opportunities for bilateral discussions, some of the participating nations (particularly Canada and India) suggested informally, before the Conference, that the representative of the United States and the Soviet Union should be cochairmen. In this way it was sought to create an institutional arrangement whereby the two parties most directly concerned with the issue of disarmament would be in a position to engage constantly in bilateral discussion and negotiation. The arrangement has already produced some results. The direct line between Washington and Moscow was negotiated and signed between the United States and Soviet delegations to the Conference;[21] the direct test ban talks between the two sides at Geneva played a vital role in leading to the Moscow Treaty of August 6, 1963;[22] and, finally, the nonorbiting in space of weapons of mass destruction, though formalized through United Nations General Assembly Resolution 1884 (XVIII) of October 17, 1963, was largely negotiated at Geneva, partly at sessions of the Eighteen-Nation Committee Conference and partly by the two cochairmen.

Another recent illustration of the centrifugal pull toward direct discussion is furnished by the summing up of the President of the Security Council, on May 18, 1964,[23] after several weeks of discussion in the Council on the Kashmir issue. This summing up recommended direct discussion between India and Pakistan for arriving at a solution to the problem. The Council returned to what is generally regarded as the norm, or even the ultimate, in negotiating techniques. It was aware that in the course of some sixteen years of consideration of the Kashmir issue it had made other suggestions, including a blueprint for a settlement and the use of good offices, mediators, and special representatives. In those circumstances, the recommendation of a return to direct discussions between the parties was all the more significant.[24]

GOOD OFFICES.   Although the Hague Convention of 1907 [25] does not specifically differentiate between mediation and good offices, there are, nevertheless, very real differences between the two techniques of negotiation. Essentially, mediation is a more formal process which entails the prior agreement of the parties to a dispute or situation, both to the use of the method and to a particular mediator. Such bilateral or multilateral agreement, as the case may be, is not an essential prerequisite in the function of good offices. When the permanent representatives at the United Nations of certain Asian and African states went as a delegation to call on Dag Hammarskjöld [26] to express their concern over the conflict in Algeria between the French and the National Liberation Front, and made suggestions as to what might be done in the situation, they were calling into operation the good offices, but not any mediatory functions, of the Secretary-General. Hammarskjöld, of course, understood perfectly. He made this clear at a press conference on August 25, 1955, at which he said:

I have transmitted to the French Delegation . . . the views expressed to me by a number of Delegations. . . . my information to the French Delegation on what had been said on the appeal from the Asian-African group was information and not a *demarche* on my side . . .[27]

Similarly, though more formally than in the aforementioned instance, the Secretary-General was still using his good offices when he complied with the following clause of a General Assembly resolution:

Invites the Secretary General to use his good offices with the Government of the Union of South Africa, in order to assist Mr. Himumuine to obtain a passport and all other administrative facilities, so that he may avail himself of the scholarship granted him by Oxford University.[28]

In neither of the aforementioned cases was there any question of agreement by the parties to the situation to the good offices role of the Secretary-General.[29]

POURPARLERS.   Pourparlers are informal discussions, generally preliminary to substantive negotiations and having the objective of promoting peaceful settlement. They are particularly useful in a delicate situation either to prepare the ground for, or even to achieve some of the purposes of, more substantive negotiation. In this respect they might be likened to conciliatory moves, but they are made directly rather than through a conciliator or a mediator. Nowadays, the term "pourparler" is used only occasionally in negotiating contexts. An example is the General Assembly resolution of December 10, 1957 on the Algerian question.[30] However, the idea contained in this word is frequently in use in modern negotiating situations.

AD HOC CONFERENCES OF STATES, AND UTILIZATION OF EXISTING CONFERENCE MECHANISMS. At one end of the gamut of the processes of negotiation is direct discussion among the parties concerned, and at the other end is conference negotiation. The latter type brings together with the parties directly concerned, other parties whose interests may be affected or who may be regarded as friendly, concerned, or neighboring states. An illustration of this type of conference was the International Conference on the Question of Laos, at which the representatives of fourteen nations—Laos itself, Burma, Cambodia, Canada, the People's Republic of China, France, India, North Vietnam, Poland, Thailand, South Vietnam, the Soviet Union, the United Kingdom, and the United States—met to negotiate. The conference drew up an international declaration, and a protocol thereto, to guarantee the independence, neutrality, and integrity of Laos. The negotiation was, as might be surmised from the list of participants, a complicated one; and although it was originally hoped that it might be completed in about six weeks, it continued in formal and informal meetings until the treaty and protocol were signed on July 23, 1962, some fourteen months after its commencement. (This was not unusual; generally speaking, conference negotiation tends to be longer drawn out than originally anticipated.)

Somewhat other criteria were operative in the selection of the nations which constitute the Eighteen-Nation Committee on Disarmament. The core participants at its sessions are the United States and the Soviet Union. (France and the United Kingdom, as nuclear powers represented at the United Nations, were naturally also named to the Committee, although France has not so far participated in Conference sessions.) The total membership was selected not on the basis of armed strength, but to create a negotiating balance. The NATO alliance is represented (or would be represented if France were to participate) by five states—the three already mentioned plus Canada and Italy. The Communist world is also represented by five states— Bulgaria, Czechoslovakia, Poland, Rumania, and the Soviet Union. To temper the confrontation of the two sides of the Cold War, eight nonaligned states were selected—Brazil, Burma, Ethiopia, India, Mexico, Nigeria, Sweden, and the United Arab Republic.

Both of the aforementioned are examples of ad hoc negotiating conferences. There also exist other multilateral bodies, established to achieve general international aims, such as the General Assembly, the Economic and Social Council, and the Security Council of the United Nations, and the Governing Board of the International Atomic Energy Agency, whose functions include negotiation.

When the General Assembly discusses issues such as disarmament, Korea, Algeria, Yemen, or the appropriate procedures to ascertain the will of a people of a trust territory on the question of their independence or self-government on termination of trusteeship status, it is engaging in deliberations which have the character of negotiation. Sometimes negotiations at the General Assembly are but one stage— often a first stage—in a long and complex process of consideration of subtle issues on the international scene.

Article 13 of the Charter gives the General Assembly the power to initiate studies and make recommendations of a character which would assist in the realization of human rights and fundamental freedoms and promote the progress of development and codification of international law.[31] Under this wide power the General Assembly has negotiated the final version of a Declaration of Human Rights, and is in the process of elaborating a Convention on Human Rights. Thus, the General Assembly has certain functions which amount nearly to the negotiation of international treaties.

Unlike the Assembly of the League of Nations, the General Assembly is not specifically endowed with the power to recommend the revision of treaties. This subject was much debated at San Francisco, the French delegate pointing out that Article 19 of the League Covenant had been utilized by Hitler and other dictators as the basis for their territorial claims.[32]

However, the General Assembly, acting under the powers given it by Article 13 read with Article 11.1 of the Charter, has amended the text of the General Act of September 26, 1928 for the Pacific Settlement of International Disputes. The amendment was adopted by an overwhelming vote on April 28, 1949.[33] In this instance a treaty was amended by the General Assembly in spite of the specific exclusion at the San Francisco Conference of powers to do so.

In general, Professor C. K. Webster was right when, in speaking for the United Kingdom at the San Francisco Conference, he described the functions of the General Assembly in the matter of conventions and agreements as follows:

The General Assembly will best safeguard the interests of the members of the United Nations by ensuring that Conventions are drawn up and submitted to Governments for approval in such a manner that before any such step is taken each question receives proper consideration and preparation by the Governments of the members themselves as well as by the Technical Committee of the General Assembly.[34]

The Security Council, when it acts for the pacific settlement of a dispute or situation under Chapter VI of the Charter, is a forum in which the Council members deliberate on and assess the situation or dispute, and then make the appropriate recommendations for a peaceful adjustment or solution. At the San Francisco Conference on International Organization, Dr. Herbert Evatt, then Foreign Minister of Australia, rightly said, "The Security Council's main work, will, we hope, lie in the peaceful conciliation of parties to important disputes." [35]

The Security Council is charged with another function which involves the most delicate and skillful negotiation—the recommendation of a suitable person to the General Assembly for appointment as Secretary-General.[36] It is also responsible for formulating plans to be submitted to members of the United Nations for a system of regulating armaments.[37] In the appropriate parts of this study we will consider the effect of the veto power, or the unanimity rule prescribed for the permanent members of the Security Council, on the functions of the Council. Article 25 of the Charter—by which members agree to accept and carry out the decisions of the Security Council—and the enforcement aspect of the Council's functions, also bear on its activities as a negotiating body.

In the various aspects of their work, both the General Assembly and the Security Council become engaged in negotiations. This is also true of the other United Nations organs, except for one of the six principal organs, the International Court of Justice, which does not and cannot function as a negotiating body.

CHAPTER THREE

The Primary Bases

THE ELEMENTAL predisposing factors in international negotiation are, first, that there must be two or more states (or entities asserting statehood and widely recognized as doing so) involved, so that the matter is international rather than purely internal—not "essentially within the domestic jurisdiction" (Article 2.7 of the United Nations Charter); and, second, that something which needs attention must have occurred or be brewing among those states or entities. This "something" might be any of a variety of possible situations, extending from the length of stay for seasonal migratory labor to overlapping claims for territory or rival interest in another area or state; or, if fairly definite contentious points have emerged from such issues, it might be in the nature of a dispute.

But just the existence of something in the air, or even of a tangible issue between two or more states, does not necessarily lead to negotiation. It might, on the contrary, lead to a rupture, to a break in relations, or even to strife or war. Therefore, there is a third elemental factor, and that is that someone—generally a state or several states acting together—must decide to do something about the matter in a peaceful manner. Need those states be parties to the situation or dispute? And need it always be a state that decides that something should be done? The answers to these questions will become apparent as we consider some actual cases of negotiation.

First, let us examine what constitutes an international dispute or situation. Many situations are not disputes at all. The commonest examples of situations which need not be disputes and which are, nevertheless, submitted to negotiation, are trade relations among countries.

It was to improve such relations that the United Nations Conference on Trade and Development met from March to June 1964 at Geneva, as a consequence of recommendations of the Economic and Social Council and the General Assembly. Through discussions and deliberations (i.e., negotiations), the General Assembly resolution stated, it might be "possible to reach at the Conference basic agreement on a new international trade and development policy." [1] The conference met not to settle specific disputes but to try to ameliorate the existing trading arrangements in the world, particularly with reference to the exports of the developing countries.[2]

Similarly, bilateral negotiations for the purpose of formulating trade agreements seldom deal with disputes. I was associated with many of the earliest of independent India's trade negotiations, between 1949 and 1951. In those years the treaties or agreements which my colleagues and I negotiated on behalf of India included the first trade agreements with Spain, Switzerland, and the Federal Republic of Germany, and letters of agreement with Sweden, Czechoslovakia, and Iraq, among other countries. In none of those cases was there any dispute to settle, but a great deal of hard bargaining and negotiating took place. This was particularly so in the discussions with Switzerland at Berne and with the Federal Republic of Germany at Delhi, for we were setting the pattern of trade between India and those two important exporters of machinery and other products in which India was and has remained most interested. Through all those negotiations, improved trade relations were established with many countries.

Contrary perhaps to the popular view, most issues which come to the United Nations are, although contentious, not termed "disputes." They are listed in the agenda as the Question of Algeria, or Palestine, or West Irian, or Indonesia, or as the India-Pakistan Question. This interrogative formulation encourages treatment of the issues as international situations rather than as disputes.

This was so in the case of one of the earliest issues brought to the Security Council with the request that appropriate action be taken under Article VI of the Charter (The Pacific Settlement of Disputes). The petitioner was Greece. Its contention was that some of its neighbors, notably Albania, Bulgaria, and Yugoslavia, were abetting the rebels in the guerrilla war in northern Greece. The issue could have been brought to the Security Council as a dispute between Greece and those neighbors, but in fact the representative of Greece wrote to the Secretary-General on December 3, 1946 asking him to bring to the notice of the Security Council "a situation leading to friction between Greece" and its neighbors. The letter concluded that the "situation if not promptly remedied," was "likely to endanger the maintenance of international peace and security." [3] The Security Council treated the issue as a situation, and the Commission of Investigation which it appointed wrote as follows in its report:

Before coming to its actual proposals the Commission felt it would be useful to recapitulate in brief the situation along Greece's northern border which these proposals are designed to alleviate and remedy.[4]

The first complaint involving Greece was made by the representative of the Soviet Union, who requested the Security Council to discuss the situation in Greece arising from the presence there of British troops.[5] This was presented unambiguously as a situation rather than a dispute. The obvious fact is that in order to promote progress toward a settlement, it is more conciliatory to describe even a fairly clear dispute as a situation, if at all possible.

The most comprehensive situation of all, and one which has been the subject of repeated and protracted negotiations, is that created by the armaments race and by the present level of armaments in the world. The Eighteen-Nation Committee on Disarmament has continuously aimed at changing the present armament situation. Its difficult marathon negotiations, to which we shall have occasion to refer in other contexts, illustrate negotiation with reference to a situation rather than to a dispute.

Another observation is relevant, however. The states concerned do not always agree that a situation or dispute exists, and when this is so there cannot be any fruitful negotiation. In September 1954, for example, the United States representative addressed the Security Council [6] about an attack on and destruction of a United States Naval plane by Soviet fighter planes. The United States said they had failed to settle the matter bilaterally, and therefore brought it to the Security Council. The Soviet representative maintained that the issue had no connection with Chapter VI of the Charter. The issue was placed on the agenda, but since the Soviet Union was unwilling to regard it as a situation or dispute to be negotiated, it was allowed to drop after the Council's inconclusive debate. (No resolution was proposed.) The Council stated it would revert to it when any delegation so requested, but none did. There was no point in going on with the discussion when one party refused to treat the issue as a negotiable situation or dispute. By allowing it to drop the Security Council inferentially took this view.

In certain other cases the Security Council has specifically refused to put an item on its agenda when one party to the issue is absolutely unwilling to cooperate. This was so when on June 26, 1956 it refused to heed a request by thirteen Asian-African Countries to put the Algerian situation on its agenda, because France opposed the request.[7]

To the elements of negotiation, therefore, we must add the qualification that the dispute or situation must be admitted as such by the parties concerned.

But the French-Algerian matter had another aspect. France as a permanent member occupies a special position on the Security Council. Even if seven members of the Council had voted to investigate the situation which had given rise to the African-Asian request, France could have eventually frustrated such an effort. The limitation placed by Article 27.3 of the Charter on the need for the concurrent votes of the permanent members of the Security Council says that in decisions under Chapter VI "a party to a dispute shall abstain from voting." But how is the Security Council to determine whether a dispute exists? A vote to determine whether there is or is not a dispute is one that might be vetoed. If the Security Council had wished to proceed on the basis that a situation existed which warranted an investigation under Article 34 of the Charter, France could presumably have used her veto, because Article 27 does not mention that parties are to abstain in the case of situations (as distinct from disputes).

Had none of the parties concerned been a permanent member of the Security Council, the Council could have investigated the situation if no permanent member had cast a negative vote and if seven votes had supported such action; and if the investigation showed that there was a dispute which was likely to endanger the maintenance of international peace and security, the Council could have taken action under Articles 36 or 37.2 of the Charter. Alternatively, the Security Council could at any stage have decided that a situation existed, and made recommendations under Article 36. The Security Council has made no general determination whether such recommendations constitute decisions to which Article 25 applies.

We should note, however, that while it is clear from a reading of Article 27 of the Charter that the Security Council may take decisions under Chapter VI which would presumably attract the provisions of Article 25,[8] the Council has tended in Chapter VI proceedings to rely on moral pressure or on persuasion to get member states to carry out its decisions.

In September 1954 Israel complained to the Security Council against the seizure of an Israeli merchantman, the Bat Galim, together with its crew, which attempted to enter the Suez Canal. Israel cited a resolution of the Security Council of September 1, 1951, wherein the Council had called on Egypt to terminate all restrictions on the passage of international shipping through the Suez Canal, wherever bound. The ship had been arrested by Egyptian authorities on the ground that its crew had used force against certain Egyptian fishermen in Egyptian territorial waters. The Council called for a report from the Chief of Staff of the Truce Supervision Organization in Palestine. About the time the report was received, Egypt informed the Council that it was withdrawing charges against the crew of the Bat Galim, and releasing them along with the ship. In these circumstances the Council did not take any decision against either side. The President of the Council made a statement commending the spirit of conciliation on both sides, and expressed the hope that it would continue.[9]

In March 1955 and in January 1956 the Security Council adopted unanimous resolutions condemning Israel for violating the General Armistice Agreements, and in the second one it came near to warning Israel. The fifth operative paragraph of the resolution read, *"Calls upon the Government* of Israel to do so [comply with its obligations] in the future, in default of which the Council will have to consider what further measures under the Charter are required to maintain or restore the peace."[10]

A few months after the second resolution, in April and in June 1956, the Security Council adopted two more resolutions on the Palestine situation. The effect of these resolutions was to request the Secretary-General to continue to use his good offices to get compliance with the Security Council's relevant resolutions and the Armistice Agreements between the parties.[11]

This sequence of events bears out the point that the Security Council, although conscious of stronger possibilities open to it, tries to act in a spirit of conciliation in dealing with cases under Chapter VI of the Charter. Fundamentally, this spirit derives from the widely realized and accepted principle that for settlements to be truly pacific —and it is with pacific settlements that Chapter VI of the Charter is concerned—the parties must be brought together. They must find a way of mutual accomodation and adjustment even if the Security Council might pressure them to do so. The recognition that the element of willingness, or at least acquiescence, is essential to pacific settlements, corroborates our statement that the parties must admit the existence of a situation or dispute.

If the parties do admit the existence of a situation or dispute, must they all be willing to take part in the negotiations? The answer might appear to be in the affirmative, but let us look at some specific cases.

France, a nuclear power, is an essential party to disarmament negotiations, and it has been so named, but President de Gaulle has refused to join in the negotiations as they are presently conducted.[12] Nevertheless, disarmament negotiations are taking place.

An even more striking case was the Suez Canal Conference called by the Government of the United Kingdom in August 1956 following the nationalization of the Suez Canal Company by the Government of Egypt on July 26, 1956. The United Kingdom issued invitations to twenty-three governments. Egypt, a principal party, did not attend the Conference, but two sets of proposals were considered and negotiations took place.[13]

Another important instance of a conference to negotiate a settlement called not at the instance of all the parties mainly involved was the Geneva Conference of 1954 to consider "the problem of restoring peace in Indochina." [14] Indeed, this Conference arose tangentially. The foreign ministers of the United States, France, the United Kingdom, and the Soviet Union met in Berlin between January 25 and February 18, 1954 to discuss a settlement on Korea, the German question, and disarmament. On February 18, 1954 they issued an agreed communiqué on these subjects. The communiqué dealt first with the calling of a Conference on Korea.

At the end of the primary paragraph dealing with the Conference on Korea, a subparagraph was added to the communiqué as follows:

[The Foreign Ministers] *Agree* that the problem of restoring peace in Indochina will also be discussed at the conference, to which the representatives of the United States, France, the United Kingdom, the Union of Soviet Socialist Republics, the Chinese People's Republic, and other interested states will be invited.

It is understood that neither the invitation to, nor the holding of the above-mentioned conference shall be deemed to imply diplomatic recognition in any case where it has not already been accorded.[15]

The Korean part of the Conference was a complete failure, but the Indochinese part resulted in the working out of settlements. Although the settlements have functioned very imperfectly in most of the succession states in the area, the fact is that the conferences were called by four foreign ministers acting for governments that did not include all the parties immediately involved.

Some six years later, when the situation in Laos deteriorated to a point where that state seemed to face disruption or a radical change in political orientation, it was Prince Norodom Sihanouk of Cambodia who proposed a conference to bring together the great powers and the countries interested or involved. As a consequence, the co-chairmen of the Geneva Conference of 1954—the foreign ministers of the Soviet Union and the United Kingdom—issued invitations for a Fourteen-Nation Conference, which met at Geneva on May 16, 1961. Prince Sihanouk was asked to inaugurate the Conference as opening speaker and pro tem chairman. V. K. Krishna Menon, Andrei Gromyko, Lord Home, and others, paid tribute to Prince Sihanouk for having initiated the Conference. Their tribute testified to the important function he had performed as head of a state which had not intervened in the civil war then being fought in Laos and which was therefore not a party involved in the situation.

A striking example of a conference to negotiate a basis for settlement, in exclusion of the involved parties, is the case of the Conference of the Six Colombo Powers of 1962, an important and interesting development in the history of international negotiation. At the end of 1962, a group of Asian and African countries, concerned about the strife between China and India, the two most populous countries in the world and the largest Asian powers, met in a conference at Colombo under the presidency of the Prime Minister of Ceylon, Madame Sirimavo Bandaranaike. It was attended by cabinet ministers from Burma, Cambodia, Ghana, Indonesia, and the United Arab Republic but not by representatives of China or India. Those six countries, after due study of the situation, including the numerous statements of Chinese and Indian leaders, made a series of substantive proposals which they suggested could be the basis for a peaceful settlement of the Chinese-Indian conflict. The proposals are of the utmost importance precisely because they suggest a disposition of the armed forces of China and India along the whole border in a manner which could well become a permanent arrangement and thus facilitate greatly the demarcation of the frontier between the two countries. On almost the whole of the frontier they recommended continuance of the present disposition of the forces of the two countries, and in the western or Ladakh sector they left room for maneuver in subsequent negotiations between China and India. In this area the six powers suggested that there should be a 12.5-mile-wide demilitarized area in which civil administration posts of both China and India would be set up by mutual agreement. The implicit suggestion was that the civilian posts should be set up in a manner which would be related to and would facilitate the eventual division of the territory between India and China. (However, in this one area the Chinese have not yet accepted the Colombo Powers' suggestion. In a note dated March 2, 1963—the Colombo Powers' proposals were made in January 1963 —the Chinese Government informed the Government of India that it had set up six check posts in this area. This was done without the discussion and mutual agreement suggested by the Colombo Powers.) [16]

If both India and China act in accordance with the Colombo proposals over the length of their common frontier, and if their actions harden into a de jure situation by mutual agreement, then the Colombo Conference of the six African-Asian Powers can be credited with virtually solving the conflict. Much in that direction has already been achieved; except in the Ladakh area the two sides are acting in conformity with the Colombo broad proposals. There are indications of efforts on the part of the Colombo Powers to try to get a basis of agreement between China and India in regard to Ladakh. It has recently been suggested that there need not be any civilian posts in the area, as it is uninhabited.

The conference of nonparty states initiated and continued efforts toward a solution, yet it can be seen from this instance that the final settlement of a dispute or adjustment of a situation will almost invariably require the presence of all the parties directly involved.

Must the parties that promote or become involved in negotiations be states, or can they be other authorities, or persons? The General Assembly and the Security Council of the United Nations frequently call for direct negotiations, suggest mediation, or ask the Secretary-General or some other person to make his services available to promote negotiations. But those actions are properly classified as the action of states working concertedly.

Article 99 of the Charter gives the Secretary-General a political function which, when exercised, could result in negotiations.[17] The scope of this power in itself might not appear to be great, but the concept underlying it has proved to be significant. On a number of occasions—at press conferences, in statements to the Security Council, in his speech to the General Assembly on his appointment to a second term of office as Secretary-General, in introductory para-

graphs to annual reports on the work of the United Nations, and in
public addresses—Dag Hammarskjöld spoke at length of the function
of the Secretary-General in taking the initiative in settling disputes:

There have been . . . various decisions taken in recent years by the
General Assembly or the Security Council under which the Secretary-
General has been entrusted with special diplomatic and operational func-
tions . . .

   This, also, represents an evolution of the procedures of the United Nations for which no explicit basis is to be found in the Charter—although
it may be said to fall within the scope of the intentions reflected in Article
99—and to which neither the League of Nations, nor the United Nations
during its earlier years, presented a significant counterpart.

   . . . in some recent cases of international conflict or other difficulties
involving Member States the Secretary-General has dispatched personal
representatives with the task of assisting the governments in their efforts.
This may be regarded as a further development of actions of a "good offices" nature, with which the Secretary-General is now frequently charged.
The steps to which I refer here have been taken with the consent or at
the invitation of governments concerned, but without formal decisions
or other organs of the United Nations.[18]

Legal scholars have observed that Article 99 not only confers upon the
Secretary-General a right to bring matters to the attention of the Security
Council but that this right carries with it, by necessary implication, a
broad discretion to conduct inquiries and to engage in informal diplomatic activity in regard to matters which "may threaten the maintenance
of international peace and security." [19]

   Both Hammarskjöld and U Thant have carried out this interpre-
tation of their function. One recent case was the designation by U
Thant of Galo Plaza of Ecuador as his personal representative in
Cyprus in May 1964.

   Both by such actions and appointments and by more direct use of
Article 99 of the Charter, the Secretary-General can initiate negotiation, and in this respect he is placed in a unique position on the international scene. Of course, there is nothing to debar any individual
with standing among the parties to an international dispute from
mediating with their consent, acting as conciliator, or in other ways
taking the initiative to open negotiations between two or more sovereign states—but there have been few such cases in our time.

   What is much more significant than any formal recourse to Article
99 is that this Article—and in some degree also Article 98 [20]—en-
dows the role of Secretary-General with a diplomatic character. It is

in this role that the Secretaries-General, particularly Dag Hammarskjöld and U Thant, have frequently acted to promote negotiation. A recent instance is the series of statements by U Thant on the subject of Vietnam. At his press conference on July 8, 1964, he said:

I have all along felt that the only sensible alternative is the political and diplomatic method of negotiation which, even at this late hour, may offer some chance of a solution. I still feel that a return to the Geneva Conference table, though perhaps belated, may produce some useful results.[21]

At his press conference on February 12, 1965, U Thant again recommended negotiations, and suggested that if there were difficulties in immediately calling a Geneva-type conference it would be worth while to explore the possibilities of private dialogues as a preliminary to a more formal conference. He repeated this suggestion at his press conference of February 24, 1965.[22]

However, the mere decision to confer is not enough; there must be an operative desire to clarify, ameliorate, adjust, or settle the dispute or situation. In short, there must be a will to move from the status quo. If this is absent there cannot be a negotiation.

The post-World War II disarmament negotiations are a graphic illustration of the key role played by the will to negotiate. A study of those negotiations shows that when the will to negotiate has been strong enough to result in substantive proposals for disarmament, then a high point in the negotiations has been reached. When it has been absent, there has been little reality in the negotiations. The three-step developments from 1952 to 1955 demonstrate this point.

The first stage, in 1952, was noted for a remarkable paper entitled "Essential Principles for a Disarmament Program,"[23] tabled by United States Representative Benjamin Cohen in the Disarmament Commission of the United Nations on April 24, 1952. This was basically the first proposal for general and complete disarmament—although these words were not used—to be made in the post-World War II period. The proposed principles provided for the reduction of armed forces of states to the point where they would serve only to maintain internal security and meet the obligations of states to maintain peace and security in accordance with the Charter of the United Nations.[24]

The response by the Soviet Union to these proposals was negative. The Soviet position was stated by Yakov Malik to be in favor of concrete measures but not mere principles. However, it can be stated objectively that the United States proposal, if it had been accepted as a basis of negotiation, would have taken us very near to the point we eventually reached in September 1961, when the United States and the Soviet Union, through teams headed respectively by John J. McCloy and Valerian Zorin, worked out in slightly greater detail just such a statement of agreed principles, which became the sheet anchor of the most successful and purposeful of disarmament negotiations so far held—the Eighteen-Nation Committee on Disarmament which has met almost continuously at Geneva since March 14, 1962.

At the first of the three-step developments, John Foster Dulles, in his statement on September 17, 1953 in the General Debate of the United Nations General Assembly, used the following words:

Given a concrete demonstration *of an equal desire* on the part of the Soviet Union to negotiate honestly and sincerely on the substance of these matters, we are confident that this work can usefully go forward.[25]

He was, of course, right in expressing the view that what was wanted was a demonstration of real desire to negotiate by both sides.

At the Eighth Session of the General Assembly, many countries, including the delegation of India, felt that one of the reasons the Disarmament Commission was making no progress might be that the powers directly involved were not doing enough talking to each other. We suggested, therefore, that those powers set up a subcommittee, and this thought was included in the General Assembly Resolution which was adopted.[26] It was when this subcommittee, consisting of the representatives of Canada, France, the Soviet Union, the United Kingdom, and the United States, began to meet that the second of the three steps was taken. The French and the British collaborated to submit a joint memorandum which introduced the idea of proceeding with a disarmament plan in stages. Admittedly, the final result to be achieved under the Anglo-French plan was somewhat short of that implicit in the United States principles of 1952. It stated the final goal—the retention by nation states of only enough armaments to meet the requirements of internal security and their obligations under the United Nations Charter—simply as something to be hoped for, a pious wish, rather than as a part of the disarmament plan. Still, it was a fairly comprehensive approach to disarmament, and the Western powers in the subcommittee pressed the Soviet representative to react. Finally, early in May 1955, the United States delegate said that if no response was made by the Soviets, he and his Western colleagues could "arrive at no other conclusion than that there is no desire to negotiate." [27] Again, one side was stressing, rightly, that there had to be evidence of a real desire or will to negotiate.

Then came the third step in this sequence. On May 10, 1955, a week after the Western powers had challenged the Soviets to show some desire to negotiate, Yakov Malik made the biggest step forward in Soviet disarmament moves up to that time. He accepted many of the proposals in the Anglo-French plan, and went further in proposals on control than the Soviets had theretofore given any hopes of doing. All the four Western representatives warmly welcomed this move forward. But a little later, on September 6, 1955, Harold Stassen, the new United States representative, placed a reservation on all the United States positions previously taken at the disarmament meetings—including the April 24, 1952 principles and the later support given by the United States to the Anglo-French proposals to which the Soviets had finally reacted so positively.

Repeatedly the Soviets returned to their proposals: at the July 1955 Heads of State Conference, at the Foreign Ministers Conference in November 1955, and on December 7, 1955 at the General Assembly when Vasily Kuznetsov made a detailed and unpolemical statement of the Soviet position. To these various efforts the reply of the West was that they desired priority for the "open skies proposal" made by President Eisenhower in July 1955 at the Heads of State meeting; and that there were now complicated technical problems, as a result of development of the hydrogen bomb, which would have to be considered.

Thus the shoe was on the other foot. Philip Noel-Baker, the British ex-Cabinet Minister and 1959 Nobel laureate for peace, had strong words for the situation created by the new Western stance. Writing his major work, *The Arms Race,* almost three years after a reservation had been placed by the United States representative on previous United States disarmament positions, he said of Stassen's statement, "The proposals [the Western disarmament proposals] were withdrawn, and they have remained withdrawn until today." [28]

On this subject of willingness or desire for some movement forward, the remarks made earlier in this chapter about the refusal of France to cooperate when certain countries sought to bring the Algerian situation to the Security Council are also relevant.

In considering the primary prerequisites for negotiation, we have seen that there must be something to negotiate about—an identifiable international dispute, or at any rate a situation giving rise to or portending friction. The parties directly involved must also admit that such a situation or dispute exists. Nonrecognition of a negotiable situation or dispute is not necessarily a function of power. Even though it might appear that between two countries the more powerful tends not to admit the existence of a negotiable situation, the assumption must be made with reservations.

In the case of the situation that existed between Portugal and India over Goa and the two other minute enclaves in India claimed by Portugal to be part of her metropolitan domain, it was not superior power that explained Portugal's refusal to negotiate with India over the termination of her possession. It might be argued that Portugal felt secure in its alliances with very powerful states, but since those states had given tangible evidence of their own renunciation of colonial positions, it is difficult to understand what could have led Portugal to consider that she could count on the support of her allies against the decolonialization current in Asia. It is also possible to argue that India took recourse to force rather than explore all the possibilities of negotiation because she knew she was much stronger on the subcontinent than was Portugal, and that Goa could be liberated without bloodshed by a mere show of strength. This is virtually what eventually happened.[29] Whatever view might be taken of the power relationships involved, the point reiterated here is that nonrecognition of the existence of a dispute or situation, for whatever reason, can frustrate possibilities of negotiation.

We have also seen that a state or states—or, as may happen, the Secretary-General of the United Nations—must be actively interested in the effort to achieve a settlement or at least a measure of accommodation. The most obvious and normal instance of this is when the parties directly concerned decide to seek a settlement. But we have also observed that it is by no means in the exclusive jurisdiction of these parties to bring the matter to a negotiating forum. Other states might decide to do so, as has been the case with some of the Indochina conferences, and the Colombo negotiations on the Sino-Indian dispute. We might also mention the initiation in the United Nations of the long round of negotiations on the cessation of the testing of nuclear weapons, as this issue was brought to the United Nations not by a nuclear power but by India, in April 1954. Jawaharlal Nehru raised the matter of the cessation of tests in the Parliament of India, and instructed the Indian representative at the United Nations to ask the Disarmament Commission to give attention to his proposal for a standstill agreement.[30] A year later, the Bandung Conference of African and Asian states repeated the proposal, and soon thereafter it started to appear in disarmament proposals, the first nuclear power to place it formally in its proposals being the Soviet Union.[31] Thereafter, each year at the General Assembly this issue has been one upon which major debates have centered. It has been placed on the agenda by India and by like-minded countries other than the nuclear states. Indeed, in the matter of nuclear testing it is not unreasonable to assert that the annual pressure of the non-nuclear powers in the General Assembly and other forums has made its contribution to the partial cessation of nuclear tests.

In the light of the foregoing consideration of some of the factors which must exist in order to make international negotiation possible, we would offer the following formulation as the first principle of negotiation:

> There must be a dispute or a situation, admitted to be such by the states concerned, which one or more parties, often those most directly involved but not necessarily so, or the Secretary-General of the United Nations, decide or desire to clarify, ameliorate, adjust, or settle.

CHAPTER FOUR

Acceptance of Peaceful Methods

WE HAVE SEEN that negotiation is based on the presupposition that there must be something that grates or jars between two or more states, and that someone duly competent must be concerned and must feel that some adjustment should be attempted.

But what of the parties to the dispute or situation? Is it not necessary that their attitudes conform to certain requirements if negotiations are to result? Clearly, if they should insist on going to war no negotiations would be possible. There are certain circumstances in which this attitude is inevitable. Under most defensive alliances it is incumbent on the members of the alliances to render military assistance to each other, i.e., to take the field in the event of an attack on any one of them. There are yet other circumstances which have traditionally led to war. For example, in 1914—leaving aside the ultimate causes of World War I—ostensibly and in an immediate sense it was not the Triple Alliance of 1907 or the Entente of 1904 which brought Great Britain into the war, but rather Germany's demand for free passage for its troops through Belgium, which had been refused by the Belgian Government. In accordance with the treaties of 1839, both Germany and the United Kingdom (as well as France, Russia, and Austria) were pledged to respect the neutrality of Belgium. The British Government demanded withdrawal, in compliance with the 1839 treaties, of the German ultimatum to Belgium. No reply came within the stipulated period, and thereafter Britain and Germany were at war. This kind of automatic unleashing of war as a result of compliance or noncompliance with treaty obligations would militate against negotiation. Is there a factor that must be present in the attitudes of states to insure recourse to procedures of negotiation? Surely there must be an effective and practical acceptance on the part of the parties directly involved of a peaceful way of solution.

In seeking the answer to this question, we encounter related questions. Is it necessary that the acceptance of peaceful methods be total, in that it exclude all other methods? And is it possible for the acceptance to fluctuate in degree without negating the possibilities of negotiation? Again, we can turn to contemporary events in our search for the answers to these questions.

Acceptance of or assent to negotiation by the parties to a dispute or situation must be dominant for negotiations to get under way. In this regard we might consider the likely effect of certain types of commitments, particularly through international treaties or through the expressed willingness to negotiate.

Let us look at the situation created by the provisions of the North Atlantic Treaty of April 4, 1949 (the NATO alliance), and its counterpart, the Treaty of Friendship, Cooperation, and Mutual Assistance of May 14, 1955 (the Warsaw Pact). Under the terms of the North Atlantic Treaty, an armed attack in Europe or North America against any member of the alliance is to be construed as an attack against all members, and the inherent right of collective self-defense is invoked against the aggressor or aggressors.[1] The Treaty goes on to stipulate in the same article that:

Any such armed attack and all measures taken as a result thereof shall immediately be reported to the Security Council. Such measures shall be terminated when the Security Council has taken the measures necessary to restore and maintain international peace and security.

Since the counterpart treaty, the Warsaw Pact, contains a similar clause,[2] the net effect of the provisions in the two alliance treaties, in spite of the deference they pay to the Security Council, would appear to be that once an armed attack occurs (which might itself be in response to an act of aggression—in other words, the circumstances of the armed attack notwithstanding) the chances of negotiation are virtually closed. The two alliances include in their membership all the nuclear powers (except China). Their clash could be of such a character that the provisions in the treaties for the Security Council to take over would be much more of theoretical than of practical consequence. Here we see how automatic implementation of the commitment of states embodied in certain treaty provisions could render negotiation virtually impossible once an armed attack had taken place.

However, the same treaty provisions might have a deterrent effect, and so long as deterrence remains operative it can be argued that the said treaty provisions actually give negotiation a chance to develop. This view is not incompatible with the tentative conclusion drawn in the preceding paragraph; the two views relate to two different phases of a theoretical situation or dispute.

Indeed, the NATO agreement and the Warsaw Pact must not be read *in abstracto*. In real life the two sides have shown that even when a situation containing the seeds of the most widespread and dangerous conflict arises, they endeavor to keep open the channels of peaceful settlement. This was most strikingly demonstrated in the Caribbean flare-up in the last week of October 1962.

The nature of the crisis, and its potentialities, will be clear from the following citations:

The letter of Adlai Stevenson, the Permanent Representative of the United States, dated October 22, 1962 to the President of the Security Council, referred to:

The dangerous threat to the peace and the security of the world which has been caused by the secret establishment in Cuba by the U.S.S.R. of launching bases and the installation of long-range ballistic missiles capable of carrying nuclear war heads to most parts of North and South America.[3]

At the meeting of the Council, spokesmen expressed the worldwide alarm:

Since the end of the Second World War, there has been no threat to the vision of peace so profound—no challenge to the world of the Charter so fateful. The hopes of mankind are concentrated in this room. The action we take may determine the future of civilization. . . . This is, I believe, a solemn and significant day for the life of the United Nations and the hope of the world community.[4] (Stevenson)

The Security Council meets today in circumstances which cannot but give rise to the gravest concern for the fate of peace in the Caribbean region and in the whole world. . . . in carrying out the measures announced by President Kennedy, it [the Government of the United States] is taking on itself a heavy responsibility for the fate of the world, and recklessly playing with fire.[5] (Valerian Zorin of the Soviet Union)

. . . representatives of some fifty Member States gathered together last night for almost three hours. There was common agreement among them on . . . the urgent need to exert every effort to save mankind from the disastrous consequences entailed in an eventual armed conflict. . . .

They have delegated the representatives of Ghana and Cyprus and myself to meet with the Acting Secretary-General in order to convey to him on their behalf their deep concern and anxiety.[6] (Mahmoud Riad of the United Arab Republic)

Upon our words, upon our deeds, hang grave events, events that may well prove decisive for the very survival of humanity.[7] (Alex Quaison-Sackey of Ghana)

What is at stake is not just the interests of the parties directly involved, nor just the interests of all Member States, but the very fate of mankind. If today the United Nations should prove itself ineffective, it may have proved itself so for all time.[8] (U Thant)

The total explosiveness of the situation was many times greater than can be conveyed in a few paragraphs. Disaster seemed very near.

But there was another side to this ominous situation. Though to some extent lost sight of in the dread portent of the crisis, there was one striking clause in each of the draft resolutions proposed by the United States and the Soviet Union. The United States draft had been appended to its letter of October 22, which had initiated the proceedings of the Council. The clauses to which I refer were first drawn pointedly to the attention of the Council by Foreign Minister Frank Aiken of Ireland, speaking for his country on October 24.[9]

The United States draft contained the following paragraph:

Urgently recommends that the United States of America and the Union of Soviet Socialist Republics confer promptly on measures to remove the existing threat to the security of the Western Hemisphere and the peace of the world, and report thereon to the Security Council.[10]

Similarly, the Soviet draft resolution, which Valerian Zorin had introduced in his statement of October 23, contained the provision:

Calls upon the United States of America, the Republic of Cuba and the Union of Soviet Socialist Republics to establish contact and enter into negotiations for the purpose of restoring the situation to normal and thus of removing the threat of the outbreak of war.[11]

The door was kept open by the major parties themselves. Without this element, which would have been absent had the two superpowers each entered the confrontation with its mind set entirely on getting the Security Council to take action in support of its own position, the possibilities of negotiation would have been very much smaller, or perhaps entirely absent. Moreover, the United States, by pressing for direct negotiation with the Soviet Union rather than with Cuba, focused its negotiating effort on its real antagonist and thus kept the issue in the realm of the practical.

Acceptance of negotiation, of course, may mean substantially different things to the parties involved in a dispute or situation. Rarely indeed do disputants find themselves wanting precisely the same goals. Nevertheless, when they bring their dispute or situation to the negotiating table they implicitly declare their willingness to search for various peaceful ways of accommodating each other. Let us return to the dangerous Caribbean crisis of 1962 to see how this process can work.

The United States asked for (a) the immediate dismantling and withdrawal from Cuba of all missiles and other offensive weapons; (b) the dispatch to Cuba of a United Nations observer to report compliance with this demand. It committed itself to (c) the withdrawal of the United States quarantine around Cuba on United Nations certification of the removal of all missiles and other offensive weapons. It was in the context of these three stipulations that the United States recommended that the United States and the Soviets confer.[12] On the other hand, the Soviet Union demanded (a) condemnation of the United States; (b) revocation of the United States quarantine; and (c) cessation of United States intervention in the affairs of other states including Cuba;[13] and asked for negotiations in this context, which was very different from that envisaged by the United States proposals. Both draft proposals were backed by statements which indicated the determination of each side to maintain its position, if necessary by recourse to arms.

What was it that brought the parties into negotiation? Certainly it would be a mistake not to assign a role in this result to the basic willingness—conditioned though it was in each case by seemingly incompatible demands—to accept negotiations while at the same time warning each other that war could break out. What is evident from this situation is that the acceptance of negotiations need not be unconditional—indeed it very rarely is—and that it need not be total, for the two sides need not abandon their determination to have recourse to arms. At no time in those three fateful days was it certain that a peaceful settlement would result. It was not certain because neither side had given any indication that it had totally abandoned the possibility of recourse to weapons.

And yet, when they swerved away from the brink of conflict and opened negotiations, both sides accepted something rather different from what they had set out to demand. The Soviets withdrew all long-range missiles from Cuba, but enough rocketry was left on the island to shoot down high-flying planes. The second demand of the United States was not pressed in the negotiations, and the terms of its third stipulation were consequently modified.

It would be a mistake to conclude that the negotiations which ensued over Cuba were a failure because neither side's position was fully met. No position can be fully met in negotiations. The Soviet position was even less accommodated than that of the United States. Certainly the United Nations did not condemn the United States. The United States withdrew its quarantine of its own accord after it had assured itself very fully that all the long-range missiles and bombers had been removed from Cuba—consequently there was no revocation of the quarantine in the sense demanded by the Soviet Union; and, finally, the United States continued to decide how it would conduct its affairs with other States without any directive from the Security Council. The Soviet Union, too, apparently found this result preferable to the one which would have been the outcome of the continuance of the Cuban crisis in the form in which it came to the Security Council on October 23, 1962.

An important point that emerges from this incident is that even seemingly imcompatible demands by the parties do not foredoom a negotiation, if the door to peaceful settlement is kept open.

Furthermore, at no point was the acceptance of negotiation by the two sides total, exclusive, or unconditional. Both expressed their realization that they were involved in a confrontation which could prove to be disastrous. Neither side renounced the use of force. Adlai Stevenson said to the Council:

We cannot believe that he [Mr. Khrushchev] has deluded himself into supposing that, though we have power, we lack nerve; that, though we have weapons, we are without the will to use them.[14]

Valerian Zorin said on the same afternoon:

There is not, and there cannot be, any doubt that the small but heroic Cuban nation will not find itself alone in its hour of need.[15]

The determination to use force unless the other side shows some signs of submission does not, therefore, preclude negotiation. On the other hand, if there are to be negotiations there cannot be a total or exclusive adherence to the determination to use force. When this is the case—when one side is convinced, as Mussolini was in respect of Ethiopia and as Hitler was on numerous occasions, that the enemy can be crushed and a total victory gained—then there is no place for negotiation. However, neither Hitler's nor Mussolini's total adherence to force and so-called total victory was more than transitory. It brought great pain and suffering in the end to the Italian and German peoples. On the other hand, negotiated settlements, which are never totally in favor of one side, have a better chance of bringing some satisfaction to the peoples involved.

The Cuban case was one of direct negotiation between the two main parties involved—the United States and the Soviet Union. The United Nations machinery in various ways played a significant role in bringing about the negotiations, but eventually there were direct negotiations.

This is not always the case, for the willingness to negotiate need not take the form of agreement to enter into direct negotiations. The case of Cyprus in 1964 and 1965 illustrates this point. In its international aspects, the Cyprus trouble is one with almost endlessly spreading ripples. However, the states primarily concerned (apart from Cyprus) are Greece and Turkey. The agreements between them (and the United Kingdom) which took form as the Treaties of Nicosia of August 16, 1960 led to the creation of Cyprus as a modern independent state. Early in 1964 the arrangements entered into at Nicosia broke down. President Myriarthefs Makarios, finding excessively onerous the exercise by the Vice President, Fazil Kutchuk, a Turkish Cypriot, of the veto powers under the Treaty of Guarantee read with the Constitution of Cyprus,[16] sought to alter the treaties and certain constitutional provisions. This led to the outbreak of large-scale violence, and resulted in the United Nations Security Council's resolution of March 4, 1964 [17] recommending the creation, with the consent of the Government of Cyprus, of a United Nations peacekeeping force on the island. The composition of the force was to be decided in consultation with the governments of Cyprus, Greece, Turkey, and the United Kingdom.

The force came into being and encountered resistance from Greek and Turkish Cypriots, who were determined to control various parts of the island, particularly those shores from which they could continue to procure arms from Greece and Turkey. Moreover, there were threats of invasion by the Turks in order to protect the Turkish minority, and counterthreats by Greece to safeguard the rights of the Greek Cypriots. All this indicated beyond doubt that the main parties were Greece and Turkey. The Prime Ministers of those two countries were invited to Washington by President Lyndon B. Johnson in June 1964 for separate talks with him. They talked with President Charles de Gaulle, and with the British Prime Minister, Sir Alec Douglas-Home.

However, the Greek Prime Minister, George Papandreou, apparently refused to enter into direct negotiations with Turkey, even at the highest level. In a message to the Greek people on June 28, 1964, he referred to his talks with President Johnson and said:

I explained that under present circumstances such a meeting at any level would, instead of leading to a detente, produce greater tension since existing complete disagreement would also be established officially.[18]

On the other hand, in his press conference on June 25, 1964 in New York after his meeting with President Johnson, Prime Minister Ismet Inonu of Turkey stated:

The question of direct talks between Greece and Turkey has been raised from the first day. I have always been in favor of it, not only in words but also in deeds. . . . In short, I believe that it is useful to get together as soon as possible and talk.[19]

Only one of the two parties was willing to meet with the other. Did this mean that negotiation was ruled out? There is a weight of evidence in support of the view that negotiations were not barred by the unwillingness of Greece to enter into direct talks with Turkey.

First, on March 26, 1964 the Secretary-General of the United Nations reported to the Security Council that, having received the agreements of the governments concerned, including Greece, he had designated Sakari S. Tuomioja as the United Nations Cyprus mediator.[20] Greece has never withdrawn her approval to the role of mediation.

Second, in the message to the Greek people on his talks with President Johnson, Prime Minister Papandreou went on to state:

After long conversations it was accepted that the initiative should be left to the United Nations Mediator, whom we should all help in his tasks.[21]

Third, during his visit to France at the end of June 1964, Prime Minister Papandreou indicated that he would welcome what would amount to mediation by President de Gaulle. He said de Gaulle "has considerable authority and France is competent to exert a moral influence in all efforts to reach a solution of the Cyprus problem. We would welcome such influence." [22]

Fourth, the United States Government decided to send Dean Acheson, former Secretary of State, to Geneva to assist in the mediation efforts. President Johnson informed the Prime Ministers of Greece and Turkey of this step,[23] and no objection to it was raised by either of them.

Thus, while Greece did not see its way to entering into direct talks with Turkey, it did not rule out other forms of negotiation. Indeed, such negotiations ensued at Geneva, and played a role in averting the long-threatened outbreak of war between Greece and Turkey.[24]

Neither Greece nor Turkey renounced the possibility of the use of force. Frequent statements were made by the leaders of both countries to the effect that they were prepared to use force. Their attitudes confirm the view that renunciation of the use of force is not a necessary prerequisite for negotiations, nor does absence of such renunciation necessarily nullify the willingness of countries to negotiate.

Indeed, it is apparent that in crises regarded as grave by the parties concerned, the alternative of the use of force (obligations under the Charter of the United Nations notwithstanding) tends to march closely with the peaceful efforts of negotiation. Obviously, the parties feel they should have recourse to arms at any moment in the event that negotiations prove unsuccessful. This is still a reality of the international situation, even in an era when a local war often contains the possibilities of escalation into a thermonuclear clash between superpowers.

India's attitude toward negotiation with China before the latter aggressed in October 1962 will illuminate this point. Prime Minister Nehru was undoubtedly keen to settle the issue peacefully, that is, by some form of negotiation. Even as late as August 6, 1962, in placing one of the series of Indian Government white papers on the Sino-Indian situation on the table of the Lok Sabha (the lower house of the Indian Parliament), he stated, "We in India are by our background and temperament peaceful by nature. We earnestly believe in the settlement of differences by peaceful discussions and negotiations." [25]

Indeed, earlier statements of his were even more expressive of the Indian background—Gandhian, nonaligned, and traditionally peaceful with China. As late as August 14, 1962, in replying to a number of speeches which had been made in the Indian Parliament on the situation along the Sino-Indian border, Mr. Nehru stated, "A great deal has been said: we must not talk to the Chinese unless they vacate. I refuse to accept that statement." [26] In short, Mr. Nehru was rejecting the pressures in India against a discussion of the issue with the Chinese. He went on to explain and defend the conversations which V. K. Krishna Menon had had with Marshal Chen Yi at Geneva at the end of July 1962; but his main defense was that these conversations did not amount to negotiation. He explained:

The Defense Minister went to Geneva where there was also the Chinese Foreign Minister. It was his absolute duty, I told him so, to meet him and to talk to him. He could not negotiate. There is no question of any negotiation . . . others were present in those meetings.[27]

In brief, one aspect of the Indian approach was to accept negotiation, or at least preliminary discussions. On the other hand, although Mr. Nehru frequently referred to the peaceful traditions of India, he made it quite clear that there had been no renunciation of the use of force should it prove to be necessary. As early as April 3, 1961, he told the Indian Parliament, "The normal policy for a country and a government to adopt even in the most serious circumstances is not to jump into war but to avoid war and also prepare for it." [28] Then, again, in his statement to Parliament on August 6, 1962 to which we have alluded, he told the legislature, "At the same time we will not hesitate to meet any threat to our territorial integrity with firmness and if necessary by force." [29] On August 14, 1962 he added, "I do think and I am quite right in saying that our capacity to deal with this situation politically and militarily has grown in the last two years or so." [30] This last statement shows Mr. Nehru treading the paths of both peaceful settlement and the use of force.

Indeed, even after the Chinese attack and withdrawal, Mr. Nehru said the following to the Rajya Sabha (the upper house of the Indian Parliament) on December 12, 1962:

Whatever the outcome may be of the efforts being made to continue the cease fire and ensure the withdrawal of the Chinese troops with a view to peaceful methods being employed later for the settlement of the boundary questions on the merits, it is clear that we shall have to continue fully our efforts at strengthening our Defense Forces in every way. We propose to do so.[31]

China too expressed its willingness to negotiate. On August 4, 1962, less than three months before the fighting broke out on the Indian border, the Chinese Government sent the Government of India a note in which it stated the following:

Since neither the Chinese nor the Indian Government want war and since both governments wish to settle the boundary question peacefully through negotiations, further discussion on the Sino-Indian question on the basis of the report of the officials of the two countries should not be put off any longer.[32]

That negotiation was regarded by the Chinese as but one of the courses open to them was made abundantly clear by the relatively uninhibited use of force by them at various points on the Indian border from 1957 on, culminating in the large-scale incursions in the autumn of 1962.

In different contexts we shall consider other factors which affect the will to negotiate, but we can now arrive at a second principle for international negotiation:

> The major parties to a dispute or situation must accept some form of negotiation as a way, though not necessarily unconditionally or as the only way—and not necessarily accompanied by renunciation of the use of force—of arriving at understanding, amelioration, adjustment, or settlement of the dispute or situation.

CHAPTER FIVE

Agreement on Objectives

EVEN WHEN the parties to a dispute or situation express willingness to engage in one form of negotiation or another, the way is still not fully cleared for the commencement of the process of negotiation. There remains the question of the objectives of the parties. It is quite possible for the parties to realize intellectually that negotiations would serve them better than deterioration of a situation or dispute into conflict; and yet their current objectives might appear so totally incompatible that superimposed on the first realization is a second—that negotiation would hardly serve any real purpose. Time and again during the extended Cold War one side or the other has stated that it would not be possible to enter into meaningful negotiations on a subject (for example, disarmament) unless there was a lessening of international tensions in general. Such statements have meant in essence that unless there was a drawing together of objectives on such issues as the future of Germany, it would not be possible to reach agreement to limit, much less to reduce and eventually abolish, armaments. Therefore, the parties' objectives—those directly involved in the issue and sometimes even those pertaining to wider or cognate issues—must at least be brought to a state of some mutual accommodation.

But the wider contextual issues do not always act as an effective brake on negotiations. The more grave and explosive a particular situation becomes, the more it tends to become divorced from the wider contextual issues. Two examples will illustrate this point.

In the matter of disarmament, while other aspects of the Cold War often militated against meaningful disarmament negotiations in the mid-fifties, after the commencement of the missile era in the latter

part of the decade the dangers inherent in military confrontation became enormously increased. Meanwhile, there was no solution to the
Berlin or German problems, the Southeast Asian situation worsened,
and competition to win the support of the third or nonaligned world
increased in intensity. The issues surrounding the Cold War were, if
anything, in a worse state of contention than previously. Nevertheless
the armaments position had become so grave, so fraught with the
possibilities of fatal mischance, that the two sides found themselves
drawn together in an effort to meet at the negotiating table.

This movement came to a head early in 1962, and is clearly indicated in an important message sent by President Kennedy and Prime
Minister Macmillan to Chairman Khruschev on February 7, 1962:

We are convinced that a supreme effort must be made and the three of us
must accept a common measure of personal obligation to seek every
avenue to restrain and reverse the mounting arms race. Unless some
means can be found to make at least a start in controlling the quickening
arms competition, events may take their own course and erupt in a disaster which will afflict all peoples, those of the Soviet Union as well as of
the United Kingdom and the United States. . . .

At this time in our history, disarmament is the most urgent and the
most complex issue we face. The threatening nature of modern armaments
is so appalling that we cannot regard this problem as a routine one or as
an issue which may be useful primarily for the scoring of propaganda
victories.[1]

The same thought is made even clearer in President Kennedy's
message to the Eighteen-Nation Committee on Disarmament Conference, which was read at the opening session, on March 14, 1962, by
Dean Rusk:

Sound disarmament agreements, deeply rooted in mankind's mutual
interest in survival, must serve as a bulwark against the tidal waves of war
and its destructiveness. Let no one, then, say that we cannot arrive at
such agreements in troubled times, for it is then their need is greatest.[2]

Mr. Khrushchev, too, saw the need to proceed with disarmament
negotiations, whatever the surrounding circumstances and unsolved
issues. In his reply to the Kennedy-Macmillan message he said:

And these questions are becoming a source of increasingly profound and
grave concern to the peoples in that the armaments race is still growing,
consuming the labour and wealth of hundreds of millions of people, while
the threat of a new war is increasing, finding material expression in the
massive accumulation of armaments.[3]

The leaders decided to carve the issue of disarmament out of the interlinked Cold War issues, and the Eighteen-Nation Committee on Disarmament (despite France's disassociation from its activities because of General de Gaulle's own rather special reasons) got down to business.

Another example of a duality of objectives—a conflict of objectives on the wider cognate issues, and yet a decision to embark on negotiations—is the case of the International Conference on Laos, which convened at Geneva on May 12, 1961. At that conference, in his opening remarks on May 16, Marshal Chen Yi made a strong and detailed attack on the policies of the United States in Southeast Asia.[4] In so doing he introduced issues wider than those that pertained directly to Laos.

Dean Rusk responded in his opening statement to the Conference on behalf of the United States. His reply is most interesting in regard to negotiating techniques. This is what he said in the relevant passage:

The real issue is whether peaceful co-existence is what normal language would indicate it means. . . .

We note the statement made by the Representative from Peiping that he is ready to work jointly with the delegations of all the other countries participating in this conference to make contributions to the peaceful settlement of the Laotian quesion. We ourselves are prepared to work diligently to discover whether there is agreement in the conference on the questions before us.[5]

The Secretary of State separated the wider question of the basic objectives of certain countries (obviously directed mainly at China) in Southeast Asia from the narrower and more specific question of a peaceful settlement in Laos. He concluded that the United States had noted that the Chinese Government [6] and the other delegations at the Conference were prepared to work for such a settlement, and on this issue the United States was willing to work toward an agreement. On that basis the work of the Conference went forward.[7]

If there is to be negotiation, therefore, there must be an effective focusing on those objectives which are directly related to the dispute or situation under consideration; and those particular objectives of the parties must not be totally incompatible.

The next question which arises in regard to objectives is perhaps even more basic. What precisely do we mean by the minimum or irreducible objectives of the parties? It is quite clear that the parties to a dispute or situation want for themselves, and will work for, the very best they can achieve. Their first objectives, or their objectives at their maximum level, are, if not one hundred percent satisfaction of their original demands, then something as close as possible to full satisfaction. At the same time, if a party to a dispute or situation is serious about negotiating, it realizes that such a high level of success is most unlikely. A party might be willing to make do with a fifty percent result, or in some situations with even a fifteen or twenty percent result. (However, for reasons of prestige and face-saving, a very low dividend of satisfaction, even when perhaps justifiable on the merits of the case, is very rarely acceptable to a state.)

Since in most cases the degree of satisfaction sought by the parties is flexible, what ultimately matters is that the irreducible objectives should not be incompatible. Sometimes it takes several rounds of consideration of an issue before the parties discover what their irreducible objectives actually boil down to.

An important and significant instance which illustrates this point is found in the progressive development of the views of the parties concerned with the Suez Canal issue in 1956.

On July 26, 1956, the Government of Egypt announced that it had taken over the Suez Canal from the Suez Canal Company. The immediate reaction in London and Paris was one of profound dismay, followed by an upsurge of all kinds of efforts to reject this decision of the Government of Egypt. Finance could not be made the main reason, or a reason, for such rejection, for the decree of nationalization provided that compensation would be paid on the basis of the market value of the shares of the Suez Canal Company as quoted on the Paris Stock Exchange on July 25, 1956.[8]

Consultations were held between the Western powers by the end of July in London, and it was agreed and declared that "the action taken by the Government of Egypt, having regard to all the attendant circumstances, threatens the freedom and security of the Canal as guaranteed by the Convention of 1888. [The reference is to the Constantinople Convention of that year.] They [the Western powers] consider that steps should be taken to establish operating arrangements under an international system. . . ." [9] Furthermore, it was decided that the British Government should call an international conference of states interested in the Canal, whether as signatories of the Constantinople Convention or as nations largely concerned with the use of the Canal.

The Government of Egypt understandably regarded it as inappropriate that an international conference to decide on operating arrangements for the Canal and on an international system to assure its operation should be convened by a country other than itself. It refused to attend the London Conference.

However, twenty-two countries gathered in London on August 16, 1956. There was an unmistakable air of crisis. Prime Minister Anthony Eden opened the Conference in tones of gravity and with a sense of severely bruised national interests. John Foster Dulles, the United States Secretary of State, opened the substantive discussion of the Conference. He said, among other things:

We suggest a plan along the following lines. . . . First, the operation of the Suez Canal in accordance with the 1888 Treaty and the principles therein set forth would be made the responsibility of an international board to be established by treaty and associated with the United Nations. Egypt would be represented on such a board, but no single nation would dominate it. . . .[10]

This amounted to international control of the Canal. Christian Pineau, the Foreign Minister of France, endorsed this proposal, saying, "So we agree this system of control envisages a system of international management of the Canal." [11]

Selwyn Lloyd, the Secretary of State for Foreign Affairs of the United Kingdom, added: "I do not believe it would be difficult to draw up such detailed plan along the lines stated by Mr. Dulles." [12]

Indeed, the position of most states at the Conference, and at that time their seemingly minimal demand, was international control and management of the Canal.

Some of the delegations, namely those of Ceylon, India, Indonesia, and the Soviet Union, took part in the Conference in consultation with the Government of Egypt, and pressed the view that full control of the Canal by Egypt must be accepted. They were unable to concur in the opposite view that the Canal should remain an international entity. In their view, Egypt, as a signatory of the Constantinople Convention, would honor its treaty obligations and would be in a position to confirm and guarantee freedom of navigation through the Canal.[13]

The Indian Delegation was in constant touch with Wing Commander Ali Sabri (later Prime Minister of the United Arab Republic),who had come to London for informal consultation with some of the delegates at the Conference. In informal agreement with Ali Sabri, and in conformity with its own views regarding Egypt's rights over the Canal, the Indian delegation prepared a detailed proposal which V. K. Krishna Menon submitted to the twenty-two nation Con-

with populations composed of all the world's races, have interceded
with South Africa to negotiate a peaceful settlement either through
the United Nations or directly with its own racial groups. Since the
support for such requests to South Africa have been worldwide, and
have come from many official representatives who happen to be of
the same race as the politically dominant faction in the Union of
South Africa, a convergence of the objectives of the South African
Government and those of the rest of the world might have been expected. But, in fact, after nineteen years this has still not been
achieved, and consequently no negotiations have been possible in
spite of the adoption of twenty-nine General Assembly resolutions
and five resolutions of the Security Council (from 1946 to the end of
1964), all seeking in one way or another to get South Africa to accept a policy of peaceful change.

In the South African case there will either be a bridging of the gap
between the objectives of those involved (or indications that this
might be possible), with resulting negotiations; or, there will be no
such developments and instead of the peaceful process of negotiation
there will be a precarious stalemate with the strong likelihood of ultimate conflict.

The Suez Canal case indicates that there can be a quite drastic
change in the view of the parties toward the contents of their irreducible minimum objectives. In the case of South Africa, we may still
hope that such radical changes will occur. The situation may be described as a "war of nerves," in which timing is of great importance.
If one side feels that it can no longer stand the war of nerves, it tends
to resort to means other than the possibilities offered by negotiation.
On the other hand, if patience can continue to prevail, what may
seem to be an entrenched position today may prove to yield in the
near future.

In the light of the foregoing analysis, a third principle for negotiation may be stated as follows:

> In order that there might be bona fide negotiations between the
> parties to a dispute or situation, their irreducible minimum objec-
> tives, which must be distinguished from their maximum declared
> objectives, must not be totally incompatible. (Irreducible minimum
> objectives tend to fluctuate with time. It follows that a situation or
> dispute which appears to be nonnegotiable at a particular time may
> prove to be negotiable after a lapse of time.)

CHAPTER SIX

Procedures

LET US NOW EXAMINE the various categories of procedure available today for the conduct of international negotiation. We have sorted out the parties, as it were, who would choose from these procedures, by identifying the necessary preconditions: a dispute or situation must exist between or among states; there must be international concern about this dispute or situation together with a desire to explore the possibilities of peaceful nonjudicial amelioration or settlement; there must be a willingness among the parties themselves to accept negotiation; and their objectives must not be marked by an unbridgeable or total incompatibility.

The first broad category of procedure with which we will concern ourselves is that termed "direct negotiation." Most governments, their statesmen and diplomats, would tend to agree that the method of negotiation most to be desired is that of direct discussion among the parties to the dispute or situation.

During the first half of the 1940s, World War II restricted the relations of most governments to matters directly connected with the pursuit of victory through a total, or nearly total, mobilization and direction of national efforts, material resources, and men. Other aspects of international relations were relatively in suspense. This fact alone prompted many states, immediately after the war, to get together to examine various neglected situations, issues, and problems. An even more strongly impelling factor, which intensified this desire, was that the destructive experiences of the war had brought governments to a mood of readiness for the establishment of mechanisms and organizations which would, as far as possible, assist in increasing the possibilities of peaceful intercourse among states.

The resulting international upsurge expressed itself in conferences which established the United Nations, the Food and Agriculture Organization, the United Nations Educational, Scientific, and Cultural Organization, the World Health Organization, the International Monetary Fund, the International Bank for Reconstruction and Development, and other agencies related to the United Nations. These developments provide some of the most significant recent cases of direct negotiation undertaken on the initiative of the governments primarily concerned, to achieve common objectives.

Governments are not always prepared to negotiate with each other, even when they admit that an international situation requires alteration. Frequently they do not come to the negotiating table until they are bidden to it—or sometimes pressured into it—by third parties. In those instances, some preliminary work may be accomplished in negotiations embracing more states than those directly concerned, and that preliminary work can become a prelude to direct negotiation among the parties concerned.

Direct negotiation might develop under any one of the following four categories:

(a) When there is a shared realization among several nations that a particular international situation should be given consideration with a view to its amelioration or settlement. Such a realization tends to occur after a traumatic international experience, such as World War II; but it can come about because of other circumstances, for example the international steps taken after President Eisenhower's address to the United Nations General Assembly on December 8, 1953,[1] which led to the negotiation to establish the International Atomic Energy Agency to foster the peaceful applications of atomic energy. In these cases the initiative generally comes from one or several of the leading countries in the international community, smaller countries accepting the invitation to join in such negotiations partly because of their own interests, either actual or potential, and partly because through such negotiations they hope to increase their participation and status in world affairs. This motivation is not entirely a selfish one. Many of the smaller countries participate in such international conferences out of the genuine though often fruitless hope of assisting in bringing about agreement among the more powerful states involved.

(b) When a powerful or large state requests a much smaller and relatively much less powerful state to undertake negotiations with it regarding a particular situation. The request from the more powerful state tends to be one which the smaller state feels unable to reject. Therefore, the invitation from the more powerful state generally results in direct negotiation.

(c) Less frequent are the cases of direct negotiation among friendly states when it is neither that a smaller state feels bound to respond affirmatively to the bidding of a larger and more powerful one, nor that the states meet to deal with international issues of wide concern, but rather that established friendship and habits of negotiation bring them together.

(d) Least frequent are those cases in which the motive for direct negotiation stems from rivalry among states, combined with sufficient good will to suggest that the rivalry might be converted, in a particular field, into coordinated or common efforts.

A historic example of the spontaneous drawing together of a number of countries for negotiation is the process that led to and included the convening of the United Nations Conference of International Organization, on April 25, 1945 at San Francisco, to reach final agreement on the Charter of the United Nations.

In another section of this chapter we will discuss the signing of the Atlantic Charter in August 1941. Concrete steps to give effect to the concepts first expressed in that Charter were taken, in the same spirit of ready association, when the representatives of the Soviet Union, the United Kingdom, and the United States met from August 21 to September 28, 1944 at Dumbarton Oaks in Washington, D.C. This meeting was followed by conversations among China, the United Kingdom, and the United States at the end of September and early in October at the same site. In those conversations the first draft of the Charter of the United Nations was evolved. When one considers how extraordinarily difficult it would be to amend a substantive clause of the Charter, and how each such endeavor has been smothered at a very early stage during the last twenty years,[2] it is all the more surprising and noteworthy that in a few brief sessions the four powers were able to draft its main provisions. The basic reason for this fortunate occurrence was that the war was a joint enterprise; had one party surrendered, the fate of the others would have been in doubt. We can justifiably surmise that the resulting sense of camaraderie among the powers, and the absence of subordinating pressures among them, had much to do with the rapid and extremely constructive formulations [3] which emerged from the Dumbarton Oaks conferences.

The only issues not agreed upon at Dumbarton Oaks were those relating to the voting procedures of the Security Council, and Trusteeship provisions. Those matters were solved in a basic sense at Yalta in February 1945. It was agreed that, except on procedural issues, the decisions of the Security Council would require the affirmative vote of seven members, including the concurring votes of the five permanent members of the Council.

The agreement on Trusteeship provisions was sketched out in the broadest outlines, to be amplified at the San Francisco Conference later that year.

At the San Francisco Conference of April 25, 1945, the strong sense of mutual involvement and concern, so marked at the end of World War II and of such influence in immediate postwar negotiations, made itself felt. In just two months the United Nations Charter was fully worked out by fifty sovereign states—a remarkable achievement and a demonstration of the effectiveness as a base of negotiations of a common realization and will in the community of nations.

Statement after statement made at San Francisco brought out the passionate and universal feeling which underpinned the Conference. United States President Harry S. Truman, said in his message at the opening: "We, who have lived through the torture and the tragedy of two world conflicts, must realize the magnitude of the problem before us. . . . We still have a choice between the alternatives: the continuation of international chaos—or the establishment of a world organization for the enforcement of peace. . . . We hold a powerful mandate from our people." [4]

Edward R. Stettinius, Jr., Secretary of State of the United States, in his first statement on April 26, referred to another aspect of the sense of a coming together to solve common problems:

Because of our common understanding that economic security goes hand in hand with security from war, United Nations conferences were held in Atlantic City, Hot Springs, and Bretton Woods on cooperative measures for relief, to meet common problems of food and agriculture and to prepare the financial basis for economic reconstruction and an expanding world economy in the post-war world.[5]

Viacheslav M. Molotov, speaking as the Foreign Minister of the Soviet Union on the same day, echoed those statements:

We will fully cooperate in the solution of this great problem with all the other governments genuinely devoted to this noble cause. We are confident that this historic aim will be achieved by joint efforts of peace-loving nations . . .

As far as the Soviet Union is concerned . . . the whole people are brought up in the spirit of faith and devotion to the cause of setting up a solid organization of international security.[6]

Anthony Eden, Secretary of State for Foreign Affairs of the United Kingdom, stated:

This hard fact is now biting deeply into the consciousness of all peoples, and they are, as I believe, ready to accept its implications and to shoulder the responsibilities which it imposes. Therein, Ladies and Gentlemen, lies the main difference between today and the lost opportunities at the end of the last world war. Today this fact is patent to all. No one will dispute it.[7]

Those sentiments were expressed not only by the world's great powers. Paul-Henri Spaak, Foreign Minister of Belgium, speaking for one of the smallest countries of Europe, said on April 27:

The peoples of the world have felt and understood the dangers that our civilization has just faced. They realize how nearly we escaped the tragedy of seeing disappear from the face of the earth, for long, and perhaps forever, all that brings a price to life and dignity to mankind. With the sure instinct that so often guides them, they are prepared today to make the effort necessary to prevent the return of such a threat.[8]

From all parts of the world the same feelings were evidenced. Pedro Leão Velloso, the Minister of State for Foreign Relations of Brazil, said:

Traditional principles, geographic imperatives, all impel us Brazilians, therefore, to prevent war and to desire the solid organization of a definitive system of security, for the peace and in war, without demanding rewards and without measuring sacrifices.[9]

From the continent of Africa, Abdel Hamid Badawi Pasha, Minister of Foreign Affairs for Egypt, said on April 28:

The keystone of this arch of peace which we seek here to build should be the deep rooted principles enunciated in the Atlantic Charter. That day in the Atlantic, in mid-August of 1941, when the Prime Minister of Great Britain and the President of the United States met and wrote down certain fundamental thoughts, they wrote a charter for all humanity.[10]

Ramaswami Mudaliar, Chairman of the Delegation of India, in his first statement, on April 28, mentioned another aspect of the universal and common feeling that brought about the San Francisco Conference:

There is one great reality, one fundamental factor, one eternal verity which all religions teach, which must be remembered by all of us, the dignity of the common man, the fundamental human rights of all beings all over the world.[11]

The United Nations Conference on International Organization was the most significant of all the postwar negotiations that were sparked by a common realization, but it was by no means unique. The negotiations to set up the International Atomic Energy Agency took place a decade later, and exemplified again the validity and strength of entering upon negotiation on the basis of a realization that has become widely diffused among the nations.

It is significant, however, that in the setting up of the International Atomic Energy Agency, although a realization of common needs developed, more effort was required than in 1945 for this point of view to become the directing factor.

President Eisenhower made his Atoms for Peace speech at the General Assembly in December 1953. At the next session, in September 1954, the United States requested the inclusion of an agenda item on international cooperation in the peaceful uses of atomic energy. When it came to the debate, the United States explained that it was in communication with the Government of the Soviet Union concerning the setting up of an agency and other aspects of international cooperation.

The discussion on this matter at the Ninth Session of the General Assembly was very brief and exiguous. The subject of atomic energy for peaceful purposes was a new one. The Assembly had not applied its mind to it, and the general feeling at the Ninth Session was to leave the issue to the atomic powers and hope for agreement among them. To most of us at the Assembly, it seemed that those powers could come to agreed conclusions—a development which would be most welcome. Consequently, a resolution which expressed the hope that an International Atomic Energy Agency would be established without delay was adopted unanimously.[12] This is how the matter was left at the close of the Ninth Session.

The next year, at the Tenth Session, the United States again asked for a discussion on the peaceful uses of atomic energy. On this occasion, somewhat to the surprise of many members of the United Nations, Senator John O. Pastore, the United States spokesman, announced that a small group of eight countries had been discussing the setting up of an International Atomic Energy Agency, that they had drafted a statute and were circulating it to all members of the United

Nations for their comments. The Assembly widely felt that the eight countries were not sufficiently representative of the international community. They were, in fact, four of the Western advanced countries: the United States, the United Kingdom, France, and Canada, and the suppliers of atomic raw materials to those countries: Australia, Belgium, Portugal, and the Union of South Africa. However, Senator Pastore attempted to assuage Assembly sentiments by announcing that the United States and its partners in negotiation would take into account the suggestions and comments of other states on the proposed statute of the agency.[13] This view was supported by Anthony Nutting, Minister of State of the United Kingdom;[14] and Paul Martin, later Foreign Minister of Canada.[15]

But this rather one-sided approach to the matter was out-of-date in the fall of 1955. In the summer of that year the first International Conference on the Peaceful Uses of Atomic Energy had been convened at Geneva. It was, at that time, the largest conference ever called by the United Nations. It enormously stimulated interest in the field of atomic energy, and vastly changed the attitudes of member states. It was in this aura that the Tenth Session of the General Assembly was considering the proposals for the creation of an International Atomic Energy Agency. In short, the matter had become one of universal concern and interest.

On October 14, A. K. Brohi of Pakistan pleaded for an agreed solution, saying that it would be disastrous to have major differences.[16] Carl Schurmann of the Netherlands echoed this sentiment;[17] and Ambassador A. M. Ramadan of Egypt pointed out that his country had joined India as a cosponsor of a draft resolution which provided that the constitution of the agency should be based on the consensus of views expressed in the General Assembly.[18] On October 18, 1955, Alsing Andersen of Denmark said that he wished to express the hope that it would be possible to organize the agency in a manner equitable to all countries.[19]

These statements, from countries for the most part allied with the United States, helped to turn the tide. Senator Pastore responded with a significant alteration of the draft resolution proposed by the United States and some other countries. He stated, and placed this idea in the draft resolution, that the eight governments sponsoring the statute would be prepared to invite all members of the United Nations and all members of the Specialized Agencies to a conference on the final text of the statute.

India, which had led the nonaligned countries in the move for a

wider based preparation of the statute, and had submitted a draft
resolution to that effect as early as October 6,[20] when the United
States had submitted the first edition of its own draft resolution,
warmly thanked the United States for this step forward. V. K.
Krishna Menon said that the very generous gesture made by the
United States and its cosponsors in putting the matter in the hands of
a world conference at a later stage was doubly welcome.[21] As sometimes happens in international negotiations, the good reception of this
concession seemed to push forward a spirit of conciliation. Senator
Pastore took most delegates by surprise when on October 25 he
announced that his Government had issued invitations to the Governments of Brazil, Czechoslovakia, India, and the Soviet Union, to join
the original eight states in the future negotiations on the draft statute.[22]

The United States had moved alongside the position of many other
member states by reconstituting the negotiating committee so as to
make it representative of most views expressed in the Assembly. In
so doing, that country took into account the universal interest which
had developed in the establishment of the agency. The universal will
had triumphed, and made possible the succeeding striking yet expected developments in the establishment of the International Atomic
Energy Agency.

On April 18, 1956, after several months of hard negotiation during
which no group of countries maintained its original position, the
Twelve-Nation Negotiating Committee for the Statute of the International Atomic Energy Agency reached unanimous agreement on a
draft statute.[23] Subsequently, in September and October 1956, the
World Conference on the Statute of the Agency, attended by 81
countries at the United Nations Headquarters, held a full and sometimes incisive debate. As a consequence, a slightly amended version
of the draft statute was unanimously adopted by the 81 countries on
October 26, 1956.[24] These were very remarkable achievements in
the field of international negotiation. They exemplified almost to per-
fection the unifying effect of a widespread common interest in an
international situation.

To turn to our second category of direct negotiations in international affairs, in recent times a large number of negotiations have
been initiated by great powers to settle situations or disputes with
relatively weaker states. One such instance is the case of the border
negotiations between the People's Republic of China and the Union
of Burma (1954–1960). All the crucial initiatives in this negotiation

came from the Chinese. In 1948 the Kuomintang Government refused to continue to receive from Burma the annual rental for the Namwan Assigned Tract, which had been assigned to Burma in perpetuity by the Sino-British Boundary Agreement of 1897.

In 1954 the Government of the People's Republic of China invited Prime Minister U Nu to Peking, and during this visit it raised the matter of the border. It was agreed, and so stated in a communiqué, that the border question should be settled "through normal diplomatic channels." [25] But in 1955 Chinese troops penetrated Burmese territory.[26] There was a clash with Burmese troops. Again, this was a Chinese initiative—though not one in conformity with the communiqué.

However, the Chinese followed up with a peaceful overture. In 1956 they again invited U Nu to China. U Ba Swe, then the Burmese Prime Minister, agreed to U Nu's visit to Peking to discuss the border problem.

In Peking, all the initiatives seemed to come from the Chinese side. As far as the Burmese delegation was concerned—it was a powerful one, consisting of most of the senior diplomats of Burma—its instructions were to stick to the status quo; that is, that the boundary which the independent Government of Burma had inherited from the British should be left undisturbed.[27] But the Chinese made a series of proposals, including recognition of their claim to the Namwan Tract, and they asked for three villages—Hpimaw, Kangfang and Gawlum, which lay on the Burmese side of the watershed between the N'Mai Kah and Salween rivers. The negotiations centered entirely upon these Chinese proposals. The area involved was not large, and there were periods in history when the Chinese had been in possession of the villages and other areas west of the watershed. For these reasons U Nu considered the Chinese request for the three villages reasonable. He felt that if the villages were given to the Chinese they would not insist on the return to them of the Namwan Tract [28] (which it must be remembered had been leased in perpetuity to Burma), and that this would be of some significance to Burma because an important highway passed through the area.

The point of real importance, however, is that to China the Namwan area was of no value, whereas the three villages which they demanded would give them a peephole into Burma from the straddled position which they would have athwart the watershed. It could be only for this contingently strategic purpose that Chou En-lai insisted on the cession of the villages by Burma in spite of the strong and fervent pleas of the leaders of the Burmese Kachin state that the territories should not be taken from them.

The Chinese initiative won the day. The Burmese gave in, and it was agreed that the villages should be ceded. The Chinese proposals were put in writing, and the Peking Government asked that they be treated as an integrated whole.[29] U Nu returned to Rangoon after a protracted stay in Peking. The Burmese Cabinet approved the Chinese proposals, and U Nu made a broadcast speech to the nation in which he explained why the Chinese proposals "were considered fair and reasonable." [30]

In December 1956 Chou En-lai paid a brief return visit to Rangoon, during which U Nu "understood that the Chinese government were prepared to agree to the transfer of the Namwan Assigned Tract to Burma on a permanent basis." [31] This was in the context of Burma's having agreed to let China have the three villages.

But the great power involved in the negotiations decided to take another initiative. In 1957 U Nu visited Kunming. "Chou En-lai was good enough to come there to meet me," he said. But at that visit Chou En-lai surprised U Nu by making another territorial demand. In effect this was a demand for another peephole about a hundred and fifty miles south of the three villages. This was the area inhabited by the Panghung and Panglao tribes, and it lay west of the 1941 line agreed to by the then Chinese Government. U Nu was taken aback. He stated:

I replied that it had been my impression, before I heard Premier Chou En-lai that a settlement of the boundary problem had virtually been reached, but that I now realized that this was not so.[32]

In January 1960 the Chinese again took the initiative. President Ne Win went to Peking, and the two tracts which the Chinese had demanded were both ceded, and a border agreement was signed.[33] The upshot thus was that the various Chinese initiatives had proved successful. The Burmese had tried to hold the frontier they had inherited, but had failed. They had not lost much territory—for obviously the Chinese were not interested in additional square mileage—but they had ceded two windows which might have strategic value to China.

I have deliberately based the above remarks on the detailed statement made by U Nu to the Chamber of Deputies of Burma.[34] The picture which emerges is that of a great power firmly holding the initiative in direct negotiations with a smaller state.

There is never complete equality of will or pressure from two parties in the direction of negotiations between them. Generally speaking, if one country is much more powerful than the other it tends to have the effect of pushing the two states concerned (to take the simplest case) into negotiation. On the other hand, the démarches of the substantially less powerful country in favor of negotiation are unlikely to be effective.

This reality notwithstanding, a distinction exists between those cases in which powerful states ask for negotiations and considerably smaller states have no alternative but to agree; and cases in which both states are impelled to negotiate by long-standing friendship and habit. The general field of relations between the United States and Canada furnishes a fair example of the latter type of negotiations, our third category.

We might look briefly at the case of the St. Lawrence Waterway, which has been the subject of one of the more difficult negotiations between the two neighboring states but which nevertheless is an example of mutual good will, friendship, and desire to cooperate. The sparring that took place between the two countries before World War II was the result not of lack of friendship but of the pressures of private, state, and regional interests on both sides of the border. At various times one government or the other had to take those influences into account, but this did not detract from their fundamental friendship and desire to cooperate.

In October 1934, the provincial leader of the Liberal Party in Ontario, Mitchell Hepburn, announced that he would not carry out the cost allocation agreement signed by his predecessor in 1932 with the Government of the Dominion. At that time no legislation had been adopted in confirmation of the 1932 agreement between the Central Government and Ontario, because Prime Minister Richard B. Bennett of Canada had feared that any legislative move by Ontario might create an impression in the United States that Canada was over-anxious to get on with the job.[35]

The outbreak of the war gave an impetus to feelings on both sides of the border that favored cooperation, and led to the basic agreement between the United States and Canada regarding the utilization of the waters of the Great Lakes–St. Lawrence Basin, signed at Ottawa on March 19, 1941.[36] This agreement, however, remained in cold storage until it was taken up again in 1951. In September of that year it was announced at the White House, when Prime Minister Louis St. Laurent of Canada visited President Truman, that both leaders considered "it would be most desirable to proceed along the lines of the 1941 agreement between the United States and Canada." [37]

Some action resulted, and eventually, on August 17, 1954, notes were exchanged between Lester B. Pearson, then Secretary of State for External Affairs for Canada, and J. C. Bliss, the United States Chargé d'Affaires at Ottawa.[38]

The note of the American Chargé d'Affaires stated that his Government "Welcomes this new opportunity for constructive and harmonious cooperation between our two countries." The note echoed a precisely similar phrase in Lester B. Pearson's note of the same day. In 1959 a Memorandum of Agreement was drawn up, together with a Tariff of Tolls, and the whole project was in good working order. On both sides of the border the two governments had had to contend with the feelings of local governments, pressure groups, and economic organizations. If a basic friendship and desire to cooperate had not existed between Canada and the United States, the individualistic and parochial forces would have won the day. Indeed, the negotiations over the St. Lawrence Waterway have been a triumph of the principle of direct talks between governments whose basic orientation is toward mutual friendship and common interest.

It is appropriate to place within the same category the historic Atlantic Charter of August 14, 1941, signed by Franklin D. Roosevelt and Winston Churchill. This declaration announced the desire to see a new world order, based on the abandonment of the use of force in international relations and buttressed by the establishment "of a wider and permanent system of general security." [39] There is little question that the Atlantic Charter could have been devised as speedily as it was only on the basis of a strong friendship between the signatory governments.

In category (d), under the general heading of direct negotiations, we have seen in recent years, as a concomitant of the slight thaw in the Cold War, a probing between the United States and the Soviet Union on various issues such as cooperation in the exploration of outer space, including, at one time, the possibility of a common endeavor for a moon shot. A recent example, and one that has been attended with a measure of success, is the successful initiation of cooperation in the field of water desalting.

In his news conference on foreign and domestic affairs held on June 23, 1964 at Washington D.C., President Johnson made the following announcement:

I am happy to announce that the United States and the Soviet Union have agreed to explore the possibility of scientific cooperation on methods of desalting sea water, including the possible use of nuclear power. As an initial step, the meeting of the United States and Soviet representatives will be held in Washington on July 14 and 15 of this year. . . . The representatives will then advise their respective governments as to the best way to proceed.[40]

White House officials stated that the initiative for the cooperation in the desalting talks had come from the Soviet Union. In the first half of 1964, at United States-Soviet scientific meetings, Soviet scientists stressed the importance to the Soviet Union of research and development in this field.[41]

The first negotiating meetings, initiated on July 14, 1964, indicated the desire of both sides to explore possibilities of cooperation. The two teams were headed by important and responsible representatives —Dr. Donald F. Hornig, the United States President's Scientific Advisor, and A. I. Churin, Chief Administrator of the State Committee on Coordination of Scientific Work in the Soviet Union.[42]

On July 16, 1964 the two sides reached an informal agreement covering the exchange of inspection visits by technical experts, exchanges of scientific reports on work being done in the field, and arrangements for small symposia to discuss projects or scientific issues. At those sessions information of value was exchanged. For example, it was learned from the Soviet team that their country had started to construct an atomic reactor to provide steam for a desalting plant in the Caspian Sea which will have a capacity of 25 million gallons a day. That will be far larger than any plant now in operation in the world.[43]

The cooperation of the two nations for the desalting of sea water is a good example of a common need and rivalry that have resulted in the pooling of efforts and resources. If the program announced as the outcome of these direct negotiations develops satisfactorily, it can have far-reaching repercussions. Almost simultaneously with the Washington bilateral negotiations, the United Nations, on July 17, 1964, published a study of water desalting needs in the developing countries.[44] Sixty-one plants in such countries were studied. As a result of the study a number of countries, including Argentina and Saudi Arabia, have asked the United Nations for assistance in this field. The successful direct bilateral United States-Soviet negotiations could, as a result of other needs, lead to multilateral negotiations under the aegis of the United Nations. This would be an example of the truism that successful negotiation tends to set up a chain reaction of negotiations. We saw this on a wide scale in the immediate post-World War II period.

Rivalry, as we can see, is not confined to the more obvious forms of competition; it permeates all areas of international endeavor, not the least of which is the enhancement of national prestige in the eyes of developing countries by such means as peace moves and the sharing of technological advances. The weight of prestige in influencing matters of war and peace will become apparent in a related context later in this chapter.

In a very real sense, rivalry in a most vital field is the explanation of the nature of General de Gaulle's proposals for disarmament negotiations. His view is that disarmament discussions must first center on the abolition of the means of delivery of nuclear weapons, and that the negotiations should be restricted to representatives of the present nuclear powers, assisted perhaps by the representatives of near-nuclear powers.[45]

A somewhat similar expression of international rivalry came from Peking immediately following the initialing of the Moscow Agreement on a limited test ban in August 1963. The Government of the People's Republic of China proposed a world disarmament conference to agree on the immediate renunciation and destruction of all nuclear weapons.[46]

While rivalry can be the basis of proposals for direct negotiation, the initiatives, in order to succeed, must be directed toward common objectives. This was so in the case of the desalination negotiations. In other cases—such as the proposal of the People's Republic of China for a world disarmament conference for the sole purpose of the abolition and destruction of nuclear weapons, and the kind of proposals which General de Gaulle offers for disarmament negotiations—the objectives of the rivals are so far apart that their proposals have not led to the negotiating table.

One of the most significant direct negotiations in recent years to arise out of rivalry has been that between General de Gaulle and Konrad Adenauer. The background of this negotiation was touched on by Adenauer in an appearance at the National Press Club, Washington, D.C., in November 1962:

. . . back in 1944 when General de Gaulle became Prime Minister of France he went to Moscow to sign a new treaty with the Russians which was again directed against the Germans, and later on he explained to me in a conversation why he had done that.

He said to me at that time in France people were concerned and afraid that the Germans, once they had recovered again, might be tempted to take their revenge on the French, and he wanted to have the safeguard against this, and that was the reason for his concluding the treaty with the Soviets. . . .

We want—and that is also the view of General de Gaulle—to establish a dike, a dam, in the heart of Europe by bringing together these two nations, not only by treaties but also by strengthening the human bonds, the human ties.[47]

To his own people Adenauer explained his ideas in a Stuttgart publication titled *Christ und Welt:*

Even those who observed it with reserve and scepticism at length remarked that this was obviously a "milestone in History." . . .

Together with President de Gaulle, I and my Government are striving simultaneously toward European unity in the wider defensive community of the Atlantic alliance.[48]

Serious negotiations commenced during General de Gaulle's visit to Germany in September 1962, and were renewed at Paris early the following year. They led to the Common French-German Declaration and the Treaty between the French Republic and the Federal Republic of Germany—both of January 22, 1963.

The Common Declaration made it explicit that what was sought by the French and German leaders was a termination of the long rivalry between the two countries. A paragraph in the Declaration is phrased:

Convinced that the reconciliation of the German people and the French people, bringing an end to the age-old rivalries, constitutes an historic event which profoundly transforms the relations of the two peoples.[49]

Maurice Couve de Murville, Foreign Minister of France, spoke of the Franco-German Treaty to the French National Assembly as follows:

The French people and the German people have understood the necessity of their final reconciliation. Since the President of the German Federal Republic and the Chancellor visited France in 1961 and 1962, and since the visit to Germany of General de Gaulle last September, this reconciliation has been consummated. . . . The two countries had already begun to act in close concert in order to harmonize their policy and their action. Of these good habits it was necessary to make a written rule and consecrate them formally.[50]

German leaders have also frequently attested their faith in the Franco-German Treaty. For example, in his first statement to the Bundestag following his election as Chancellor, Professor Ludwig Erhard said:

This treaty [the Franco-German Treaty] demonstrates the reconciliation of the two nations and should become a motive power for the unification of Europe. All problems of European policy center around the relations between the German and the French people. The Treaty on Mutual Consultation and Cooperation of January 22, 1963, will progressively have to be filled with life. The cooperation between the two nations is based on mutual understanding and confidence.[51]

In the context of history it is far too early to assess the outcome of the Franco-German treaty of January 22, 1963, but its making furnishes a notable example of direct negotiations resulting from a base of deep rivalry accompanied by sufficient understanding of a common destiny as geographical neighbors.

We have so far examined the category of direct negotiations, either bilateral or multilateral, initiated by the parties directly concerned. Direct negotiations may also be initiated either with the assistance of other states or persons, or under the influence of other states or persons. The United Nations furnishes many instances of attempts toward negotiations of this character, some of which have been successful.

In recent years attempts at direct negotiations have also taken place outside the organs of the United Nations, and some results have been achieved. One example is the case of the border dispute between Algeria and Morocco.

In our examination of direct negotiations under the influence or pressure of other parties, certain general rules or tendencies suggest themselves. One is that the more powerful the parties involved, the less feasible is it for third parties to bring to bear effective influence or pressure for negotiations between them. This suggests that the voice of power is more likely to succeed in bringing the parties together than the voices of weakness. However, this general proposition is not an absolute, as was manifest in the period of strong bipolarization which existed throughout the 1950s and for a year or two thereafter. In this period, the main protagonists in the Cold War were sensitive about the acceptance of their postures in world affairs by their allies as well as by the growing number of nonaligned or uncommitted countries. This being so, the great powers have sometimes appeared to pay some attention to the desires of other countries. However, such cases have not been frequent, and broadly speaking are not to be found in situations in which the prestige, or vital interest, of the great powers is directly concerned, such as the questions of Germany, Southeast Asia, the Western Hemisphere, and certain aspects of armaments and security.

When the leading power on one side shows some readiness to negotiate over crucial issues, it will be found on analysis that it has felt itself under the pressure of the strength of the other side, rather than of third parties. This would appear to have been the case in 1955, when at the Heads of State Conference representatives of the Governments of France, the Soviet Union, the United Kingdom, and the United States instructed the foreign ministers of those countries to work out a security pact for Europe, or a part of Europe, and also made the following declaration regarding the German question:

The Heads of Government, recognizing their common responsibility for the settlement of the German question and the re-unification of Germany, have agreed that the settlement of the German question and the re-unification of Germany by means of free elections shall be carried out in conformity with the national interests of the German people and the interests of European security. The Foreign Ministers will make whatever arrangements they may consider desirable for the participation of, or for consultation with, other interested parties.[52]

No progress was made on any aspect of the directive by the four heads of government. The Soviet Union, which at the beginning of the Conference felt itself under the pressure of Western nuclear strength, soon made rapid strides in the development of missiles, the balance of power was readjusted at a new level, and the 1955 directive was no longer in conformity with the realities of the situation.

The general propositions relating to direct negotiations which ensue as a result of the interest, influence, or pressure, of single or multiple third parties, may be stated as follows:

(a) Pleadings or urgings by third parties are successful in inverse proportion to the degree in which the vital interests of a party or parties are involved in the dispute or situation in question.

(b) When pleadings are made by a large section of the world community, then even the great powers may consider it to be in their own interest to respond to such pleadings.

(c) In periods of dangerous deadlock involving the prestige more than the basic vital interests of the great powers, third-party urgings or pleadings may provide a plausible and acceptable possibility for retreating from the brink of armed conflict and thus for the initiation of direct negotiations.

The validity of (a) above is manifest when this proposition is stated in traditional terms, namely that there are certain things (what they consider their most vital interests) that countries would rather fight for than compromise. This has proved to be the case time and time again in the post-World War II era.

South Africa, although repeatedly asked by the United Nations, has been adamant in its rejection of negotiations regarding its recent policies, because the present Government believes that the very existence of the Union is threatened by the issues raised.

The case of Algeria in its struggle for independence may, on the contrary, be regarded as illustrating the positive aspect of this principle (since direct negotiations resulted), particularly as it is a case in which the interpretation by a major power of its own vital interests went through a considerable transformation.

The General Assembly discussed the question of Algeria for seven consecutive years, from 1955 to 1961; and during that period the issue also came before the Security Council. During the Tenth General Assembly Session France walked out of the Assembly, so strong was its antagonism to any United Nations involvement in the issue, and so clear-cut was its conception of its own vital interests. Although a face-saving resolution introduced by India saved French *amour propre*,[53] and France joined in the discussion of the case in 1956 and 1957 when resolutions seeking to promote negotiation were adopted by the Assembly unanimously,[54] no substantive discussions between France and Algeria resulted immediately. France maintained the position that no settlement would be possible that eliminated her sovereignty and presence from Algeria, while the National Liberation Front maintained that Algeria must reemerge as a fully independent state. There was a continued clash of avowed vital interests, and the broad-based urging of the world community remained largely ineffective.

It would not serve our purpose to trace all the steps taken at the United Nations. However, note must be taken of the resolution adopted on December 19, 1960 by a vote of 63 in favor, eight against, and 27 abstentions. (Those voting against were six of France's associated states in Africa, plus Portugal and the Union of South Africa.) France itself did not take part in the vote. This resolution asserted the right of the United Nations to insist on the application of the relevant provisions of the Charter in the settlement of this issue. The third operative paragraph of the resolution reads as follows:

Recognizes further that the U.N. has a responsibility to contribute towards the successful and just implementation of this right [of self-determination].[55]

By this time serious negotiations had commenced between France and accredited representatives of the FLN. General de Gaulle had substituted for insistence on preserving the French presence in Algeria the acceptance by his Government of the principle of self-determination. Obviously, looking back at the situation, one reason which made it possible for France to make this shift was that it had firmly decided to embark on becoming a nuclear power, and a nuclear power, as has been seen in the case of the superpowers, becomes less and less dependent for the preservation of its vital interests on the maintenance of foreign military bases and other direct manifestations of its presence abroad.

The self-determination of peoples was introduced into the Charter of the United Nations, although it had found no place in the Covenant of the League of Nations. The very first Article states it to be a purpose of the United Nations:

To develop friendly relations among nations based on respect for the principle of equal rights and self-determination of peoples.

Nevertheless, in the early years of consideration of the Algerian case by the United Nations, the almost annual insistance on the application of these rights to Algeria did very little to shift the situation. It was only after the reconsideration by France of the nexus between its own vital interests and Algeria that the United Nations did perhaps influence the course of events. Without the pressure of the General Assembly at that stage for the application of the Charter principle of self-determination, it is likely that France would have continued, for some time at any rate, to seek some other adjustment.

To a certain extent, the case of Algeria also reflects our second general proposition. Even the great powers may, on occasion, consider it to be in their own interests to respond to pleadings from a large section of the world community. However, there were other important factors directing the Algerian case—the long duration and the bitterness of the military conflict, and then the exclusion of the issue from the category of France's vital interests.

The admission to membership in the United Nations of sixteen states on December 14, 1955 was a significant example of the decision of great powers to heed the urging of a large section of the world community.

Some of the sixteen states had been applicants for membership ever since 1946 (Albania, Mongolia, Jordan, Ireland, and Portugal). Although a trickle of other applicants, such as Pakistan, Indonesia, Yemen, Burma, and Israel, had been allowed in by the great powers, the list of applicants on whom agreement could not be reached had swelled to eighteen by negative Security Council decisions on the cases of Austria, Bulgaria, Cambodia, Ceylon, Finland, Hungary, Italy, Nepal, and other states. In exasperation, the General Assembly in 1949 asked the International Court of Justice for an advisory opinion on whether the admission of a state to United Nations membership could be made effective by decision of the General Assembly, when the Security Council had made no recommendation for admission.[56] The Court advised that admission to the United Nations could not be granted on a vote of the General Assembly alone.[57]

In 1953,[58] the General Assembly appointed a Good Offices Committee to try to persuade the great powers. However, no tangible progress was made. The attitude of the Soviet Union was that it could not agree to the admission of the non-Communist states on the list of eighteen applicants unless the Security Council would simultaneously recommend the admission of the five Communist applicants.

In the General Assembly in 1954 and 1955, pressure continued to build steadily for the admission of applicant states. Finally, heeding this nearly unanimous pressure, the United States and the Soviet Union decided to accept each other's position. This amounted to agreement between them that the United States and its friends would help to insure at least seven positive votes in the Security Council for the applications of the Communist states, provided the Soviet Union would refrain from vetoing any of the thirteen non-Communist applicants. This crucial decision reflected a yielding of the great powers to world public opinion, as expressed by the overwhelming majority votes in the General Assembly.[59] However, when the Security Council met on December 10, 1955 to consider the eighteen applications, the representative of the Republic of China vetoed the application of Mongolia, whereupon the Soviet Union vetoed the applications of the thirteen non-Communist applicants on the ground that its agreement with the United States had not been honored by the Republic of China.

The atmosphere in the United Nations was one of profound dismay and anger at the frustration of the efforts of the vast majority of its membership. The essential question was whether the great powers would heed the pleadings of the world community. An enormous pressure developed in favor of the admission of at least a great majority of the applicant states. Behind the scenes activities were conducted by a number of delegates. Paul Martin of Canada, Victor Belaúnde of Peru, and members of the Indian delegation, were among them. A formulation was evolved privately which would entail holding back one non-Communist applicant against the application of

Mongolia, which the Republic of China continued to oppose. Fortunately, the leaders of the Soviet Union, Nikolai Bulganin and Nikita Khrushchev, were visiting India and Afghanistan at that time. V. K. Krishna Menon, the leader of the Indian delegation, sent a strong plea to Jawaharlal Nehru asking him to use his good offices with the Russian leaders. This tactic was helpful, and Yakov Malik, the representative of the Soviet Union, told us informally on the morning of December 14, 1955 that he had received fresh instructions from his Government to facilitate the entrance of all the eighteen applicants except Japan. Since the Republic of China had continued to be adamant in its opposition to Mongolia, this meant that Mongolia and Japan would not be admitted. Each side would keep out one state from the other side. The events in the Security Council on December 14, 1955 corresponded to these positions, and sixteen states were admitted to United Nations membership.

As a result of strong international urgings, the great powers altered the entrenched positions which for some nine years had held up the development of the United Nations as a near-universal body. Once the position had been so significantly breached in 1955, the Soviet Union decided not to maintain its objections. Japan and the Sudan were admitted, and very soon thereafter Mongolia too attained membership. Before the breakthrough of December 1955 the United Nations had a membership of sixty states, but then a process started which resulted, by the end of 1965, in a United Nations membership of 117—a tribute both to the great powers and to the force of strong urgings by a large number of third parties.

Other instances could be cited where the great powers have yielded to third-party urgings, for the most part at the United Nations. At various stages of the disarmament issue this has been true, and particularly in 1960. As a result of their insistence that year that there should be agreement between the two great powers, or no resolution at all in the General Assembly, the growing number of nonaligned countries were able to defeat the attempt of Canada to give priority to a largely Western resolution on disarmament. The draft resolutions of the Soviet Union and its allies were also placed in cold storage by the action of the nonaligned countries.[60] This insistence of a growing body of United Nations opinion on agreement between the United States and the Soviet Union, more particularly as the dangers of the missile era became increasingly evident, prepared the way for the unusual developments in 1961, when the United States and the Soviet Union, for the first time in fifteen years, introduced jointly sponsored resolutions on disarmament which were adopted unanimously by the General Assembly.[61]

Another instance of the influence of joint urgings by a number of states on a great power may be seen in the events at the Third Emergency Special Session of the General Assembly following developments in Lebanon in 1958. The United States decided, at the request of the President of Lebanon, to land a group of Marines in that country during the summer of 1958, although at the behest of the Security Council a substantial group of United Nations observers was already in Lebanon. This action resulted in the immediate convening of the Third Emergency Special Session on August 8, 1958.

We are not now concerned with all the facets of the Middle East situation at the time of the landing of United States Marines in Lebanon and the sending, again at the request of the Government of Jordan, of a small contingent of British troops to Amman. We are concerned rather with the negotiating pressures which developed in the United Nations Emergency Special Session in regard to the relations of the two great powers with Lebanon and Jordan.

The United States regarded the situation as so significant and internationally fraught with possibilities of mischance that it took the unprecedented step of sending President Dwight D. Eisenhower to make its opening statement to the Emergency Special Session.

President Eisenhower made a far-ranging appeal for peace in the Middle East, and he proposed a six-point plan to achieve this objective.[62]

But the mood of the Assembly, particularly of the Arab states and of most Asian and African states, was completely focused on the withdrawal of the troops which had been sent into Lebanon and Jordan. Foreign Minister Mahmoud Fawzi of the United Arab Republic, the first of the Arab spokesmen and the one who spoke at the same meeting as had President Eisenhower, said:

What we are all facing now, is the immediate withdrawal of these armed forces [those of the U.S. in Lebanon and of the U.K. in Jordan]. We welcome the announcement by the Government of the United States of its intention to withdraw its armed forces from Lebanon, and of the actual beginning of this withdrawal. But we are deeply perturbed by the failure of the United States to indicate, until now, the time during which that withdrawal will be completed, and we are anxiously waiting to hear such an indication. . . .

The Assembly has before it a clear and an extremely moderate draft resolution submitted by the delegation of the Soviet Union (A/3870) recommending the withdrawal from Lebanon and Jordan respectively of the United States and United Kingdom armed forces which are stationed there. It is the view of my delegation that this draft resolution completely deserves our full, serious and sympathetic consideration.[63]

That this was the nature of the issue before the Assembly was clear from the statements of the Arab delegates, most of the Asian and African delegates, and some others, and even more so from the intensive diplomatic activity in the corridors of the United Nations and in delegation offices and hotel suites on the East Side of New York City. Some Western delegates considered it likely that the Arab states and their friends would vote for a draft resolution they had presented to the Assembly. This was particularly the view of the delegates of Canada and Norway, who, among other states, cosponsored the draft resolution.

However, the Canada-Norway draft resolution [64] made no mention of the withdrawal of the troops which had been stationed in Lebanon and Jordan—although this was the primary issue before the Assembly in the understanding of most states. The United States was not unfavorably disposed to the Norway-Canada draft resolution. Mr. Dulles said so when he commented on it before the Assembly. But the draft offered no solution.

On August 19, 1958 Mr. Dulles asked me, as the leader of the delegation of India, to see him. Henry Cabot Lodge took me to the office of the Secretary of State in the United States suite in the United Nations building, facetiously remarking on the way that my attitude had been responsible for the erosion of an assured two-thirds majority for the Canadian-Norwegian resolution. He said Mr. Dulles was anxious to know why India could not at least abstain on that draft resolution. I had a forty-five minute talk with Mr. Dulles, and explained my position. The Canadian-Norwegian draft was silent on the withdrawal of the troops of the United States and the United Kingdom, but this omission I was willing to let pass in view of the stated assurances of the United States and the United Kingdom that they would withdraw their forces as soon as adequate United Nations measures had been adopted by the General Assembly. What was much more difficult to accept was that the only mention of the landing of the troops, which was in the preamble of the draft resolution, was couched in such terms as might be construed as the General Assembly's acceptance of the need for troop landings. I said that, in view of the stand of Nehru on the use of troops in other countries, I could not associate myself with this resolution, but on the contrary would have to vote against it. I added that I had no power to influence other member states in their attitude toward the draft resolution, but I had naturally explained the Indian position when asked to do so.

These explanations had perhaps led some of the other delegates to re-consider their own positions.

I was struck by the receptivity of Mr. Dulles to this statement. He appeared to accept its validity—for me although not for himself!—and instead of attempting to persuade me to accept an opposing line of thought he spent a good deal of time commenting on the policies of Ernest Bevin in regard to the Middle East in the immediate post-World War II period. Those reminiscences are hardly relevant to this study, nor would I feel free to mention their full content, as they involved Mr. Dulles' views on some still sensitive Middle Eastern issues. The relevant point is that the conversation might have had some influence on the subsequent decision of the United States and its allies not to insist on the Canada-Norway draft (which probably could not have obtained the necessary majority and would have sharply divided the Assembly), but to encourage others to try to find a solution. As long as the Canada-Norway draft was being vigorously pressed—and this understates the efforts made by its sponsors and friends to win acceptance for it—the diplomatic capacities of most of the Arab states and their friends were absorbed in the task of counter-ing the arguments presented to them. This phase ended when the United States decided not to put its great weight behind that draft.

The Arab representatives were aware of the contents of an alterna-tive draft which I had prepared. Taking into account this alternative, and the contents of the Canada-Norway draft, and, of course, basing their stand mainly on the unity of thinking which the ten Arab states had been able to develop in their own deliberations outside the meet-ings of the Assembly, they succeeded in cosponsoring and introducing in the Assembly on August 21, 1958 a draft resolution in which the salient clauses included the following statements:

Noting that the Arab States have agreed, in the pact of the League of Arab States, to strengthen the close relations and numerous ties which bind the Arab States and to support and stabilize those ties . . .

Requests the Secretary General to make . . . such practical arrange-ments as would adequately help in upholding the purposes and principles of the Charter in relation to Lebanon and Jordan in the present circum-stances, and thereby facilitate the early withdrawal of the foreign troops from the two countries.[65]

Immediately after the draft resolution had been introduced by For-eign Minister Mohamed Ahmed Mahgoub of Sudan, Mr. Dulles made a statement on behalf of the United States in which he said:

This is an event of happy augury, and the United States, I may say, supports the Arab draft resolution . . .

. . . The result arrived at justifies the great faith which the United States has always placed in the General Assembly, which operates free of veto power and where free world opinion has an opportunity to crystallize along sober and constructive lines.[66]

There had, indeed, been a statesmanlike development, made possible in essence by the willingness of a superpower, the United States, to change its position.

My own statement in the General Assembly, made almost immediately after Mr. Dulles', expressed the feeling of the Indian delegation:

This is an Arab draft resolution. It asks for peace and prosperity in the Arab world. It asks that the foreign troops now in Lebanon and in Jordan should be withdrawn at an early date. I think it is a matter also for great gratification in this Assembly that the representatives of the United States and the United Kingdom have said they will support fully this draft resolution.[67]

On the same day the General Assembly adopted unanimously [68] the draft presented by the ten Arab states. The Western powers in voting for this resolution endorsed a decision which was completely silent on two of the six points in the program presented by President Eisenhower (a United Nations peace force, and steps to avoid a new arms race spiral in the area), and which met the other points only by implication and in a degree.

From this exploration of the developments at the Third Emergency Special Session of the General Assembly, we can see the effective influence of the urgings of the United Nations on two great powers, the United States and the United Kingdom, in regard to certain aspects of their relations with Lebanon and Jordan.

In considering the influence of third parties in issues involving prestige more than vital interests, it is important to remember that the vital interests of the disputing parties are not likely to be engaged in precisely the same degree. Clearly, it can hardly be said that the degree of American vital interest involved in Hungary is as great as that of the Soviet Union. (This statement does not imply a value judgment of whether or not a country should have vital interests which extend beyond its own borders.) Again, the vital interests of the United States are much greater in Cuba than are those of the Soviet Union. Consequently, when a situation between the superpowers arises concerning an area such as Cuba or Hungary, their involvement, in terms of vital interests, is unequal. The power whose vital interests are only minimally or insignificantly involved, or whose prestige rather than vital interest is involved, will be the less inclined to overstep the brink of actual conflict.

Even though Cuba is an independent national entity, the powers directly confronting each other in the crisis of 1962 were the United States and the Soviet Union. The fact that the vital interests of the former were seriously involved—much more so than those of the latter—explained the nature of President Kennedy's statement of October 22, 1962 announcing that the Republic of Cuba had been placed in quarantine.

The next day the issue went to the Security Council, but there was no immediate evidence of a reappraisal of posture by the side which was the less vitally concerned. The Soviet Union stood firmly with its Cuban ally. As Soviet and other ships approached Cuban water, bringing various military supplies and equipment, the hour of fatal collision seemed inevitably to approach.

It was difficult to see the possibility of a retraction by the Soviet Union of what it, and perhaps many other countries, seemed to regard as an unavoidable concomitant of its alliance with Cuba.

Can one assert that President Kennedy's statement of October 22, 1962, and the statement of Adlai Stevenson in the Security Council on the following day, would necessarily have been more successful in averting a crisis than was the British Government's note of August 3, 1914 to the German Government? One cannot say—but the facts of international life had changed somewhat between 1914 and 1962.

A major organ of the United Nations was brought into session on October 23. Eleven countries participated directly in its discussions, and around them stood the foreign ministers or other senior representatives of another hundred or so countries. The representatives of two countries in the Security Council, Ghana and the United Arab Republic, introduced a draft resolution asking "the Secretary-General promptly to confer with the parties directly concerned on the immediate steps to be taken to remove the existing threat to world peace." [69]

Fortunately for the world, U Thant made his appeal directly to President Kennedy and Premier Khrushchev.[70] On the next day, October 25, 1962, both Mr. Kennedy and Mr. Khrushchev replied to U Thant broadly to the effect that they were willing to consider his suggestion of a conference.[71] In keeping with the fact of its lesser involvement in terms of vital interest, the Soviet reply was somewhat the more receptive of U Thant's suggestions. As a third party, the Secretary-General of the United Nations pleaded with the two leaders and through the very nature of his endeavor gave them—particularly the leader whose country's vital interests were less heavily involved

—an opportunity to draw back from the brink of what could have been a shattering conflict. After that the United States and the Soviet Union were able to commence direct negotiations both in New York and in Washington.

It is by no means always easy to categorize the interests of a power as vital, or as secondary, to its prestige. For example, is Aden really of vital interest to the United Kingdom today, after the attainment of independence by India, Pakistan, Burma, and Ceylon? And yet in the discussions of 1964 regarding the setting up of an independent South Arabian federation, to include Aden, there were references to the United Kingdom's need for installations or a base at Aden.

A more complicated case is that of the Aksai Chin area in Ladakh, the northeastern part of the state of Jammu and Kashmir. In this area the Government of the People's Republic of China has constructed a road and has consolidated its possession of some 12,000 square miles of territory. The area has little or no stable population, but is used for the grazing of flocks by pastoral people from neighboring Ladakhi territories. It could, therefore, be argued that India's interest in this area could not be described as vital.

On the other hand, it might be argued that to the Chinese Aksai Chin is of very considerable strategic importance because it offers a short route from western Tibet to Singkiang. However, these two statements would not by any means give a complete picture of the relative stakes of the two countries. The Chinese presence in so considerable a portion of Ladakh territory would give China a strategic opening to the rest of Ladakh, and even to the rest of Kashmir and other parts of India such as Lahaul and Northern Himachal. It could also be argued that such presence was evidence of Chinese expansionism in the border territory. It is unlikely that any official of the Chinese central government had ever set foot in the Aksai Chin area in the three hundred years prior to the time the Chinese got there around 1950. This new Chinese activity in itself might, with some justification, have led to an upgrading of the Indian interest in Aksai Chin to the category of vital interests. However, it could in turn be argued that as the Aksai Chin area is on the far side of the Karakorum Mountains, it is outside India's natural geographic boundaries.

And let us recall the nature of the attitudes of China and India toward the proposals made by the six Colombo powers (Burma, Ceylon, Cambodia, Ghana, Indonesia, and the United Arab Republic) regarding this area. India has accepted the Colombo proposals. Most Indians would argue that India's acceptance indicates that Government's desire to reach a settlement with China on a fair basis, rather than any lack of Indian interest in the Aksai Chin area. However, it is perhaps more realistic to take the view that India's readiness to negotiate on the basis proposed by the Colombo powers, even though this involves a considerable retreat from its original position, is determined primarily by a realization that the Aksai Chin area is not of really vital interest to the country. China, on the other hand, is unwilling to accept negotiations on terms which might appear to bring into question again the possession of territory near its Trans-Aksai Chin road.

In this issue the pleadings and urgings of third parties have provided a plausible and acceptable way of retracting from armed conflict, as far as India is concerned; and as far as China is concerned they have at least kept open the way to negotiation. In view of this provisional conclusion, the Sino-Indian border issue can be included in the category presently under discussion. However, it is also relevant to the first of the categories we have formulated, namely, that such urgings are successful in inverse proportion to the degree in which the vital interests of a party are involved.

As a consequence of the foregoing analysis, we might now suggest the following general principle regarding direct negotiations:

Negotiations may be directly conducted by the parties concerned in a dispute or situation either on their own initiative or as a result of the influence or pressures of a third party or parties.

Negotiations directly initiated by the parties to a situation or dispute tend to develop in one or another of the following four circumstances:

(a) When there is a more or less spontaneous and shared realization, generally by a number of countries, that a particular situation should be the subject of negotiations;

(b) When a relatively powerful or large state suggests negotiations to a relatively small or less powerful state;

(c) When there is a tradition of friendship and common discussion among two or more states;

(d) When there has been strong rivalry between states which has come to be accompanied by a mutual realization of common interest to end or moderate that rivalry, in regard to a particular aspect of the relations of the states concerned.

When negotiations are directly conducted but made possible as a result of the influence or pressure of third parties, three categories of cases emerge:

(a) The pleadings or urgings of third parties are successful in leading to negotiations in inverse proportion to the degree in which the vital interests of a party or parties are involved.

(b) In certain cases states, not excluding the great powers, show responsiveness to the urgings or pleadings of a large section of the world community, and agree to negotiate.

(c) When the prestige of a country which is a party to a dispute or situation is the primary basis of its involvement in that dispute or situation, then the urgings of third parties will frequently provide a plausible and acceptable way for retracting from the brink of armed conflict.

CHAPTER SEVEN

Mediation, Conciliation, and Good Offices

WE HAVE SO FAR been concerned with procedures leading to direct negotiation among the parties involved in an international situation or dispute. Although direct negotiation is generally the final goal of all efforts in the broad field of the pacific settlement of international disputes and situations, there are times when it cannot be achieved. For example, when the political and economic factors involved, such as competing claims to a piece of territory, have become part of the emotional life of the people of one or more of the states which are parties to the dispute or situation, and when those emotions are strong enough to affect the political leaders themselves, then circumstances which are not amenable to direct negotiations have come into existence.

We see such a state of affairs in the case of Kashmir, which involves India and Pakistan, and in the case of that part of the Tyrol which is inhabited by Germanic peoples but is under the sovereignty of Italy. In such emotionally charged situations a substitute for direct negotiation is generally desirable. The obvious first priority as a substitute is likely to be the injection of an acceptable third party, either a state or an individual, to act as an intermediary between the parties, make suggestions to them, and if he cannot bring them together face to face, to mediate in a Janus-like role.

Often an element of direct negotiation is not entirely absent, but this element would be missing if it were not for the efforts of the mediator or conciliator; it falls into the place of a significant secondary factor in the process of peaceful consideration of the dispute or situation.

The issue of Kashmir illustrates how the need for mediation can develop even between neighboring countries which are bound together in common association as members of a larger group [1] and by a common tradition and shared history.

It was understandable that when India and Pakistan emerged as modern independent states in August 1947 there should have been many issues that had to be solved between the two countries. Those problems extended from arrangements for petty trade in fresh vegetables across the border to the flow of enormous numbers of refugees, property claims, public debt division, the sharing of the waters of rivers, and rivalry to obtain possession of the beautiful hinterland of Kashmir.

Nevertheless, when the Kashmir situation first arose as an international issue by India's letter to the Security Council on January 1, 1948, it seemed to the Government of India that a solution could be found without too great difficulty.

Prime Minister Nehru's position was that although the state had acceded to India in accordance with the Government of India Act, 1935, of the Parliament of the United Kingdom, which had been accepted as the applicable legal basis by both Pakistan and India in respect of such matters, India would see to it that the people of Kashmir were given the opportunity to determine their own future by a free vote.

Since Pakistan, too, wished for the opportunity of a free vote in Kashmir, it seemed that this common objective could be quickly reached.

However, in the meanwhile certain other events occurred. The refugee situation put a clamorous and often intolerable strain on both Governments. The loss of property and wealth by the refugees was enormous. Other issues, such as division of the public debt, the apportioning of defense stores, trade matters, water disputes, all contributed to the general deterioration of relations between India and Pakistan. What could have been smarting and superficial hurts began to fester and entered the blood stream of the two nations. These events contributed to the basic causes for the delays in implementing the type of pacification of Kashmir prescribed by the Resolutions of 1948 and 1949 of the Security Council and the United Nations Commission for India and Pakistan.

In the new psychological mood, neither country felt it could sufficiently trust the other to justify withdrawal of its forces from Kashmir.

Although there were stray remarks between Indian and Pakistani leaders about the Kashmir issue at London during (but not at) Commonwealth prime ministerial conferences, and at supposedly chance meetings at airports, direct negotiations were hardly possible in the supercharged emotional situations that had become nationwide in both India and Pakistan.

This state of affairs continued until 1957, when the Security Council, at the insistence of Pakistan, returned to the issue. Although the Security Council did not use the direct language we are using here, its members realized that it would hardly be possible for the Governments of India and Pakistan to get anywhere with direct negotiations, even though India claimed that this was the "best course [as indeed theoretically it might have been] to adopt." Some members of the Council proposed that Ambassador Gunnar Jarring of Sweden should "examine with the governments of India and Pakistan, any proposals which, in his opinion, are likely to contribute towards the settlement of the dispute, having regard to the previous resolutions of the Security Council and the United Nations Commission for India and Pakistan." [2]

Gunnar Jarring visited India and Pakistan from March 14, 1957 to April 11, 1957. He held discussions with governmental teams of both countries headed by their Prime Ministers. As far as the two Governments were concerned, his mediatory functions—for that is what they were—were fully accepted. His own words were:

It is a pleasure for me to report that the co-operation of the two Governments, envisaged in the second operative part of the Security Council resolution has been complete in all respects. Our conversations took place in an atmosphere of complete frankness and cordiality.[3]

Mediation had to be resorted to in this indirect manner, because of the high emotional involvement of the peoples and Governments of India and Pakistan. Such an atmosphere militates strongly against constructive and objective consideration of the issues by the parties directly concerned. It was not until 1959, that the general atmosphere in the two countries had been somewhat ameliorated by the settlement of another major dispute, namely, the division of the waters of the Indus and the five rivers of the Punjab (which had been promoted by Eugene Black, then President of the International Bank), that it again became possible for India and Pakistan to embark on direct talks on the Kashmir issue—although still without reaching mutually acceptable results.

The Cyprus issue of 1964, which we have referred to in connection with the willingness of countries to negotiate, is particularly germane to our study of negotiation through or with the assistance of third parties. There are certain general similarities between the Cyprus case and the Kashmir issue. An important territory is involved, and the emotions of two neighboring states have become thoroughly stirred. The Mediterranean, like the Indian subcontinent, is an anciently settled part of the world, and emotions over real estate in either region might seem to outsiders to rise out of all proportion to the intrinsic or objective value of the issue concerned. However, in studies of international affairs, an axiom that is often overlooked is that an issue which seems unimportant when viewed from a certain part of the world will be measured against a different scale of importance in other parts of the world.

The Cyprus issue, in its psychological factors, is especially illustrative of this rule. Obviously, the emotional and political involvement of the Greek and Turkish Cypriots is total. Almost equally strong is the involvement of Greece on the one side and Turkey on the other. It is clear also that other countries have a degree of involvement. Some of the Arab states have not forgotten the use of the British bases on Cyprus in the 1956 attack on the Suez. Nor have they forgotten the long period of Turkish rule over much of the Arab world. Both of these factors operate to stir up Arab feelings in some degree over the Cyprus issue. Then again, Greece and Turkey are both members of NATO. Their affairs are of concern to their allies, particularly to their major ally, the United States. Another international embroilment arises out of the fact that by the treaties leading to the independence of Cyprus the United Kingdom has two bases on the island and holds sovereign authority over them. Cyprus is a member of the Commonwealth of Nations, and at the same time is an active member of the large Afro-Asian group at the United Nations.

Each of these half-dozen international involvements creates a zone of interest in the Cyprus issue. The result is the existence of a number of competing ideas for a solution of the problems of the island. In the present section of our study we are concerned only with those processes and activities which relate to efforts at mediation, or other third-party assistance in ameliorating the international aspects of the situation.

Apart from the two formal efforts to mediate, one sanctioned by the United Nations and the other launched by the United States through Dean Acheson, there have been third-party efforts of one description or another by other states and individuals. As noted in Chapter Four, the Prime Minister of Greece has actually welcomed the possibility of mediation by President de Gaulle, and it may be assumed that the French leader or his Government has made informal behind-the-scenes suggestions to the parties more directly involved. Both the Greek and Turkish Prime Ministers have also visited Prime Minister Douglas-Home, whose country is by treaty in possession of part of Cyprus. It was reported at one stage that the Spanish Foreign Minister, who was visiting Turkey, was offering the services of his Government to assist in resolving the issue. Amid these divers efforts, of various degrees of informality, the two main mediatory efforts went forward.

In the first resolution adopted by the Security Council in 1964 on the Cyprus Question, the Secretary-General of the United Nations was asked to "designate in agreement with the Government of Cyprus and the Governments of Greece, Turkey and the United Kingdom, a mediator." [4] Consequently, the Secretary-General, on March 25, 1964, designated Sakari S. Tuomioja as United Nations mediator.[5] In this case the mediator had not only the operative sanction behind him of the Security Council, but that sanction was so drawn that it committed four governments to the acceptance of the mediator.

The other mediatory effort, that performed by former Secretary of State Dean Acheson, was a less formal one. Indeed, the terms of his assignment have not been disclosed. It is perhaps best, therefore, to refer to it as a third-party effort to assist in resolving the issues under contention. The move might be interpreted as an effort of mediation or conciliation, or merely the offering of the good offices of an expert statesman, from a country which is not only directly interested but which because of its international status cannot remain unconcerned about any situation that might develop into a major conflict. However, the *New York Times,* in a message datelined from Washington, stated that:

Former Secretary of State, Dean Acheson, at President Johnson's request, is flying to Geneva in an effort to help mediate the dispute between Greece and Turkey over Cyprus.[6]

In another message from Washington datelined July 30, 1964, State Department officials said that Dean Acheson, as unofficial mediator, had had only separate meetings with Greek and Turkish officials.[7]

It appears that the reaction of at least two parties involved in the dispute were more in favor of mediation by the United Nations mediator than by Dean Acheson. After his visit to the United States, Prime Minister George A. Papandreou told the Parliament of Greece on July 3:

We agreed that the [United Nations] Mediator must be left to continue his task and that we should give him, all of us, every possible assistance, that was the conclusion of my talks in the United States.[8]

The Greek Prime Minister went on to mention his visit to the Secretary-General and the mediator in New York. He spoke in the highest terms about U Thant, and added that he told Sakari S. Tuomioja, "We are absolutely willing to help him in his task: . . . we respect everything he may do in pursuit of his mission.[9]

As far as Mr. Acheson's efforts are concerned, the Greek and Turkish representatives at Geneva appear to have been cooperative, but the representative of Cyprus did not join in any discussion with him. On July 30, President Makarios spoke in adverse terms about an alleged Acheson plan for Cyprus which he said was "absolutely unacceptable"; he also referred to "self-appointed mediators." [10]

Regarding the mediatory efforts of the late Sakari S. Tuomioja, President Makarios is reported to have said that he did not consider those efforts to be useless, but added, "I am not optimistic about their outcome." [11]

From the cases of Kashmir and Cyprus, certain factors relevant to mediation appear to emerge. One is that the official agreement of *all* the parties directly involved to the initiation of a mediator into his task is a highly desirable prerequisite. In the case of Cyprus even more formally than in the case of the Gunnar Jarring mission to India and Pakistan, the agreement of the parties directly involved to the designation of a particular United Nations negotiator had been obtained. In both cases the parties concerned had, in effect, decided to welcome and assist the negotiator.

Another factor which was operative in both cases begins to become apparent first from the Security Council record, which indicated that Pakistan was more receptive to the Jarring mission than was India. Second, the Greek Cypriots do not seem to be happy about the idea of unofficial mediation any more than India was when President Kennedy suggested early in 1962 that India and Pakistan should accept Eugene Black's assistance in resolving the Kashmir issue. India turned down this suggestion, while Pakistan was favorable to it. In a sense, the political position of India in Kashmir is analogous to that of the Greek Cypriots. India in regard to Kashmir, and the Greek

Cypriots in regard to Cyprus, are the powers in major occupation. Neither of them is keen to have third parties meddling in the affair.

The Greek position is that the issue is for the Cypriots to settle. Prime Minister Papandreou has said this about the Greek position on Cyprus: "Unrestricted independence . . . includes the right of self-determination, and the protection of the Turkish minority even by international guarantees." [12] This proposal supports the Cypriots' right to decide their own affairs in the exercise of the right of self-determination. Similarly, the Indian position on Kashmir has been that Pakistan has no locus at all in the case, the people of Kashmir are part of the citizenry of India, and no outside involvement, no matter how well-meaning, is acceptable; the people of Kashmir take part in general elections, enjoy universal franchise and the secret ballot, and they have made their choice.

These observations would seem to indicate that parties in possession are less receptive of third-party efforts than are parties who feel that such efforts are likely to result in a solution or adjustment more favorable to them than the continuation of the status quo.

The events after the Chinese invasion of India in the autumn of 1962 do not refute this provisional conclusion. Again, the Western powers suggested that India and Pakistan accept third-party assistance in regard to the issues that sharply divided them. India, now less sure of her possession of Kashmir, and conscious of her weakened position, responded favorably to the offer. Pakistan, on the other hand, perhaps expecting India to be further weakened by the recrudescence of events on her border, was cool to the suggestion. Pakistan may have felt that Kashmir would soon be in its grasp and possession and for that reason was not willing to submit the issue to third-party suggestions which would be unlikely to favor entirely the position of either India or Pakistan.

The case of West Irian is a most significant one among recent international issues which have been the subject of mediation. West Irian, or the western half of the island of New Guinea, is a considerable territory of what was for some time the Netherlands East Indies. It remained under the jurisdiction of the Netherlands when Indonesia became independent at the end of 1949.

From 1949 to 1954, Indonesia sporadically pressed its claim for West Irian. However, no negotiations of any consequence took place, and in the autumn of 1954 the issue was brought to the United Nations. The Indonesian request was a very simple one. It was that the General Assembly should urge the two parties—Indonesia and the

Netherlands—to enter into negotiations on the question of West Irian. The General Assembly record of the First Committee states that Tjondronegoro Sudjarwo of Indonesia made the following plea:

Indonesia sought. . . . only further negotiations with the encouragement and guidance of the United Nations. But Indonesia attached great importance to a recommendation of the United Nations.[13]

However, the Netherlands was adamant in the view that it was sovereign in New Guinea, and that under Article 2.7 of the Charter no one had any business to interfere in the issue. Foreign Minister J. M. A. H. Luns stated his position categorically in the following terms at the plenary session of the General Assembly on September 24, 1954:

. . . my Government reserves all its rights under the Charter, including those under Article 2, paragraph 7. In order that there may be no possibility of doubt on this point, let me repeat here once again my Govenment's unalterable decision to maintain and to uphold its lawful sovereignty over the territory of Netherlands New Guinea.[14]

In 1955, a development in the situation came after the April Bandung Conference. At that Conference the 29 nations present had urged the two Governments to enter into negotiations. Both Governments seemed responsive to the urgings, and on December 7, 1955 they announced that they had decided to hold a conference, which among other matters would consider problems relating to West Irian, without either party's giving up its stand regarding sovereignty over the territory.

This information was welcomed by the General Assembly, which expressed the hope that the negotiations referred to in the joint statement of December 7 would be fruitful. A brief resolution to this effect was adopted unanimously on December 16, 1955.[15]

However, in view of the strongly divergent positions of the two Governments, nothing came of the negotiations between the Netherlands and Indonesia. In the following year Indonesia again came to the General Assembly and asked for a resolution which would invite the two countries to negotiate, but the Netherlands opposed the move, and the Indonesians, while obtaining a simple majority for their proposal, failed to muster a two-thirds vote. In those circumstances, no resolution was adopted by the General Assembly.

In 1957, Dr. Subandrio, the Foreign Minister of Indonesia, again urged the General Assembly to bring the two parties together for further negotiations. For example, the record has him saying:

A United Nations recommendation for further negotiations would enhance the Organization's prestige, and Indonesia was prepared to accept
a resolution establishing such a precedent for peaceful settlement.[16]

Foreign Minister Luns was again adamant on the question of the
sovereignty of the Netherlands:

An effort was being made to violate the territorial integrity of the Kingdom of the Netherlands by the use of threats and the misuse of the
General Assembly, and to brush aside as irrelevant the principle of equal
rights and self-determination of people.[17]

Throughout those years the Netherlands remained in firm possession of West Irian and was not likely to agree to negotiations which
might alter its status in the territory. However, the situation was
becoming increasingly delicate. The Dutch strengthened their garri-
sons in New Guinea, and the Indonesians commenced small-scale
infiltration and guerrilla tactics. It was in those circumstances that the
issue returned to the General Assembly in 1961.

At that stage the Netherlands, finding that its possession was no
longer secure, expressed willingness to hand over the administration
of the territory to an international authority under the United Nations.[18] But the Minister of Foreign Affairs of Indonesia stated that
the Netherlands was continuing its preparations to cut West Irian
loose from Indonesia by force of arms, and that if this were to continue a time would come when Indonesia would liberate West Irian,
also by force.[19]

At the General Assembly both sides presented resolutions in support of their views, but neither was able to obtain a two-thirds
majority. The effect, if any, of the infructuous 1961 General Assembly consideration was to give an impetus to nonpeaceful settlement.
Indonesian paratroopers landed on the territory and there were also
sea-borne landings. The Netherlands responded by increasing its
forces in the area.

It had become apparent that if the situation was to be peacefully
resolved some form of third-party assistance would be necessary. The
Acting Secretary-General suggested that the parties should meet, with
the assistance of a mediator. Early in March 1962, the United States
Government offered the services of Ellsworth Bunker, who had recently completed a very successful tour of duty as Ambassador of the
United States to India. He evolved a plan which provided that the
Netherlands would relinquish the administration of West New Guinea
not directly to Indonesia, but to a United Nations temporary author-

ity, which in its turn would make it over to Indonesia. Originally the idea was that the United Nations should remain administrator for as long as two years, but when the agreement was finally signed on August 13, 1962 it provided for administration by the United Nations for only six or seven months. Face was saved by the fact that the agreement also provided that Indonesia would make arrangements to give the people of the territory the right to exercise freedom of choice (Article XVIII). Article XX provides that the act of self-determination will be completed before the end of 1969. Indonesia will make arrangements for the act of self-determination with the assistance and participation of a United Nations representative and his staff.[20]

A very dangerous and delicate issue, which not only had reached the brink of conflict but in which confrontation of the forces of the two sides had actually started, was saved from becoming a major threat of war by skillful use of the techniques of mediation. On August 21, 1962, Garfield Barwick, the Minister for Foreign Affairs of Australia, gave an interesting statement on the issue in the Australian House of Representatives, and made a perceptive comment on the techniques of negotiation which had been applied to this case:

Whilst the negotiation was primarily between the two parties to the dispute, Honourable Members will bear in mind that the third member present at the negotiations represented the Acting Secretary General of the United Nations. The technique of negotiation followed in this case seemed sound to the Australian Government. . . . The solution which has been reached stems to a considerable degree from the initiatives of the Acting Secretary General and of his designated representative, Mr. Bunker: it carries with it the authority of the Secretary General's office, it is obviously regarded by him as a practical and reasonable proposition, and it will have his support when the agreement comes before the United Nations for approval.[21]

Behind the active involvement of a third party in the form of a mediator, there was also the encouraging and responsible factor of the good offices of the Secretary-General of the United Nations. There were thus two levels of involvement of third parties.

Let us turn now to another international issue. At the end of September 1963, both Algeria and Morocco reported that there had been border attacks in the western Sahara region, where each side accused the other of aggression. Since communication is more effective in the early stages of a dispute, the two heads of state acted by getting in touch with each other. King Hassan II of Morocco sent a personal

envoy, Abdelhadi Boutaleb, his Minister of Information,[22] to Algiers
to talk things over with President Ahmed Ben Bella. The talks helped
to ease the situation, but they did not get down to the substance of
the claims of the parties. On October 10, 1963 the Moroccan Council
of Ministers noted the report of Mr. Boutaleb and took "a certain
number of measures aiming at insuring the protection of the national
territory." [23]

This really meant that the countries were continuing to engage in
armed conflict. However, on October 12, 1963 the last effort at a direct bilateral settlement was made when the Algerian Government
repeated a proposal for a joint investigating commission.[24]

But national emotions had by that time become greatly aroused on
both sides, and from then on all efforts to mend the situation were
made through third parties. The first of these was an effort at conciliation. President Habib Bourguiba sent envoys to Algeria and
Morocco with appeals for a peaceful settlement. They carried personal messages of a conciliatory character for President Ben Bella
and King Hassan.[25] But armed conflict continued. Conciliation
which simply appealed to good will was no longer sufficient. The
Algerian Government decided to put the issue before the Organization of African Unity. Meanwhile, on October 15, 1963, President
Ben Bella issued an order for general mobilization of the Liberation
Army.[26]

However, by now several mediatory efforts were active. Emperor
Haile Selassie visited Morocco and Algeria; a meeting of the Arab
League on October 20, 1963 voted unanimously (the belligerents
abstaining) in favor of an immediate cease-fire; Ghana's Foreign
Minister also visited the capitals of the warring nations on a mission
of mediation; President Bourguiba made a new appeal; and an Iraqi
delegation arrived at Algiers. These efforts crystallized into a proposal to meet at Bamako, the capital of Mali. Here two mediators—
President Modibo Keita of Mali and Emperor Haile Selassie of
Ethiopia—met separately with King Hassan II and President Ben
Bella, who did not wish to meet face to face. The mediation of the
two heads of state was effective, and the Agreement of Bamako was
signed on October 30, 1963. It secured a cease-fire and withdrawal of
the forces of both sides to the positions held at the end of September.
The zone from which the forces withdrew was to be supervised by
Ethiopian and Malian officers.

The next step in the process of third-party assistance in resolving
the dispute was a meeting of the foreign ministers of the members of

the Organization of African Unity at Addis Ababa, in the middle of November 1963. At that meeting a seven-nation commission of African states (Ethiopia, Mali, Senegal, Ivory Coast, Republic of Sudan, Tanganyika, and Nigeria) was set up to resolve the dispute.

Although the seven-nation commission refrained from making recommendations on the basic issues, the complex of third-party efforts resulted in the return of stability, on a broadly acceptable basis, to the western Sahara region. In this degree, the efforts which started with conciliation and went on to a good offices visit by Emperor Haile Selassie to both Rabat and Algiers, and then developed into full-scale mediation by two heads of African states, had succeeded. This episode shows that as a dispute gathers momentum and becomes a national issue, it often reaches proportions which are unmanageable in direct negotiations. Second, it tends to show the advantages of bringing to bear on a situation the views of more than one mediator or conciliator. In this respect there is a similarity to the joint efforts of the six Colombo powers in regard to the Sino-Indian border dispute; and the case is not as different from that of West Irian as might first appear, in that in the settlement of the dispute between the Netherlands and Indonesia there was not only the direct mediation of Ellsworth Bunker, but also the good offices of the United States Government and U Thant. In addition, strenuous efforts at the United Nations, although no consensus had emerged as to the best method of handling the dispute, had demonstrated that world opinion was strongly in favor of a peaceful solution of the West Irian issue.

In regard to the Suez Canal issue before the outbreak of hostilities, so much attention has been focused on the London Conferences that it is sometimes overlooked that in October 1956 there were extremely significant meetings of the Security Council and unique and historic meetings in Dag Hammarskjöld's office at the United Nations.

Early in October the United Kingdom and France on the one hand, and Egypt on the other, brought counter-complaints relating to the Suez Canal to the Security Council. The Franco-British item was, in paraphrase, a request for consideration of the situation created by Egypt's action in nationalizing the Suez Canal Company. The Egyptian complaint was that actions against Egypt by France and the United Kingdom were a threat to international peace. The Council inscribed both items on its agenda, and on October 5, at its 735th meeting, it started consideration of the Franco-British item. That meeting was historic in that the Security Council met virtually at foreign minister level (cf. Art. 28.2 of the United Nations Charter). Foreign Minister Christian Pineau of France was in the chair, and other Foreign Ministers present were Paul-Henri Spaak of Belgium, Mahmoud Fawzi of Egypt (by invitation), D. T. Shepilov of the Soviet Union, Selwyn Lloyd of the United Kingdom, John Foster Dulles of the United States, and Koca Popovic of Yugoslavia.

The United Kingdom and France immediately introduced a draft resolution [27] which sought the approval of the Security Council for the arrangements proposed by 18 of the 22 countries which had attended the first London Suez Conference in August 1956. The Franco-British draft resolution had the support of Mr. Dulles.[28]

However, without the support of the Soviet Union, Yugoslavia, and possibly other countries for the Franco-British draft resolution, it could not have been adopted. Had this happened, the situation could have looked even more dangerous than it became later in the month when France and Britain attacked the Suez area. This view is based on the fact that at the Security Council meeting of October 5, the United States had apparently committed its support to the United Kingdom and France. Had the Western draft resolution been vetoed, there would have been a direct confrontation between the United States and its allies on the one hand, and the Soviet Union on the other. At this stage another most significant and invaluable initiative in international negotiation took place. The Security Council, after meeting in open session from October 5 to October 9 (735th–738th meetings), held three closed sessions—a most unusual procedure —on October 9, 11, and 12, 1956. Indeed, this was the first time the Security Council met in closed session to consider a complaint of a member state.

Those meetings succeeded in blunting the edge of the confrontation, and led to a new development, which was that Christian Pineau and Selwyn Lloyd met with Mahmoud Fawzi in Dag Hammarskjöld's room on the 38th floor of the United Nations Secretariat building. At a series of informal sessions, under the effective guidance of the Secretary-General, who made his good offices available and who was acting in that capacity rather than as mediator or conciliator, a self-contained set of six agreed points was worked out which created a framework for the settlement of the crisis.

When the Security Council reconvened in open session at its 742nd meeting on October 13, 1956, Selwyn Lloyd made the first substantive statement, in the course of which he made the following important disclosures:

Other discussions have taken the form of conversations between the President, in his capacity as Foreign Minister of France, the Egyptian Foreign Minister, and myself, in the presence of and, indeed, under the roof of the Secretary-General of the United Nations, whose able and tactful assistance has been of the greatest help to us all. . . . and we now have agreement, so I believe, on the basic requirements, which any settlement of the Suez Canal should meet. Thus we have established, so to speak, the framework within which a basis for negotiation can perhaps be constructed.[29]

As a result of the success of the efforts of the Secretary-General with the Foreign Ministers of France, Egypt, and the United Kingdom, the old draft resolution of France and Britain was scrapped and a new draft resolution was introduced.[30] We need not go into the substance of the proposals in the new resolution. However, Selwyn Lloyd stressed that there was agreement among all three countries on the six requirements for the Canal, as set out in the new draft proposal. Christian Pineau was the next speaker. He immediately paid tribute to the Secretary-General:

First of all, I wish to join with Mr. Lloyd in thanking the Secretary-General of the United Nations for the tact and good will which he has shown in the past few days, and which, there can be no doubt, have made possible very useful conversations.[31]

Mahmoud Fawzi revealed that it was Dag Hammarskjöld who at a previous closed meeting had presented to the Security Council the six agreed principles:

The first part of the draft resolution, in which six basic principles are outlined, coincides with what was presented by the Secretary-General to the Council yesterday and was generally accepted.[32]

A representative of a non–great-power member of the Council, Djalal Abdoh, speaking for Iran, said:

My delegation wishes to express its gratitude to the Secretary-General who, mindful of the responsibilities conferred on him by the United Nations Charter, has made so valuable a contribution to the conversations which have been held, and which have proved fruitful and constructive.[33]

D. T. Shepilov also paid tribute to the Secretary-General:

We are gratified to find that, as a result of the exchange of views between the Ministers of Foreign Affairs of the United Kingdom, France and Egypt, with the active and fruitful participation of the Secretary-General of the United Nations, Mr. Hammarskjöld, it has become possible to agree on a number of general principles.[34]

John Foster Dulles said the following:

It is a tribute to this Council, and above all, to the Foreign Ministers of Egypt, France and the United Kingdom, and to our Secretary-General that the problem has been considered here calmly and constructively and that important agreements have emerged.[35]

These tributes underline the fact that although it was perfectly possible for the members of the Security Council and the Foreign Minister of Egypt to get together and talk, this eminent group of statesmen, who were used to handling crises, found it desirable and apparently necessary to utilize the good offices of the Secretary-General of the United Nations. Even this most complex problem, and one which raised strong emotions (Mr. Dulles said in the Council, "The Suez Canal problem is one of vast importance and great complexity and it easily arouses great emotion.") could be brought within a reasonable framework of reference through the assistance and participation of a highly intelligent, subtle, and determined third party—in this case, Dag Hammarskjöld as Secretary-General of the United Nations.

The new Franco-British draft resolution contained not only the six agreed principles but, and not so fortunately, also the Anglo-French view as to how those principles should be interpreted. In this part of their draft resolution the two countries asked the Security Council to take the view that the proposals of 18 of the countries which had attended the first Suez Canal Conference in London, in August 1956, corresponded to the six agreed principles. This, of course, was unacceptable to Egypt and to other countries. When it came to the vote on the Anglo-French draft resolution, the first part of the draft, setting out the six agreed principles, was adopted unanimously. On the second part there were negative votes by the Soviet Union and Yugoslavia. Since the Soviet Union is a permanent member of the Security Council, the second part was not adopted. Mr. Dulles' statement after the vote was not entirely unoptimistic, particularly in regard to the possibly beneficial effects of the continuing use of the Secretary-General's good offices:

I think, of course, that it is understood that the Council remains seized of this matter and that the Secretary-General may continue to encourage interchanges between the Governments of Egypt, France and the United Kingdom—a procedure which has already yielded positive results.[36]

In fact, Dag Hammarskjöld did hold talks with Foreign Minister Fawzi between October 13 and 19, 1956 with a view to exploring possible agreement on the implementation of the six agreed principles. On October 24, Hammarskjöld reached the view that he had come to agreement with Fawzi, and addressed a detailed letter to him on the subject. Before a reply could be received, the inexplicably precipitate armed attack on the Suez took place. A few days later, on November 2, 1956, Foreign Minister Fawzi sent his reply to Hammarskjöld. His communication was to the effect that the arrangements suggested in the Secretary-General's letter of October 24 were acceptable, with one small exception.[37]

Some of the real reasons for the attack on the Suez region at the end of October 1956 would take us into questions totally unconnected with the present stage of our study. It is quite clear from what Mr. Dulles said at the conclusion of the Security Council meetings, that on October 13 there was no apprehension in his mind of an attack against Egypt by the French, British, and Israelis. No one can have known more intimately the attitudes of the United States' close allies (the United Kingdom and France) at the time than Mr. Dulles. We can only conclude that the armed attack was the result of a headstrong diversion from the path of negotiation, along which progress was being made under the guidance of Dag Hammarskjöld.

From these cases we may draw some conclusions regarding third-party activities such as mediation, conciliation, and the lending of good offices:

Mediation and conciliation are often methods of bringing the main parties together, either at a common table (as in the case of West Irian) or indirectly (as in the case of the Algerian-Moroccan dispute).

Particularly when national emotions are strongly aroused (Kashmir, Cyprus, and the Suez) the best solution—direct discussions between the parties—becomes impracticable. In those circumstances a mediator, conciliator, or good officer becomes more than an intermediary. He takes on the substantive function of a maker of proposals or suggestions. Often his proposals come to be accepted (Hammarskjöld in respect of the Suez in 1956; Bunker in respect of West Irian in 1962). In such cases, third parties, while working modestly as mediator, conciliator, or good officer, become the major determinant of the course of negotiations.

The wider the circle of international concern represented by third parties, the more effective the resulting mediation, conciliation, or good offices tend to be. We have observed how in the case of West Irian, although there was one mediator, there were other strong international factors at work through the good offices of the United States and the United Nations Secretary-General, and behind them was the universal interest in the United Nations, expressed not through a resolution but in the full debates at the sixteenth Session of the General Assembly (1961). In the case of the Sino-Indian border dispute, we could see that some effectiveness accrued from the fact that the six Colombo powers acted together.

Among the parties to a territorial dispute or situation, the party in possession is, generally speaking, the one which is less amenable to any negotiations and thus also to third-party involvement. In the case of the Sino-Indian dispute Mr. Nehru suggested referral to the International Court of Justice and also other forms of third-party involvement, but since the Chinese had taken possession of what they wanted they showed no interest in those proposals.

From these conclusions, therefore, we may draw up another principle of international negotiation:

Negotiations between the parties to a dispute or situation may be conducted through or with the assistance of one or more mediators, conciliators, or providers of good offices; but when territory is at stake the party in possession tends to resist third-party involvement, although it is just such involvement which might eventually assist in resolving the issue, particularly when the national emotions of the parties are aroused.

The influence or effectiveness of third parties in negotiation tends to increase when a plurality of states (and the Secretary-General of the United Nations and/or other designated person) constitute the third party, or have made explicit their support for the efforts of the third party.

CHAPTER EIGHT

The Wider Forums

WE HAVE SO FAR considered procedures relating to direct negotiations, bilateral or multilateral, among the parties concerned, and negotiations stimulated by or undertaken through third parties. We come now to wider forums, negotiations through conference.

Negotiation takes place by conference when the parties directly involved in a dispute or situation agree to its peaceful consideration by a larger number of states, and, rarely, selected individuals from other than the parties themselves. On one basis of analysis it will be found that conference negotiation falls into two categories. The first consists of those conferences at which the parties have not surrendered their decision-making powers. Some examples are the General Assembly of the United Nations, the Trusteeship Council, other United Nations bodies, and perhaps the Security Council in respect of most of its actions under Chapter VI of the Charter. The second category consists of those conferences at which the parties have surrendered a substantial power of decision. An example is the Laos Conference of 1961–62. The parties directly involved in that Conference were Laos and those states which were supporting or assisting the various Laotian factions struggling for supremacy in the county. However, there were other countries participating in the Fourteen-Nation Conference, such as Burma and India, which had not supported any of the Laotian factions. The parties directly involved agreed to abide by conference decisions arrived at by unanimous vote, that is, decisions that would be influenced, even considerably so, by countries not directly involved. From those decisions emerged a draft treaty which was signed by the representatives of all fourteen governments. While some governments had to go through processes of ratification of the Laos

Agreement, the fact remains that by agreeing to submit the issue to a conference, consisting of a larger number of countries than the direct parties, the parties directly involved had agreed to the working out of a solution in collaboration with other states.

In this connection we might consider the nature of Security Council decisions under Chapter VI (The Pacific Settlement of Disputes) of the United Nations Charter. While states have held that they are not bound by recommendations of the Security Council formulated on questions brought before the Council under Chapter VI,[1] it is not absolutely certain that this attitude is in accordance with the Charter.

As far as nonmembers of the United Nations are concerned, the Charter specifically lays down that if they bring issues under Chapter VI to the Security Council they must accept in advance the obligations of pacific settlement provided in the Charter.[2] There is no reason to think the Charter treats member states on a different basis. This would lead to the conclusion that Article 25 of the Charter [3] applies also to the pacific settlement of disputes. It would seem to follow that when the Security Council considers a matter under Chapter VI, and after discussion takes a decision on a procedure for pacific settlement, that decision is binding on the parties, even if it is a decision to recommend a certain course of action.[4] Therefore, the Security Council acting under Chapter VI should be regarded as a significant example of a forum for negotiation through conference of a larger number of states than the parties to a dispute or situation, in which the decision-making power vests in the conference.

On the other hand, no such binding characteristics apply to the decisions of the other negotiating conference organs of the United Nations, namely the General Assembly, the Economic and Social Council, and the Trusteeship Council. This is true to an even greater extent of the subsidiary organs of the United Nations which may be created under Article 7.2 of the Charter. Some examples of those bodies would be the Human Rights Commission, the Transport Commission, the Committee on Information from Non-Self-Governing Territories, and the Population Commission.

However, even when the decisions of negotiating conferences are not binding on a party to a dispute or situation, they generally have a considerable effect on the subsequent attitudes and actions of the parties. This general rule does not apply when some of the parties to a dispute or situation have not acquiesced in the consideration of the matter by the negotiating conference.[5]

Conferences, Decisions of Which Are Not Binding

In a world bristling with international problems arising out of disputes and situations among nations, one would imagine that there would be a preponderance of activity in such international organs as are best fitted to arrive at clear-cut findings and to enforce what the majority of countries would regard as just solutions. There are two organs, accepted by over one hundred states, which in terms of the powers conferred upon them by international treaty could come to clear-cut solutions or could enforce them: the International Court of Justice and the Security Council of the United Nations.

In actuality, however, at the present stage of relationships among nation states, such procedures are applied exceptionally rather than as a general rule. That is because a nation state generally refuses to part with its discretion to determine the extent to which it will, in each individual case, be prepared to diminish or compromise its own vital interests as it conceives those interests.

Moreover, it could be stated as a psychological axiom in relations among sovereign states, that if x were to be taken from or required of state A in order to arrive at a solution of a dispute or situation with state B, state A would prefer to undertake or accept x if persuaded to do so by its peers (or by superior powers), rather than if obliged to do so as the result of findings of a judicial character in a courtroom. In other words, the public exhortations, the invitations to Washington and Moscow, the wooing by important powers, praise for the acumen and wisdom of its statesmen, appeals in the interest of world harmony, and the spotlight and the publicity of international conferences, go to make up a much more acceptable political context for action by most governments than a courtroom or than wholly quiet diplomacy.

It is largely for these background reasons that negotiation through large conferences makes so strong an appeal in our time to most nation states. The large conference, par excellence, is the General Assembly of the United Nations with its 117 member states at the end of 1965. Consequently there has been a steady tendency for international issues concerning world peace, security, and disarmament to be brought to the General Assembly rather than to more restricted forums.

There is, of course, another important reason. This is that the Security Council, which under the terms of the United Nations Charter has the primary responsibility for the maintenance of international peace and security, is essentially a great-power body. Five of the large powers, with their vetoes, dominate it. The chances of getting them to accept the point of view of a small state are almost nonexistent. Generally speaking, from the point of view of a small state the great powers appear to be rather fearsome and rigid entities. A small state feels it has very little hope of influencing any of them, especially the superpowers, although purely tactically, in a Security Council vote, one or the other might help out.

On the other hand, in the General Assembly the situation is very different. There are numerous fairly strong regional caucuses, some of which are connected with nonregional international organizations or dispositions of states. An African country can hope to persuade some thirty-five other African states of the justice of its cause in a particular case. This having been done, the issue can then be placed before the Afro-Asian group and might emerge with the support of more than half the membership of the United Nations. It might even be possible, unless the state in question is strongly committed to one side or the other in the Cold War, to acquire the support of nonaligned states from regions other than Asia and Africa. Eventually, the country may find it has built up general support for its case among some seventy-five [6] member states.

With the support of seventy-five states, it obviously suits such a country much better to bring its troubles to the General Assembly, rather than to go to the Security Council or use quiet negotiating tactics. Of course, this can be done only within limits. The General Assembly is active for roughly three months in the year, although there is a tendency to increase the length of its sessions, whereas the Security Council is so constituted that it is available to the world community at all times.[7]

It is partly for these reasons that the Security Council has lost ground to the General Assembly.[8] It is to the latter that problems of peace and security such as disarmament, the questions of West Irian, Aden, Malta, Fiji, Nyasaland, British Guiana, and Korea, and the denuclearization of Latin America,[9] are brought.

A significant example of how the influence of the General Assembly can prove to be as binding as a decision of the Security Council was provided in 1958 in connection with the crisis in Lebanon and Jordan.

During the Lebanese and Jordanian crisis, on July 20, 1958, Premier Khrushchev proposed a summit meeting consisting of the heads of the Governments of the United States, the United Kingdom, France, India, and the Soviet Union, together with the Secretary-General [10] of the United Nations, to resolve Middle Eastern problems. The Security Council being meanwhile seized of the issue, on August 1 the representatives of the United States, Canada, and the United Kingdom requested a special meeting of the Council in accordance with Article 28.2 of the Charter. However, no meeting at the level of foreign minister was held because the Soviet Union indicated in a message dated August 5, 1958 that it had decided to ask for a meeting of the General Assembly in emergency special session to discuss the problem.[11]

When the issue moved to the General Assembly, it certainly could not be assumed or even anticipated that in this larger, more unwieldy forum great-power differences could be eliminated. On the contrary, it was to be expected that each side in the Cold War would try to muster support for its own position and that, consequently, the General Assembly would find itself sharply divided.

However, contrary to apprehensions and to reasonable anticipations, the General Assembly was able to adopt unanimously a resolution on the Lebanon and Jordanian situations.[12] How did this seeming miracle occur? In a basic sense one of the impelling causes was that the General Assembly made it possible for a much wider, more varied, and less tense series of urgings and informal negotiations to be brought to bear on those who were directly involved in the issue. Inevitably the Security Council members, although of course not technically barred from or closed to suggestions from other diplomats at the headquarters of the United Nations, tend to act as a separate group, and they do so in accordance with the instructions of their governments. Moreover, the permanent members of the Security Council constitute an inner group, and the run-of-the-mill permanent representative of a smaller country tends to have some inhibitions about offering suggestions to that group.

The General Assembly has an egalitarian effect on the totality of the United Nations membership. There the great powers are, of course, focuses of attention, but they are at the same time equal colleagues with the smaller and larger member states.

To return to the specific case of the Third Emergency Special Session in August 1958, more than a score of Asian, African, and other friends of the Middle Eastern states were discussing matters and exchanging views with the Arab states, some more closely and intensely than others. A similar number of countries were meeting with the representatives of the United States and some of its allies, and a number were also meeting with the Soviet Union's representatives. It would be difficult to convey the intricate crisscrossing and permutation of meetings among the representatives of the members of the Assembly. The net effect of their activity, which focused on the need for stemming the dangers of big power confrontation in the arena of the Middle East, and on the opportunity offered to rise above and eliminate at least some of the frictions in the area, was the working out of the terms of a resolution which drew to itself the adherence of every single member state of the United Nations.

It would be fallacious to convey the impression that complete peace and calm was ushered into the Middle East by this unanimity at the General Assembly. The complexities of international affairs are such that no single event, no matter how constructive, achieves a complete solution to any problem. From our point of view what is of special significance is that the General Assembly vote exemplified the potentialities of this form of conference negotiation, with no binding obligations, at their highest. Even if decisions of the Security Council under Chapter VI of the Charter are binding on the parties involved, the power of enforcement of a Security Council decision is a separate matter, which derives from the subsequent Chapter (VII), and binding decisions that are made without invoking powers of enforcement may remain merely rhetorical.

On the other hand, a unanimous decision of the General Assembly, even without any sanctions or means of enforcement, has behind it the weight of world opinion, which for the average state is a factor that cannot be treated lightly. There are two exceptions to this general appreciation.

The first exception has already been mentioned. That is when action is taken in the General Assembly against the wish of one or more parties to the dispute or situation. Such are the Hungarian, the South African, and the Korean cases. The other exception, which in a sense is subsumed in the former, is when the General Assembly tries to go against a great power. In 1961 the Assembly by a very large vote appealed to the Soviet Union to refrain from carrying out its intention to explode a fifty-megaton bomb. Only the Soviets, their allies, and Cuba voted against the resolution, and Mali abstained, while 87 countries voted in favor,[13] but the Soviet Union went ahead with its atomic tests. Another telling example is that at the Seventeenth Session of the General Assembly, the nonaligned countries supported by others introduced a draft resolution on the cessation of nuclear tests which was not fully to the liking of either the United States and the United Kingdom on the one hand or the Soviet Union on the other. Owing to the strong world sentiment in favor of the ending of nuclear weapons testing, the resolution was adopted by a very large majority,[14] but the great powers abstained on it. The United States and the Soviet Union were on the same side in refraining from endorsing the resolution. Consequently, adoption even by an overwhelming majority did not immediately and directly change the great powers' attitude toward nuclear weapons tests.

On the issue of disarmament, a preference has come to exist—the provisions of the Charter notwithstanding—for the forum of the General Assembly over the Security Council at the United Nations. The Charter states that "the Security Council shall be responsible for formulating . . . plans to be submitted to the Members of the United Nations for the establishment of a system for the regulation of armaments." [15] The General Assembly, on the other hand, "may consider . . . the principles governing disarmament and the regulation of armaments. . . ." [16] The Security Council has a categorical duty in this respect. The General Assembly has only a permissive jurisdiction of a general character. However, without conscious decision, the issue of disarmament has come to be almost entirely a preserve of the General Assembly. Disarmament cannot be achieved by compulsion. Even a small country prefers to feel that at least once a year it has an opportunity to join in the consideration of this issue so intimately welded to the most vital interests of nations.

No single item now takes as much of the time of the most important Political First Committee—*primus inter pares* among General Assembly bodies—at the annual session of the Assembly as does disarmament.

At the very first session of the General Assembly, the first resolution adopted [17] concerned disarmament, but the content of that resolution was simply to set up a commission to deal with problems raised by the discovery of atomic energy, and to work out agreements on such matters as elimination of nuclear weapons under effective safeguards. The Commission which was set up by this resolution was fully in accordance with the intentions of the Charter. It consisted of the members of the Security Council plus Canada (unless that country happened to be a member of the Council). Thus, the Commission was virtually the Security Council itself; and, what is more, the Commission was to make its reports and recommendations to the Security Council (to itself!).

Before the year was out, at the same First Session of the General Assembly a second resolution on disarmament was adopted. That resolution, too, consisted almost entirely of recommendations to the Security Council regarding the general principles to which that body might give some attention in its consideration of issues relating to disarmament. It asked member states to make available certain information and to give all possible assistance to the Security Council and the Atomic Energy Commission.[18] In this manner the General Assembly in its First Session placed the responsibility for disarmament where the Charter meant it to be—in the Security Council. Having done so, the General Assembly paid no attention whatsoever to disarmament at its Second Session.

But the Security Council and its Atomic Energy Commission started to run into difficulty. The Baruch Plan was not accepted by the Security Council. The General Assembly expressed its deep concern at the impeding of the important work of the Atomic Energy Commission, and called upon the Commission to hold informal meetings and to reach agreement.[19] Still unwilling to take disarmament into its own lap, the General Assembly adopted another resolution at the same session asking the Security Council and a Commission on Conventional Armaments (which was again the Security Council itself) to pay some attention to the reduction of conventional armaments.[20]

At its Fourth Session, the General Assembly continued to pin responsibility for disarmament on the Security Council.[21]

At the Fifth Session, while disarmament remained the general theme, and while the General Assembly established a Committee consisting of the members of the Security Council plus Canada, it asked that Committee to report to the Assembly on the best means of coordinating the functions of the Atomic Energy Commission and the Commission for Conventional Armaments.[22]

It was not until 1952 that the General Assembly adopted a resolution which gave some directions of principle to a Disarmament Commission, a body which it set up by the same resolution (again comprised of the Security Council plus Canada), and which was directed now to report to the Security Council *and the General Assembly*. At last the General Assembly decided to take a more direct interest in disarmament.

However, it was not until 1954 that disarmament started to shift to the center of the stage at the General Assembly. This happened after the Government of India had taken the initiative in April of that year to raise the question at the United Nations of the cessation of nuclear tests, and after the success of largely Indian-initiated efforts to end the difficulties regarding the repatriation of the Korean prisoners of war. I mention these two points because to an extent they are indicative of the commencement of an interest in disarmament and other matters relating to world security among the nonaligned countries and other smaller countries of the world. Hitherto the disarmament issue at the United Nations had been a matter virtually for a handful of great powers and a few of their close allies. But in 1954, after a lengthy debate, notable for the contributions of such countries as India, Australia, Egypt, and the Philippines, the General Assembly adopted the first unanimous resolution on disarmament since 1946.[23] That resolution laid down principles for disarmament under effective international control, "the whole program to be such that no State would have cause to fear that its security was endangered." [24] Furthermore, the resolution broke new ground in remitting to the Disarmament Commission a number of proposals relating to disarmament made to the General Assembly by various countries.[25] Finally, it gave further emphasis to the role of the General Assembly by transmitting to the Disarmament Commission the records of the General Assembly at which the disarmament issue had been considered and debated. There was but one mention in this resolution of the Security Council. As far as the totality of membership in the United Nations was concerned, the Security Council had, from then on, been deprived of supremacy in regard to disarmament.

In a sense, this was tantamount to a legislative alteration of the terms of the Charter. No formal amendment had been thought of or proposed, but in substance a change had occurred, and it had occurred because of the advantages of flexibility and the full impact of the weight of world opinion on an important issue which could be brought to bear in the near-universal forum of the General Assembly, but not in the Security Council.

Undoubtedly, if the great powers had been asked to agree on an amendment to the Charter in the aforementioned sense, they would have rejected the proposal; and yet so powerful was the cumulative force of the technique of wide-open conference negotiation, that an amendment had tacitly been accepted by the great powers. This is a striking illustration in the post-World War II period of the effectiveness of international parliamentary negotiation.

Since 1954, the sole occasion on which the Chamber of the Security Council was used for the discussion of disarmament was in July

1956, when India [26] and a few other countries asked for a meeting of
the nearly moribund Disarmament Commission (at that time the members to the Security Council plus Canada) to make one last effort to
push that body into activity. The effort failed. The Disarmament
Commission was unable to make any real contribution by way of
fruitful consideration of disarmament possibilities.

   The Security Council forum for the disarmament issue was so
hopelessly ineffective that the General Assembly spontaneously began
considering steps to sever the remaining connection of the Security
Council with the agenda item of disarmament. A series of informal
negotiations was begun behind the scenes, culminating in a resolution in the General Assembly in 1957 to set up a Disarmament Commission of twenty-five member states.[27] However, even this Commission was unacceptable to the Soviet Union, and in 1958 the General
Assembly completely usurped the functions of the Security Council
by constituting a Disarmament Commission which was, in fact, itself,
that is, all members of the United Nations. This proposal was introduced by the Yugoslav representative and myself (for India). We
certainly realized that a Disarmament Commission composed of the
full General Assembly membership could not effectively negotiate the
details of disarmament agreements, but we had to get a consensus on
a body which represented world opinion, and at that time the only
consensus we could get was on the basis of including all member
states in the Disarmament Commission.[28] Thereafter, it has been exclusively to the General Assembly, among the organs of the United
Nations, that disarmament issues have come. At the General Assembly in 1961 a historic event took place, in which the United States
and the Soviet Union for the first time cosponsored a substantive
resolution on disarmament.[29] That Assembly unanimously endorsed
the agreement reached by the United States and the Soviet Union to
constitute a new negotiating committee for disarmament, which has
come to be known as the Eighteen-Nation Committee on Disarmament, and which has already had a more fruitful life in the negotiation of disarmament issues than any previous disarmament commission. In keeping with the trend we have been observing is the striking
fact that this negotiating committee for disarmament was asked to
make its reports to the General Assembly, and in certain circumstances to the Disarmament Commission (which in membership is
identical with the General Assembly), but not at all to the Security
Council.

   Since then, the relationship of disarmament to the General Assembly through the committee of the eighteen nations has been an integral one, and the Security Council has retained no place whatever in disarmament negotiations.

The growing jurisdiction and powers of the General Assembly in regard to disarmament show how, in an area of vital interest to the world community, the widest kind of conference negotiation asserts itself as the preferred forum for international consideration.

Many other examples of this tendency could be cited. A number of the questions on the agenda of the Eighteenth Session of the General Assembly not only could but should, in accordance with the Charter, have gone before the Security Council, for that body has "primary responsibility for the maintenance of international peace and security," and the members of the United Nations "agree that in carrying out its duties under this responsibility the Security Council acts on their behalf." [30]

When in 1954 the Indonesian Government first brought the issue of West Irian to the General Assembly, one of its grounds for so doing was that the prevailing state of affairs might constitute a threat to the peace and security of Southeast Asia.[31] But this ground was relevant primarily to the function of the Security Council. Indeed, this aspect of a threat to the peace became the main ground for United Nations concern as the West Irian issue remained unresolved. However, the issue was not taken to the Security Council in spite of the wording of the Charter. Finally, when the parties reached agreement, with the help of the mediation of Ellsworth Bunker and the good offices of the Secretary-General of the United Nations and those of the United States, they decided to report the matter not to the Security Council but to the General Assembly. The agreement, signed on August 15, 1962, contains the following provisions:

1. The present Agreement will enter into force upon the date of the adoption by the General Assembly of the resolution referred to in Article 1 of the present Agreement.

2. Upon the entry into force of the present Agreement, the Secretary-General of the United Nations will register it in accordance with Article 102 of the Charter.[32]

Article 1 of the Agreement states that "Indonesia and the Netherlands will jointly sponsor a draft resolution in the United Nations. Under the terms of it the General Assembly of the United Nations takes note of the present Agreement, acknowledges the role conferred upon the Secretary-General of the United Nations therein, and authorizes him to carry out the tasks entrusted to him therein." [33] In terms of the Charter, all this should have been referred more appropriately to the Security Council

It is sometimes suggested that the General Assembly has increased in importance because of the Cold War and the consequent frequent inability of the Security Council to arrive at decisions. It is true that the Security Council is subject to possible vetoes, but this is not the main reason why the General Assembly has increased in power. The Security Council veto provisions can be adduced as the operative reason only in cases in which the great powers were in direct confrontation in the Council, or cases that involved the vital interests of one of the superpowers. Such cases amount to a small minority of those which have been brought before the Security Council.

In instances where the Soviet Union has used its veto power because it wished to support the point of view of a particular small state, the Soviet Union might have taken a view supported by a large number of states of the region concerned. Similarly, when the Western powers have together abstained and a particular draft resolution has failed to obtain the requisite number of affirmative votes for adoption, the Western stand has often reflected the wishes of a large number of countries in the region of the world to which the dispute or situation relates. The willingness of one side or the other in the Cold War to respond to the points of view of countries in the various regions of the world, while it might explain the inability of the Security Council to adopt resolutions, is not necessarily a reason which would drive countries away from the Security Council. In short, the voting provisions in the Security Council cut both ways; they are not always unacceptable to other states.

Fundamentally, what explains the general urge of states to repair to the General Assembly is that there they can muster wide support for their positions. Even if they cannot obtain passage of resolutions in their favor (in all the years that the West Irian case was brought to the General Assembly by Indonesia only once was a resolution adopted), the publicity, the expressions of the sentiments, aspirations, fears, will, and determination of a large number of countries, are all stimulated by discussion in the General Assembly rather than in smaller forums of negotiation. And these expressions of feeling, in turn, stimulate the process of "harmonizing the actions of nations in the attainment of . . . common ends." [34] The countries of the world have begun to feel that the main organ for the peaceful settlement of their problems is the General Assembly, even though this large conference of states is a purely recommendatory body with no Charter powers to take enforcement action.

From the General Assembly experience, one can say that the larger the conference, the weaker and the less influential is any individual member of it. Even very weak states by acting together can acquire a certain strength in large conferences.

Conferences, Decisions of Which Are Binding

It would appear that, in a technical sense, binding decisions in conference negotiation are not a characteristic of large general conferences such as the General Assembly of the United Nations, the General Conference of the International Atomic Energy Agency, or the general conferences of the Specialized Agencies of the United Nations. Such conferences are in essence global. In the nature of things, they depend for their authority not on the binding character of their decisions but on the fact that they serve as vehicles of international opinion in a wide sense, and at times of the international will and determination in the same sense.

Not all small conferences take binding decisions, but it will be found that binding decisions are generally a function of small conferences. This has been true of the Security Council (11 member states until the end of 1965), the Laos Conference (14 member states), the Organ of Consultation of the American States (at the time of writing, 20 states), the Arab League Meetings (about a dozen states), the Negotiating Conference for the Statute of the International Atomic Energy Agency (12 states), and the Board of Governors of the International Atomic Energy Agency (originally 23 members and now 25).

Conferences which make binding decisions are generally small, and there is a tendency either to require by the provisions of the relevant statute, or to establish as a working rule, that the decisions of those bodies should be taken by a relatively large vote. Indeed, in regard to issues which raise important problems of international peace and security, the tendency is to require unanimity for the decisions of such bodies, or to require the unanimity of an inner core group of states —which in its turn virtually insures unanimity.

As far as the Security Council is concerned, we have touched on the application of Article 25 of the Charter to decisions of the Council taken pursuant to findings under Chapter VI. In regard to Chapter VII, which relates to decisions by the Council with respect to threats to the peace, breaches of the peace, and acts of aggression, no doubts of any significance have been raised as to the relevance of Article 25.

The veto provisions in regard to the Security Council practically insure that any effective decision has to be unanimous or very nearly so. The permanent members represent not only their own views but tend to accommodate themselves to the views of their allies and other friendly states. When all the permanent members subscribe to a particular point of view, the rest of the members tend, as allies or friendly states, or states wishing to promote agreement among the great powers, to add their vote of assent to the consensus among the permanent members, or at any rate not to cast a negative vote.

If we look at the resolutions of the Security Council of 1955 and 1956 on matters of substance, we will find that those resolutions which were adopted were voted affirmatively by all members. Where there was no unanimity, there was in fact no resolution. At its 695th meeting on March 29, 1955, for example, the Security Council unanimously condemned an attack by Israel as inconsistent with the obligations of the parties under the General Armistice Agreement between Egypt and Israel and under the United Nations Charter.[35]

On September 8, 1955, at its 700th meeting, the Council unanimously adopted a resolution noting that there had been a rupture of talks initiated by the Chief of Staff of the Truce Supervision Organization, and calling upon the parties (Egypt and Israel) to bring about order and tranquillity in the area.[36]

On January 19, 1956, the Security Council unanimously adopted a draft resolution condemning Israel for an attack against Syria and warning Israel that if it did not comply with its obligations, the Security Council would have to consider what further measures under the Charter were required to keep the peace.[37]

On April 4, 1956, the Security Council again unanimously adopted a resolution asking the Secretary-General to make a survey of the various aspects of enforcement of and compliance with the four general armistice agreements and the Council's relevant resolutions.[38]

On June 4, 1956, the Security Council unanimously adopted a resolution requesting the Secretary-General to continue his good offices and thus to obtain full implementation of its resolution of April 4, 1956 and full compliance with the armistice agreements.[39]

During the year 1956 the Security Council also adopted four brief resolutions unanimously recommending to the General Assembly that Sudan, Morocco, Tunisia, and Japan be admitted to membership in the United Nations.

In the one case in which it was not possible to reach unanimity, no resolution was adopted. This related to the complaint of Israel against Egypt concerning restrictions on passage through the Suez Canal of ships trading with Israel. In this instance, on January 13, 1955 the President of the Council summarized the general trend of discussion and stated that most representatives in the Council regarded its resolution of September 1, 1951 as having continued validity.[40] This resolution had called on "Egypt to terminate the restrictions on the passage of international commercial shipping and goods through the Suez Canal wherever bound and to cease all interference with such shipping beyond that essential to the safety of shipping in the Canal itself and to the observance of the international conventions in force." (This resolution was somewhat of an exception, for it was not adopted unanimously. China, India, and the Soviet Union abstained.)

Since there had been no motion before the Security Council to revoke its resolution of September 1, 1951,[41] there was obviously no question but that it continued to be in force. The January 1955 summary of the President of the Council amounted to a shelving of the issue, and the case shows a strong need in the Security Council to arrive at complete unanimity, or at near unanimity with perhaps one or two abstentions.

Again, three Security Council resolutions were adopted between March and early August 1964 regarding Cyprus, and in none of them was a negative vote cast. The first [42] called for order and restraint, and recommended the creation of a United Nations Peace Force and the designation by the Secretary-General, in agreement with the Governments of Cyprus, Greece, Turkey, and the United Kingdom, of a mediator. The second Council resolution [43] reaffirmed the previous one. Then on August 9, 1964 the Security Council adopted its third resolution,[44] calling for an immediate cease-fire and restraint by the parties. This resolution was adopted by a vote of nine in favor with two abstentions (the Soviet Union and Czechoslovakia).

These examples point toward the conclusion that the graver the issue in terms of international peace and security, the more closely we approach the need for unanimity. In such cases lack of unanimity is virtually synonymous with international disorder. The Security Council saw such situations arise in 1956 when unanimity broke down over the attack on Suez, again when it broke down over the troubles in Hungary, and in 1958 when it broke down over the situation in Lebanon and Jordan.

The International Conference on Laos (1961 and 1962) attests to the validity of this view. When the Conference started, Mr. Gromyko, on May 16, 1961, stated as the Chairman for the day (the chairmanship alternated on a daily basis between the cochairmen, the heads of the delegations of the Soviet Union and the United Kingdom):

The Delegations of the Soviet Union and of the United Kingdom, as co-presidents of the conference, have prepared a memorandum of the organizational questions connected with this conference. This paper has been circulated to all delegations and has been approved by the participants of the conference.

May I take it then that these arrangements as set out in the memorandum are approved?

It is so decided.[45]

In other words, the Conference arrangements and rules were adopted without discussion. They included the provision that there would be no voting at the Conference. This meant that all decisions, both of substance and of wording, would be reached only when all the fourteen nations attending had given their assent. The unanimity rule, adopted without question, worked better than might have been anticipated, considering that there were views and objectives as dissimilar as those of the United States, the People's Republic of China, the Democratic Republic of (North) Vietnam, the United Kingdom, Canada, France, and Thailand. Many persons would have prognosticated complete failure for the Conference, but there was no possible basis of success other than unanimity.

The positions which were furthest apart were those of the United States and the People's Republic of China. However, if an international agreement was to be formulated, its terms would have to be such that neither of the two states would find them unacceptable. Let us see what their representatives and other participants said, at various stages, about reaching agreement.

On May 16, 1961, Marshal Chen Yi, the Foreign Minister of the People's Republic of China, stated:

Provided *all the countries* participating in this conference have the sincerity to truly settle the question, there is no reason why our conference cannot achieve positive results.[46]

At the end of the Conference, Lord Home (as he was at that time), speaking as Chairman and on behalf of the United Kingdom, stated on July 21, 1962:

. . . today we are reaching complete accord and an international agreement to which we all subscribe, and that agreement assures the Royal

Laotian Government and nation that all the governments here in this room will respect not only the unity and independence of Laos but also its neutrality.[47]

Dean Rusk, speaking for the United States on the same day, referred to the agreement reached by all members of the Conference:

. . . the task before us was to "discover whether we can agree that the people of Laos should be permitted to live in their own country without interference and pressures from the outside." It is satisfying to come back today and to participate in this session during which it is being recorded that such an agreement has been reached.[48]

In commenting on the agreement reached, Maurice Couve de Murville, the realistic and lucid Foreign Minister of France, said:

The texts now before us are the fruit of long negotiations and mutual concessions. . . . They show what active and discreet diplomacy can do when patient work makes it possible to define the means for achieving a common purpose.[49]

From these statements one can get some idea of how strongly embedded and how unequivocally accepted was the idea that unanimity had to be achieved. This realization had nothing to do with adherence to a rule of procedure. It stemmed solely from the fact that the realities of the situation demanded nothing less than unanimity. As a participant at this Conference, I would add that at no time was this realization in doubt. This in itself was a striking fact, because on several occasions in the detailed negotiations it looked as though it might not be possible to find common ground between the views of some of the Western participants on the one hand and the Asian Communist states on the other. This was particularly true when it came to the powers of the International Commission for Supervision and Control—consisting of Canada, India, and Poland, with the representative of India as the Chairman—in regard to the investigation of cases where there was reasonable ground for considering that violations of the agreement had occurred. Rather than veer from the need for unanimity, the heads of the delegations of the inner group of six countries, namely, China, France, India, the Soviet Union, the United Kingdom, and the United States (I served for India at these meetings), spent many difficult weeks working on a few crucial aspects of the powers and functions of the International Commission. Necessity, not procedure, impelled us forward.

In a sense, a similar necessity urged us on in the preliminary negotiations for the statute of the International Atomic Energy Agency.

Twelve nations—Australia, Belgium, Brazil, Canada, Czechoslovakia, France, India, Portugal, the Soviet Union, the Union of South Africa, the United Kingdom, and the United States—met at Washington, D.C., from February to April 1956, in the midst of the Cold War.

The negotiators decided that on important matters decisions would be taken by a two-thirds majority. Since there were only two Communist countries in the group, only one country from the growing Asian-African section of the General Assembly, and no other non-aligned countries, the chances that a two-thirds majority would not be available to the Western countries and their allies were very small. A two-thirds majority was, obviously, inadequate if a widely acceptable statute was to be drawn up.

Negotiation was not at all easy. In addition to the Cold War confrontation, there was the fact that India felt it should press strongly for the views of the "have-nots"—those countries which would presumably go to the Agency for assistance in the development of peaceful atomic energy industries. On all technical matters the spokesman for India was the distinguished atomic scientist, Homi J. Bhabha, who in 1955 had been the President of the First United Nations International Conference on the Peaceful Uses of Atomic Energy. This led to a detailed and searching technical analysis of the justification of proposed language of the statute on the subject of the appropriate international controls to insure that atomic materials were not diverted from peaceful pursuits to use in weapons. Then again, on the administration of the Agency and on questions of its political aspects, it fell to me to speak for the Indian delegation and press hard for adequate representation for the "have-not" section of the potential membership of the international agency.

These issues took many of the sessions late into the night. There was voting on various points, but when it came to the final round of consideration of the wording of the draft statute to be presented to the World Conference at the Headquarters of the United Nations, enough give-and-take had occurred in the long negotiations over the substance of the draft statute for all its proposed articles to be adopted unanimously.

These several instances of negotiation illustrate the tendency toward unanimity in smaller conferences, especially when it is realized that lack of unanimity would so split those engaged in the negotiation as to produce chaotic results. In the case of the International Atomic Energy Agency, obviously a body which was satisfactory only to the highly developed countries would not have been practicable. (And a statute for such a body could have emerged from the Washington, D.C. negotiations if certain countries had insisted on upholding their position on the two-thirds vote.) The highly developed countries were not in need of an atomic energy agency for giving assistance to each other! Other countries were the potential recipients. It was necessary to work out draft articles which could be acceptable also to the "have-not" countries. As the president of the Statute Conference in New York put it, "The Draft Statute is not the perfect instrument that it may become . . . it represents however, a common denominator, a balance struck between reality and aspirations." [50]

Djalal Abdoh of Iran also drew attention to the spirit of compromise present at the twelve-nation negotiating committee:

First of all, we congratulate ourselves that the efforts to prepare the draft statute did not prove in vain, and that we have before us a text which is, generally speaking, balanced, and which has made allowance to a large extent for the views of different countries. No doubt this is the result of the spirit of compromise evidenced by the sponsoring countries.[51]

The Vice President of the Conference, Dr. Pavel Winkler, spoke the following words, which are all the more significant as they came from the representative of Czechoslovakia at a time when Cold War tensions were high:

The deliberations in Washington were marked by an endeavour to achieve mutual understanding and by an effort to find, by means of negotiation, the solution of controversial issues. In this spirit it was possible to reach agreement even on issues which, in the past, had been the subject of considerable dispute.[52]

James J. Wadsworth, speaking for the United States, was in a position of special vantage when it came to conveying the nature of the Washington negotiations. He said:

We found that the differences of view were often great. But even greater was the will to bridge those differences. All the delegations, without exception, showed patience and persistence equal to the task. . . . As a result the draft statute before us today was adopted unanimously.[53]

Mongi Slim, a veteran statesman of Tunisia and until November 1964 his country's Foreign Minister, said:

To prepare a draft statute for an international agency which could gain the support of all nations, was difficult indeed and required great patience and a spirit of mutual understanding. This is why my delegation feels called upon to express its praise to the twelve-nation committee which is at present placing the draft before us.[54]

Indeed, most of the eighty odd countries present at the Conference drew attention to the significance of the fact that the twelve-nation negotiating body, representing several strongly entrenched and differing points of view, had reached unanimous agreement on the draft of a statute. They were implicitly observing that the inherent laws of negotiation are more powerful than the rules of procedure adopted by a particular body. In small conferences the rules of procedure become secondary, and voting itself becomes only a background possibility rather than a day-to-day reality.

For students of political organization, such developments are of particular interest, for they bear out the frequent emergence, even in complex international affairs, of a kind of general will.[55]

In the sphere of international conferences, we might move somewhat further away from the United Nations and look at the Organization of American States. The decisions of the Organ of Consultation are taken by a vote of two-thirds of the signatory states, which have ratified the Inter-American Treaty of Reciprocal Assistance (the Rio Treaty). The Organ of Consultation constitutes, in our terms, a binding conference. One aspect we have suggested to be typical of binding conferences is clearly evident, in that this is a relatively small body of countries, at present twenty. But does the second element which we have been tracing exist in this case—the element of unanimity?

In the case of the meeting of the foreign ministers of the Latin American states in July 1964 on sanctions against Cuba in accordance with Article 8 of the Rio Treaty, four countries, Bolivia, Chile, Mexico, and Uruguay, voted against the resolution on the application of certain measures to the present Government of Cuba. However, as loyal members of the Organization, all twenty nations signed the resolutions adopted by the affirmative votes of sixteen member states. Immediately after such signing, a *New York Times* correspondent in Washington expressed the view that Bolivia, Chile, and Uruguay would comply before long with the sanctions suggested by the resolutions.[56]

On August 12, 1964, the *New York Times* carried a news item datelined Santiago, Chile, August 11, to the effect that the Government of Chile had broken "diplomatic relations with Cuba tonight, in response to last month's call by the Organization of American States, for political and economic sanctions against Havana." [57] In this case, what appeared to occur was a somewhat delayed *ex post facto* (in terms of the resolutions of the OAS) achievement of near unanimity. This would again indicate that no matter how contentious the issue, in small negotiating conferences which take binding decisions there is a clear tendency toward near unanimity.

In this category we might finally look at an organization from another part of the world, the Arab League. An interesting case occurred in 1961, that of Kuwait. In 1899 the sheikdom, in spite of the fact that it was then part of the Ottoman Empire and owed allegiance to the Turkish Government, entered into "a Lawful and Honourable" Bond with the United Kingdom Government, which in effect made Kuwait a protectorate of the British.[58] Shortly after the outbreak of World War I, the British Government asked the Sheik of Kuwait to attack various neighboring points held by the Turkish Forces. For these services, His Britannic Majesty's Consul General in the Persian Gulf stated:

I make to you on behalf of the British Government certain promises concerning your Excellency personally, viz: . . . That the British Government does recognize and admit that the Sheikdom of Kuwait is an independent Government under British protection.[59]

Finally, on June 19, 1961, the British Political Resident in the Persian Gulf wrote to the ruler of Kuwait terminating the agreement of January 23, 1899 "as being inconsistent with the sovereignty and independence of Kuwait." [60]

The recognition of the full independence of Kuwait by its former protector, did not however, settle the status of Kuwait. Iraq claimed the sheikdom as an integral part of its own territory. The issue went before the Political Council of the Arab League on July 13, 1961. The Committee of the League debated Iraq's case. It decided against Iraq, and adopted a resolution recommending that Kuwait be made a member state of the Arab League, and that the League assist Kuwait to gain United Nations membership. Furthermore, it recommended that the Arab League should secure the independence of Kuwait. (In this way it sought to nullify that part of the agreement between Kuwait and the United Kingdom which stated that the latter would always be willing to provide assistance if demanded by Kuwait.) This resolution in the Political Committee of the Arab League was adopted by the affirmative vote of all the members other than Iraq. The League has held that unanimity cannot be expected necessarily to include the vote of the party or parties to a dispute.

The issue then went to the Arab League Council. Iraq did not present itself at that meeting. The Council unanimously adopted the recommendations of the Political Committee. Here again we see how a relatively small body (its total membership including Kuwait is thirteen states) works on the basis of the principle of unanimity, bearing out the general propositions we have been observing in regard to small international conferences composed of more states than the parties directly involved in the issue or dispute.

In the light of the foregoing analysis we now suggest the formulation of another general principle which appears to have emerged regarding negotiation by conference:

Negotiations conducted by conference of a larger number of states than those which are directly parties to an international situation or dispute tend to fall into one or the other of the following categories:

(a) Conferences, the decisions or recommendations of which are not binding on the parties. These tend to be general conferences composed of most or all of the states in the international community, and arrive at their decisions or recommendations by a majority vote. Unless a party to the dispute or situation at issue has categorically opposed this form of consideration, the decisions or recommendations of such conferences, although not binding, tend strongly to influence the actions of the parties concerned.

(b) Conferences, the decisions of which are binding on the parties. These conferences tend to be restricted to a relatively small number of states, and decisions, regardless of the prescribed or adopted rules of procedure, tend to be arrived at by consensus, unanimity, or near unanimity.

CHAPTER NINE

The Optimum Scope

NOW THAT WE HAVE formulated a concept of international negotiation, examined the elemental factors, and analyzed some procedures through which international negotiation may be conducted, we must look more deeply at the question of its scope. By setting the prerequisites, we have by implication indicated some of he practical limits created by the attitudes of states or furnished by the circumstances surrounding individual international disputes or situations. We have, however, also observed that attitudes of states change; that irreducible objectives and vital interests shift; that power relationships fluctuate. So too do the efforts of the international community as a whole, and so too does the understanding of states of their duties under international treaties and agreements. All in all, it is necessary to examine further the matter of the scope of negotiation.

Take, for example, the basic obligations of member states of the United Nations: "All Members shall settle their international disputes by peaceful means in such a manner that international peace and security, and justice, are not endangered." [1]

This obligation in effect rules out any use of force. In issues between states members of the United Nations, we need not say "except in self-defense," because when the obligation is fully implemented by all member states there is no occasion to use counteracting force in self-defense. In fact, the Charter goes even further than the obligation cited above:

All Members shall refrain in their international relations from the threat or use of force against the territorial integrity or political independence of any state, or in any other manner inconsistent with the Purposes of the United Nations. [2]

If these obligations were fully observed, *all* disputes and situations would become either negotiable or justiciable. Strict compliance with these Charter provisions would largely nullify such restrictions on the scope of negotiation as we have mentioned—unyielding national interest, incompatible irreducible objectives, the effect of superior power together with the fact of possession of a territory in dispute, and so on.

Perhaps no member state of the United Nations which has been involved in a dispute or situation with another state can claim to have adhered fully and strictly to the aforementioned provisions of the Charter. Since all member states have agreed that their obligations under the Charter take unqualified precedence over any other international obligations, there can be no excuse for failure to comply with its terms. For whatever reason, it did become a dereliction of a solemn Charter obligation when India used force—even if the use was minimal and nominal—to take over Goa. It may be argued that since the General Assembly had held unequivocally that Goa was a colony and furthermore had held that all colonial relationships were to be terminated without delay, consideration should have been given by the United Nations to the devising of effective measures to reinstate Goa to its rightful status. But these arguments, boiled down to practicalities, would require India to bring its point of view to the United Nations and to obtain from the Security Council or General Assembly agreement either that Portugal should be persuaded by some form of negotiation to give up its colonial possession of Goa or that the United Nations should consider other steps to hasten the decolonialization of Goa. No state which is a member of the United Nations may arrogate to itself the powers of enforcement which are to be set in motion by decision of the United Nations under the relevant provisions of the Charter.

In view of the obligations undertaken by states through adherence to the Charter of the United Nations, no member state is likely to state that it rejects the method of peaceful settlement, and in general that of negotiation, in dealing with international disputes or situations. Let us take the two most contentious of recent situations, those of Cyprus and Southeast Asia.

Early in August 1964 the use of force on and around Cyprus took on an indisputably international character. Turkish aircraft attacked Cyprus for several days, dropping bombs and strafing certain areas of the island. In one raid as many as 64 planes took part.[3] On the same date it was reported that Greek planes had flown sorties over Cyprus.

However, they did not discharge the contents of any weapons or bombs.[4] It was reported from Paris that Turkey had withdrawn some of its air units and some of its bases from the NATO Command, to use them in its national interest in the Cyprus crisis.[5] The Security Council, on August 9, 1964, called for an immediate cease-fire by all concerned.[6]

The situation had become one of actual armed conflict. Nevertheless, on August 11, 1964, the Turkish representative at the United Nations, Ambassador Orhan Eralp, informed the Council that Prime Minister Ismet Inonu of Turkey had sent "a warm and conciliatory message to the Prime Minister of Greece expressing the hope and the anticipation that the question of Cyprus may be solved within one month." [7] The Turkish Ambassador then read the message of his Prime Minister, which included the following statement:

The dangers involved in the continuation of the present grave conditions are apparent; for this reason there is an imposing necessity to find a political solution to this problem in the shortest possible time. It is, therefore, of a great importance to accelerate the Geneva talks and to come to an agreement as quickly as possible. It will be possible to reach an agreement within a month . . .[8]

Indications quickly came that at Geneva both Greece and Turkey had yielded a little in the talks taking place through the United Nations mediator.[9]

In the Cyprus dispute, even when hostilities had broken out (in violation of the terms of the Charter), there were expressions at the highest level of willingness to negotiate. This case provides evidence that no matter how complicated the situation, or how weakly present the prerequisites for negotiation, the theoretical fact that all international disputes or situations are negotiable tends to become converted into a reality.

The situation in Southeast Asia is even more complex than that of Cyprus. Two of the states very intimately involved are not members of the United Nations—the Republic of South Vietnam and the Democratic Republic of North Vietnam. The seat of China is held by the Nationalist Government from Taiwan, whereas the Peking Government, the People's Republic of China, whose authority runs over the vast mainland of China, is not in the United Nations. Although the Charter makes it possible for a nonmember of the United Nations to bring before the Security Council or the General Assembly any dispute to which it is a party,[10] it is not practicable to regard United

Nations processes as being fully available to such states. A proud
state, whether China or Germany, is not likely to bring its problems
to the United Nations unless it is fully represented at the organization. The Democratic Republic of North Vietnam even spurned the
request of the President of the Council [11] to make available information relating to the complaint contained in the United States letter
dated August 4, 1964.[12]

In practice, the major available processes for negotiation of international disputes are for the time being virtually closed to certain important states in Southeast Asia. But it does not follow that those
states are opposed to international consideration of the situation. On
the contrary, the Government of the Democratic Republic of North
Vietnam stated in its reply to the Security Council that it considered
the Southeast Asian situation one which should be put before the
Geneva Conference—the group of countries which met in 1954 (perhaps to be supplemented, as in the case of the Conference on Laos of
1961–62) and made agreements for the transfer of power from
France to the two Vietnams, Cambodia, and Laos.[13]

The situation in the Vietnams and Laos, and to some extent in
Cambodia, was not a peaceful one in the middle of 1964. Indeed, it
had been steadily deteriorating so that by July 1964 the United States
announced that it would increase its personnel in South Vietnam by
several thousand men, a step which it was believed would bring
United States military advisers and technicians in that state to a
strength of about twenty thousand. As far as North Vietnam was
concerned at that time, no official information was available of foreign military assistance to the Government, but early in 1964 there
were indications that the People's Republic of China had sent MIG
jet fighter planes to North Vietnam.[14]

In Cambodia, United States military personnel had been withdrawn at the request of that Government, and there were frequent
complaints by Cambodia of Vietnamese incursions alleged to have
been supported by United States personnel and armaments. There
had been a Security Council mission on this subject, which had reported that United Nations observation of the international frontier
between Cambodia and South Vietnam was desirable.[15]

In Laos there had been armed conflict for some months between
the Pathet Lao on one side and the neutralist and right-wing forces on
the other. For a short period, Prince Souvanna Phouma had been put
under surveillance by two generals of the army. This crisis had been
surmounted. Souvanna Phouma remained Prime Minister, but order

had not returned to Laos. The Governments of the People's Republic of China and the Soviet Union, and the Pathet Lao, had suggested reconvening the Fourteen-Nation Geneva Conference. Poland had suggested that the three Laotian factions and the three member states of the International Commission (Canada, India, Poland) should meet preparatory to the calling of a Fourteen-Nation Conference. India had supported both these suggestions. France had also supported the idea of a Fourteen-Nation Conference, but the United States and the United Kingdom, while not opposing the Conference, felt that certain preconditions would have to be satisfied, namely an effective cease-fire and the return of the Pathet Lao to the positions it held before it started its military offensive early in 1964. However, these proposals and counter-suggestions did not stop the fighting. The brief lulls, from time to time, seemed to be dictated by problems of commissariat or weather.

To return to the case of the complex issue involving the peace of the two most populous states in the area, South and North Vietnam, the United States and the United Kingdom had not seen it possible in 1964 to agree to the calling of a negotiating conference, in spite of the wishes of France, India, China, the Soviet Union, the Democratic Republic of North Vietnam, Cambodia, Laos, and Burma, and the urgings of the Secretary-General of the United Nations.

On July 23, 1964 President de Gaulle held a press conference in Paris, at which he stated:

Thus it seems that, locally, a military solution cannot be expected. . . . But, although they [the Americans] certainly dispose of all the desired means, it is difficult to assume that they wish to take the tremendous risk of a generalized conflict.

Lacking a decision by war, it is peace which thus must be made. Now, this implies returning to what was agreed upon ten years ago and, this time, complying with it, in other words, this implies that in North and South Vietnam, in Cambodia and in Laos, no foreign power any longer intervene in any way in the affairs of these unfortunate countries. A meeting of the same order and including, in principle, the same participants as the former Geneva conference would certainly be qualified to make a decision and to organize an impartial control.[16]

As it happened, President Johnson held a news conference on the following day. Regarding the possibilities of a negotiating conference for Vietnam, he said:

Other friends suggest that this problem must be moved to a conference table. And, indeed, if others would keep the solemn agreements already signed at a conference table, there would be no problem in South Vietnam.

If those who practice terror and ambush and murder will simply honor their existing agreements, there can easily be peace in Southeast Asia immediately. But we do not believe in conferences called to ratify terror, so our policy is unchanged.[17]

When the Security Council met on August 5 and 7, 1964, as a result of the aforementioned suggestion of Ambassador Stevenson, Ambassador Roger Seydoux of France repeated the French suggestion for a conference.[18]

Ambassador Stevenson referred to certain aspects of Ambassador Seydoux' brief intervention, but he did not comment on the proposal to call another Geneva-type conference. He reaffirmed the United States position that North Vietnam should comply scrupulously with the agreements of 1954 and then the United States and South Vietnam would have no cause for military defensive measures.[19]

The Secretary-General of the United Nations, in a press conference in New York on July 8, appealed for a return to the conference table. He said that "military methods will not bring about peace in South Vietnam." [20]

Since the United Nations organs of negotiation were not readily available for some Southeast Asian situations and disputes, and in view of the differing approaches to the possibility of other forms of negotiation regarding that region, it appeared superficially that the major issues, at any rate through 1964, were not negotiable. But subsequent events showed that this was a short-term view. The military situation in Vietnam deteriorated sharply in 1965, and yet on April 7, 1965 President Johnson stated that his Government was ready for "unconditional discussions."

Indeed, no conclusion regarding the negotiability or otherwise of a situation should be drawn from focusing on a short period in its overall duration. No position could have been firmer than that of France in its rejection of the idea of negotiation over Algeria. When the issue of Algeria was first brought to the General Assembly, Ambassador Hervé Alphand of France, speaking in the General Committee on September 22, 1955, stated that "Algeria was as much a part of France as Britanny, or Auvergne. If Algeria has been conquered this was true also of Flanders, Burgundy, Aquitaine, Roussillon." [21]

France was so determined that this issue would not be the subject of international negotiation that it sent its Foreign Minister, Antoine Pinay, to attend the plenary session of the General Assembly on September 30, 1955. When the question of the inclusion of this item was to be finally decided, he was more adamant than Hervé Alphand had been. He said:

If the territorial unity of any State and all frontier treaties old or new could at any time be placed in question that would be the end of security for many and of independence for the weak.[22]

In spite of Antoine Pinay's strong plea, which was supported by Paul-Henri Spaak of Belgium and by the delegates of the United States and the United Kingdom, the Assembly voted to place the question of Algeria on its agenda. As a result of this decision, the French delegation headed by Foreign Minister Pinay walked out of the General Assembly and did not attend any of its sessions until action had been taken by the Assembly to unseize itself of the item on Algeria.

In the well-known story of how France shifted its position, the highlights were President de Gaulle's statement of September 16, 1959 recognizing the right of the Algerian people to determine their own future; the endorsement of de Gaulle's policy by France in a referendum on January 8, 1961; and the Evian Agreements, which were ratified by the French on April 8, 1962 and by the Algerians on July 1, 1962. In the Security Council, when Algeria's application for admission to the United Nations was being considered, Ambassador Roger Seydoux said:

But France upheld its great traditions. It remained faithful to its ideal of liberty, and mindful of the duties it has assumed, toward the people for which it has assumed responsibility . . .[23]

These words of Roger Seydoux carried a meaning almost diametrically opposed to that of the words spoken seven years previously by Hervé Alphand; and in the intervening period France had negotiated with Algeria and agreement had been reached. What had been absolutely and emphatically nonnegotiable had become negotiable and had been satisfactorily settled.

On January 1, 1961, Prince Sihanouk of Cambodia proposed a conference on the question of Laos. The suggestion was not at first very welcome to the United States, but eventually that country agreed to attend, and at the end of fourteen months of negotiation it subscribed to the International Agreement and Protocol which emerged. In doing so it signed documents which were also signed by the People's Republic of China and the Democratic Republic of North Vietnam, and it agreed to adhere to more substantive and consequential documents than those it had not seen fit to sign in 1954. There had been a significant increase of flexibility in the approach of the United States to this Southeast Asian problem.

It should be also noted that the United States position in 1964 and 1965 on negotiations on the problems of Vietnam and Laos was that it was ready to implement fully the existing Geneva agreements. In short, it does not maintain a position of insistence on a military solution for the problems of Vietnam or Laos. On the contrary, the United States, by asking for the full implementation of the 1954 and 1962 agreements, and more specifically in President Johnson's statement of April 7, 1965 and subsequent statements, demanded a return to peaceful conditions. The difference between the United States' position and that of many other countries interested in the area is reduced to the question of how to get to the negotiating table.

Sometimes what appears to be a refusal to negotiate is the rejection rather of a particular form or method of negotiation. This is exemplified by the debates in February, March, and May 1964 in the Security Council on the question of Kashmir. In those debates some member states, including the United States and the United Kingdom, raised the possibility of mediation by the Secretary-General to assist the parties in the settlement of the issue. This method of approach was supported by several other countries. Another method of approach which was mooted and received some support was the implementation of the first resolutions on the Kashmir issue adopted by the Security Council and the United Nations Commission on India and Pakistan in 1948 and 1949. However, neither of these two approaches was acceptable to India. Its representative insisted that the only way of settling the matter would be direct negotiations between India and Pakistan. There was no real objection from any quarter to this view, and after full debate the representative of Brazil suggested that the President of the Security Council should draw up a statement of the consensus of the members. In a statement on May 18, 1964, Ambassador Roger Seydoux of France, the month's chairman, announced that he was unable to reach complete agreement with all his colleagues on the content of a presidential statement. He therefore made a statement in two parts, the first setting forth the points of agreement and the second the points of disagreement. Among the points of agreement was the following:

. . . the members of the Council expressed the hope that, in the light of our recent debates the two Countries concerned would resume their contacts as soon as possible in order to resolve by negotiation their differences, in particular their differences relating to Jammu and Kashmir.[24]

In this case we see obduracy in opposition to certain forms of negotiation, but openness to another form. The conclusion to be drawn is that the Kashmir issue is not unamenable to negotiation. In spite of the great difficulties that beset the pursuit of constructive negotiations directly between the parties involved, it would seem that this form of negotiation cannot be ruled out. As to other forms, India had even shown some interest in the possibilities of mediation or good offices toward the end of 1962.

In its absolute sense, the word "nonnegotiable" does not exist in the dictionary of international relations. At most, the word may correspond to the facts and circumstances at a given time. It may also correspond to approaches toward one or another possible form of negotiation.

However, to leave a dispute between nations unnegotiated for a long period may provoke armed conflict between the parties. In the case of India's relations with Pakistan, this has become a real hazard. Early in August 1964, the Indian authorities announced that in the first seven months of that year there had been 349 armed clashes on the Kashmir border.[25] General Robert H. Nimmo, the Chief Military Observer of the United Nations, proposed that both sides withdraw their forces to positions 500 yards from the cease-fire line, creating a zone of 1000 yards free of the military patrols of either side. On August 10, 1964 India's Defense Minister, Y. B. Chavan, announced acceptance of this suggestion.[26] It was clear, however, that with the rate of cease-fire violations reaching almost two per day in mid-1964, the situation became so explosive that large-scale conflict could easily result if the agreed United Nations peace-keeping machinery was not strengthened or if meaningful negotiations were not instituted to solve the dispute.[27]

This analysis leads us to the formulation of a principle on the optimum scope of negotiation which would appear to correspond to the current facts of international relationships:

> All international disputes and situations are, at one stage or another, negotiable, either directly between the parties concerned, or through other agreed forums or procedures. (Since the longer a dispute or situation remains unnegotiated the greater the cumulative risk that it might become an occasion for the use of force, this principle might cease to be valid if negotiation is indefinitely postponed, or if it is engaged in without a seriousness commensurate with the issues involved.)

CHAPTER TEN

Three Factors Which Impede Negotiation

A DIFFERENCE IN THE power levels of the countries concerned is one of the factors of prime importance which affect movement toward negotiation. A country which insists on following its own policies and has the power to do so is not the one that is most disposed to negotiate an issue, for negotiation would result in some modification, however slight, of its policies and practices in regard to that issue.

This factor impedes and controls movement toward negotiation even more when the vital interests of the more powerful country are involved. That is to say, a great preponderance of power, plus the conviction that its vital interests are involved, can lead a state to reject or defer the question of negotiation.

The international commitments of a country may also militate against negotiations, particularly where its prestige is at stake, and so may the personal pride, anger, or even the vanity of its rulers. Indeed, once a situation or dispute begins to affect the personal feelings of the head of a state or government, those personal feelings play an extremely important role in international affairs.

Let us look at some cases in which these three factors seem to operate.

Disparities in Power Levels, or a Sense of Buoyant Power

In our time, General de Gaulle has spoken of the influence of power on international relations more clearly than most leaders have. On July 23, 1964, he said:

At the end of the last World War, the distribution of forces in the world was as simple, as brutal, as possible. It appeared suddenly at Yalta. Only America and Russia had remained powers and all the more considerable powers in that all the rest found themselves dislocated, the vanquished engulfed in their unconditional defeat and the European victors destroyed to their foundations.

Then again, in the same statement:

It is clear that things have changed. The Western States of our old continent have rebuilt their economies. They are rebuilding their military forces. One of them—France—is becoming a nuclear power.[1]

He goes on to imply that now that continental Western Europe, through France, is becoming a nuclear power, it is rising to new heights of strength and is about to adopt an independent policy.

It might be argued that such an independent policy is not necessarily incompatible with negotiation. As far as France itself is concerned, we have seen how General de Gaulle has frequently called for negotiation of the problems of Southeast Asia. But in making these calls, France is not dealing with an issue to which she is a party, and we are here concerned with attitudes of the great-power countries in situations or disputes that directly relate to them. In such matters France's growing power does not appear to have been a factor that has been conducive of negotiation.

For example, France's growing power has been a factor in the rebuffing of British desires for membership in or association with the European Common Market. Another expression has been France's attitude toward the Eighteen-Nation Committee on Disarmament. It is true that France is not as powerful as the United States or the Soviet Union, but there is now a great disparity of power between France and the other members of the Committee (excluding the two just mentioned and the United Kingdom). It is this great disparity which has led General de Gaulle to say, quite frankly, that in regard to disarmament he shuns negotiation with the puny nonnuclear powers of the world. Here we have a clear case where a disparity of power militates against negotiation—at any rate in the forum favored by all other countries.

This point becomes even more vivid when we consider the attitudes of the superpowers in concrete situations. One example is the position of the United States in regard to the Castro Government in Cuba. Early in July 1964, Fidel Castro gave an eighteen-hour interview to Richard Eder, who then reported fully in the *New York Times*.

Eder wrote that Castro gave definite form to rumors about his desire "to explore a rapprochement with the United States." Castro suggested that the time had come when an extensive discussion of the issues between the two countries would be useful. He said that "Cuba would commit herself to withholding material support from Latin American revolutionaries if the United States and its American Allies would agree to cease their material support for subversion actively against Cuba." Eder continued, "Dr. Castro was obviously eager to make his statements about the United States as conciliatory as possible. There was an almost total absence of bellicose pronouncements and several times he restated his points, invariably altering them for the milder."

Regarding aid to rebels in neighboring Latin American countries, Dr. Castro's thesis, according to Eder, is that if one state violates an international norm, and he holds that the United States has done so by aiding rebels from Cuba, the other state has a right to do so as well. Eder then quotes Fidel Castro's statement as follows: "But we can discuss this question with the United States; if they're ready to live with us in subjection to norms, then we would feel the same obligation."

Discussing the background of relations between the United States and Cuba after the Cuban Revolution, Castro said that both countries were to blame but that the United States as a mature, powerful nation had a much greater share of responsibility. He added, "It could be said, however, that both sides did very little to prevent matters from getting where they did." [2]

On July 6, 1964 a United States Department of State spokesman, Richard I. Phillips, when questioned about Castro's proposals, read the following statement:

Taking into account decisions reached within the Inter-American System we have consistently maintained that there are two elements that are not negotiable: Castro's ties of dependency with the Soviet Union, which are tantamount to the Soviet domination of the regime; and the continuance of Castro's promotion of subversion elsewhere in the hemisphere. [3]

At his news conference on July 10, 1964, President Johnson was asked what his attitude or response was to Castro's offer to negotiate. The President replied:

I have seen newspaper reports purporting to reflect his attitude. I am much more interested in the deeds than the words, and I shall carefully watch for any actions that I think would be in the best interest of the people of Cuba and the people of the world. I am much more interested in deeds than words.[4]

On July 21, 1964, Fidel Castro's brother, Raoul, said that Cuba would consider stopping its demands for an end of the economic blockade and reconnaissance flights as conditions for talks with the United States. He amplified this and said that "if the United States wants to hold discussions without Fidel's five points, perhaps we might agree in dropping them." [5] The five points were those suggested by Fidel Castro on October 28, 1962 during the missile crisis: ending of the economic blockade of Cuba; halting subversive activities and the arming of exiles; halting pirate attacks from the United States and Puerto Rico; halting violations of Cuba's air space by United States reconnaissance planes; and finally, United States withdrawal from the Guantanamo base.[6]

However, Administration thinking seemed to remain firmly opposed to negotiation. In his statement to the Consultative Meeting of American Foreign Ministers at Washington, D.C., Secretary of State Dean Rusk is reported by the *New York Times* to have referred to the Castro interview with newsman Eder and to have said:

In this interview, Castro also tried to put Cuba's subversive activities on the bargaining counter. I wish to make one point very clear, that as far as the United States is concerned the encouragement and support of subversion by the Cuban regime against other countries of this hemisphere is not a subject for bargaining. It simply must stop and when it does the hemisphere will know it, without the need for discussions with Castro's regime.[7]

A few days later it was reported that Mr. Rusk, speaking on an ABC program, "Issues and Answers," said that "Castro has no future in Cuba or this hemisphere."

It would seem that in mid-1964 United States officials were not disposed to favor negotiations with the Castro Government. It appeared not unlikely that the reasons of the United States were not restricted to charges of intervention in the affairs of other states. Mexico, for example, has felt that this charge against Cuba has not been proved.

The obvious fact is that Cuba needs negotiations much more than does the United States; relatively it is weak and feels insecure. The United States, on the other hand, is highly powerful and has no reason to feel insecure in relation to Cuba. There is, of course, the factor that Cuba has a very powerful ally in the Soviet Union, and this alliance is an annoyance to the United States. However, the fact is that since the withdrawal of Soviet missiles and bombers and most of its ground forces, Cuba is militarily virtually isolated from the Soviet Union. If there were any evidence of renewed Soviet military movement toward Cuba, there is little doubt that the United States would feel compelled to take measures as it did in 1962 to cut off such movement.

It might be said from this instance that immense military might and power can deter the other side from aggression, but it can also deter the possessor from responding to calls for negotiation. Since such power controls or contains the situation, the strong country has no drastic or compelling need to discuss the issue. On the other hand, a weak country which feels itself subjected to the immense power of the other party tends to seek negotiation with a view to exploring the possibilities of altering the situation.

This general proposition can also be illustrated in the great power of the Soviet Union vis-à-vis situations of interest to it. Had it not been for the great disparity of power between the Soviet Union and Hungary, the situation which occurred in 1956 and so fundamentally involved the relations of those two states might well have become a subject for negotiation. As it was, however, the Soviet found it simpler to utilize its strong arm before it entered into discussions regarding its future relations with the Government of Hungary.

Another example of the effects of the disparity of power on possibilities of negotiation is furnished by recent developments in the relations between the United States and a much weaker state, Cambodia. In May 1964 Cambodia brought charges against the United States and South Vietnam involving the violation of its frontier. In this connection, Ambassador Voeunsai Sonn of Cambodia told the United Nations Security Council on May 19, 1964 about several measures which his Government had suggested. One of these was that the United Nations send a commission of inquiry. He said, however, that such a Commission would have only a limited role to play. He added:

It would not replace the control of the frontiers by the International Control Commission, which is a permanent body which is consecrated by the International Agreement which flowed from the Conference of Geneva in 1954.

A meeting of a new Conference of Geneva appears to be indispensable in order to make clear the attributes of this International Control Commission and to give it the necessary means to take up the control of the frontiers. . . . Since August 1962, we have ceaselessly requested the convocation of a Geneva Conference in order to obtain recognition and international guarantees of our neutrality and our territorial integrity.[8]

Ambassador Stevenson, in his reply to Ambassador Sonn, stated:

Now it is suggested that the way to restore security on the Cambodian-Vietnamese border is to reconvene the Geneva Conference which ten years ago reached the solemn agreement, which I have just read to the Council. While I hesitate and dislike to disagree with my friend from Cambodia, I submit that we can surely do better than that, and that there is no need for another such conference. A Geneva conference on Cambodia could not be expected to produce an agreement any more effective than the agreements we already have.[9]

In fairness, it should be added that Ambassador Stevenson did not just take a negative stand. He made a proposal for improvement of the situation in the following terms:

We would suggest that . . . it would be useful to ask the Secretary-General of the United Nations to offer assistance to Cambodia and to the Republic of Viet Nam in clearly marking the frontiers between the two countries.[10]

However, it remains true that for long the United States strongly opposed another negotiating conference on Cambodia's neutrality and independence. Although several countries in the neighborhood of Cambodia (Burma, China, and India) have supported Cambodia's plea, no conference would be of any avail unless the United States were also a willing participant. When in May 1965 the United States showed some willingness to participate in a conference on Cambodia, it was reported in the press that its idea was to use the conference as an opportunity for talks on Vietnam. This was unacceptable to Prince Sihanouk.

Another instance to note is that when the situation in Laos was going strongly against the right wing militarily, in spite of the substantial military and financial assistance to General Phoumi Nosavan (the right-wing military commander), and when it became clear that further military assistance could not be usefully absorbed by the right wing, the United States did agree in 1961 to a conference on Laos. It would appear, therefore, that only when the situation between a powerful country and a relatively weak one reaches the point when all other practical means of obtaining an acceptable rearrangement have failed, is the powerful party disposed to negotiate. Moreover, it is not easy for a powerful country to reach the point of admission that all other means of solution have been exhausted.

In the case of South Vietnam, there is a significant outpouring of seemingly dispassionate, friendly, and well-meaning views of governments and responsible individuals to the effect that no military solution is possible—that as long as force is used in South Vietnam, the Vietcong and their friends will remain involved in the confrontation. In spite of this view, the United States, motivated perhaps by its continuing feeling that it could deploy more power if necessary in the region than hitherto, for a long time did not agree to the calling of a negotiating conference or to any other form of negotiation. A primary cause of the United States' reluctance to negotiate was its vastly superior power in comparison to that of the other parties in the conflict.

In the cases we have mentioned, the stronger party or the party with a sense of growing power has been a nuclear power. It is obvious that the possession of nuclear weapons adds a new dimension to a country's strength. However, instances can be cited when a nonnuclear power has been sufficiently puissant in comparison with the other party to a dispute or situation to affect the relations between them and the chances of negotiation. For example, when President Sukarno stated that 100 million Indonesians would mobilize against Malaysia, and when he referred to the smallness of the enemy, he was saying clearly enough that his much greater strength would enable him to settle the issue. Such expressions are not compatible with negotiation, and it is significant that the efforts which took place first under the sponsorship of the Thai Foreign Minister, Thanat Khoman, and later in Tokyo, quickly broke down. Since then there has been little serious talk of negotiation.

Another significant instance of the operation of power levels upon possibilities of negotiation has been furnished by the assumed changes in strength between India and Pakistan. The Indians took the initiative in bringing the Kashmir issue to the Security Council in 1948. At that time both countries had just become independent and neither had a tangible sense of power. Once frustrated in its efforts to get Pakistani forces and personnel out of Kashmir through United Nations action, India relied increasingly on its own capacities. There was no dramatic build-up of military power, but gradual and minor developments of the military machine took place. Moreover, in general economic development and in the expansion of its industrial complex, India enjoyed greater progress than Pakistan throughout the

1950s. These factors combined to increase India's sense of strength and discipline.

During the whole of this period, India remained less open to ideas of direct or indirect negotiation with Pakistan over the Kashmir issue. We recall that it was not particularly responsive to the Security Council's move in 1957 to send Ambassador Gunnar Jarring to the subcontinent on a mediatory mission. Nor did it take sustained steps to promote direct negotiations with Pakistan.

Then came the jolt to India's power status through the surprising swiftness of the Chinese invasion of its northeastern and northwestern borders late in 1962. Prime Minister Nehru, before his death, had become much more conciliatory toward Pakistan over the Kashmir issue and had encouraged the Government of Kashmir to release Sheik Abdullah from his long incarceration. He had indicated his willingness to meet with President Ayub Khan, and had encouraged Sheik Abdullah to discuss the issue with the head of the state of Pakistan. All this took place after India had reason to think that it was not as powerful vis-à-vis her neighbors as it had previously thought. In this case, an assumed significantly greater power had played a role of arresting possible approaches to negotiation. When the assumption proved to be incorrect, the country showed more willingness to negotiate.

As the power status of India declined, Pakistan became less keen to negotiate. In initiating a debate on the international situation in the Lower House of the Indian Parliament on November 23, 1964, Swaran Singh, the Indian Minister of Foreign Affairs, made the following observations:

. . . we proposed to Pakistan in July last year that there should be a meeting between the representatives of the two countries to find ways and means of eliminating needless conflict and loss of life on both sides which only tended to heighten the atmosphere of tension and further to embitter the relations between the two countries. In September the Pakistan Government replied agreeing to our suggestion and after mutual consultations through diplomatic channels it was arranged that a delegation from India should visit Karachi for talks on November 2, 1964 with the representatives of the Pakistan Government on the restoration of tranquillity along the ceasefire line and along the international boundaries between India and Pakistan. However, on the eve of the talks the meeting had to be postponed at Pakistan's request.

After weeks of diplomatic consultations the Pakistan Government had suggested a date after November 22, for talks in Rawalpindi between the Home Ministers of the two countries. We agreed to have these talks in Rawalpindi from November 23, 1964, that is, from today for two days. The Indian delegation was announced and the necessary preparations had been undertaken for the meeting. But again the Pakistan Government a few days ago asked for a postponement of the meeting.[11]

A manifest decline in India's power would not unnaturally result in a relative rise in Pakistan's sense of power—particularly as long as China, India's powerful antagonist in Asia, expresses warm friendship for Pakistan. The sense of closeness between China and Pakistan cannot but create for either of them a sense of powerfulness in relation to India. This new sense may well have something to do with Pakistan's coolness toward the negotiation to which Swaran Singh was referring, and for its direct-action approach in the Rann of Cutch in April and May, 1965.

Claims of International Commitments

In the post-World War II period, the vital interests of the major states have expressed themselves in part through a series of international commitments. There are, for example, NATO, the Warsaw Pact, SEATO, CENTO, and the Inter-American system. In these alliances the two sides to the Cold War, headed by the superpowers, the United States and the Soviet Union, have sketched out their interests and their international commitments.

But this is true not only of the military alliances entered into in the post-World War II period. Even India, which has repeatedly affirmed that it has no military alliances, has international defensive responsibilities. For example, Prime Minister Nehru, in speaking in the Indian Parliament on December 8, 1959 about such responsibilities, said:

Apart from the obvious responsibilities of defending India and Indian territory, our responsibilities undoubtedly extend to the neighbouring countries, Sikkim, Bhutan and Nepal. We have to stand by them whatever the consequences. . . . This treaty between India and Nepal, a treaty of peace and friendship was signed on July 31, 1950. . . .

Now, apart from the treaty—but as an essential, operative part of that—there was an exchange of letters between the two Governments in identical language, as is the custom. In these letters there is this sentence: "Neither Government shall tolerate any threat to the security of the other by a foreign aggressor. To deal with any such threat, the two Governments shall consult with each other and devise effective counter-measures." [12]

It is clear from this statement that India regards the defense of Nepal, Sikkim, and Bhutan as vital to the preservation of its own interests.

Similarly, when President Kennedy in his radio and television address on the Cuban crisis on October 22, 1962 stated the following, he was giving precision to the United States' concept of its obligations arising out of its commitments and interests:

But this secret, swift, and extraordinary buildup of Communist missiles—in an area well known to have a special and historical relationship to the United States and the nations of the Western Hemisphere, in violation of Soviet assurances, and in defiance of American and hemispheric policy—this sudden, clandestine decision to station strategic weapons for the first time outside of Soviet soil—is a deliberately provocative and unjustified change in the status quo which cannot be accepted by this country.[13]

Adlai Stevenson, in presenting the United States case on the Caribbean crisis to the Security Council on October 23, 1962, developed this theme as follows:

The principle of the territorial integrity of the Western hemisphere has been woven into the history, the life and the thought of all the people of the Americas. In striking at that principle, the Soviet Union is striking at the strongest and most enduring strain in the policy of this hemisphere. . . . To allow this challenge to go unanswered would be to undermine a basic and historic pillar of the security of this hemisphere.[14]

When the crisis had been surmounted, Chairman Khrushchev wrote to President Kennedy on December 19, 1962, saying that "the definite improvement which has taken place in the international situation should facilitate" endeavors to reach a nuclear test ban. He then laid down a basis on which the United States and the Soviet Union could work to avoid a thermonuclear war. He said:

To prevent this from happening, we must, on a basis of complete equality *and due consideration for each other's interests,* develop peaceful relations between us and resolve all controversial questions by means of negotiations and mutual concessions.[15]

Khrushchev thus indicated that he accepted the position of taking into account the interests of both sides. Negotiations would be conducted on the basis of safeguarding such interests.

When the vital interests or commitments of a state are ignored, trampled upon, or seriously threatened by another state, the tendency of the injured party is to react in deeds rather than in words. In short, it is apt to take steps to protect its interests and honor its commitments, rather than restrict itself to the region of pure discussion and peaceful negotiation.

The reaction of the United States to the sending of missiles and bombers to Cuba by the Soviet Union was essentially of this character.

In keeping with this view, President Kennedy's statement of October 22 contained the following significant phrase:

This nation is prepared to present its case against the Soviet threat to peace, and our own proposals for a peaceful world, at any time and in any forum—in the OAS, in the United Nations, or in any other meeting that could be useful—*without limiting our freedom of action.*[16]

In the case of Cyprus, Ambassador Orhan Eralp of Turkey told the Security Council that the action of Turkey in bombing and strafing the island had been "taken under its solemn rights emanating from existing international agreements." [17] He identified completely the interests of the ethnic Turks on Cyprus with those of the Turkish Government. Only if we accept such unequivocal identification can we understand his words that his Government had "been constrained to act in legitimate self defense." [18] Greece, too, is committed to the Greek Cypriots. These sets of commitments and avowals of vital interest have inhibited, although they have not foreclosed, processes of negotiation.

Another striking case of the inhibitory effect of commitments on the possibilities of negotiation is furnished by the positions of China and the United States in Southeast Asia. The United States' position was made clear in President Johnson's statement of June 23, 1964, when he opened a news conference:

The policy of the United States toward Southeast Asia remains as it was on June 2, when I summarized it in four simple propositions:
1. America keeps her word.
2. The issue is the future of Southeast Asia as a whole.
3. Our purpose is peace.
4. This is not just a jungle war, but a struggle for freedom on every front of human activity.[19]

President Johnson put first and foremost as a determinant of policy America's unswerving adherence to its international commitments. Such commitments express a strong linkage between states and weld them together in the pursuit of common purposes. As far as China is concerned, the Government of the People's Republic, after the military events in Tonkin Bay early in August 1964, issued a statement in which it referred to China and North Vietnam as being "closely related to each other like the lips and the teeth." [20]

What is the effect on Chinese policy of this fact of identity of interests with North Vietnam? Is it a demand that there should be negotiations regarding former Indochina? While in a general sense it is true that China has supported the demands of the Democratic Republic of North Vietnam for a Geneva-type conference on Vietnam, the reaction to the Gulf of Tonkin military events has not been a demand for negotiations. On August 17, Marshal Chen Yi, the Foreign Minister of China, flatly refuted the United States view (as he stated it) that the matter was closed. His riposte was:

This is a fraud. We hereby tell them frankly that the matter is far from being over. The aggressor must be punished. The debt of blood must be repaid. . . . The initiative is entirely in our hands.[21]

There is no semblance here of urgings for or even readiness to consider discussion, conciliation, or other peaceful means of settlement or adjustment. And since August 1964 this Chinese attitude appears further to have hardened.

The commitments of a powerful state can restrict approaches to negotiation in the settlement of disputes or situations involving weaker states. The hypothesis which we are advancing applies both to the United States' commitment in South Vietnam and to China's commitment to the Hanoi Government.

Although only incipiently a nuclear power, China regards itself as extremely powerful, and, in a nonnuclear war, a match for any country. Members of the Chinese delegation to the Laos Conference of 1961–1962 (including Chang Han Fu, the Deputy Foreign Minister of China) frequently said to me that in Korea they had defeated the United States in spite of the fact that the United States was substantially assisted by other important powers, such as the United Kingdom, Canada, Australia, and Turkey. It would appear that in Southeast Asia they regard themselves as equal to the military demands of the situation. Recently, Marshal Chen Yi is reported to have given an extensive interview to Dr. Hubert Portisch, the Editor of *Der Kurier* of Vienna. On the issue of a possible military conflict with the United States, the Chinese official said:

And—incidentally, we have told this to the Americans—this will not be a second Korea. Korea is a narrow peninsula and it is impossible for many millions of soldiers to operate there. The space is too narrow. In South East Asia it is quite different. A very wide and a very broad front can be set up there. Such a war would not remain isolated in a narrow space. It would also involve Vietnam, Laos, and Cambodia, perhaps also Thailand. . . .

If they [the Americans] want a small war, well, then a small war it will be. If they want a big war, then it will be a big war. . . .

The Americans threaten with atomic bombs, and my friend Khrushchev is also afraid of this. What do they want to achieve with atom bombs against China? They could destroy cities like Shanghai and Peking with atom bombs.

But China? Do you know how big China is? [22]

These remarks, which seem to me typical of Marshal Chen Yi's thinking,[23] indicate that China regards itself as a match for a United States military effort in Southeast Asia. The result of this situation is the overlapping but contradictory commitments of two very powerful states toward relatively weak states. (While I describe North Vietnam as a relatively weak state, I am reminded of the fact that Ambassador Jacques Roux once told me that the French regard the North Vietnamese as some of the finest infantry men in the world.) Because of these overlapping commitments, the situation in Southeast Asia is both highly dangerous and extremely difficult to bring to the negotiating table.

Personal Feelings of Heads of States

In his monumental work on the Second World War, Winston Churchill tells us that he "had continuous difficulties and many sharp antagonisms with him [General de Gaulle]." [24] In the same paragraph Churchill goes on to say that while he "understood and admired . . . [he] resented his [General de Gaulle's] arrogant demeanor . . . he [de Gaulle] had no real foothold anywhere. Never mind, he defied all. Always, even when he was behaving worst, he seemed to express the personality of France—a great nation with all its pride, authority, and ambition." [25] In many passages in his work, Churchill cites instances of difficulties with de Gaulle. We might take note of two such instances.

In May 1943, when Churchill visited North Africa, one of the issues which engaged his attention was rivalry between the French commanders. In describing the situation, Churchill makes the following observation:

De Gaulle would not accept Giraud as Supreme Commander of the French forces. Giraud was anxious to keep the French Army of North Africa intact and clear of Free French influences. This attitude of de Gaulle on the question of military command exacerbated American dislike and distrust of him.[26]

It is hardly likely that de Gaulle could have forgotten the attitude which Churchill describes in the last sentence of the above citation. Immediately before the D-day operations, Churchill briefed de Gaulle on the project. De Gaulle raised the question of the administration of liberated France. This nettled Churchill, who tells us that de Gaulle's remark made him speak bluntly. His description of what he said to de Gaulle is as follows:

. . . if there was a split between the National Committee of Liberation and the United States, we should almost certainly side with the Americans. About the administration of liberated French soil, if General de Gaulle wanted us to ask the President to give him the title-deeds of France the answer was "no." If he wanted us to ask the President to agree that the Committee was the principal body with whom he should deal in France, the answer was "Yes." De Gaulle replied that he quite understood that if the United States and France disagreed, Britain would side with the United States. With this ungracious remark the interview ended.[27]

These last two sentences record another incident which de Gaulle is most unlikely to forget.

There can be little doubt that de Gaulle has continued to be influenced by his fateful wartime experiences and the assessment he then made of the relationship between the "Anglo-Saxon" powers.

On June 12, 1964, in a tour through northern France, de Gaulle declared in a speech at Amiens that "France wants, recommends and will obtain one day, the end of these interventions on both sides." He was referring to Vietnam, Laos, and Cambodia, and spoke of those countries as having been "unfortunate and torn" because of "interventions that have occurred there." [28]

Rhetorical though these words might sound, they represent the strong feelings of the head of a most important European state, one which is increasingly showing its determination to act in the exercise of its own unfettered judgment. In the particular case of Southeast Asia, de Gaulle is pressing for negotiation. But in other cases, such as that of the possibility of negotiation between the United Kingdom and the European Common Market countries, his attitude has been one of strong skepticism and emotional opposition.

Indeed, the very force of his statements in favor of negotiation in Southeast Asia tends to create a reaction against his position, and thus to diminish the chances of negotiation. Strong countries (as the United States is in comparison with France) do not like being pushed into positions even of negotiation, particularly by a head of state whose feelings and sentiments through the years have not been very favorable to the strong country concerned. De Gaulle's statements continue to show his unfavorable emotional attitude toward the United States. Recently he said:

In reality, the fact that Europe, not having a policy, would be subject to the policy that came to it from the other side of the Atlantic appears to them, even today, normal and satisfactory. We have seen many people, quite often, what is more, worthy and sincere, advocate for Europe not an independent policy . . . but . . . an Atlantic system, in other words, American, and consequently subordinate to what the United States calls its leadership.[29]

Referring to the current position in Southeast Asia, he stated:

It can be added, without any intention of being derogatory, that their conviction of fulfilling a sort of vocation, the aversion which they had to any colonial work which had not been theirs, and finally the natural desire in such a powerful people to ensure themselves of new positions, determined the Americans to take our place in Indochina.[30]

The sentiment which informs and pervades statements such as the above is not conducive to a spirit of conciliation and negotiation; if anything, it tends to harden positions by putting the powerful country, whose activities have been referred to in a somewhat derogatory way, to the test. That country then naturally tends to explore the possibility of other courses of action. A tangential force away from negotiation is generated. Difficult and hazardous as the path of negotiation regarding Southeast Asia may be, most uninvolved and friendly observers regard it as fully worth exploration to its utmost limits. The emotionally charged remarks of the great French leader may have deterred those involved in the region from this valuable, and eventually necessary, exploration.

Those who have been directly concerned with the settlement of adjustment of international situations or disputes know how frequently the characteristics of individuals enter into and affect possibilities of negotiation. Even so controlled, sensitive, and brilliant an international figure and negotiator as Dag Hammarskjöld occasionally missed a step or two, because of a tendency toward personal involvement in the situation at hand. In the late summer of 1956, after the failure at the London conferences on the Suez Canal, and the rejection by the first of those conferences of the compromise Indian plan for the future arrangements for the operation of the Canal, Dag Hammarskjöld had striking success in working out with the foreign ministers of France, Egypt, and the United Kingdom a series of six points to govern the operation of the Canal. This was a remarkable negotiating achievement. However, in talks with Dag Hammarskjöld at that time directed to suggesting certain possibilities to him, one could not but sense a certain overconfident brushing aside of other possibilities which, as it turned out, might have been valuable in intensifying discussions just when the United Kingdom, France, and Israel were planning an attack on the Canal Zone. Perhaps it was his view that as the basis of a peaceful settlement had been found—largely by him— there was no reason to give ear to suggestions which other diplomats considered likely to be useful. This arose out of what I have called a personal involvement. I do not wish to give the impression that this kind of involvement was typical of Dag Hammarskjöld. Far from it. Almost invariably he was rather like a great bird that flew rapidly above the situation—observing it clearly and in detail, seeing its dangers, its human foibles, and its humorous aspects. But this was an instance of behavior resulting from the personal involvement of a man in a highly sensitive and responsible position, who normally remained uninvolved although intensely concerned. This is not a criticism of Dag Hammarskjöld but an illustration of the fact that at times the roles of the main actors are so played that personal feelings or emotions rise (in Dag Hammarskjöld's case very rarely) to a position of control or dominance.

Again, in 1958, after the landing of United States Marines in Lebanon, there was a brief period when Dag Hammarskjöld's personal predilections raised some difficulties in the pattern of negotiation. A draft resolution, in part his own work, which was being canvassed with members of the Third Emergency Special Session of the General Assembly by the delegations of Canada, Norway, and a few others, was not one which would have met the needs of the situation. Yet it was being pressed very hard on the delegates. Hammarskjöld seemed confident that the opposition would crumble. He gave the Western powers to understand that he could get the Arabs, notably Foreign Minister Mahmoud Fawzi of the United Arab Republic, to accept it. In this assessment he turned out to be mistaken, but it should also be mentioned that he was, at the same time, advising the

Arabs to get together and draft an alternative proposal. The latter, in fact, is what happened, but only after the first draft had nearly been brought to a vote.[31]

There is no question that India's Jawaharlal Nehru was a man singularly lacking in pettiness and meanness. At the same time he was a man of uninhibited feelings. This added to his charm, directness, and, in most situations, to his effectiveness. However, in international affairs these obtrusions of feeling—through minor emotional outbursts—did not conduce to peaceful negotiations. There was one such uprush in 1960, when the King of Nepal, as head of state of that country, issued a proclamation on the failure of his Cabinet's Government to carry out its tasks. The King terminated the session of Parliament, dismissed the Cabinet, and took over the Government himself. When this news came to Delhi, Prime Minister Nehru did one of the most extraordinary things a statesman could have done. He made a speech in the Indian Parliament, on December 20, 1960, expressing his shock at the action of the King, criticizing him sharply for the complete reversal of the democratic process, and saying that the development was to be viewed with considerable regret.[32]

These were the lofty sentiments of a true democrat, but they were totally out of place, for they constituted public criticism of the head of a friendly and neighboring state. They resulted in a very considerable cooling of relations between India and Nepal, and obliquely contributed to the advancement of the interests of other powerful states in the region. They added considerably to the difficulties of the continuing process of discussion of many matters of interest both to India and its Himalayan neighbor.

There were other occasions when Prime Minister Nehru's feelings deflected India from the course of negotiation. In the long period from 1956 to 1962, Sino-Indian relations steadily deteriorated. There was ample reason for negotiation and plenty of desire on both sides for it. However, in this period the Chinese press and government officials opened a campaign of rude invective directed personally against Jawaharlal Nehru. He was a sensitive and proud person and was particularly nettled by criticism from a Government whose interests he had personally championed at international conferences, including the yearly efforts which the Indian delegation made at the General Assembly of the United Nations to secure the rectification of the credentials of the delegation of China.

While the Chinese attacks on the Prime Minister were in bad taste and pernicious, they should have been regarded as a hazard of

Nehru's public life, and he should not have allowed them to affect his attitude toward China. Unfortunately, however, they did. I recollect reporting to him personally on the progress of the negotiations at the International Conference on Laos. I was making my oral report in September 1961 at Belgrade, where Jawaharlal Nehru was leading the Indian delegation at the Conference of Heads of State or Government of Non-Aligned Countries. When I described the attitude of China, Nehru's expressive eyes flashed; he looked up and said, "The Chinese are extremely rude." This remark was irrelevant to what I was reporting to him. It was clear that his feelings had been deeply wounded by the Chinese verbal barbs. He had come consequently to dislike the idea of dealing with them, and this was undoubtedly one of the reasons why several opportunities for negotiation were neglected. For example, since the Chinese for most of 1961 and a large part of 1962 had responsible high officials at Geneva from their Foreign Office at Peking, India could have shown some willingness to talk with them there on Sino-Indian problems. Marshal Chen Yi was there for several weeks, and his chief lieutenant, Vice Minister Chang Han Fu, was there almost continuously. However, no desire was indicated from the Indian side to negotiate on the difficulties. Even if the Indian Foreign Office believed that talks might be initiated at Geneva, knowing Mr. Nehru's feelings it would not have broached the subject to him. My own suggestions in that direction in September 1961 were met with a frozen silence on the part of the Prime Minister.

In fairness, I should add that the Chinese were unreasonably nettled and testy about India. Marshal Chen Yi blustered to me about the Indian press. He said; "Your newspapers attack China all the time, they tell lies about China, they're antagonistic to our people and our Government." I explained to him that our newspapers were privately owned and expressed different sections of public and private opinion. The Government of India did not control the press. Marshal Chen Yi brushed this aside. He would not accept the explanation. The Government could, he insisted, stop this kind of writing about a friendly and neighboring country. His feelings were strong and antagonistic because of what he construed to be either a deliberate press campaign in India inspired by the Government, or a campaign at which the authorities connived.

It would be possible to cite other instances in which the personal feelings of responsible officials played an important role in international relations in general and in the possibility or conduct of negotiation in particular. I hesitate, however, to multiply such instances, as they would involve persons who are still active in international life. It would not be in keeping with the purpose of this study to arouse the ire of responsible leaders! The reader can undoubtedly supply this hiatus by extrapolating from his own experience, and understanding what the feelings of persons in greater or lesser positions of authority must be under provocative circumstances.

I can only emphasize that personal feelings are of profound importance in international affairs; and since it is the most dramatic, delicate, and tense situations that are most apt to rouse feelings, there are few crucial international issues in which the personal reactions of the responsible officials concerned do not have some bearing on the possibilities and practices of negotiation.

The three factors considered in this chapter are elements that sometimes deflect or impede the course of international negotiation. The following principles may be derived from an observation of those factors in operation:

> When there is a real or assumed significant disparity of power between the parties to a dispute or situation, or when one of the parties is imbued with a sense of growing power, then such disparity or sense of buoyant power may militate against resort to negotiation to settle the dispute or ameliorate the situation.
>
> When, together with the difference in power level, the international commitments of the more powerful party are involved, then those commitments tend to exclude the concerned dispute or situation from, or render it less susceptible to, negotiation.
>
> The personal feelings of heads of state or government or other responsible persons, when aroused, may seriously affect possibilities of and attitudes in negotiation, not only with respect to the situation or dispute in the course of which feelings have been aroused, but in all situations or disputes with the state whose rulers or representatives have been responsible for arousing those feelings.

CHAPTER ELEVEN

Vital Interests

WHAT ARE THE VITAL interests of a country? In the early 17th century King James I of England dismissed his ambassador, Sir Henry Wotton, who had scribbled on an album at Augsburg the now famous phrase, "An ambassador is an honest man sent to lie abroad for the commonwealth." And of course, a century earlier Machiavelli floated his ideas of international statecraft. Those ideas were not new. They had appeared, for example, in the *Arthashastra* (*Treatise on Material Gain*), attributed to Kautiliya, the minister of the Indian emperor Chandragupta Maurya, who lived approximately during the time of Alexander the Great.

The doctrine that the safety and interests of a state are sacrosanct is an old one and has never died. As Harold Nicolson points out in his work, *Diplomacy,* the doctrine, "My country right or wrong," makes a powerful appeal to many millions of quite civilized people.[1]

Since the implication of this old theory is that in defense or promotion of its vital interests a state has much latitude in its actions irrespective of the interests of other states, it is obviously a concept that is becoming increasingly difficult to fit into a developing world community seeking to live by a common code or charter.

The Charter of the United Nations allows for legitimate self-defense, and it provides that a government's actions in its essentially domestic affairs are outside United Nations intervention; but it does not allow a country to plead that, impelled by its vital interests, it has to have recourse to force or to threats of force for furthering or protecting those interests.

Although the Charter does not give a country the right to act in the name of its vital interests, old habits die hard. One of the most constant and persistent motivations among states is the autistic urge to act in promotion or defense of vital national interests—strategic, economic, or even prestigious. This urge creates a powerful, though intangible and elusive, factor in international relations which often retards or interferes with the possibilities and processes of negotiation.

Who decides when the vital interests of a country are concerned? The answer is, the government of the country itself. Obviously, therefore, the "vital interests" of one country are often in opposition to those of another.

Although modern states tend not to rely on the idea of vital interests in stating their terms, at times we see this thought emerging in various forms in international negotiation, or in connection with disputes or situations.

In 1948, when the Security Council was first seized of the Kashmir issue, it appointed a United Nations Commission for India and Pakistan. The Interim Report of the Commission contains the following statement purporting to convey the views of Mohammed Zafrullah Khan, who was then the Foreign Minister of Pakistan:

The Minister for Foreign Affairs dwelt at length on economic and strategic considerations. He argued that India, if it had control of Jammu and Kashmir, would be in a position to divert all five rivers of the Punjab, i.e., the Chenab, Jhelum, Beas, Sutlej and Ravi. The last three being already under Indian control and thus could reduce to a desert ⅓ of the irrigated areas of the West Punjab.[2]

Krishna Menon referred to this statement in one of his interventions before the Security Council on the same issue, as follows:

Sir Mohammed Zafrullah Khan said that there are strategic interests. Well, I would argue first of all that the strategic interests of a country should not always be placed in the picture when we are talking about the fortunes of the people of that country. But let us leave that alone. What if there are strategic interests? The strategic interests of a country like India, with its big land mass in the Indian Ocean, are at least as vital in the world as the strategic interests of its neighbour.[3]

The great powers are generally even more cautious about the use of such phrases. On the other hand, their concept of vital interests tends to be wider than those of other states, and it is difficult for them to exclude this important factor from their dealings.

President Eisenhower, in his letter to Soviet Premier Bulganin on August 4, 1956, mentioned a reduction which had then taken place in the level of Soviet armed forces. On this measure he commented:

However, I doubt that such reductions of this particular kind as our governments may make in their respective national interests will contribute effectively to eliminate the fear, and the vast cost, generated by national armaments.[4]

Later in the same communication, President Eisenhower wrote regarding Germany:

We also agreed that Germany should be reunified by means of free elections carried out in conformity with the national interests of the German people and the interests of European security.[5]

The Russians, however, had an entirely different idea of where their interests lay, and therefore they did not respond to President Eisenhower's plea for discussion to promote or reach agreement on the basis of his concept of the national interests of Germany or of the security of Europe, or, again, of disarmament and international security.

When Premier Khrushchev wrote to President Kennedy on December 19, 1962 regarding a fresh round of negotiations for a nuclear test ban, he suggested a basis (outlined herein in Chapter Ten) which included "due consideration for each other's interests." While this was an effective basis for initiating negotiations, it was difficult to build upon. How, precisely, was due consideration to be given to "each other's interests?" The Soviet Union had one idea of how this should be done, while the United States had another. It did not prove possible for the two ideas to coincide. A third party could have proposed various ways out of the impasse, which would have involved relatively minor shifts of the positions of the two superpowers. However, such shifts were not to be obtained, because the two sides had very clear and categorical ideas about the requirements of their respective national interests.

The negotiation which resulted from the Khrushchev-Kennedy exchange of letters of December 1962 was unexpectedly brief and infructuous; "national interests" had supervened, and what had been a very promising opening brought no results. It is not our intent here to condone or justify the fact that national interests exist and are regarded as vital or essential. We are concerned only with their effect on the possibilities or the processes of negotiation.

Although vital interests, as such, are not brought into negotiating forums very often, it is obvious that they must play an important part in negotiations. No country is likely to expose itself knowingly to security hazards or economic disadvantages, or even serious loss of face, just to enhance some concept of international well-being. This does not mean that countries are always in a position to resist negotiation, or even other forms of readjustment, which might adversely affect their vital interests. The United Kingdom for long considered it a matter of vital interest to defend its far-flung empire. Nevertheless, in the last twenty years we have seen the virtual disappearance of that imperial dominance which held sway over as much as a quarter of the world. In a material sense, the giving up of the Empire has certainly cost Britain something, and in prestige there has also been a cost— although in this latter respect the United Kingdom has also gained respect and good will by its divestment of empire.

Indeed, it is difficult for an international readjustment to take place without a corresponding readjustment of the net assets, as it were, of the states involved. In the short run those changes in net assets often go against one state and favor another. However, in our age of technological progress, it is much more possible than in previous times for states to offset their losses by concentration of effort on the development of their resources or their trading capacities. Small countries, such as Belgium and the Netherlands, which drew considerable material advantage from their relatively large empires, have not, as a result of losing those empires, fallen to a lower economic level. The loss of empire has been offset by the productivity of new enterprises and investments. Compensating factors such as these counteract in some degree the normally strong reluctance of a state to submit to negotiation a situation which would touch upon its vital interests.

Contemporary events furnish a number of specific instances of the intrusion of the concept of vital interests (whether openly stated as such or not) on the possibilities and processes of negotiation.

The German question is clearly one which brings into play the factor of vital interests. Obviously, the vital interests of Germany itself are involved. But in a power sense, after the German defeat in World War II the more significant involvements have been those of the West on the one hand and of the Soviet Union and its new allies on the other. There are very real reasons which make the Western countries, and the Soviets and their allies, wary and concerned about what happens in Central Europe. As might be expected, therefore, both sides are taking positions in terms of their vital interests.

At a news conference on July 12, 1962 in Washington, D.C., when Secretary of State Dean Rusk was asked a question about Soviet announcements to the effect that they would make a separate peace treaty with the German Democratic Republic, he replied as follows:

But it has been very clear all along that the Western position on what we have referred to repeatedly as our vital interests is very simple, very firm, and the problem is if there are disagreements, handling those disagreements without a major crisis. . . . If the only thing that is to be discussed is Western interests, vital interests, and the only purpose of such discussion is to seriously reduce or to eliminate Western positions then there is no basis for serious negotiations in that direction.[6]

In January of the same year, President Kennedy had expressed similar thoughts about Berlin in his State of the Union Message:

In these last six months the allies have made it unmistakably clear that our presence in Berlin, our free access thereto and the freedom of 2,000,-000 West Berliners, would not be surrendered either to force or through appeasement. And to maintain those rights and obligations, we are prepared to talk, when appropriate, and to fight if necessary.[7]

The Russians have acknowledged that the consideration of vital interests enters into the problem of Germany. On August 21, 1961, Chairman Khrushchev wrote a letter to American readers which appeared as the preface to a book on the Soviet stand on Germany. In that letter he stated:

The West German Government is supported in its position by the Governments of the United States of America, Great Britain and France, all of whom reject the proposal on the conclusion of a peace treaty with the Federal German Republic and the German Democratic Republic, though such a decision does not infringe in any way on the direct interests of the Western Powers. On the contrary it conforms to the vital interests of the Americans, the British, the French and the Germans and also to the interests of all the peoples of the earth.[8]

One of the most comprehensive of recent statements elaborating the position of a power with extended vital interests in the world was made by Secretary of State Dean Rusk at a news conference on July 31, 1964. He is reported to have stated:

Where our vital interests and the vital interests of our allies are concerned, the United States is just as tough and just as stubborn as is necessary to protect our vital interests. And that has been, I think, eminently demonstrated time after time.

I think we ought to bear in mind that when the other side considers that their vital interests are at stake, they are going to be stubborn, too. And I think it would be unrealistic to suppose that they will roll over and play dead on the basis of anything that we say and do that might affect their vital interest.

Now, the problem arises where there are conflicts of interest. . . .
But we ourselves would not yield to pressures against our vital interests
or threats against our vital interests. We have to be cautious about supposing that others would.[9]

Here we have a clear statement of the dominant part played by a
country's understanding of its vital interests in the whole problem of
international negotiation, and particularly in the process of selecting
issues for negotiation at a given time.

The practical application of the concept of vital interests tends to
shift, and from the point of view of enhancing the scope of negotiation this is a welcome fact. We can start from the hypothesis that in
times of gravely heightened international tension the outlines of national interest tend to spread themselves as far as possible. This is
because when there is a strong possibility or apprehension of international conflict, the countries involved are unwilling to consider any
withdrawal from positions, lest such withdrawal harm them strategi-
cally or politically, or give the other side an impression of weakness.
To take the example we have just been discussing, it is this factor of
the hardened periphery of the exposed vital interests of both sides
which makes it difficult to bring within the ambit of serious discussion
possible approaches to the lessening of tension in and around Berlin.
Another example is Southeast Asia. Now that tensions are high in
that area, the vital interests of the various contestants are spread to
their farthest limits, and the more extended the limits of a particular
side the more seriously is that side restricted in its willingness to submit issues to negotiation.

But there are times when the lines of vital interests seem to recede
and blur. Perhaps we are approaching the threshold of such a situation as certain more relaxed manifestations arise in the ideological
struggle between the West and the Soviet-oriented Communist states.
In the 1950s there was no doubt that any enlargement of Communist
influence was, per se, a threat to the vital interests of the Western
world. However, in the 1960s Western statesmen have enunciated
their belief that it is the right of countries freely to determine their
own forms of political and social organization. In reply to a question
put to him by Alexei I. Adzhubei, the editor of *Izvestia,* on November 25, 1961, President Kennedy said:

If the people of any country chose to follow a communist system in a
free election, after a fair opportunity for a number of views to be presented, the United States would accept that.[10]

Then again, in his radio and television address in October 1962, President Kennedy addressed certain remarks to the Cuban people. In the course of this statement he said:

But this country has no wish to cause you to suffer, or to impose any system upon you . . . and I have no doubt that most Cubans today look forward to the time when they will be truly free. Free from foreign domination, free to choose their own leaders, free to select their own system.[11]

The Soviets, on their side, have split with the Chinese Communists on the question of war to promote their ideology, and even for assisting liberation movements in colonial territories. Chairman Khrushchev addressed the World Congress for General Disarmament and Peace on July 10, 1962 at Moscow on one aspect of this issue:

We believe that if either side works for the victory of its ideology and policy by augmenting its armed forces and its threats of war, things will surely move towards a world-wide nuclear war. We declare to the whole world that the policy of starting a world war in order that the Communist ideology should win is foreign to us.

We base ourselves on the fact that there are two systems in the world —one system of States based on capitalistic principles and another based on the Marxist-Leninist doctrine, on socialist principles. An ideological and political struggle is in progress between these two systems. We believe that this struggle should not be developed into a war between States with different social systems, but that matters should be settled through peaceful competition.[12]

It would appear that as far as the Soviet Union is concerned, there has been some movement away from the use of armed force to promote Communism. At the same time there has been a gradual growth toward a more relaxed position in the non-Communist world about social, economic, and political systems, provided such systems are not the tools of a foreign power.

These two complementary developments mean that the two sides (the United States and the Soviet Union) are no longer as strongly poised for conflict over ideological matters as they were a few years ago. To state it in other terms, it is no longer so clearly in accordance with the vital interests of either side to avoid negotiations simply on the ground that ideological differences are unbridgeable. To the extent that there is developing a degree of will to live and let live provided there is no intervention in or subversion of one system by the other, the potential scope of negotiation is widening. I believe that it is this general approach which has made it possible for the United States and the Soviet Union to continue for a record time with active negotiations on disarmament. This persistence would not have been feasible ten years ago.

The vital interests of powerful countries are much more in evidence than those of the lesser powers. However, the lesser powers too stake out their claims, and once these are in confrontation movement toward negotiation becomes difficult.

An example of this type of situation is the Cyprus issue. When the issue was first brought to the United Nations in 1954, both the Greeks and the Turks set out their claims in terms of their interests. The remarks of Ambassador (later Foreign Minister) Selim Sarper of Turkey, made at the General Committee of the General Assembly three years later, have been summarized by the United Nations:

[He] pointed out that the people and Government of Turkey had a direct interest and concern in any discussion dealing with the status of Cyprus. Since the island lay off the shores of Turkey, a part of the population was Turkish, and Turkey had been a signatory of the Treaty of Lausanne, which laid down the current status of Cyprus. . . . Cyprus was situated 40 miles off the shores of Turkey, and nearly 700 miles away from Greece.

The direct interest of Turkey in Cyprus was valid because Cyprus was an island off the Turkish mainland, commanding the vital routes of communication, defense and trade of Turkey; from that point of view, Cyprus was of no importance to Greece.[13]

On the other hand, the Greek representative, Foreign Minister Avengelos Averoff-Tossizza, stated:

The distance from Cyprus to the Turkish and Greek coasts was 40 and 135 miles respectively, not 40 and 700 miles; the Aaland Islands were not one island but a group of 300, 80 of which were inhabited by a population of 21,000, a very different matter from one island inhabited by a population of 500,000.[14]

The two mutually exclusive positions regarding the interests of Greece and Turkey held up meaningful negotiations for several years, that is, until 1959. At that time the Greeks and Turks held discussions and reached agreement on the future of Cyprus, but within a few years the complicated arrangements to preserve a balance between the communities on the island broke down. One is tempted, however, to wonder whether the placing of the two communities in separate compartments, as laid down in their arrangements, was devised not so much for the good of the communities as to give Greece and Turkey the levers which each of them appeared to want in order to influence and engage in the affairs of Cyprus in pursuance of their respective vital interests.

The real reasons for Turkey's interest would appear to be strategic. Soon after violence erupted again on Cyprus in 1964, the *New York Times* carried a story, the relevant part of which read:

When American and other foreign officials arrive in Ankara, they are nearly always shown a map of Turkey. To the north is the Black Sea, and beyond it the Soviet Union. On the East are the Soviet Union and Iran, Iraq and Syria are to the South. Bulgaria and Greece are to the northwest and the Greek-owned Aegean and Dodecanese islands to the southwest.

Cyprus is regarded as a potential "cork" in the south. Military leaders call it the "cork in the bottle of Iskenderun," the big south Turkish naval base. Therefore, it is argued to keep the south open, a Turkish military presence on Cyprus is a necessity.[15]

It is not our intention to judge between Greece and Turkey, but to observe that the close identification of those two countries with the affairs of Cyprus—an area which both claim is vital to their interests—makes the process of negotiating a settlement for the future of Cyprus extremely difficult and complex.

A striking illustration of how obstacles can be placed in the path of negotiation by pronouncements of leaders regarding the vital interests of their countries is furnished by a leader who adopted a policy of conciliation in international affairs. Jawaharlal Nehru, who had been molded into thinking along conciliatory lines by his intimate relationship with Gandhi, which extended over a period of thirty dramatic and highly important years of his life, and who must have been conscious of India's obligations as a member of the United Nations not to use force in the settlement of international issues, told the Indian Parliament as long as three years before the armed clash with China: "We believe firmly that peace is better than war. Nevertheless, if the Country's freedom or its integrity or its honour is attacked, we have to defend it with war if necessary."

Prime Minister Nehru felt that a country should go to war, if necessary, in defense of "its honor." This is a far-reaching concept of the vital interests of a country, and yet it must be regarded as a very natural one if a man like Nehru so readily brought it into play.

The chances are that when a country feels—justifiably or not—that its honor is at stake, its emotional state renders negotiations extremely difficult. In the case of China and India, no full exploration of the various possibilities of a negotiated settlement was made between 1956 and 1962. This does not mean, of course, that negotiation would necessarily or inevitably have brought a peaceful adjustment or settlement between China and India. However, the nature of the involvement of vital interests was partly responsible for constricting the possibilities of negotiating the issue. The high degree of pride and bluster on the Chinese side created a complementary obstacle, and finally there were the "hurt feelings" of the leaders on the two sides.

While the vital interests of a country, as defined by itself, generally contribute impediments to negotiation, two factors operate to mitigate the effectiveness of this tendency in certain circumstances.

One is the power level of the country whose vital interests are involved. Representatives of small countries no doubt feel strongly about the affairs of their states. For example, representatives of Cyprus are reported to have said that even if it meant war, Cyprus would not give up its just claim to self-determination. But this sort of statement does not alter the fact that the basic issues involved have become the subject of negotiation, even if those negotiations are not to the liking of the Government of Cyprus. The Cypriot Government had spoken scathingly of the attempts of former Secretary of State Dean Acheson to mediate the issue. It also appeared to have been somewhat reluctant about the efforts of the United Nations mediator. However, a small and relatively low-powered country is not always able successfully to oppose negotiations or to divert them into channels which will support or protect its vital interests. Cyprus' position that the only issue is that of self-determination virtually precludes that country's support of negotiation, but it does not determine the course of events.

A second factor is the growing use of conference negotiation. The Charter of the United Nations brings one forum, the Security Council, virtually into permanent session, and experience has shown that the General Assembly can be convoked in emergencies to supplement its annual session which fills a quarter of the year. This being so, in the post-World War II period conference negotiation is readily available, especially at the behest or in the interests of the smaller states. General Assembly sessions have played an important role in bringing the great powers into negotiation, their vital interests notwithstanding. The same has been true of the Security Council. Two relevant cases will demonstrate this point.

When the United States Marines landed in Lebanon in 1958, President Eisenhower said to the Third Emergency Special Session of the General Assembly on August 13, 1958:

The United States troops will be totally withdrawn whenever this is requested by the duly constituted Government of Lebanon or whenever, through action by the United Nations or otherwise, Lebanon is no longer exposed to the original danger.[16]

The Emergency Special Session acted with surprising speed. We have noted the manner in which it came to adopt the Arab resolution unanimously on August 21, 1958. This resolution was of a general character, and contained only one reference to Lebanon. It requested the Secretary-General to make "such practical arrangements as would adequately help in upholding the principles and purposes of the Charter in relation to Lebanon and Jordan in the present circumstances and thereby facilitate the earliest withdrawal of the foreign troops from the two countries." [17]

In short, the process of negotiation in the Emergency Special Session of the General Assembly took its own course and went its own way, and the terms of settlement did not correspond to the ideas of the great powers. Nevertheless, these developments were accepted by as powerful a country as the United States. But for the largely unforeseen developments obtained through conference negotiation and their effect on the situation, it is reasonable to suppose that the United States would have wished for, and sought to obtain, in its long-run vital interests, a clearer guarantee of Lebanese independence before removing its troops from that country.

Although, as we have observed, no extensive direct negotiations have resulted from the Security Council meetings on Kashmir, those meetings in themselves, it must not be overlooked, have been a kind of negotiation of the dispute. The parties involved have made full statements of their case, other countries have made suggestions, and at the very least the meetings have had the effect of stemming the drift toward armed conflict.[18] India and Pakistan each feels that Kashmir is of vital interest. They have both shown (and India more than Pakistan) a reluctance to engage in direct negotiations, but, their vital interests notwithstanding, the Security Council has remained seized of the dispute and its processes have had a limited measure of success in handling the situation.

The effects of vital or essential interests on the chances and processes of negotiation suggest another relevant governing principle:

> States formulate their own views as to which interests are vital or essential to their survival, security, or fundamental welfare; and in regard to such interests they seek to retain for themselves the power of action or decision, and are reluctant to expose themselves to the hazards of international negotiation, their international obligations (such as those in the Charter of the United Nations) notwithstanding.

> The degree in which this principle is effective is in direct relation to the level of power of the country concerned.

> The availability in our era of forums for conference negotiations tends to mitigate the capacity of a country, large or small, to exclude an issue involving its vital or essential interests from the scope of international negotiation.

CHAPTER TWELVE

Third-Party Intrusions

IN AN ERA OF alliances, few countries stand alone when it comes to negotiation. This is true not only of the members of the various military alliances, but also of other groups which have appeared or have become strengthened in recent years. For example, the Organization of American States is becoming increasingly effective, at least as far as negotiations within the Western Hemisphere are concerned. There is the Organization of African Unity, created as recently as 1963 at Addis Ababa, which has already shown some capacity in promoting negotiations or in undertaking them on behalf of African states. The same may be said of the Arab League.

One of the loosest of all international associations is the (ex-British) Commonwealth of Nations, and yet behind the scenes it stimulates discussion among its members on international issues. It often promotes a degree of international negotiation, and sometimes gives a slight boost to the negotiating strength of a member state which happens to be involved in a dispute or situation with a non-Commonwealth state.[1]

Even neutral Sweden and Finland are part of an international association, the Nordic group of countries, and this association is not without international implications when it comes to certain negotiations, for example in regard to the composition of the membership of the Security Council.

In this chapter it is our purpose to observe the disparity in power levels which may be created between the parties to an international dispute or situation when one of them succeeds in obtaining the support of an important state or a group of states, and to notice the effect of such disparity on negotiation. What happens when, let us say,

Kuwait (a small Arab state) has a dispute with Iraq (a larger but not unduly powerful Arab state) and the United Kingdom (a great power) becomes involved? The injection of the United Kingdom into the dispute creates an imbalance in favor of Kuwait, and in addition brings the United Kingdom into the negotiations, if any should follow. We have, in such a case, both an imbalance and a third-party involvement. Another matter to be considered is the correction of a disparity in power levels between the parties to a dispute or situation when the weaker party secures the support of a strong party or of a regional power, which then comes to be associated, in some degree at least, in such negotiations as may ensue. A third matter of concern is the possibility that the circle of engagement of outside parties can widen to the extent of involving the superpowers.

These considerations and factors are in some measure in juxtaposition to one of the principles formulated at the end of Chapter Ten: When there is a real or assumed significant disparity of power between the parties to a dispute or situation, or when one of the parties is imbued with a sense of growing power, then such disparity or sense of buoyant power may militate against resort to negotiation to settle the dispute or ameliorate the situation.

Indonesia and Malaysia are involved in a dispute over some parts of the territory of North Borneo. Indonesia claims that the adherence of North Borneo to the Federation of Malaysia is not based on a fair expression of the wishes of the people. It demands that a more direct process of ascertainment of the wishes of the people should be adopted than the sampling of views, which was undertaken in 1963 by a United Nations mission. On June 25, 1964, President Sukarno addressed a mass rally held to observe Jakarta's 437th anniversary, during which he said:

We, the Indonesian nation are prepared to recognize "Malaysia" only if that is the will and the wish of the North Kalimantan people themselves. If the North Kalimantan people rise against the neo-colonialist project of the "Malaysia," then the Indonesian people will render their support and aid to the greatest possible extent.

He added, "For now we are completely free to implement our confrontation and People's Two-Fold Command [to crush Malaysia]." [2]

Indonesia is decidedly a stronger power than Malaysia. It has a considerable army and an air force equipped with rockets. Malaysia sought to redress this imbalance by invoking Article VI of the Agreement concluded on July 9, 1963 in London by the United Kingdom with all of the states composing the Federation of Malaysia. This article provides that the terms of the Agreement on external defense and mutual assistance between the United Kingdom and Malaya of October 12, 1957 shall apply to all the territories of Malaysia. Article VI of these arrangements provides for consultation between Malaysia and the United Kingdom, so as to insure cooperation between the two, and Article VII states the following:

In the event of an armed attack against any of the territories or forces of the Federation of Malaya or any of the territories or protectorates of the United Kingdom in the Far East or any of the forces of the United Kingdom within the Federation of Malaya, the Governments of the Federation of Malaya and of the United Kingdom undertake such action as each considers necessary for the purpose of meeting the situation effectively.[3]

Malaysia has invoked its Agreement with the United Kingdom, and joint military action is being taken on the concerned borders of North Borneo and elsewhere in the Federation. Indonesia will undoubtedly closely watch the situation to assess whether the military balance has turned against it. Dr. Subandrio, Deputy Prime Minister and Foreign Minister, said on June 24, 1964, after meeting with Ambassador K. C. Shann of Australia, "I will also ask for aid if the Tunku asks for aid." [4]

However, no markedly superior force has been deployed by either side. There have been small-scale border skirmishes and relatively minor instances of infiltration, but neither side has proved superior strength. In these circumstances, Indonesia has the satisfaction of feeling it is militarily a match for a great power, the United Kingdom. On the plane of general diplomatic activity it is doing all it can to humiliate Malaysia. The Peking Government and its friends in Asia and Africa have come to the support of Indonesia, and in a statement to a huge rally in Jakarta on May 23, 1965, President Sukarno opposed Malaysia's participation in the Afro-Asian Conference to be held in Algeria (the second Bandung Conference), and claimed that "a majority of Asia and Africa are of the same opinion as Indonesia and oppose the participation of Malaysia." [5] At this writing it can be said that if Indonesia is able to exclude Malaysia from the Afro-Asian Conference it will in a measure have established its negotiating superiority in the dispute with Malaysia. Whether Malaysia will be able to redress the negotiating balance remains to be seen. It will be difficult to do so if, indeed, a large majority of Asian and African states express views in opposition to or unsympathetic toward its position in Borneo. But the Federation has had some success. For example, although the Philippines does not recognize the Federation of Malaysia it is supporting Malaysia's right to be present at an Asian-African Conference.[6] These are moves by two parties to strengthen their negotiating position by calling in the support of friendly states.

No further negotiations directly on the Indonesian-Malaysian dispute have been attempted since an abortive summit conference among the leaders of the two countries and the Philippines at Tokyo in June 1964. However, it is quite likely that should any further negotiations take place they will be on a conference basis and will involve either directly or indirectly the powers which are giving significant, assistance to one side or the other.

Kuwait regained its full independence on the basis of notes exchanged on June 19, 1961, between the Political Resident of the United Kingdom in the Persian Gulf and the ruler of Kuwait.[7] Those letters stated that "the relationship between the two countries shall continue to be governed by a spirit of close friendship," and that the United Kingdom Government would remain ready "to assist the Government of Kuwait if the latter request such assistance."

However, the independence of Kuwait was immediately followed by a demand from the Iraqi Premier, General Kassim, for the union of Kuwait with Iraq. Kassim described the letter of June 19, 1961 as "illegitimate," and said that the Kuwait leaders were "irresponsible people under the sway of imperialism." [8] The London *Times* published a report from Baghdad on June 27, 1961 to the effect that the Iraqi Army had pledged to support Kassim in his claim to Kuwait.

The Kuwait Government could have counteracted the relative strength of Iraq with British support alone, but it was able to bring itself into a position of even greater strength in the region. On June 26, 1961, it applied for membership in the Arab League. The United Kingdom also immediately took military measures, converging on the Persian Gulf. The *Manchester Guardian* reported that warships were moving from as far as Hong Kong and Singapore and from nearer Karachi.[9] On July 2 Prime Minister Harold Macmillan said that while he still trusted that threats against Kuwait were no more than words, "The British force was today moved into the State of Kuwait and placed at the Ruler's disposal." [10] On July 3 Macmillan told the House of Commons that there was a big Iraqi military build-up near Basra, about thirty miles from the border of Kuwait. About the British forces, he said that they would be withdrawn "as soon as the

Ruler considered that the independence of Kuwait is no longer threatened." Macmillan added, "We do not, of course, rule out any solution by the United Nations or other force." He referred to the need for negotiation and said, "We must look at the longer issues, because these are heavy burdens on our economy. We want to create a general state of harmony in the Arab world and we are encouraged by the degree of understanding that we have had from the Arab countries as a whole." [11]

Early in July 1961, the issue came before the Security Council. On July 7 the Soviet Union vetoed a British resolution, and this phase of the negotiation ended in frustration. The veto showed that while Kuwait, on the one side, had raised its power level with British assistance, Iraq, on the other side, had called into the situation the more than compensatory power of the Soviet Union.

Kuwait then pressed forward on the road of power readjustment open to it, namely, the support of the other Arab states. It agreed to accept forces from Arab states in replacement of those of the British.[12] Simultaneously, the Arab League admitted Kuwait to membership as a fully independent state, and on October 19, 1961 Kuwait informed the President of the Security Council that the British forces had been withdrawn, having been replaced by Arab League forces.[13]

However, Iraq was still fighting to redress its negotiating strength, and on November 30, 1961 the Soviet Union vetoed a draft resolution of the United Arab Republic in the Security Council recommending that the General Assembly admit Kuwait to United Nations membership.

But the Kassim regime in Iraq was overthrown. The Arab League became more united, and in May 1963 the Security Council recommended the admission of Kuwait.[14] At its Fourth Special Session, the General Assembly admitted Kuwait to the United Nations on May 14, 1963.

In the Kuwait case we see the interplay of third, fourth, and fifth parties in regard to the issue of its emergence into statehood. The British, the Arab League, the Soviet Union, and the United Arab Republic, all played important roles in the negotiating phases of the issue. As a result of their roles, the relative power levels of Iraq on the one side and Kuwait on the other fluctuated. In the long run, Kuwait was able to maintain the stronger position in the region be-cause of the continuing support of the Arab League. When the League became completely united in its support of Kuwait, Iraq lost the assistance of the Soviet Union, and its case for the annexation of

Kuwait dissolved. This case shows that the strong and united support
of the countries geographically in the region of the dispute or situation is, in the long run, a greater advantage than the temporary support of even one of the superpowers.[15]

In Oman, also in the Persian Gulf, there has been in recent years,
and continues in some measure to be, a power struggle between the
ruler of Oman and a rival group. This struggle has led to some interesting negotiating developments which have come to involve third
parties—the Arab states on one side and the United Kingdom on the
other.

On August 13, 1957 the eleven Arab member states of the
United Nations called for a meeting of the Security Council to consider what they described as acts of aggression by the United Kingdom against Oman. However, on August 20, 1957 the move of the
Arab states mustered only four votes in the Council, and the issue
was not inscribed on the Security Council's agenda. The United States
abstained on the issue and did not take sides. The other superpower,
the Soviet Union, voted in favor of the item. The United Kingdom, of
course, opposed it and contended that Oman was not an independent
state.[16]

Thereafter, from time to time the General Assembly of the United
Nations has been seized of the issue of Oman at the initiative of the
Arab states. In April 1961 a draft resolution was presented to the
Assembly by the Arab states together with Afghanistan, Guinea,
Indonesia, and Yugoslavia—the non-Arab states indicating a widening of the zone of third-party interest. This resolution would have
recognized the right of the people of Oman to self-determination and
independence. However, no vote on the draft resolution was taken at
that session of the Assembly. It was deferred by unanimous acceptance of a proposal to do so made by India.[17] The success of this
move indicated the existence at that time of an approximate balance
between the negotiating strengths deployed by the two sides.

At the next session of the General Assembly (the Sixteenth), in
December 1961, the resolution was brought to the vote. Although it
obtained a majority, the margin in favor fell short of the requisite two-
thirds. The Soviet Union sided with the Arab states, while the United
States sided with the United Kingdom.[18]

At this juncture of the negotiating struggle in the organs of the
United Nations, this was the lineup in terms of power levels: The
Arab member states were united. On the other side, the United King-
dom had succeeded in enlisting the support of the United States and

had raised its power level far above that of the Arab states. However, those states had the general support of the Soviet Union and of many of the nonaligned Asian-African states, such as Afghanistan, Ghana, India, and Indonesia. The latter group is, at times, important in a negotiating sense but does not add significantly to the power level of the party it supports. Therefore, it may be said that in 1961 the United Kingdom had been able to maintain a power superiority for its own side. It fought the battle for the Sultan of Oman in the strongly contentious debates of 1960 and 1961 in the General Assembly. Even if there had been a two-thirds majority in favor of the independence of Oman, it would not necessarily have constituted a definitive negotiating defeat for the United Kingdom. The United Kingdom and its friends could have found various ways of counteracting the General Assembly resolution, some of which they did subsequently use and which are permissible in the interplay of international negotiation.

In 1962 eleven Arab states again asked for, and this time obtained, the inclusion of an item on the "Question of Oman" on the agenda of the Seventeenth Session of the General Assembly.

The United Kingdom then circulated a telegram addressed by the Sultan of Muscat and Oman to the President of the General Assembly. This telegram stated that the Sultan would refuse to permit any further moves to intervene in matters which fell exclusively within the domestic jurisdiction of the sultanate. This did not impress the Arab states. Their case was that the Sultan of Muscat was oppressing the independent people of Oman and denying them their rightful international status. The United Kingdom contended that Muscat and Oman constituted one entity, and that British forces had intervened at the request of the ruler to resist rebellion in 1954 and 1957. Their assistance had been effective, and later the forces had been withdrawn.

At the Seventeenth Session of the General Assembly, eighteen countries introduced a draft resolution purporting to recognize the right of the people of Oman to independence. In the Special Political Committee the draft resolution obtained more than a two-thirds majority (41 in favor and 18 against). Again the United Kingdom and the United States voted against, while the Soviet Union voted in favor. Significantly, the vote of India shifted to abstention. This was after the Chinese attack on India. The Indian delegation felt it wiser to abstain in what was becoming increasingly a power struggle between the two sides to the Cold War.

The United Kingdom's reaction to this adverse voting situation was interesting and intelligent. In the Plenary Session, where there was a high expectation that the resolution in favor of the independence of Oman would be adopted, the representative of the United Kingdom stated that he was authorized to say, on behalf of the Sultan of Muscat and Oman, that while maintaining the view that the question of Oman was an internal issue, outside the scope of the United Nations, the Sultan was prepared to invite, on a personal basis, a representative of the Secretary-General, who could obtain first-hand information about the situation. In these circumstances the United Kingdom representative hoped that the Assembly would not prejudge the issue by final adoption of the resolution. This astute move once again swung around the voting balance. The draft resolution did not retain its two-thirds majority, and failed to be confirmed. The Secretary-General appointed as his personal representative Ambassador Herbert de Ribbing of Sweden. The Eighteenth Session of the General Assembly took the view that the de Ribbing report was not sufficiently comprehensive, and resolved to appoint an ad hoc committee to examine the question.[19]

The structure of the power confrontation has not altered much in these years. The basic confrontation is between the small sultanate of Oman and Muscat on the one hand and the independent Arab world on the other. It is extremely difficult for the former to maintain its stand against the latter, and in the long run it might prove impossible to do so. However, the Sultan of Oman has the direct support of the United Kingdom. In a power sense this more than matches the present Arab strength. The United Kingdom has faithfully born the brunt of negotiations at the United Nations for the sultanate. The ultimate powers have chosen more or less opposing positions. This means, in effect, that the present power level is against the independent Arab states. Added to this is the wealth of experience in parliamentary negotiating techniques of the British. Here, then, is an issue in which third-party involvement is so great as to have become the major factor in the situation.

In 1962 a popular revolt shook the foundations of the old order in Yemen, and the Imam (the spiritual head, who also exercised secular political authority) just managed to escape with his life. A Republic was proclaimed and was quickly recognized by most countries, including the United States, the Soviet Union, the United Kingdom, and India. However, in the Arab world there was no unanimity. This lack of agreement has made the Yemen problem an international issue.

Saudi Arabia sent arms and other assistance to the Royalists (the Imam and his followers), and the United Arab Republic came to the assistance of the Arab Republic of Yemen. Thus the two Yemenese contenders had started on the road of raising their respective power levels. In the beginning the Royalists were the weaker of the two sides. They were, however, aided to some extent by the mountainous terrain in which they had taken refuge. Assistance from Saudi Arabia immediately gave them a great advantage over the new Republican Government. There is a completely open frontier between Saudi Arabia and Yemen, and no obstacle existed to the flow of Saudi aid for the Royalists.

Reports of this highly disruptive situation reached the United Nations and the important states in the organization. U Thant sent Ralph Bunche on a mission to Yemen, Cairo, and Saudi Arabia. Ellsworth Bunker was sent on a similar mission by the United States. These missions confirmed that large-scale assistance to the respective sides had been provided by Saudi Arabia and the United Arab Republic. Both countries had become deeply involved in the affairs of Yemen. The Secretary-General presented a report to the Security Council which brought out these factors.[20]

The Secretary-General was able to promote negotiations behind the scenes, in the course of which he obtained assurances from both Saudi Arabia and the United Arab Republic that they would disengage themselves from the affairs of Yemen. The terms of the proposed disengagement were reported as follows to the Security Council by the Secretary-General:

The Government of Saudi Arabia, on its part, will terminate all support and aid to the Royalists of Yemen and will prohibit the use of Saudi Arabian territory by Royalist leaders for the purpose of carrying on the struggle in Yemen. Simultaneously, with the suspension of aid from Saudi Arabia to the Royalists, the United Arab Republic undertakes to begin withdrawal from Yemen of the troops sent on request of the new Government, this withdrawal to be phased and to take place as soon as possible, during which the forces would withdraw from field activities to their bases pending their departure. . . . A demilitarized zone to a distance of twenty kilometers on each side of the demarcated Saudi Arabian–Yemen border is to be established from which military forces and equipment are to be excluded. In this zone, on both sides, impartial observers are to be stationed to check on the observance of the terms of disengagement. . . . The United Arab Republic and Saudi Arabia have further undertaken to cooperate with the representative of the United

Nations Secretary-General or some other mutually acceptable intermediary in reaching agreement on the modalities and verification of disengagement.[21]

In order to implement disengagement, the Secretary-General recommended that a small United Nations observation mission be sent to Yemen. His anticipation was that it would "be needed for three or four months, at the most." [22] The Secretary-General followed this up by other reports, including one in early June which indicated that Saudi Arabia and the United Arab Republic would pay the cost of the observation mission.[23] The Security Council met on June 11, and there was general agreement on observation, the smaller countries on the Security Council fully supporting the Secretary-General's position. Ghana and Morocco introduced a draft resolution asking the Secretary-General to initiate the proposed observation. This proposal was adopted by a vote of ten in favor and none against, the Soviet Union abstaining.[24] The great powers thus kept out of the confrontation. The Soviet move to condemn Saudi Arabia had failed, and nothing had come, on the other hand, of the efforts of the Yemen Republic to implicate the United Kingdom in the build-up of the military strength of the Royalists.

The disengagement of Saudi Arabia and the United Arab Republic proved to be a much more long-drawn-out affair than the Secretary-General had anticipated. However, the two countries continued to pay the cost, and the observation mission remained on until September 4, 1964. The purpose of the mission was not so much to conduct comprehensive observation as to act as a reminder that Saudi Arabia and the United Arab Republic had agreed to terminate their involvement in the affairs of Yemen. From this point of view, its effect was highly salutary. It enabled the Secretary-General to stimulate peaceful discussions behind the scenes among Yemen, Saudi Arabia, and the United Arab Republic. Eventually, high-level negotiations took place in which King Hussein of Jordan is said to have played a role during an unofficial visit to Cairo in August 1964.[25]

The two sides to the dispute (the two contenders for power in Yemen), in seeking to raise their power levels, implicated the third parties of Saudi Arabia and the United Arab Republic in the process of negotiation. There was also a wider involvement in the negotiation, to include the Secretary-General, the Security Council, and in some degree, the United States.

We are clearly dealing with a phenomenon created by the operation of a virtually universal force—the impulsion that leads small or relatively weak parties, in their disputes with relatively strong parties, to seek a champion. And we find that as a by-product of such championing, complications in negotiation set in, for the champion or champions become parties to the situation or dispute. In general, this phenomenon tends to arise on the geographical borderline between the main powers. In Europe there is the example of the two German states and a divided Berlin, with the whole of the Western world behind the major fraction of that country while the Communist countries stand behind the smaller fraction. But in this case, unlike the cases we have mentioned in the Middle East and somewhat similar situations which exist in Southeast Asia, the potentialities of conflict are too serious for either side to venture over the brink. There is, therefore, a stalemate on the ground.

Perhaps paradoxically, this stalemate does not appear to encourage the development of major negotiation between the two sides. This factor is worth observing, because it is sometimes assumed that if a situation or dispute between states can be cooled off, and open armed conflict avoided, there is a strong likelihood that the disputants may develop a frame of mind conducive to discussion or negotiation. This does not necessarily hold in international life, and specifically it does not hold when the process of negotiation would have to address itself not to evolving some provisional via media (for this already exists), or to a slight shift in the relationship between the two sides, but rather to securing a basic readjustment of attitudes. Such basic alterations are obviously very difficult to achieve. Good will and the exchange of ideas around a table will not necessarily produce them. We see here, then, a determined obstacle to the development of negotiation when the champions which have been called in are the two ultimate powers and when both of them are convinced that their vital interests are involved.

This being so, we must frame any general principle with caution, but we must also not make the error of concluding that we cannot in these somewhat unclear circumstances identify a general trend or principle.

If the German question seems unyielding to direct negotiation—the word "direct" is used with respect to negotiations which attempt to deal with the situation frontally rather than with surrounding relevant factors—it does not follow that all forms of negotiation are ruled out; or that confrontations over the vital interests of the two sides to the Cold War are nonnegotiable.

We have seen that Southeast Asia has come to be included in the geographical sphere of vital interests of the United States. We might reinforce this observation by reference to a statement of President Eisenhower dating back to the precise period when the United States first decided to give effect to its concern by active support for the Government of the Republic of South Vietnam. At a press conference on April 7, 1954, President Eisenhower was asked the following question:

Mr. President, would you mind commenting on the strategic importance of Indochina to the free world? I think there has been, across the country, some lack of understanding on just what it means to us.

The President's reply was as follows:

You have, of course, both the specific and the general when you talk about such things.

First of all, you have the specific value of a locality in its production of material that the world needs.

Then you have the possibility that many human beings pass under a dictatorship that is inimical to the free world.

Finally, you have broader considerations that might follow what you would call the "falling domino" principle. You have a row of dominoes set up, you knock over the first one, and what will happen to the last one is the certainty that it will go over very quickly. So you could have a beginning of a disintegration that would have the most profound influences.

Now with respect to the first one, two of the items from this particular area that the world uses are tin and tungsten. They are very important. There are others, of course, the rubber plantations and so on.

Then with respect to more people passing under this domination, Asia, after all, has already lost some 450 million of its peoples to the Communist dictatorship, and we simply can't afford greater losses.

But when we come to the possible sequence of events, the loss of Indochina, of Burma, of Thailand, of the Peninsula, and Indonesia following, now you begin to talk about areas that not only multiply the disadvantages that you would suffer through loss of materials, sources of materials, but now you are talking really about millions and millions and millions of people.

Finally, the geographical position achieved thereby does many things. It turns the so-called island defensive chain of Japan, Formosa, of the Philippines and to the southward; it moves in to threaten Australia and New Zealand.

It takes away, in its economic aspects, that region that Japan must have as a trading area, or Japan, in turn, will have only one place in the world to go—that is, toward the Communist areas in order to live.

So, the possible consequences of the loss are just incalculable to the free world.[26]

Partly on this philosophy, the United States has maintained a steady and indeed an increasing involvement in Southeast Asia, thereby raising to a great height the power level of the side which it espouses.

But the opponents of those supported by the United States in Southeast Asia are not without their champions. In the Laotian struggle in early 1961, the planes of the Soviet Union were making air drops in the Pathet Lao areas. By that time another important champion had arisen—the People's Republic of China. At the Laotian Conference in 1961–1962, the Chinese delegates rapidly made it clear that they would not stand for any foreign domination (meaning the United States) in Southeast Asia. Marshal Chen Yi, their Foreign Minister, welcomed the determination of the Laotians to set up a neutral government under Prince Souvanna Phouma, and he added, "The Chinese Government has constantly supported, and will continue to support this desire." Later on he added:

The Chinese Government firmly supports the struggle of the Democratic Republic of Vietnam and the Vietnamese people to uphold the Geneva agreements and to achieve the peaceful unification of their motherland. The Chinese Government has consistently supported Southeast Asian countries in their just cause of practicing a policy of peace and neutrality, safeguarding national independence and opposing interference and aggression from outside.[27]

The Laos Conference was significant, not so much because it attempted a settlement for Laos, but because it demonstrated that the involvement of outside powers, in support of one party or another, could become the major factor in the situation.

The Laos Conference was a complex and hard-fought negotiation between the United States and the People's Republic of China. The efforts of the other important countries at the Conference—the Soviet Union and the United Kingdom as cochairmen; France, as the previous colonial power in the area; and India as the chairman of the International Control Commission which supervises the International Agreements in Vietnam, Laos, and Cambodia—all were in some degree directed toward bridging the positions of the United States (with Thailand and South Vietnam) on the one hand, and China (with North Vietnam) on the other.

At the Laos Conference there was thus a major confrontation between two powers, one an ultimate power and the other a world power potentially in the top category. Furthermore, although China could count in a degree which was not calculable on the support of the other ultimate power (the Soviet Union), the differences between the two sides were successfully negotiated. All those who took part in this negotiation realized, and continue to realize, that in order to be fully successful the Laos settlement has to be accompanied by settlement in Vietnam. It is in Vietnam, the largest of the states of former Indochina, that the main confrontation is taking place between the United States and China. As long as this confrontation continues in the form of armed conflict, the peaceful settlement of Laos will remain a paper reality rather than a tangible political, national, and international fact.

The events surrounding the Laos Conference confirm the view that the support of outside states to the parties involved in a dispute creates disparities in power levels, which are then sought to be corrected by the engagement of a strong state or states on behalf of the side which feels weaker, and this process tends to continue to the limits of today's possibilities, namely to embrace the ultimate powers. Finally, all the powers so involved become part of the negotiating complex.

This development, in the acute form in which we see it today in Asia, Europe, increasingly in Africa, and even in the Western Hemisphere (the Caribbean), is a significant development of the post-World War II era. Until then, and certainly until 1914, there was a tendency for the major states to respect each other's spheres of influence. Today our world is physically too small for spheres of influence; and, much more important, the magnitudes and capacities of power deployment are such that they can easily be made to affect situations in any part of the world.

From our analysis of the nuances of some of the factors relating to negotiation, we may outline the following general principle:

> A significant disparity in power levels between the parties to a dispute or situation may result from the support which one of those parties obtains from another state or other states, particularly of states in its region, and in such cases the supporting state or states tend to become involved in the situation or dispute and also in any negotiations which might ensue.
>
> A significant inherent disparity of power levels between the parties to a dispute or situation, or such a disparity created by the support given to one of the parties by another state or states, may be cor-

rected by the weaker party's obtaining the support of a strong power or a significant neighboring state or states; and those supporting powers or states also tend to become involved in any negotiations that might ensue.

The escalation of involvement on either side of powerful states tends to continue until it reaches those powers which have an ultimate responsibility for, or stake in, the present world security arrangements.

CHAPTER THIRTEEN

Alliances of Powerful States

THERE ARE two main motivations which have led to the mutual treaties of defense and support that characterize the post-World War II era. On the one hand, smaller countries and lesser powers tend to cling to the greater powers. This was the old habit which Aelius Aristeides noted in the middle of the second century A.D.: "To find oneself under the dominion of one's superiors is a 'second best' alternative; but this 'second best' proved to be the best of all in our present experience of the Roman Empire. This happy experience has moved the whole world to cleave to Rome with might and main. The world would no more think of seceding from Rome than a ship's crew would think of parting company with the pilot. . . . The thought of being abandoned by Rome is so appalling that it precludes any thought of wantonly abandoning her." [1] In short—there is a tendency for the weak to cleave to the strong.

At the same time, there has been the tendency in our era for the superpowers to strive to win the friendship and the alliance of as much of the world as possible. Each side of the Cold War has wished to extend or harden the periphery of its system so as to limit the other side in its capacity for geographical and ideological deployment. This thought underlies the views which President Eisenhower expressed in 1954, quoted in our previous chapter, in regard to a region as remote from the United States as Southeast Asia. And the same motivation is present when the Soviet Union places some of the elements of its military strength on the distant island of Cuba.

The countries of the world have been made acutely aware in the post-World War II period of the interest in them of the two superpowers. This factor has given small countries a value in the international power struggle which is out of all proportion to their real strength. Each side in the major confrontation seems to work on the basis that each country gained, in alliance or friendship, is not only an addition to its own power but a gain in prestige and a subtraction from the power of the other side and a diminution of its prestige.

This attitude of the two powers extends to those countries which have entered into military alliances with them, and also applies to their dealings with the nonaligned countries. The latter category of countries has received economic assistance and has acquired military hardware from both sides, often on favorable financial terms. Numerous statements have emanated from the superpowers to the effect that economic assistance is given to those countries as part of the arrangements to maintain or enhance their security. Countries such as India, although not members of either a Western- or Soviet-sponsored military alliance, receive economic assistance from Washington under the latter's Mutual Security Program, and so do many other countries.

From a purely strategic point of view, the need of the superpowers for the alliances or friendship of the lesser powers has diminished sharply in the missile era. Both the United States and the Soviet Union are now able so to arrange the placement of their strategic missiles that they are almost entirely independent of foreign military bases and other facilities which they might otherwise hope to procure through mutual security pacts and alliances. Nevertheless, the old habit of alliances has continued.

There is no indication yet of any marked decrease of enthusiasm for winning the friendship or alliances of foreign countries. This may be partly explained by the fact that in what has become the main forum for mustering world opinion and for constructive international diplomacy and negotiation, the United Nations and particularly its General Assembly, each country counts. At the General Assembly Iceland with its 140,000 people has the same one vote as the United States; and of course each of the new member states from Africa and elsewhere has a vote. Neither side of the Cold War wishes to appear in the world community without friends, and each side is normally keen to win the battle of votes.

There are observable beginnings of an attempt to revivify the Security Council, where the great powers are not so dependent on what one might call the mass vote of the ever-increasing number of member states of the United Nations. However, it appears that the tendency toward alliances will persist until there is a fully integrated world security system. Until then, the weak will cleave to the strong as they did in the time of Aelius Aristeides; and the great will seek tangible expression of their greatness through gaining the adherence of the lesser countries.

Added to these basic motivations is the growing realization among the richer countries—particularly among the leading states of the world—that international peace and good order are promoted by aid to the world's developing countries.

This phenomenon of alliances and close friendships, arising as it does from deeply ingrained factors, profoundly influences the negotiating postures of the great countries, particularly vis-à-vis the countries with which they conclude their alliances and other arrangements.

Let us consider first the situation which has developed between the United States, as the acknowledged leader of the Western alliance, and one of its most powerful allies, France.

In 1959 General de Gaulle announced that France was determined to become a nuclear power. Over the years he has made various statements on his concept of the Western alliance. On June 8, 1959, a spokesman of the Quai d'Orsai indicated that France would undertake no new commitments to NATO until it had received satisfaction of its demands. These, it was explained, were recognition by its allies of its right to a larger role in the affairs of the alliance and to allied aid in becoming a nuclear power.[2]

Here then is the crux of the matter: France's desire for a larger role, since expressed by de Gaulle and other French leaders to be a role based on the equality of France (or of Western Europe) with the United States on the one hand and the Soviet Union on the other.

One result of this desire for a larger and more independent role has been de Gaulle's decision to withdraw the French fleet from NATO control. President de Gaulle explained his attitude at his Press Conference on March 25, 1959. We should look at his argument in some detail:

I remind you that the possible zone of action of N.A.T.O. does not extend south of the Mediterranean. The Middle East, North Africa, Black Africa, Madagascar, the Red Sea, etc., are not part of it, everybody knows. But nobody can deny that France may at any time have to act in these countries.

How would she do so within the framework of N.A.T.O. . . . ?

For analogous reasons, two other great powers, the United States and Great Britain, have taken their measures so that the greater part of their naval forces should not be integrated into N.A.T.O. as it exists now. As well, they keep in their own hands alone the essential element of their power, atomic bombers.

As to the fact that France has taken back the disposal of the fleet, I do not think that this can prevent her, should the occasion arise, from taking part in the common battle in the Mediterranean, and I do not think the alliance is weakened by it.

I even think the opposite, for it seems to me that the alliance will be the more alive and stronger . . . where each pays his way rather than . . . where the states and peoples and governments see themselves, within the sacred domain of their own defense, deprived more or less of their role and responsibilities.[3]

Although de Gaulle argued that his approach would strengthen NATO—and this may or may not have been the case—the fact remained that the very closeness of the United States' alliance with France notwithstanding, de Gaulle (far the weaker partner in the alliance) was creating difficulties for the United States. This was borne out by President Eisenhower's remarks at his press conference on June 17, 1959:

I'm going to make a special effort to meet him [de Gaulle], because there are differences of opinions between our two Governments, and I think he believes and I believe that a personal conversation between the two of us might ease some of the rough points in these arguments and possibly solve them.

He and I are old friends, comrades of the war and since, and I would be hopeful that here would be one place that because of the special character of the problems, so many of them having to do with defense, that maybe two heads of governments who both by coincidence have been old comrades-in-arms, we might have some solution that wouldn't otherwise be apparent.[4]

However, the meeting at the summit between the two leaders, and the added fact of wartime comradeship, did not resolve the issues as President Eisenhower hoped they would. France continued her acts of disengagement (without dissociation) from some of the intimacies of the NATO alliance. On August 26, 1959, the *New York Times* announced that 50 United States fighter planes had shifted to Germany in a dispute with France over the NATO nuclear arsenal. It was added that the remainder of the 75 combat aircraft of the 49th Tactical Fighter Wing would complete the transfer from France in the next few days.

Did the United States take corresponding action to show its disapproval of France's moves? The answer is in the negative, and the reason is that the more powerful country in such circumstances is, paradoxically, often the keener of the two to maintain the alliance. Its intrinsic strength may gain little from the particular relationship at stake, but its sense of leadership, its understanding of its own over-all responsibility, its prestige, and its fear lest the principle of the falling dominoes come into play, all contribute to its attitude. In an operative sense, they tend to make the stronger party the weaker *negotiating* partner when it comes to the nuances of the alliance.

When it came to the development of its own nuclear deterrent, France, after listening to the United States' advice and the United States' ideas regarding how best the purposes of the NATO alliance could be served, brushed aside that advice and went ahead on her own. Again, the stronger negotiating partner seemed to be the weaker of the two in the process of negotiation. President Kennedy was asked about this at his press conference on June 27, 1962. Here is the question put to him, and his reply in full:

Question: Mr. President, Secretary [of State Dean] Rusk has just about completed his rounds of the Western European Capitals. I wonder if you could give us an evaluation of his trip with particular reference to whether this government has now averted France's determination to build its own nuclear power and whether we will seek to coordinate and integrate that power into the NATO system?

Answer: We have always accepted its determination to do so. What we have not agreed to is to participate in the development of a national deterrent. We believe that that is inimical to the community interests of the Atlantic Alliance, that it encourages other countries to do the same.

Now France has determined to do so. She's going to do it. But I think that for the United States to associate with that effort, to associate with the concept of additional independent national nuclear deterrents, to play our part in its development would be a mistake, both from the point of view of the United States, of the Atlantic community and peace, because then other countries will feel compelled to do the same, and in my judgment, the NATO alliance and the steps we've taken to implement the NATO alliance give adequate security to Europe and the United States.

I think we should stay with that. Now the French do not agree. And they are going ahead. We accept that, but we do not agree with it.[5]

In short, the United States felt that France's action was inimical to the interests of NATO, and that it would be a mistake from the point of view of the United States and NATO and the preservation of peace. However, the weaker partner in the alliance had its way, and again there was no retaliatory move by the United States. It is fair to say that in the negotiations between the United States and France in the last few years in regard to defense and mutual security, we see one side consistently having its way against the views and wishes of its more powerful ally, without that ally's reacting against the weaker party.

When he has expressed his views on his nuclear force, de Gaulle has done so with scathing criticism directed against the general view of his powerful ally, the United States. At his press conference on January 14, 1963 he said:

In politics and in strategy it is as in economics, monopoly quite naturally appears to him who holds it as the best possible system. Then one hears a multiple chorus of officers, specialists, American publicists, violently, strongly attack our autonomous armament. The atomic force with which France claims to equip herself is and will remain, they say, infinitesimal with regard to those of the United States and Russia.

To build it would be losing many efforts and much money for nothing. Furthermore, within the alliance, in any case, the United States has a crushing superiority, so let us not go counter to their virgin action. It is perfectly true that the quantity of nuclear means which we will be able to equip ourselves with, will be far from matching the mass of those of the two giants of today.[6]

To those in the United States and elsewhere who reject France's nuclear power as not constituting a credible deterrent, de Gaulle answers:

We are in a position to think that six years from now our deterrent means will reach a total instantaneous power of 2,000 Hiroshima bombs. That is what certain, obviously unthinking, opponents call France's "little bomb." [7]

France under de Gaulle has continued to go its own way, and in particular has acted in opposition to the views of the United States, and also against the United Kingdom, which is at present more powerful than France. Is it increasing power which enables France to act in this manner? In other words, does France's self-confidence stem wholly from its own intrinsic strength? If this were so, then we should not see the pattern being repeated when it comes to less powerful allies of the United States or of the Soviet Union.

Let us examine certain aspects of the relationship between the United States and Pakistan. For nearly ten years, United States funds have accounted for about one-half of the funds available to the Gov-

ernment of Pakistan. The degree of Pakistan's dependence on the
United States would appear to be crucial, not only for the well-being
of Pakistan but even for the survival of that country at anything approaching its present level of governmental effort. However, Pakistan
has acted to strengthen its ties with China (and China has acted with
equal diplomatic ingenuity and self-interest to strengthen its ties with
Pakistan), and in doing so has made moves which have not been
favored by the United States.

It is widely assumed that the dissatisfaction of Pakistan with the
United States and hence its turning toward China commenced with
the military assistance which the United States offered to India after
the Chinese attack on the Indian frontier in November 1962. This
however, is not the case. From 1960 on, Pakistan and China have
worked hard for a close relation with each other—that is, ever since
it became apparent that China and India were involved in a serious
border dispute. In June 1961, I raised this matter informally with
Marshal Chen Yi and his deputy Chang Han Fu at Geneva. Chang
Han Fu and I, being colleagues at the Laos Conference, had developed friendly and good working relations. It puzzled me that Communist China should be entering into a close alliance with a country
which had often boasted of its staunch alliance with the Western
world,[8] and which had, moreover, not always espoused the cause of
the Peking Government for membership in the United Nations, or
supported Peking at a large number of other conferences which I had
attended. On the other hand, India had gone out of its way at international conferences to support the full participation of the Peking Government. India had not let the border dispute interfere with its generally friendly attitude toward China, or disrupt its conviction that
China should play its rightful role in the international community.

Marshal Chen Yi and Chang Han Fu were most embarrassed by
my raising the question of the reorientation of their relationship with
Pakistan. They first tried to laugh off the matter. However, I pressed
them and cited instances which indicated the movement of the two
countries toward each other. My Chinese friends, decidedly uncom-
fortable, tried to turn the tables on me by asking why the Indian
newspapers were so critical of the Chinese Government!

It seems clear, and this is by no means regarded as reprehensible in
international affairs, that China and Pakistan, impelled by a common
animosity for India arising out of their territorial claims, started to
come together. President Ayub Khan began to express his dissatisfaction with the United States considerably before the Chinese attack on
India, or the offer of military assistance by the United States to India.

On May 10, 1962, President Ayub Khan was reported to have said that the trend of United States relations with India might force some of India's neighbors "to look for protection elsewhere." [9] Although India was receiving no military assistance from the United States, President Ayub Khan continued: "The feeling is emerging in the minds of many countries surrounding India, that with American assistance, India is enlarging her military powers as a pretext of opposition to China." [10]

On June 27, 1962, in the period before the Chinese attack on India and, again, before any military assistance from the United States was given to India, the Foreign Minister, the late Mohammed Ali, declared in the Pakistan National Assembly that his country was looking forward "to the closest possible ties with China."

After the attack by China, the Pakistan leaders, in spite of being partners of the United States in military defense alliances, and with no apparent reason to distrust either the capacity or the will of the United States to honor its alliance, swung further in the direction of China. On July 8, 1963, President Ayub Khan declared at a meeting of the Moslem League Party that the small nations of Asia would be forced "to seek protection which would only be available from China, if India continued to receive Western military assistance." He added that the West was contributing to the spread of Communism in Asia by forcing into Chinese arms those countries which feared India's military build-up.

About the same time, Pakistan entered into an air communications agreement with Peking which involved the flight of Boeing 707s into China. Pakistan decided to place some of her Boeing parts in China. This led the United States to reconsider a grant she was about to make for the development of airport facilities in East Pakistan. However, after a few months' delay the United States made the grant.

The *New York Times* carried the following news item relating to the views of Zulfikar Ali Bhutto, the Foreign Minister of Pakistan, regarding the reorientation of his country's foreign policy:

The situation arising from the Chinese-Indian border conflict and the dispatching of arms to India, Mr Bhutto said, has required the people and the Government of Pakistan to reconsider her foreign policy. He said the foreign policy was being reshaped. He said that Pakistan would like to halt the deterioration in relations between Pakistan and the West but that the initiative would have to come from the West.[11]

In the same statement, Mr. Bhutto said to the National Assembly of Pakistan that an attack on his country "could involve the territorial integrity and security of the largest Asian state." The London *Times,* commenting on this remark, stated that "Parliamentary circles believed Mr. Bhutto's remarks implied an undertaking between Rawalpindi and Peking on mutual defense." [12] We should remind ourselves of the authoritative statements before the dispatch of arms aid from the West to India, to the effect that Pakistan was seeking and entering into close ties with China.

Assuming that the comment of the London *Times* represented the facts of the situation, it would seem that Pakistan had arrived at the interesting position of being in military alliance with both the United States and Communist China! Certainly this illustrates very clearly the dilemma of a strong power (the United States) in its relations with a weaker power (Pakistan).

It is not only the Western powers which face difficulties in their negotiating relationships with their weaker allies. Although it is more difficult to obtain full information about the relations of the Eastern European states with the Soviet Union, it is now known that Rumania has recently refused to join in the largely Soviet-directed economic plan for Eastern Europe. The *New York Times* gave the following report regarding a statement carried by the major Rumanian newspaper, *Scinteia:*

The analysis also made it clear that Bucharest would defend its economic position in the Eastern bloc and would resist Soviet attempts to curb Rumania's industrial development in favor of more raw material and food production.

The statement said that the project of a supranational control body in Comecon—the Soviet Bloc's Council for Mutual Economic Assistance— "is not in keeping with the principles that underlie the relations between Socialist countries."

"The idea of a single planning body for all Comecon countries," the statement declared, "has the most serious economic and political implications. The sovereignty of the Socialist State requires that it holds in its hand all the levers for managing economic and social life." [13]

It is also known that Rumanian leaders did not see eye to eye with Khrushchev regarding relations with China, and did not support Khrushchev's plan for a meeting of the Communist parties of the world at this juncture when there were sharp differences between the Soviet and Chinese policies.

In August 1964 Rumania entered into a commercial agreement with France with a view to lessening her dependence on the Soviet Union and other Communist countries.

Here again we have the case of an extremely powerful country (the Soviet Union), which in spite of a military alliance and common ideology with a weaker partner, is unable to get its way in its negotiations with that partner. Again, the reason would appear to be that the strong party does not wish to take any step which would widen the rift between itself and the weaker party. The Soviet Union knows that in spite of difficulties there are other countries to which Rumania could look. This inhibits the Soviet Union in its negotiations with Rumania.

When the Laos Conference of 1961–1962 was convened at Geneva, the United States was giving large-scale assistance to the Royal Government of Laos, which at that time was in the hands of a "right-wing" group whose strong man was General Phoumi Nosavan. As the Conference progressed, the general feeling—shared by most of the Western delegates as much as by the nonaligned delegates—was that General Phoumi was not being particularly cooperative in regard to working out a settlement with the two other main Laotian factions (the Centerists under Prince Souvanna Phouma, and the left-wing Pathet Lao). Most of the delegates felt, and conveyed this view to the relevant quarters, that as long as the United States continued its assistance to General Phoumi Nosavan, and as long as he was assured of such assistance, he would continue to be recalcitrant. On February 12, 1962, the *New York Times* reported:

Some Western diplomats believe General Phoumi Nosavan wants to make an "all or nothing" gamble on the political future of his faction. To this end . . . he has insisted on having the two key ministries despite the fact that the United States, the Soviet Union and other interested parties want them to go to the neutralists. . . .

It was said [that] if he stands firm to the point that the other factions break off the talks, General Phoumi Nosavan probably believes that the United States would have no other course than to support him fully should the fighting resume on a broad scale.

As the representative of India at the Laos Conference, I am in a position to say that the foregoing report states fairly accurately the attitude at the time of Phoumi Nosavan. It was clear that he felt he could exploit his anti-Communism to his own advantage. This he felt put him in a very strong position vis-à-vis the United States. At one stage he said, "We do not have to change our position because we and the United States are both fighting Communism." [14] His tactics worked for some time. However, late in March 1962, when Averell Harriman visited Laos, the United States withheld its monthly payment to the right wing.[15] In correspondence with the King of Laos, President Kennedy upheld the United States position of support for Prince Souvanna Phouma.[16]

The United States continued its pressure on the right wing, and this was among the factors that contributed significantly to the final achievement of an accord on Laos and its signing on July 23, 1962.

In the case of Laos in 1961–1962, we see an instance of a very weak party using various tactics to maintain the support of its very strong partner, and by doing so affecting the course of negotiations. It was not until the United States refused to let its weak partner have its way that the negotiations could go forward to a successful conclusion. In this case the strong partner asserted its strength. It should be added, however, that by the time this took place it had also become clear to the weak partner that there was no other power to which it could turn for assistance. In the other cases we have so far cited, the weaker partners have felt that there were other powerful arms ready to embrace them.

In the relations between small Cuba and its superpower ally, the Soviet Union, there have also been indications of the disproportionate strength in negotiation of the weaker partner.

Immediately after the high point of the Caribbean crisis of October 1962, Fidel Castro refused to allow on-site or at-port inspection of the dismantling of Soviet missiles. It seemed that the Soviet Union, which had sent Anastas Mikoyan, then its First Deputy Premier, to reason with Castro, failed to get the Cuban leader to agree to any such inspection. In fact, Castro turned the Soviet Union's own willingness to be inspected on the high seas into a reason against inspection of Cuba. In a statement broadcast on November 1 he said:

I wish to answer regarding the Red Cross inspection. We are equally against that inspection at our ports. I ask myself that if the Soviet Union authorizes the inspection of its ships at the high seas, why would it then be necessary to inspect them again in the Cuban ports.[17]

He used the following argument in the same broadcast against inspection:

And if one of them does not need any additional guarantee, that is the compromise of the United States not to invade Cuba, why is it the compromise of the Soviet Union of retiring its strategic arms requires the additional guarantee of inspecting us? [18]

Not only did the Soviet Union fail to persuade its small ally, Cuba, to accept certain measures in the wake of the crisis of October 1962, but in 1963 it failed to secure Cuba's adherence to the partial test ban treaty signed at Moscow on August 6 of that year. Cuba was the subject of a rebuke in an officially inspired article in *Pravda* on September 12, 1963. The *New York Times* reported that the article contained an admonition to Fidel Castro to show more restraint, and to accede to the treaty for a limited test ban. The article, stated the *New York Times,* praised the test ban treaty as inspiring "all mankind." It also said, "The world public awaits from all governments further steps, normalizing the situation, relaxing international tension and strengthening peace." [19]

Although documentation is not equally available on the relations of the two superpowers, it would appear that both are in much the same position in regard to their attempts to negotiate with or through their weaker partners in an alliance.

It would appear from our analysis that there is ample post-World War II evidence to support the following principle:

When a powerful state enters into or becomes dependent upon alliances or other close arrangements with less powerful states, in order to protect or advance its own interests, it may find that its negotiating position vis-à-vis such states is vulnerable, particularly when they are able to turn to alternative sources of power.

CHAPTER FOURTEEN

Deterrent Force

DETERRENT FORCE normally signifies the possession of a nuclear weapons capacity of such a character as to constitute an effective brake on massive aggression against the possessor by any other country in the world.[1] By "such a character" we imply that in the event of aggression the nuclear weapons could be deployed to mete out incapacitating punishment to the aggressor. At the present time the nuclear arsenals of only two countries, the United States and the Soviet Union, fully meet the requirements of this definition. However, two other countries, the United Kingdom and France, possess nuclear weapons, and are probably in a position to deter aggression by any country other than the two superpowers. China may be in the same category fairly soon. We propose to regard the United Kingdom and France as possessors of a deterrent force, although it is true that the French *force de frappe* is still in the early stages of development. As we have seen, General de Gaulle recently told the world that in six years his country would possess a nuclear capacity equivalent to 2,000 Hiroshima bombs.[2] This might or might not be sufficient to deter the superpowers (although it seems clear that the French calculation is that if effectively carried and propelled, it would be). However, it will certainly amount to a considerable nuclear weapons capacity, and will be strongly deterrent in almost all world confrontations involving France. Under these circumstances, it is realistic to place France in the category of those countries in possession of deterrent power. And at the rate at which China is developing its nuclear capacity, that country may be in the same category in a few years.

As far as the United Kingdom is concerned, no striking disclosures of nuclear weapons capacity have been made, but it is estimated that the United Kingdom has 180 medium-range bombers armed with nuclear bombs in the megaton range. This constitutes a large nuclear force, and preparations are said to be afoot to launch five Polaris nuclear weapons carrying submarines. Even the present United Kingdom nuclear armament capacity, stated in terms of Hiroshima bombs for comparison with the projected French force, seems to be of the order of 9,000 such bombs. The United Kingdom, therefore, now possesses what might be termed a real deterrent capacity, although its means of delivery would have to be modernized to make this capacity fully effective.

It is apparent that the capacity of some countries to kill scores of millions of human beings and to cause enormous destruction of property and natural resources must affect the balance of negotiating power. Since most major world confrontations tend to line up the present superpowers on opposite sides, we shall direct our discussion mainly to the relationship between negotiation and deterrent force in those cases in which deterrence may be assumed to be possessed by both sides. But we shall also pay some attention to other negotiating situations in which a nuclear deterrent force is held by only one side to a confrontation.

The leaders of nonnuclear countries have in various ways given their views on the effect of the possession of nuclear deterrence on the general negotiating posture of a country. The late Prime Minister Nehru remarked, while replying in the Indian Parliament to the debate on the President's address on February 25, 1955:

I believe that we have helped, occasionally, in regard to the solution of some problems, and in the relaxation or lessening of tension. We might take due credit for that, but let us not go beyond that. After all a country's capacity to influence events is determined by various factors. You will find that India is lacking in most of those factors. If we have been successful in some measure, the success has been due not obviously to any kind of military strength or financial power, but because we took a correct view of events.[3]

We observe from these remarks that Mr. Nehru, whose background was such that he might be expected to downgrade somewhat the influence of the might of nations, considered that military strength was perhaps the primary factor (this was the first factor he mentioned) among those which give a country the capacity to influence world events. Since the present peak of military strength is nuclear strength, Mr. Nehru implied that nuclear strength greatly enhances a country's capacity to influence events. And since normally the influ-

encing of world events does not take place through the exercise of
military capacity, but rather through restrained techniques of bringing
military strength to bear on a situation without its actual use, we are
not stretching Mr. Nehru's remarks in attributing to them the implication that the possession of great military strength (deterrent force)
can have a very real influence on world events, through various negotiating forums such as the United Nations General Assembly, ad hoc
conferences, or quiet bilateral negotiations.

The position of Germany in regard to the influence of nuclear
weapons on negotiation is not quite so clear. Perhaps this is in part
related to the fact that in one of the Protocols of Paris amending the
Brussels Treaty, establishing the Western European Union in October
1954, the Federal Republic of Germany undertook not to manufacture in its territory any atomic weapons.[4]

The Federal Republic, while in its NATO capacity seeking equality
of armaments for its contingents, has not generally thought of itself as
a potential nuclear power, if we are to judge by the statements of its
leaders. Indeed, in those statements there has been a welcome corela-
tionship between disarmament and the eventual solution of the problems of Germany. On May 28, 1957, in the Communiqué and Joint
Declaration issued by President Eisenhower and Chancellor Adenauer, it was stated:

The President and the Chancellor agreed that, if a beginning could be
made toward effective measures of disarmament, this would create a degree of confidence which would facilitate further progress in the field
of disarmament and in the settlement of outstanding major political
problems, such as the re-unification of Germany.[5]

Then, again, in 1960 the *New York Times* stated that before Chancellor Adenauer left Bonn to visit President Eisenhower, he made it
clear that disarmament, and not Berlin, was the vital question for the
proposed East-West summit meeting.[6]

However, until there is agreement between the powers to disarm,
Germany does not see why it should be on the lower level of strength,
and this would imply that it, too, counts on nuclear power to give it
added negotiating strength. This is not to say that West Germany is
necessarily intent on acquiring its own nuclear weapons—although
most East European statesmen and diplomats insist that this is precisely the intention of that country. The latter are, indeed, able to
produce a considerable volume of evidence in support of their view.
An informative document on this subject is Soviet Ambassador

Semyon Tsarapkin's statement at the Eighteen-Nation Committee on Disarmament Conference at Geneva on August 13, 1964.[7]

There may well be a certain degree of ambivalence in Germany regarding the acquisition of nuclear weapons as a means of increasing strength. Such weapons exist around German territory and upon it, but Germany itself is not a nuclear power. Under those circumstances, its leaders have been restrained in statements about the effects of nuclear power on negotiation.

Another view on this matter was expressed when Marshal Chen Yi was in Geneva for the Laos Conference of 1962. He appeared on the National Swiss Radio, and in the course of his remarks stated:

. . . We have powerful bodies which are carrying out research. . . . this research also concerns the manufacture of the atomic bomb. We are carrying out this research because the imperialists believe that so long as we have no atomic bombs we shall be weak and contemptible.[8]

Marshal Chen Yi obviously considers that the possession of nuclear weapons gives a country added stature in world affairs. It cannot be the Marshal's intention that nuclear weapons should be used in the day-to-day conduct of world affairs; what he would seem to mean is that in international relations, in the pressures which countries exert on each other to obtain for themselves the most favorable results in situations and disputes, the additional stature attained by the possession of nuclear weapons would be of significant value. Privately, too, he and his deputy, Chang Han Fu, made it clear that China had no intention of remaining in a lower armaments category than any other world power. (In this connection, Prime Minister Nehru, although conscious of the weight in international affairs that accrues from great military strength, both in public and in private was resolutely opposed to the manufacture of atomic weapons by India. He remained steadfast in this view to the end.)

The views of another country in the nuclear galaxy were stated on January 1, 1964, when President de Gaulle broadcast a New Year's message to France. In the course of his message he said:

It is a fact that, while reducing by half the length of military service, we are, through the creation of our first atomic weapons and the modernization of our forces, in the process of taking our destiny in hand, which had, since 1940, been in the hands of others.[9]

This is indeed a striking statement about the decisive characteristics of nuclear weapons. President de Gaulle considers that nuclear weapons are now an essential component in the articulation of his country's independence. Independence in international affairs does not signify a self-contained anarchic concept of national life. Certainly de Gaulle was not speaking in this sense. What he meant was the restoration of his country's ability and capacity to express, in international situations, its own view rather than a view which would be refracted by the impact on France of such considerations as: "We cannot take up *x* position, because we fear the nuclear power of *y*, an inimical country"; or, "We cannot take up *x* position, because we are dependent upon the support of *y*, a nuclear power, and what would that nuclear power think if we were to adopt *x* position?" The desire to be independent in this sense should not be regarded, as it sometimes is, as an aberration of the President of France. On the contrary, most countries, and indeed in certain circumstances all countries, hope to possess this kind of independence in international affairs.

Later on in the same New Year's message President de Gaulle returned to this point, obviously because he regarded it as extremely important:

Firstly, we must pursue the effort which should equip us with a thermonuclear arsenal, the only one with a power adequate to the threat of aggression and consequently the only one which allows us independence.[10]

In short, France, within the threshold of the possession of nuclear power and set on the road to deterrent power, considers nuclear weapons as a guarantee of its capacity to act as an independent nation. This view is also implicit in the remarks made by Marshal Chen Yi.

What of the view of the United Kingdom, the third state in the nuclear hierarchy? It is not the habit of the United Kingdom to publicize its nuclear position. However, from time to time the Government has made it clear that its nuclear weapons must serve the national interests first and foremost. It is difficult for the Government to make a stronger statement than this, particularly because there is considerable opposition in the United Kingdom to the continuance of Britain as an independent nuclear power. Although a minority opinion, it is wide enough to be taken into account by both the major political parties. Under these circumstances, assuming Britain continues to remain an independent nuclear power, it is doubtful that it will resort overtly to nuclear diplomacy, namely, that it will use its nuclear strength too obviously to buttress its negotiating positions. There are two other reasons for the United Kingdom's reticence in this regard.

First, the United Kingdom, of all the powerful allies of the United States, has remained the closest in step with the senior partner and leader of NATO. In circumstances which involve its security and survival it can count upon the strength of the negotiating position of the United States. Second, most of the confrontations to which the United Kingdom is still a party, for example in Arabia, in Southeast Asia, and in South America, are confrontations of a colonial character. As was made clear in the Suez clash of October 1956, when it comes to a colonial confrontation the United Kingdom cannot count on the support of its ally, the United States. In the United States' view, the maintenance or defense of a colonial empire is not within the scope of a nation's essential and vital interests. This being so, the United Kingdom is obliged to play down nuclear diplomacy when it deals with colonial questions. In this respect there seems to be a clear difference in the mind and approach of the United Kingdom on one hand, and France on the other. We recall that part of de Gaulle's press conference of March 25, 1959 in which he stated that NATO did not extend south of the Mediterranean, or to the Middle East, North Africa, Black Africa, Madagascar, the Red Sea, etc., and then added: "But nobody can deny that France may at any time have to act in these countries."

The Prime Minister of the United Kingdom will tend to content himself with a lower-keyed statement. In the statement on nuclear defense systems attached to the Nassau Communiqué issued by President Kennedy and Prime Minister Macmillan, we find these words:

These [British] forces, and at least equal United States forces, would be available for inclusion in a NATO multilateral nuclear force. The Prime Minister made it clear that except where Her Majesty's Government may decide that supreme national interests are at stake, these British forces will be used for the purposes of international defense of the Western Alliance in all circumstances.[11]

However, the British Government has recognized the close relationship between its nuclear deterrent and its negotiating position. The annual White Paper on Defense for 1961 contains the following illuminating remark regarding Britain's separate nuclear capacity: "Our contribution also substantially increases our influence in negotiations for a nuclear test agreement, disarmament and reorganization of NATO strategy."

In the House of Commons debate on the 1963 Defense White Paper, on March 4 of that year Peter Thorneycroft, then Defense Minister, moving for the approval of the statement on defense, reaffirmed the British Government's decision to continue its nuclear deterrent, claiming that to scrap it would "gravely impair the independence of Britain's foreign policy." The impairment of which the Defense Minister spoke would not be of just Britain's capacity to defend itself, but of its foreign policy, which is translated into action mainly through various forms of negotiation.

We have referred to the Nassau Agreements of December 1962, and to the statement on nuclear defense systems which accompanied that communiqué. In the debate in the House of Commons on those documents, Harold Macmillan in January 1963 gave various reasons in favor of the United Kingdom's continuing to keep its own nuclear deterrent. One of the reasons mentioned was that the possession of a nuclear force in the past meant that the United Kingdom had been able to make "a valuable contribution in many fields of international discussion."

On February 26, 1964, in the debate on the Defense White Paper for that year, Mr. Thorneycroft, when announcing that a fifth Polaris submarine would be built for the United Kingdom Navy, stated:

The greatest force for peace is the existence of the nuclear deterrent. For the first time governments know that major war would mean destruction of the world, and because they know this, the forces of diplomacy are brought forward at a very early stage in disputes, even in minor disputes.

The views of the leaders of the United States and the Soviet Union regarding the relationship between deterrent power and international negotiation are of real significance to this issue. They show, among other things, the effect of the knowledge of the massive destructive power of nuclear deterrence on the orientation of states toward negotiation. Both the American and the Soviet leaders have repeatedly drawn attention to the need to negotiate in order to change the nature of the military confrontation between the two sides. To take some of their statements chronologically, I would refer first to an address by Secretary of State Christian Herter at the National Press Club, Washington, D.C., on February 18, 1960. The Secretary of State spoke on disarmament. He ended his statement with the following words: "The perils that confront every man, woman, and child in the world today are too great to admit of anything but the most strenuous, devoted, and persistent effort to this end [disarmament]." [12]

President Kennedy, in his State of the Union Address to Congress on January 30, 1961, emphasized the strengthening of the military tools of the United States. He quoted from his statement on taking the oath of office:

Only when our arms are sufficient beyond doubt can we be certain beyond doubt, that they will never be employed.

. . . we must sharpen our political and diplomatic tools—the means of cooperation and agreement on which an enforceable world order must ultimately rest.[13]

President Kennedy saw no contradiction between a strong nuclear deterrent and the diplomatic tools—to be used largely through negotiation—to reach agreement and to stimulate cooperation among the nations of the world.

In an address on March 20, 1961 at the University of California at Berkeley, Secretary of State Dean Rusk in a sense amplified this position by explaining just why negotiation for disarmament, concurrent with maintaining a strong nuclear posture, was necessary: "The path toward disarmament is tortuous and full of pitfalls. There are risks along that path, but there are more frightful risks if we do not try once more, with the combination of deep purpose and clear thought we shall require." [14]

President Kennedy threw additional light on the attitude of his Government on this issue by some of the statements in his defense message to Congress on March 28, 1961. He stated:

The primary purpose of our arms is peace not war. . . . to provide backing for diplomatic settlement of disputes . . . diplomacy and defense are no longer distinct alternatives, one to be used where the other fails—both must complement each other.[15]

Speaking at Brussels on May 9, 1964 at a Belgian-American luncheon, Dean Rusk was reported to have said: "From our position of combined strength, we have been able to see, hopefully, some prospect of easing tensions in relations with Eastern Europe." [16] Mr. Rusk then referred to the few very limited agreements which had been achieved; and he made it clear that his view was that NATO's military might, which includes nuclear deterrence, had helped in working out those negotiated agreements.

The Soviet leaders have likewise made statements which indicate that they too see a close relationship between their deterrent power and the need to negotiate.

On January 14, 1960, Prime Minister Khrushchev addressed the

Supreme Soviet on disarmament and also on Soviet armed strength. He stated:

. . . we already have so many nuclear weapons, both atomic and hydrogen, and the necessary rockets for delivering these weapons to the territory of a potential aggressor, that should any madman launch an attack on our state or on other socialist states we would be able to literally wipe the country or countries which attack us off the face of the earth.[17]

On the next day, the Supreme Soviet issued a disarmament appeal to all countries. In that appeal strong emphasis was placed on negotiation. A passage in it read:

The visit by N. S. Khrushchev, Chairman of the Council of Ministers of the U.S.S.R., to the United States and his discussions with President Dwight Eisenhower have opened a new chapter in world relations—one of peaceful negotiations for the settlement of the international issues left unsettled since the Second World War or created during the years of the arms race and the "cold war." Negotiation is the only possible way to solve the issues in dispute.[18]

It would thus appear that the possession of nuclear power at a deterrent level does not mean that the Soviet Union is unwilling to negotiate disputes, or in particular to negotiate to change the present military confrontation.

Khrushchev was explicit about the relationship between deterrence and the need to reach agreement on disarmament in his message to the Ten-Nation Committee on Disarmament on March 14, 1960:

Today, when weapons of terrible, destructive power—atom and hydrogen bombs and intercontinental missiles—have been created, the question of disarmament has become the major and most vital problem of the present time.[19]

In 1961, in addressing the 22nd Congress of the Communist Party of the Soviet Union, Khrushchev touched on Soviet military strength and then added:

The situation which has developed requires the urgent solution of fundamental international problems on the basis of the principles of peaceful coexistence. . . . The most important component of the foreign policy activity of our party is the struggle for universal and complete disarmament.[20]

Tass published a summary of a report made on February 14, 1964 by Mikhail A. Suslov, a Secretary of the Soviet Communist Party's

Central Committee. Mr. Suslov was writing on the quarrel of his party with the Peking Communists. He said:

The Chinese leaders are trying to paralyze the efforts the Soviet Union and other socialist countries are making to avert the threat of a world war. . . . The Soviet Union's atomic weapon is a reliable guarantee of the defense not only of our country but also of the entire Socialist camp, including China. The leaders of the C.P.R. are well aware of this fact. Nonetheless, they are out to put their hands on nuclear weapons.

It thus turns out that the possession of an atomic bomb which the Chinese leaders call a "paper tiger" is their cherished goal.[21]

As far as the United States and the Soviet Union are concerned, we observe a constant interplay between the strengthening of the nuclear deterrence on the one hand, and the need to negotiate, particularly to modify the present balance of terror, on the other. But what is the attitude of the possessors of nuclear deterrence at any given time when they are waiting for, or preparing for, or are uncertain about, the immediate desirability of negotiation to deal with a particular international situation?

After the Vienna summit of June 1961, at which a mutual verbal show of strength took place, Khrushchev made an address in which the following significant passages occurred:

We shall sign the peace treaty and order our armed forces to administer a worthy rebuff to any aggressor if he dares raise a hand against the Soviet Union or our friends. . . .

We must perfect our weapons, improve our skill in handling arms so that they fire without fail and with pin-point precision.[22]

Statements such as these bring out the fact that nuclear deterrence can be a countervailing factor to the trend to negotiate. In his State of the Union message on January 30, 1961, President Kennedy stressed the need for an over-all review of the defense posture of the United States so as to create an invulnerable missile force and generally to strengthen the already considerable United States deterrent power. In the context of development of this strong deterrent position, President Kennedy referred to the situation in Castro-dominated Cuba and said, "Communist domination in this hemisphere can never be negotiated." [23]

The position of the President was not a theoretical one. The Bay of Pigs action, and the handling of the Cuban crisis in October 1962, both indicated a substantial determination to implement this approach. These events took place under the aegis of the great fact of

United States deterrent strength. In short, deterrent strength gives each side a capacity to undertake certain actions which in previous eras might have produced war. This was patently the case in regard to Hungary in October and November 1956, the erection of the Berlin Wall in 1961, and Cuba in 1961 and 1962.

Deterrent force leads to another set of difficulties in the possibility of negotiating disputes and situations. It can give rise to defiance, and evasion or secrecy.

The fact that nuclear weapons are potentially mass destructive and if used on a considerable scale would undoubtedly cause unprecedented damage, does not on occasion deter countries which are not in possession of nuclear weapons from provoking or indulging in conflict, even with the knowledge that such activities could result in nuclear war. When the representative of Cyprus at the United Nations says that his Government will maintain its position even if this should lead to large-scale war over Cyprus, he is acting in this manner. So, too, when the Foreign Minister of Pakistan states that an attack on his country could involve China, the largest power in Asia, he is showing something of the same defiance.

China particularly has exhibited a spirit of defiance regarding deterrent force. There is, for example, the statement made by Mao Tse-tung to Khrushchev in October 1959. This was quoted by *Izvestia* shortly after the signing of the partial test ban treaty. The relevant excerpts are:

"Can one guess," Mao said, "how great will be the toll of human casualties in a future war? Possibly it would be a third of the 2,700 million inhabitants of the entire world—i.e. only 900 million people. I consider this to be even low, if atomic bombs would actually fall.

"Of course it is most terrible. But even a half would not be so bad. . . .

"I had an argument about this with Nehru. In this respect he is more pessimistic than I am. I told him that if a half of humanity were destroyed, the other half would still remain but imperialism would be destroyed entirely and there would be only Socialism in all the world, and within a half of a century or a whole century the population would again increase even by more than a half." [24]

In the above statement Mao Tse-tung shows complete confidence in the ideological selectivity of nuclear weapons, fallout, and the genetic effects of radiation.

The Chinese have stated this same position in other ways. For example, they have glorified man and belittled atomic weapons—a most appealing point of view, especially to other underdeveloped countries.

On the 34th Anniversary of the founding of the Chinese People's Liberation Army, the Chinese *Bulletin of Activities* quoted Mao Tsetung as saying, "Although important, weapons are not the decisive factor in war; it is man and not material things that decides the issue." [25]

Another Chinese approach in belittling deterrence has been to point out—and this is more realistic than the previously cited posture—that other countries could also develop their own deterrence. The *Chinese People's Daily* recently said:

On the other hand, the United States can use this [a test ban treaty] to create pressure of public opinion to prevent other Socialist countries than the Soviet Union from conducting nuclear tests and possessing nuclear capability, and thus preventing the Socialist camp from re-inforcing its power of resisting United States nuclear blackmail.[26]

The *People's Daily* also reported the Chairman of the China Peace Committee, Kuo Mo-jo, as saying at the Peking rally commemorating the tenth anniversary of the Korean armistice:

The present attempt by a small number of countries to control the destiny of the people of the world by means of monopolizing nuclear weapons will almost certainly be smashed in the not too distant future.[27]

Another limitation of deterrence is that a certain amount of reliance is still placed by countries on their ability to conceal the full picture of their military strength. The Soviet Union has made this explicit. Some countries which engage in the development of nuclear and other weapons of mass destruction, while following the same policy, have compounded it by secrecy regarding the weapons they conceal.

Prime Minister Khrushchev, in his address to the Supreme Soviet at Moscow on January 14, 1960 stated:

The territory of our country is immense. We have the possibility of dispersing our rocket facilities, of camouflaging them well. We are creating such a system that if some means earmarked for a retaliatory blow were put out of commission one could always send into action the means duplicating them and hit the targets from reserve positions.[28]

These attitudes of secrecy and various kinds of defiance may ostensibly be based on defensive requirements, but they often fortify the truculence of parties to disputes or international situations, and thereby decrease the likelihood of effective negotiation. Undoubtedly China's general attitude of defiance, now fortified by her specific posture in regard to nuclear deterrence, partly explains her tough approach to negotiation in general, and in particular to such issues as her border dispute with India and Southeast Asian questions.

The above analysis indicates some of the complexities and cross-currents which are operative in the field of negotiation as a result of nuclear deterrence. These factors render extremely difficult the task of formulating with precision the relationship between deterrent power and international negotiation. However, three principles would appear to indicate the major effects of deterrence on negotiation:

> When the deterrent force available to both sides in an international dispute or situation is such that its use could devastate much of the structure, productive enterprises, and human content of the community on either side, the knowledge that this could be so might dispose the parties to negotiate some modification of the nature of their military confrontation.
>
> International situations in which the possession of deterrent force by one or more parties acts, at least temporarily, as a bar to the outbreak of hostilities, might encourage or promote limited provocative actions rather than negotiation.
>
> Deterrent force approaches its minimum efficiency and tends to harden states against the possibilities of negotiation when a state involved in a dispute (no matter how small or large that state), considers that its very existence is at stake, or that the destructive effects of nuclear power have been exaggerated, or that it is possible to build countervailing power, or to practice secrecy in the deployment of defensive and offensive military capacity.

CHAPTER FIFTEEN

Economic Weakness

IN A FINANCIALLY and commercially interdependent world, the relative economic levels of countries become factors of much greater relevance in their attitudes toward each other than they were at a time when communities subsisted, for the most part, on the products of agriculture and small-scale industry of the cottage type. Moreover, modern means of travel and communication have spread the urge for a high standard of living to the remotest corners of the world. No community is now content merely with what its local soil can produce. The counterparts of the social and economic revolutions of nineteenth-century Europe are likely to visit the economically "un-revolutionized" countries of Asia, Africa, and Latin America with all the more impact because of modern means of communication, which have stimulated a vivid awareness of the fruits of the social and economic revolution in evidence in the now developed countries of the Atlantic world and in the Soviet Union and Japan as well.

Then again, certain economic needs are so basic to human beings that denial of their satisfaction creates desperation, which can drive governments to certain extreme attitudes toward their neighbors or toward more prosperous states in general. Such attitudes need not always be truculent. On the contrary, economically weak governments will often feel that their best hope is not truculence but the soft ingratiating word. But since this sort of softness is put into practice only in situations of dire threat to survival, weak governments more frequently will think in terms of common approaches, cooperative endeavors, and joint activities or positions, in their relations with more powerful states. Therefore, economic weakness, which is invariably coupled with the desire for economic betterment but might also at times lead to a desperate and irresponsible mood, will affect the posture which a country will adopt toward other countries in the world.

Economically weak countries will tend to get together in dealing with economically powerful countries. Then again, a country which is weak often takes advantage of multilateralism in its economic negotiations, without directly engaging in it. It will negotiate simultaneously, or nearly so, with the United States on the one hand and the Soviet Union on the other, and perhaps also with France, the United Kingdom, or Germany. This procedure serves to protect the weaker country by confronting one strong country with the fact that it is possible for the weak country to go to a competing source for its required goods and services. These two stances—of getting together and of placing two or more economically strong countries in competition —account for the negotiating postures which predominate in the developing world.

However, such countries also make bilateral arrangements in regard to their economic needs. In the post-World War II world there has been an especially large number of such deals. They have been partly a concomitant of the Cold War, partly an effect of the awakened conscience of wealthy countries, and partly the result of the realization that unsatisfactory living conditions in a country or area may become breeding grounds for international discord. Thus motivated, the two superpowers have given military and economic assistance mainly to their allies, although also to other countries. Generally, the initiative in proposing bilateral aid has come from the superpowers or from their wealthy allies. It would obviously be ridiculous for the poorer countries to reject such freely proffered assistance. The nonaligned countries have received considerable economic assistance from the superpowers and their allied states, although less per capita than the aid given to the aligned countries.[1]

Our concern, however, is with the question of what happens when a country, being relatively poor, has to seek out either assistance or the widening of commercial channels for the satisfaction of its needs. When such aid or increased trade has been obtained, it has generally come within the category of internationally negotiated assistance or economic cooperation. (Aid and assistance are terms sometimes used in this chapter, as in other studies, in a wide sense, to cover not only financial grants or gifts of goods, but also commercial transactions such as barter agreements or loans for the acquisition of capital equipment and for other development requirements.)

The less developed countries of Asia and Africa have set certain guidelines for their economic dealings with the wealthy countries. The first significant occasion on which this was jointly done was the Bandung Conference of April 1955. Of the twenty-nine countries assembled, all of them with the exception of Japan were in the category of "less developed" countries. The communiqué issued at the conclusion of the conference recommended a multilateral approach in economic relations with the wealthy countries; and it also recommended collective discussion and action and unified approaches even when individual African or Asian countries were to undertake bilateral negotiations with the developed countries. Paragraph 3 of the communiqué stated:

The Asian-African Conference recommended: the early establishment of the Special United Nations Fund for Economic Development; . . . the early establishment of the International Finance Corporation which should include in its activities the undertaking of equity investment, and encouragement of the promotion of joint ventures among Asian-African countries in so far as this will promote their common interest.[2]

Both of the United Nations organs to which the communiqué refers were at that time under consideration by the General Assembly and the Economic and Social Council. Both were conceived as cooperative institutions to foster the economic growth of the less developed countries. At Bandung a number of those countries got together to press for their establishment, although some of the economically powerful countries had made it clear that they were not in favor of action to set them up at that time.

On the economic front, the Bandung communiqué turned next to the matter of trade in commodities of most interest to the less developed countries:

The Asian-African Conference recommended that *collective action* be taken by participating countries for stabilizing the international prices of and demand for primary commodities through bilateral and multilateral arrangements, and that as far as practicable and desirable, they should adopt a *unified approach* on the subject in the United Nations Permanent Advisory Commission on International Commodity Trade and other international forums.[3]

There was to be collective action even in cases of bilateral negotiation. At the United Nations a unified approach was to be encouraged.

Shipping is an important aspect of international trade, and on this subject the Bandung communiqué said:

The Asian-African Conference attached considerable importance to shipping and expressed concern that shipping lines reviewed from time to time their freight rates, often to the detriment of participating countries. It recommended a study of this problem, and *collective action* thereafter to induce the shipping lines to adopt a more reasonable attitude.[4]

These recommendations were heeded in varying degrees by the countries present. The united front of the participants and other underdeveloped countries at the United Nations for the establishment of a Special Fund for Economic Development is an apt illustration of the effectiveness of their collective efforts.

Work on the matter of a fund for economic assistance to the less developed countries through the United Nations started as early as 1950.[5] The Cold War was on, and the poorer member states saw much advantage in being able to go to the organization for the financial aid they sought for their development. If they could go to the United Nations, they would not incur direct obligations to one side or the other in the Cold War. However, it was not until 1952 that the General Assembly conceived the idea of a Special Fund to assist the less developed countries. Under pressure from Egypt, India, Indonesia, Pakistan, and other countries of Asia and Africa, joined by countries such as Mexico and Yugoslavia from other areas, and encouraged by the responsiveness of certain Western nations, notably the Netherlands, the General Assembly expressed the belief that "detailed plans for action . . . must be initiated without delay if such plans are to be translated into action within a reasonable period of time." [6]

The same resolution went on to ask the Economic and Social Council to prepare for the consideration of the next session of the General Assembly a detailed plan going into "the size, composition and administration of the special fund," [7] the manner of collecting contributions and the character of those contributions, as well as "the policies, conditions and methods to be followed in making grants and loans from the special fund to under-developed countries," [8] and other matters.

The pressures of the less developed countries acting together had, however, taken matters further than some of the most important potential donor countries considered wise, or practicable, at the time. As a result, the same resolution contained a clause entering a caveat against the reading of any commitment into the assent of the highly developed countries to the proposed studies. That clause reads:

Cognizant of the fact that, although the necessary acceleration of the economic development of under-developed countries requires foreign financial aid, the study and elaboration of the plans mentioned in the preceding paragraph cannot and must not be regarded as in any way committing the governments participating in such study or in the elaboration of such plans to join in implementing those plans in any degree, whether financially or otherwise.[9]

From then on, the united forces of the less developed countries were locked in a struggle with most of the highly developed countries on the issue of establishing a United Nations Special Fund for economic development. Due to the dilatoriness of procedures, the Economic and Social Council was not able to make its recommendations on the details of a plan for a Special Fund to the Seventh Session of the Assembly. However, the less developed countries continued their joint pressure. As the Cold War increased in intensity, the idea of resorting to a United Nations Fund, rather than relying on bilateral assistance from the great powers, became increasingly attractive to the smaller and economically weak countries. Again, at the Eighth Session of the General Assembly, a resolution was adopted on the Special Fund, but contrary to the direction in which the resolution of 1952 had pointed, all that the new resolution was able to do was to appoint Raymond Scheyven of Belgium (then president of the Economic and Social Council) to examine the issue further with interested governments. The same resolution clearly reflected the reluctance of the more highly developed countries. One clause of the resolution read:

Considering that the General Assembly should keep under review the question of the establishment of a special fund and, in particular, be attentive to any changes either in world conditions or in the attitudes of the governments of the Member States, which might be propitious to the establishment of such a fund in the near future.[10]

Doggedly, the less developed countries pushed ahead. Mr. Scheyven was helpful, and obtained promises of support from certain governments of developed countries, notably France and the Netherlands. Together with an eight-member advisory group of experts, he prepared a report entitled "A Special United Nations Fund for Economic Development." [11] As a result of this report, the General Assembly appointed an ad hoc committee of the representatives of sixteen governments to analyze further the comments of governments

on the proposal. The United States and the United Kingdom retained
the view that it was to be hoped that more favorable conditions would
soon be created through international disarmament, so that funds
should become available for the proposed Special Fund.[12]

When the matter returned to the Economic and Social Council for
consideration, the United States representative repeated the view that
the success of the fund depended on genuine multilateral support
which would be possible only when international agreement on disarmament had been reached.[13] Nevertheless, at the Eleventh Session
of the General Assembly the less developed countries introduced a
draft resolution sponsored by 41 states—more than half the membership of the Assembly—which asked for the drawing up of a draft
statute for SUNFED (Special United Nations Fund for Economic
Development, as it was then called). Delegate after delegate from the
less developed world sponsored the cause of SUNFED and explained
its proposed nature and functions. The representative of Greece,
Constantin P. Caranicas, is recorded as saying that "what was really
needed was a source of international funds sufficiently large to build
up the infrastructure of the under-developed countries." [14]

The delegate of Iraq, Faisul Damluji, said that "The sooner the
United Nations as a collective body assumed these tasks, fulfilled
them, and proceeded to assume still others, the sooner would such
objectives be attained." [15]

And the representative of Sudan, Mohammed Khogali, said that
"Newly independent countries were rather suspicious of assistance
offered by the countries from which they had gained their independence, and of assistance which was subject to conditions. The Sudan
therefore welcomed the establishment of SUNFED." [16]

However, a number of countries, including Australia, Belgium,
Italy, Japan, the United Kingdom, and the United States, doubted the
wisdom of such a move. Finally, in deference to the views of an important group of highly developed countries, the Assembly decided to
continue to work on studying the legal and economic aspects of the
proposed Fund. The forty-one sponsors of the previous draft resolution accepted this compromise, which was unanimously adopted by
the Assembly.[17]

At the next General Assembly, the Twelfth Session, India introduced a draft resolution, sponsored by eleven states, calling for the
establishment of the Special Fund by January 1, 1960. However, the
Netherlands alone of the more developed countries joined in cosponsoring the draft resolution. The United States made it clear that

it would not only vote against the draft but would refuse to participate in the work of the proposed preparatory commission to set up
the Fund.[18]

Although the less developed countries were united, it was clearly
impractical to go ahead with SUNFED as conceived, against the
opposition of the United States. There was a protracted negotiation
between a group of representatives of the less developed countries,
including India, Egypt, Mexico, and Yugoslavia, and representatives
of the United States. Finally, a compromise resolution was adopted
unanimously on December 14, 1957, whereby the nature of the
Special Fund was altered from an investment-providing institution to
one which would assist countries in assessing their own resources,
making surveys, and undertaking other "seed" activities to promote
the development of investment projects.[19]

Thus concluded the long negotiation during which the less developed countries, acting together, achieved not only partial success in
the tangible form of a United Nations Special Fund, but also the safeguarding of their position through a clause in the aforementioned resolution which read:

Decides that as and when the resources prospectively available are considered by the General Assembly to be sufficient to enter into the field of
capital development, principally the development of the economic and
social infrastructure of the less developed countries, the Assembly shall
review the scope and future activities of the Special Fund and take such
action as it may deem appropriate.[20]

Subsequently, enthusiasm for even the more limited version of the
Special Fund became so great that in 1963 105 member states of the
United Nations and its Specialized Agencies contributed to it. Of
these, over 75 countries would be generally accepted as falling within
the category of less developed countries. As many as 63 of them had
then received assistance from the Special Fund.[21]

Although the Cold War is less of a factor today than it was when
pressure for the Fund was originally applied, the fact that this institution still commands such wide support from the less developed countries vividly illustrates their preference for a multilateral United Nations institution to which they can turn for economic assistance. The
General Assembly, again under strong pressure from the increasing
number of less developed countries, has now embarked upon the task
of converting the Special Fund into a Capital Development Fund.

A draft statute for a United Nations Development Fund was drawn up by the special committee which had been appointed by a General Assembly Resolution of 1961. However, most of the highly developed countries find themselves in opposition to this project, much as they opposed the original concept of SUNFED. But the pressure is strong and in 1962 the Resolution in the General Assembly on continued study of the project was sponsored by 37 member states, all in the less developed category except for Denmark, the Netherlands, Norway, and Sweden.[22]

Meanwhile, by a resolution of the 1965 General Assembly, the operations of the Special Fund became merged with those of another United Nations body set up to aid developing countries, the Expanded Program of Technical Assistance. The merged operations are going forward under the new name of the United Nations Development Program.

Another important piece of evidence indicative of the general attitude of the less developed world is contained in the Declaration of the Belgrade Conference of Non-Aligned nations held in September 1961. The Declaration states:

The participants in the conference recommend the immediate establishment and operation of a United Nations Development Fund. . . .

The participating countries invite all the countries in the course of development to cooperate effectively in economic and commercial fields in order to face the policies of pressure in the economic sphere, as well as the harmful results which may be created by the economic blocs of the industrial countries.[23]

There could hardly be a more categorical statement of how the less developed countries feel in regard to negotiations with the more highly developed countries.

The idea of the importance of remaining free from economic domination was expressed by Jawaharlal Nehru in his inaugural address to the Third Session of the United Nations Economic Commission for Asia and the Far East on June 1, 1948. He said:

But a long period of foreign domination has made the countries of Asia very sensitive about anything which might lead to some visible or invisible form of domination. Therefore, I would beg of you to remember this and to fashion your programmes and policies so as to avoid anything savouring of the economic domination of one country by another.[24]

This is the attitude of most of the less developed countries, and it explains in great measure their strong preference for multilateral economic negotiations, and for such institutions as the United Nations Special Fund, now functioning as the United Nations Development

Program, in which there is no direct relationship between aid received and any one highly developed country.

No wonder, either, that in 1961–62, the African states which were first associated with the European Common Market jointly negotiated the pattern of their association. The sixteen African states attended the special session of the European Parliamentary Assembly held at Strasbourg from June 19 to June 24, 1961. Standing strongly together, they put up a determined fight for their demands. The *New York Times* reported that "The Africans won nearly every point they asked." [25] The *Manchester Guardian* was even more categorical. It stated, "The African countries have the running in Strasbourg and all the resolutions reflect their thinking rather than European thinking." [26]

Later, in 1962, there were protracted negotiations about the amount of aid which the European Common Market countries would give to the associated African states. Again, the African states, now numbering eighteen, negotiated hard, and the amount of aid agreed upon for the five years beginning June 1, 1963 was raised from the original offer of $780 million to $800 million. The final convention between the European Common Market and the eighteen African states was signed at Yaounde, capital of the Cameroun Republic, on July 20, 1963,[27] and records the considerable successes achieved by joint efforts on the part of the African states.

Thirty-two African states which met at Addis Ababa in May 1963 negotiated the Charter of the Organization of African Unity. This Charter mentioned the need for a joint stand in economic matters, and included in its purposes "Economic Cooperation, including transport and communications." The Charter was signed on May 25, 1963 by the heads of the 32 states.[28]

The position of the less developed countries was similarly strong at two recent United Nations conferences. One was not on economic development but was related to it, namely the 1963 United Nations Conference on the Application of Science and Technology for the Benefit of the Less Developed Areas. There was a double multilateralism expressed when the Conference considered the problems of industrial development. The official report reads:

Whatever the less developed countries can achieve by their own efforts, the more advanced nations must cooperate to the full in helping them to reach maturity, "to leap across the centuries." [29]

The report tells us that throughout the sessions of the Conference the following points were stressed:

An international organization should be set up within the United Nations to co-ordinate the efforts of the specialized agencies to find ways and means to encourage research on the application of science and technology in less developed countries.

More intensive international co-operation is essential to avoid widening the gap still further between more and less developed countries.[30]

The second United Nations conference to which we refer was more directly concerned with the issue before us—the Conference on Trade and Development held in the spring and early summer of 1964 at Geneva. The most striking fact of this Conference was the unified stand of 75 of the less developed countries from Africa, Asia, Europe, and Latin America. U Maung Maung, speaking for Burma on May 4, 1964, said, "the experience of the past sixteen years showed quite clearly that G.A.T.T. had worked essentially in a manner consistent with the commercial policy of the major trading nations." [31] Mr. Vohra of India made several proposals, including the following:

The policies, rules and procedures of G.A.T.T. should be amended . . . so that it would be better fitted to tackle the problems of world trade especially those of developing countries.[32]

Octavio Augusto Dias Carneiro of Brazil asked for "a new structure [in the field of world trade] capable of accelerating the economic development of developing countries." [33]

Mr. Shemirani of Iran proposed, among other points, "Consideration of international trade not solely as an instrument of profit, but also as an instrument of developing countries." [34]

Quotations such as these could be multiplied many times. The pressure all through the Conference was to set up an organization which would maximize trade opportunities for the less developed countries, protect them from the uneconomic and unprofitable exploitation of their raw material resources, and assist in the diversification and strengthening of their economies. The partial success achieved at the Conference was owed entirely to their unity of effort and purpose.

We find, therefore, in the post-World War II era, a strong tendency among the economically weaker countries to use existing forms of international organization to present the more highly developed countries with a united front. When their purposes are inadequately served through the existing institutions they unitedly demand the creation of new institutions or express their views in ad hoc meetings. This age of developing international organization is also an age of cooperation by the economically weak countries in their search for a fuller life for their peoples. An impetus has been given to such cooperation through the establishment under the aegis of the Economic and Social Council of regional economic commissions for Africa, Asia and the Far East, and Latin America.

Let us now examine the effect of economic weakness within countries on their attitude toward negotiation. Our suggestion is that economic weakness, if it is fairly persistent, will frequently encourage a country to focus its vision on some foreign situation, real or imaginary. In this way an emotional outlet for internal frustration is provided, while sometimes the essentially tedious path of peaceful negotiation is avoided.

Obviously, no leader would state or admit that because of internal problems he or his government is whipping up antipathy among his people against a neighboring state or a group of states. Therefore, in this instance we are obliged to go to secondary sources for evidence to test our hypothesis.

In Istanbul, early in September 1955, there was a serious outbreak of violence against the Greek population of the city, ostensibly on the Cyprus issue. The Government said it was Communists who had inspired the activity. However, the *New York Times* in attempting to analyze the situation stated: "Communist organizations have been rigorously suppressed for many years." [35] Michael L. Hoffman, the *Times* correspondent, went on to report:

For three successive years Turkey had undergone an inflation that, according to monetary experts, has amounted to nearly 30 per cent annually. The mob was particularly robust in destroying hardware and textiles, the prices of which, since they are mostly imported, reflect this inflation. Foreign observers believe economic distress explains to a great extent the violence of the outbreaks, whoever may have been responsible for organizing them.[36]

It is only fair to add that in the trial in 1960 of Adnan Menderes, Prime Minister of Turkey at the time of the disorder, and his Foreign Minister, Fotin Rustu Zorlu, no report was made public confirming or denying the theory of economic causes for the disturbance which took the form of focusing attention on the Greeks. However, economic difficulties including severe inflation had undoubtedly been a constant irritant to the Turkish people for some years, and it is very possible that economic frustrations converged to express themselves in an antisocial eruption among the populace while the unnegotiated situation with the Greeks acted as an instigating cause.

Portugal firmly holds on to over 800,000 square miles of colonial territory inhabited by more than twelve million people, not merely because it espouses a theory of colonialism which is obsolescent in the world of today. Theories have something to do with it, but certain obtrusive factors of an economic character inevitably fill much of the skyline when one views the broad situation. Portugal is about twice as poor per capita as the next poorest major Western European country. Its per capita income of $230 per annum is out of line with the Western standard of living. Both Angola and Mozambique, the two largest Portuguese colonial territories,[37] are of considerable economic value to Portugal. They are rich in minerals and in agricultural produce, and on the whole Portugal has jealously retained for itself much of the wealth of the colonies. A United Nations report observes:

The Special Committee on Territories under Portuguese administration has pointed out in its report that economic integration of the overseas territories has long been one of the main cornerstones of Portuguese policy. In 1961 legislation was enacted setting up the basis for a common market which was to come into effect in ten years.[38]

The Special Committee's report contains a number of statements relevant to our inquiry. The representative of Ethiopia on the Committee made remarks which are summarized in the report as follows:

. . . all the large estates are still in the hands of non-Africans as witness the statistical fact that the land cultivated by 6.5 million Africans was estimated at between 450,000 and 500,000 hectares, while that of non-Africans covered 1.5 million hectares. Labourers' wages were completely inadequate, and the Africans were still being exploited.[39]

The representative of Mali stated:

The existence of a system of forced labour had been confirmed by Mr. Marcelo Caetano, a former Portuguese Colonial Minister, and by such writers as Basil Davidson and John Gunther. Under agreements signed with South Africa and Southern Rhodesia, Portugal annually provided each of those countries with 100,000 African workers from Mozambique, for which it received $6 a head; in addition, South Africa guaranteed that 47.5 per cent of maritime traffic originating in the Johannesburg and Pretoria areas passed through the port of Lourenço Marques in Mozambique. A further example of economic exploitation of the African population was the use of the police to supervise work on the Mozambique cotton plantations.[40]

James Duffy, writing in *Foreign Affairs* in April 1961, made the following comments:

In recent years the two largest of the colonies, Angola and Mozambique, have come to occupy an important position in the nation's total economy . . . a large part of Portuguese exports, notably wine and cotton goods, is destined for Africa and increasing percentages of Portuguese African products—coffee, tea, sisal, copra, diamonds—go into the world market. The economic picture is not entirely favorable, but it has never been better, and without the African provinces continental Portugal's economy would suffer seriously.[41]

The same authority, writing in another publication, stated:

For the first time since the hey-day of the slave trade, Portuguese Africa, principally the two large colonies of Angola and Mozambique, is prosperous, contributing as much as 25 per cent of Portugal's national budget.[42]

These factors, embracing the continued economic weakness of Portugal itself and the exploitation of its colonial territories, would appear in very large measure to explain Portugal's posture regarding its colonies and its refusal to negotiate on the question of independence for them.

Let us turn to another part of the world where a strong economic urge stemming from a basic insufficiency would seem to promote strife rather than negotiation or even the observance of previously negotiated settlements. In 1962 a British expert on Vietnam, P. J. Honey, edited a book on North Vietnam, in which Nguyen Ngoc Bich, a leading representative of an important section of Vietnamese opinion, said:

Thus, in the final analysis, the success of the Five-Year Plan [of North Vietnam] will depend upon the problem of feeding the people of North Vietnam, a problem which cannot be easily resolved without increased supplies of rice from South Vietnam. . . .

. . . the war of subversion which has clearly been declared against Ngo Dinh Diem and the U.S.A. might well be understood as a struggle unleashed simply for the purpose of conquering rice. . . . It is because of the enormous economic benefits which will accrue to North Vietnam from national reunification that the DRV campaigns so vigorously in its favour. . . .

However, it is precisely because North Vietnam is fighting to secure rice that the war is, from the purely national point of view, a legitimate one.[43]

From the recent attitudes of the Peking Government, it would appear that Chinese foreign relations and postures have grown in truculence since 1959, when the Soviet Union started to withdraw its economic and technological assistance. The *New York Times* correspondent writing from Hong Kong on September 28, 1963 stated, "Peking has accused Moscow of 'tearing up' hundreds of agreements since their relations began to deteriorate and has attributed the present serious plight of the Chinese Communist economy to Soviet 'betrayal.' " [44]

Premier Chou En-lai painted, on the whole, an optimistic picture of Chinese economic conditions on October 13, 1963 when he gave his first comprehensive interview to a Western newsman since 1960. He was talking to Gerald Long, the General Manager of Reuters. Chou admitted that there had been three consecutive years of natural disasters which had affected the economy of China, but he added: "With our experience in the past years and our experience this year [1963] in dealing with partial natural calamities, we shall be better prepared to meet them." [45]

At a banquet in September 1963 on the occasion of the 14th anniversary of the founding of the People's Republic of China, Chou referred to "difficulties arising out of serious national calamities from 1959 through 1961." [46] These references by Premier Chou give some substance to the contention that economic difficulties were severe and chronic in China at the time. This period coincided with important movements of troops in the coastal area facing Formosa, truculence in relations with India, including the military activities in the fall of 1962, and a strong stance in Southeast Asia. It is perhaps permissible to draw the conclusion that although other factors have also been at work, there is a connection between economic deprivation in China and aggressiveness in its foreign postures; and in such postures it would be apposite to include the much more militant Chinese Communist support of national liberation movements, and its attitude on the dissemination of Communism in contrast to that of the Soviet Union, which emphasizes coexistence and peaceful competition with the Western world.

The hypothesis that chronic economic weakness might encourage a country—in this case major countries rather than small ones—to adopt militant postures, has not been so easy to establish because published primary sources are, obviously, not available. However, there is substantial evidence in support of it from secondary reports. Moreover, it is a general observation that economic discontent is often a base for an upsurge of militancy. Hitler's rise was assisted by the desperate economic plight of Germany after the Treaty of Versailles. A clearer example is that of Italy just before World War II. Mussolini's fascist build-up at home, and his military action in an attempt to recover Italy's lost African colonies, were the direct result of that country's desperate economic plight during the 1930s.

Because there is no single cause for militant attitudes, we shall formulate our next principles without reference to military action as an alternative to negotiation when a country is in economic difficulties. There is little doubt that economic weakness affects negotiating postures, and our principles therefore can shed light on the behavior of states in negotiation at certain phases of their development.

Economic weakness predisposes countries to engage in joint negotiations in economic situations or disputes to which those countries are party. It may, in the alternative, lead an economically weak state to seek simultaneous negotiations with two or more economically powerful states in competition with one another. However, offers of economic assistance by powerful states tend to result in direct bilateral negotiations which stand outside the general rule.

Chronic economic weakness, particularly in a large country, may cause the government of that country to elect to focus the attention of the people on imagined or real foreign threats or other international situations, to the neglect of attempts to alleviate such imagined or real threats or situations by the processes of international negotiation.

CHAPTER SIXTEEN

Economic Development and International Trade

ECONOMIC DEVELOPMENT and international negotiation are mutually supportive processes. Countries which seek to raise the standard of living of their people, unless they have reached a state of desperation in this endeavor or unless they feel their vital interests are involved, will desire peace and will therefore be disposed toward the negotiation of international disputes and other situations.

Another important relationship between economics and international negotiation is the effect of international trade on negotiating postures. A few countries are not primarily dependent on international trade. Others, such as the United Kingdom, have developed a tradition as international traders. A sharp alteration in trade patterns has occurred in the post-Industrial Revolution world. For example, if one goes back to the British trade statistics of about 1800, one finds a considerable import into Britain of manufactured goods, mainly textiles, from India. A hundred years later, after Britain had experienced the Industrial Revolution, its trade statistics show large exports of machine-manufactured textiles to India, a large import of raw cotton, and practically no import of manufactured textiles from that country. The export volume of the manufacturing nations has grown tremendously since 1800, and the value of the exports of the primary-product countries has not kept pace. Nevertheless, trade is of special significance to many of the less developed countries because through the exchange of their raw materials and semifinished goods for the capital goods of the more developed countries they hope to effect their own peaceful economic revolutions.

The basic concern of the newly liberated countries in Asia and Africa regarding the present low standard of living of their people has manifested itself in a number of ways. For example, one of the earliest thoughts expressed by the representative of India in addressing the United Nations General Assembly on the problem of disarmament negotiations was that part of the savings which would accrue to countries as a result of disarmament should be made available to finance development projects in the underdeveloped world. This view came to be widely supported, and as long ago as 1953, at its Eighth Session, the General Assembly adopted a resolution in which it formally declared that "Member States of the United Nations . . . stand ready to ask our peoples, when sufficient progress has been made in internationally supervised world-wide disarmament, to devote a portion of the savings achieved through such disarmament to an international fund, within the framework of the United Nations, to assist development and reconstruction in underdeveloped countries." [1]

Recently both the Economic and Social Council and the General Assembly have focused their attention more strongly on this possibility. An Economic and Social Council Resolution of August 2, 1963 concerned itself partly with the advantages which disarmament could have for economic and social programs in less developed parts of the world.[2]

The General Assembly itself negotiated and adopted carefully worded resolutions on this matter at its Seventeenth and Eighteenth Sessions.[3] The resolution of December 11, 1963 frankly states that the subject of diversion of additional funds to economic development has received an impetus from recent efforts in the field of disarmament. Its consideranda state:

Encouraged by the conclusion of the Treaty banning nuclear weapon tests in the atmosphere, in outer space, and under water,

Hopeful that further agreements will be reached which will lessen world tensions and lead ultimately to general and complete disarmament under effective international control, . . .

These two paragraphs of the Resolution make explicit the close interrelationship which the vast majority of United Nations members consider as existent between disarmament negotiations and development. The support of many member states for disarmament is related directly to their need of resources to raise their standards of living.

The resolution of December 11 underlines this point by expressing the hope that all governments will intensify their efforts to achieve general and complete disarmament, impelled by the desire to realize the benefits for mankind which had been set out in the form of a declaration in the relevant resolution of 1962.[4] That declaration is a striking affirmation of a belief in the betterment of human conditions. The 1962 resolution reads:

Declares that it firmly believes in the triumph of the principles of reason and justice, in the establishment of such conditions in the world as would forever banish wars from the life of human society, and replace the arms race, which consumes enormous resources of funds, by broad and fruitful co-operation among nations in bettering life on earth.[5]

Indeed, carried away by the hope that disarmament might now be around the corner, the resolution goes so far as to encourage the drawing up of development plans which might be accelerated by the application of funds released by disarmament. This part of the resolution is again worthy of noting in detail:

Invites the Secretary-General and the Goverments of developing countries to intensify their efforts to establish and implement soundly conceived projects and well-integrated development plans of a national and regional character, as indicated in General Assembly resolution 1708 (XVI) of 19 December 1961, the implementation of which may be accelerated at such time as additional resources are released following an agreement on general and complete disarmament under effective international control.[6]

Moreover, the resolution "solemnly urges" governments "to multiply their efforts for a prompt achievement of general and complete disarmament under effective international control." [7]

Here we have a two-layer effort in negotiation, directed toward a settlement of the primary issue of disarmament and toward getting a world consensus for the secondary issue, the use of funds which would be released by success in such negotiations. The obtaining of such a world consensus has in itself been a long-drawn-out negotiation at the United Nations. There has been reluctance and hesitancy on the part of the great powers to tie savings which might result from disarmament directly to efforts to raise standards of living in the vast underdeveloped areas of the world.

In a nationwide television and radio broadcast from Washington, D.C., on December 18, 1956, Jawaharlal Nehru stated:

India has experienced both good and ill, but throughout her chequered history she has remembered the message of peace and tolerance. . . . We are now engaged in a gigantic and exciting task of achieving rapid and large-scale economic development of our country.[8]

Other underdeveloped countries have expressed their concern for the settlement of present-day conflicts by one or another of the various procedures offered by international negotiation, in order that economic development might progress rapidly. The Charter of the United Arab Republic proclaimed by the National Congress of that country on June 20, 1962 contains the following statements:

The sincerity of their call for peace arises from their dire need for it. Peace is the sure guarantee of their ability to pursue their sacred struggle, for the sake of development. . . . Again, it comprises the propagation of the idea of transferring the huge funds spent on the manufacture of nuclear weapons to the service of life, instead of menacing and jeopardizing it.[9]

Among the highly developed countries, Sweden is a foremost example of a state which has resolutely negotiated for and maintained an unbroken dissociation from international conflict for a century and a half. In this context of peace the prosperity of Sweden has been built. Swedish diplomats—peacemakers and peacekeepers—are prominent at the headquarters of the United Nations, in the field wherever trouble threatens, and at disarmament negotiations in Geneva. Prime Minister Nehru was struck by the prosperity and peace which reign in Sweden, and he referred to those factors in an address he made at a banquet in New Delhi on December 19, 1959 in honor of Mr. Tage Erlander, the Swedish Prime Minister. He said:

You have built up a society which is free, democratic, progressive, and which has ensured to its people a high standard of living and social security. . . . You have been free from war for 150 years. As a result of that and of other qualities, you have built up Sweden as she is today.[10]

The intense desire of the underdeveloped world for the concurrence of disarmament and development is reflected in the records of their conferences. At the Bandung Conference, the participants declared on April 24, 1955:

All states should cooperate especially through the United Nations in bringing about the reduction of armaments and the elimination of nuclear weapons under effective international control. In this way international peace can be promoted and nuclear energy may be used exclusively for peaceful purposes. This would help answer the needs, particularly of Asia and Africa, for what they urgently require are social progress and better standards of life in larger freedom.[11]

Again, the declaration issued at Belgrade by the heads of non-aligned governments on September 6, 1961 included this plea:

The participants in the conference urge the great powers to sign without further delay a treaty for general and complete disarmament to save mankind from the scourge of war and to release energy and resources, now being spent on armaments, for the peaceful economic and social development of all mankind.[12]

The declaration of the Belgrade Conference immediately went on to suggest that the nonaligned countries should be represented at future negotiations. The train of thought was that those countries would give added emphasis to the negotiations because of the close connection between their successs and the economic and social betterment of a large number of human beings.

Both the superpowers concede that the successful negotiation of disarmament would make large resources available for economic development. The Foreign Ministers of the United States and the Soviet Union, in their opening remarks to the Eighteen-Nation Committee on Disarmament Conference at Geneva, expressed this view. Secretary of State Dean Rusk said in his opening statement on March 16, 1962:

Our objective, therefore, is clear enough. We must eliminate the instruments of destruction. . . . In so doing . . . we can lift the burden of the arms race and thus increase our capacity to raise living standards everywhere.[13]

Foreign Minister Andrei Gromyko turned some striking phrases in developing the same idea in his opening statement on the same date:

What electric computer can calculate how many people could have been saved from hunger and disease if but a part of the funds expended on armaments had been diverted to the improvement of the living conditions in those countries, which, through no fault of their own, lag many decades, or even centuries behind the present-day levels of technology, education and medicine? [14]

President Kennedy went further than acknowledging that disarmament would assist in raising living standards in less developed countries. In disposing of the suggestion that disarmament might deal a very severe blow to the economy of the United States, he said at a news conference on February 7, 1962:

We could never have a change comparable to the change we had in 1954 when we went from a tremendously high expenditure, at a time when our gross national product was far less than it is today, into a bitterly sharp dive, and had three very prosperous years of full employment, so that would be the last reason, I think, that we would benefit. We can do so many more useful things from a social point of view if we had the funds that were available, so I don't think that's any argument against disarmament.[15]

Premier Khrushchev too, indicated that he felt the urge to swing away from tremendous financial outlays on armament so that resources could be released for the benefit of the people and the raising of their standard of living. In a radio broadcast from Moscow, March 16, 1962, he said:

Comrades, we desire to solve the disarmament problem because we understand well what a heavy burden is shouldered by the peoples through the tremendous expenditures on armaments and to what terrible consequences the armaments race can lead. With what joy the peoples would breathe if the resources now spent on the manufacture of destructive weapons would be used for raising the material well-being of people, the development of science and culture, and peaceful constructive work! [16]

From statements such as these it would appear that there is a strong and widespread predisposition toward negotiation so that all the peoples of the world should attain or maintain a high standard of living.

Is there a connection between the need of countries for international trade and their disposition toward negotiation?

The importance of maintaining its trade relations has been a very real factor in the case of the United Kingdom; so great that when Winston Churchill made his perilous journey across the Atlantic at the height of World War II to meet his great ally, President Franklin D. Roosevelt, and the two leaders inscribed the Atlantic Charter, Churchill wrote into that expression of hope for peace with justice:

Fourth, they will endeavour, with due respect for their existing obligations, to further the enjoyment of all States, great or small, victor or vanquished, of access, on equal terms, to the trade and to the raw materials of the world which are needed for their economic prosperity.[17]

When Britain did engage in what might have become a major post-World War II military conflict, it did so to protect its trade routes. It is difficult to appreciate the strong feeling which was aroused by the decision of Egypt to nationalize the Suez Canal Company, a feeling based on a long history of economic and political patterns. In actual fact the nationalization of the Suez Canal Company has left unchanged the traditional sea lanes, but it was impossible for most Englishmen to anticipate this in the summer of 1956.

On October 30, Prime Minister Anthony Eden sent President Eisenhower a telegram in which he said:

We have earnestly deliberated what we should do in this serious situation. We cannot afford to see the canal closed to or lose the shipping which is daily on passage through it. We have a responsibility for the people in these ships. We feel that decisive action should be taken at once to stop hostilities.[18]

It might be held that this incident shows that a nation which is dependent upon trade will be disposed to go to war in an international situation that threatens its trade routes. However, this statement would be a gross oversimplification.

First, the British did try to arrive at a peaceful and negotiated settlement of the situation. They called a conference in August 1956 at London to try to work out a proposal for the future administration of the Canal. This conference was not able to come to a consensus. Thereafter, a second conference was called at London. And following that conference there were discussions at the Security Council, to which we have referred in another context. The period from August to October 1956 was, in fact, one of intensive diplomatic and negotiational activity.

Second, the British maintained that they were entering the Suez not to fight Egypt but to keep Egyptian and Israeli forces from warring in that area, so that the Canal should remain open. Even when the Security Council convened to deal with the situation, Anthony Eden apparently still thought that Britain aided by France could have succeeded in this self-given mission. Eden is highly critical of Henry Cabot Lodge for the speed with which he pressed to a vote in the Security Council the United States resolution, on the night of October 30, 1958. This was the resolution which led Britain to use the veto at the United Nations for the first time.[19]

In regard to the events of that tense and dramatic night and the following day, Anthony Eden implicates the present writer. Referring to the fact that it was Yugoslavia, then a member of the Security Council, which proposed to take the Suez issue to an emergency special session of the General Assembly, Anthony Eden holds that it was the Indian representative (myself) who urged the move on Ambassador Joza Brilej, the Yugoslav representative on the Council. He has said:

The next move, by the Yugoslav delegation, was fateful in its consequences. Prompted from the sidelines by the Indian representative, Yugoslavia sought to transfer the dispute from the Security Council to a special session of the General Assembly, under the procedure known as "Uniting for Peace," originally devised at the time of the Korean conflict.[20]

While it is true that my friend, Joza Brilej, and I were in close and constant communication at the time, Yugoslavia itself was responsible for the action, although it received encouragement from others, including some of the friends or allies of the United Kingdom, to invoke the "Uniting for Peace" resolution.

As an elaboration of negotiating procedures at the United Nations, this was a most important step, because it led to a vote by the Soviet Union in favor of the Yugoslav proposal. (The United States also voted in favor, and against her French and British allies.) This meant that the Soviet Union, which had hitherto strenuously opposed the "Uniting for Peace" resolution as being *ultra vires* of the Charter, had given its assent to activating just that crucial part of the resolution which it had most strongly opposed. By this vote, the Soviet Union assented to the principle that issues of peace and security may be transferred from the Security Council to the General Assembly in certain circumstances. And, in the particular case concerned, the Council had patently been dealing with a matter that fell within the purview of Chapter VII of the Charter, which concerns action to be taken to deal with aggression.

Hostilities did break out, and the United Kingdom was engaged in them, but the conflict of views became so sharp that Anthony Eden eventually had to resign as Prime Minister. The decision to attack Egypt was not in keeping with many other moves which the British have made in the post-World War II era. It did not have great popular support at home, and was widely recognized abroad as an exception to Britain's usual action. Besides, as far as the United Kingdom was concerned, it later became known that the decision to resort to arms was made by a sick man. One therefore cannot maintain, on the basis of the Suez case, that trading nations quickly take up arms to defend their trading arrangements. At most, the case shows that when vital trading interests become involved, the likelihood of negotiation may be lessened but does not cease to exist.

During the succeeding phases of United Nations negotiation on the Suez issue, the members of the United Nations addressed themselves to the question of obtaining the quick clearance of the Canal because their trade was suffering and would continue to suffer as long as it remained blocked by the ships which had been sunk. In order to spur the withdrawal of the British and French forces from the Suez area, a series of resolutions was adopted at the General Assembly. The debate at the commencement of the Eleventh Session largely focused on this issue. The late Prime Minister of Ceylon, S. W. R. D. Bandaranaike, said:

There is another important thing, of course: the early clearing of the Suez Canal. This is very important to all of us, particularly to my country. Most of the trade of Ceylon—75 per cent of it—passes through the Suez Canal. . . . it is important that the Suez Canal be cleared as early as possible.[21]

Gregoire Cassimatis of Greece said on November 24, 1956:

The Canal has been blocked, and not only Europe, not only the countries of the eastern Mediterranean, but virtually all countries are beginning to suffer the effects of these events. Fuel shortages are beginning to be felt, and the situation is anything but favourable to that progress and well-being of humanity which is one of the fundamental objects of our Organization.[22]

Paul-Henri Spaak, the Foreign Minister of Belgium, sought to amend an Asian-African resolution on the withdrawal of the forces of the United Kingdom and France. Nevertheless, he too wanted prompt withdrawal and vigorous action by the United Nations. He urged the following:

Surely we have a common interest, Egyptians as well as British and French, Europeans as well as Africans and Asians, in beginning as soon as possible to clear and open up the Canal. Surely, this is a positive item of our policy.[23]

Mr. Spaak was speaking on behalf of the Benelux group of countries, Belgium, the Netherlands, and Luxembourg. He was representing a very important trading complex.

Foreign Minister Halvard Lange of Norway, a country with a very large mercantile marine and one of the most important users of the Canal, struck a new note in favor of a negotiated settlement to ensure that the Canal would be usable. He said:

Those of us who are important users of the Suez Canal—and, as a user, my country comes second, cannot rest content until a solution of these problems has been worked out on the basis of the six principles (S/3675) agreed upon by the Security Council at its 743rd meeting on 13 October 1956.

There is urgent need for the United Nations not only to see to it that the Canal is cleared with the utmost speed possible, but also to exercise its good offices with a view to bringing about direct negotiations between Egypt and the principal user nations on the future regime of the Canal.[24]

The representative of Ethiopia, whose geographical situation makes it dependent on the Canal, also urged a speedy settlement. Ambassador Yilma Deressa's words were:

Ethiopia warmly applauds the understanding reached with the Egyptian Foreign Minister for the reopening of the Canal, since it can well be questioned whether the national economy of any Member of the United Nations, still less that of any Member of the continent of Africa—where the Canal after all is situated—stands to lose more than the national economy of Ethiopia, almost all of whose exports pass through the Canal.[25]

The dependence of many countries on the considerable volume of international trade which flowed through the Canal was one of the major factors against the continuance of armed conflict in the Suez area. It stimulated the United Nations' efforts to clear the Canal and to secure peace.

The term "dependence on international trade" must be interpreted broadly, to include not only the great trading countries of the world but those countries which could not meet their basic requirements for social and economic development without trade. Although the total trade of the Republic of the Ivory Coast is extremely small compared with that of Belgium, nevertheless the Ivory Coast is dependent upon international trade because without it that country would be unable to earn the foreign exchange necessary for the import of capital goods required to diversify its economy, to produce employment, and to stimulate the technological revolution essential to the struggle for better living conditions. Dependence, therefore, is to be measured not simply by the volume of trade, but by its nature. The General Assembly resolution at the Seventeenth Session regarding arrangements for a world conference on trade and development highlighted this thought. One of its paragraphs read:

Convinced that the promotion of higher rates of economic growth throughout the world and the evolution of a new and more appropriate pattern of international trade will require the adoption of the institutional framework for international co-operation in the field of trade.[26]

Among the significant motives that led to decisions in the General Assembly and the Economic and Social Council to convene a world trade conference was the need to negotiate those terms of trade which adversely affected the exporters of primary products. This thought, too, is contained in the resolution we have just cited. Another need was to eliminate obstacles and discriminatory practices in world trade, and to secure diversification of the exports of the developing countries.[27]

A complex of many factors—all aspects of the urge to negotiate about the various elements in international trade—was brought to a focus in the widespread demand of the underdeveloped countries for a United Nations Conference on Trade and Development. This was a multilateral effort of countries to avoid disputes by creating a forum for what turned out to be a massive international trade negotiation. Before that Conference met, the General Assembly adopted its final resolution on the subject on November 11, 1963.[28] To this resolution was attached a declaration made at the Eighteenth Session by 75 developing countries, which concluded with an expression of hope regarding the type of negotiations to be undertaken at the Trade Conference. It read:

The developing countries expect that the Conference will offer an opportunity for the manifestation, in the field of trade and development, of the same political will that was responsible for the Charter of the United Nations signed at San Francisco and the creation of the Organization. They are confident that, in this spirit, the decisions of the Conference will bring about fuller international co-operation and that greater progress can be made towards the attainment of collective economic security. International trade will thus become a strong guarantee of world peace and the Conference will be a landmark in the fulfillment of the Charter.[29]

At the Conference, the connection between the development of international trade and the maintenance of international peace was repeated in statement after statement. One typical statement was summarized in the official records of the Conference as follows:

Mr. Goenka (India) said that his delegation attached the utmost importance to the work of the Second Committee, the establishment of which was based on a clear recognition of the need for rapid expansion in the exports of manufactured and semi-manufactured goods from developing countries to bring about the required structural changes in their economies. A new pattern of international co-operation in trade and development assistance had to emerge, not only in the interest of mutual trade but also in the interest of peaceful coexistence.[30]

The United Nations Conference on Trade and Development adopted its Final Act on June 15, 1964, a massive and important document. Certain striking findings were summed up in the preamble and unanimously accepted:

The share of the developing countries in world exports declined steadily from nearly one-third in 1950 to only slightly more than one-fifth in 1962. . . .

The developing countries' surplus of exports over imports in 1950 became a deficit in 1962 of $2.3 billion. . . .

According to United Nations Secretariat estimates, this gap [between the import requirements of developing countries and their export earnings] could be of the order of $20 billion a year in 1970. . . .[31]

The Final Act included fifteen general and twelve special principles, which were adopted by overwhelming majorities. Their purpose was to achieve broad agreement on measures to deal with the problems that would result from action on the *Findings* of the Conference. Moreover, the principles adopted are based on the recognition, recorded in the Final Act, "that universal peace and prosperity are closely linked."

The disposition to seek trade negotiations, and economic negotiations generally, is not confined to the less developed countries. The penchant of the United Kingdom in this regard has often been expressed, as on the occasion of the drawing up of the Atlantic Charter, by a solemn reiteration of the importance of trade, with the implication that peace must be preserved—that is, issues must be negotiated rather than permitted to become a ground for armed conflict. Churchill was consistent in this endeavor. In the Joint Declaration issued by President Eisenhower and Prime Minister Churchill on June 29, 1954, the two leaders stated: ". . . we will seek every means of promoting the fuller and freer interchange among us [friendly countries] of goods and services which will benefit all participants." [32]

Two more recent developments in relations between countries on the two sides of the great divide between East and West might be observed. The first concerns the attitude of the main trading countries in Europe to the general question of relations with the Soviet Union. Although those countries do not yet have a large trade with the Soviet Union and its Eastern European allies—in 1962 and 1963 it amounted to no more than 3 to 4 percent of imports and exports—there seems to be a strong desire in many of them for more relaxed relations so as to permit expansion of trade, which is needed for the continued prosperity of Western Europe. Referring to the new role of

Britain in the world, Prime Minister Alec Douglas-Home told the House of Commons on June 17, 1964: "Britain has had a crucial role in lessening East-West conflict and a crucial role in averting conflict between North and South, between the developed and undeveloped countries." [33]

The United States, farther removed from the Communist countries, more prosperous than the countries of Europe, and not as dependent on trade expansion as is most of Europe, has for years held that terms of credit to the Soviet Union and other Communist countries should be restricted to five years. Longer credits amount to aid, in the United States' view.[34] This contention had been frequently discussed among other significant trading countries, yet by mid-1964 there was a marked tendency on the part of many countries to break with the United States' position.

On September 7, 1964, the British overstepped the accepted guidelines in trading relations with the Soviets by advancing a very substantial amount of credit (more than $67 million) for a period as long as fifteen years to enable them to purchase in Britain a large polyester fiber plant.[35] Edward du Cann, the United Kingdom Minister of State for the Board of Trade, signed the export credit guarantee, and gave figures to show that the United Kingdom-Soviet trade was steadily increasing. The official position was confirmed by Paul Chambers, Chairman of Imperial Chemical Industries, who also expressed the view that the Soviet Union had become a fast-growing market of great potential for the chemical industry.[36]

The next day, September 8, Robert J. McCloskey, the United States State Department spokesman, said: "We disapprove of granting long-range credits to Communist countries and therefore we regret the action taken by the British." [37] But the British have been undeterred by the reaction of the State Department to this transaction.[38]

It was reported from Paris on September 14, 1964 that the United States was still striving to discourage further long-term credits to the Soviet Union and its allies. But the same message reported that "France is chafing at this restraint in view of longer term credits being offered by Britain." [39] The French attitude was implicit in President de Gaulle's New Year's message to France on January 1, 1964. He stated:

. . . we must envisage the day . . . when, perhaps in Warsaw, in Prague, in Pankow, in Budapest, in Bucharest, in Sofia, in Belgrade, in Tirana, in Moscow, the Communist totalitarian regime, which still succeeds in constraining confined peoples, will gradually come to an evolution compatible with our own transformation. Then there should be open to Europe as a whole prospects in keeping with its resources and its capacities.[40]

On the other side of the world, Japan was also breaking loose from the constraints imposed by the five-year rule with respect to credits to the Communist countries. In September 1964, Premier Khrushchev told a Japanese delegation that Moscow appreciated Japan's granting of long-term credits to the Soviet Union. This was an acknowledgment of recently granted eight-year Japanese credits on sales to the Soviets.[41]

It is well known that a number of countries—including Japan—have initiated agreements with the Soviet Union and offered inducements of a financial character to that country for an increase of trade. The desire of industrialists and governments to be assured of returns on capital they have already invested will be a factor predisposing many countries toward negotiated settlements with the Soviet Union so as to lessen the chances of armed conflict.

There is also a new trend in negotiations by the Federal Republic of Germany, another front-rank trading country. Impelled by its need or desire for increased trade, it has recently negotiated new types of agreements with the countries of Eastern Europe. In March 1963, Poland and the Federal Republic concluded negotiations for arrangements for three years, running to the end of 1966, which enabled Germany to open a commercial mission in Warsaw to provide for increased trade between the two countries.[42] A similar agreement was reached with Hungary in November 1963.[43]

In September 1964, the Federal Republic stepped up its policy of conciliation, that is, of negotiation, toward the Communist East. A team left for Czechoslovakia at that time to talk about an exchange of trade missions between the two countries. A little earlier Secretary of State Rolf Lahr had gone to Yugoslavia for talks which embraced political and trade matters.

The Federal Republic of Germany is, thus, taking steps which involve an element of political compromise in its relations with states that recognize the German Democratic Republic, in order to ensure its own position as an important trader in the world.

Our analysis of the relationship between trade and development on the one hand, and negotiation on the other, would suggest the following principles:

The urge of a government or a people toward, or their commitment to, the attainment or the maintenance of high living standards, tends to predispose that country to negotiate international situations and disputes.

The greater the degree of dependence of a country on international trade, the more will it be disposed to resolve international disputes or situations through negotiation, particularly if such disputes or situations might lead to conflict which would impede the flow of international trade of interest to it; and the more will it take advantage of any relaxation of the international situation, obtained through negotiation, so as to stimulate the development of its trade.

CHAPTER SEVENTEEN

Two Underlying Inhibitory Factors

WE HAVE DEALT with some elements of the influence of power on international negotiation, but we have yet to consider the effects on the negotiating postures of relatively less powerful countries of the existence in our era of magnetic centers of great power which have created systems of alliances. By adhering to one alliance or another, a less powerful state can bolster its own negotiating position.

Why is it, for example, that the Government of East Germany is able to insist on its own terms, or the terms of its allies, as a basis for significant political negotiations with the considerably larger part of Germany which is known as the Federal Republic? Why is it, again, that North and South Korea are so strongly inhibited in the matter of significant negotiations between themselves? No single cause will, of course, provide a full answer to these and similar questions. However, the fact that both Germanies and both Koreas are linked by systems of alliance to extremely powerful blocs is one of the root causes that inhibit their negotiation. Such inhibition occurs not only in the case of divided countries, for the same consideration applies between Cambodia and Vietnam and between Pakistan and India (although in both cases the element of division is still perhaps a background factor), or between Indonesia and Malaysia. When a state feels it can count on the backing of another very powerful state, it tends not to be forthcoming in negotiating a dispute unless it can be sure of the support of its backer for the particular position it chooses to adopt.

The use of force, or a too-great readiness to use force, are of course not compatible with negotiation. Blatant threats to resort to force normally remove an issue from the sphere of negotiation to that of conflict. Certain countries in certain phases of their development tend to be more aggressively postured than others. For example, states which consider themselves to be on the advancing tide of history or among the "new emerging forces" will often be inhibited by these postures in the matter of peaceful settlements, which is to say that they will be inhibited in regard to negotiation.

In the case of the two Germanies we have recently seen instances in which East Germany has been willing to negotiate with West Germany on minor issues such as passes for West Berliners who wish to visit East Berlin, and on trade matters. Indeed, East Germany seems willing to negotiate on a number of issues, provided such negotiations do not challenge its existence. When it comes to the issue of possible unification of Germany, then its terms stiffen and, in consequence, its attitude becomes significantly different. The basic reason for this change of gear is to be found in the support on which it can count from the Soviet Union.

This was strikingly displayed in 1955 at the Geneva Conferences, first of Heads of State and then of Foreign Ministers, which attempted to negotiate the German issue. The idea of unification was not at first dismissed by the leaders of the Soviet Union. Their proposals of July 20, 1955, presented at the negotiations among the Heads of State and Government, included the following:

Pending the formation of a united, peace-loving, democratic German state, the German Democratic Republic and the German Federal Republic may be parties to the Treaty [a General European Treaty on Collective Security] enjoying equal rights with other parties thereto. It is understood that after the unification of Germany the united German State may be a party to the Treaty under general provisions hereof.[1]

When the Conference ended, the Heads of State and Government gave a directive to their Foreign Ministers in which they "agreed that the settlement of the German question and the re-unification of Germany by means of free elections shall be carried out in conformity with the national interests of the German people and the interests of European security." [2]

In spite of this clear directive, when it came to the Foreign Ministers' meeting later in 1955, no progress was made toward reunification. Neither East Germany nor its strong supporter, the Soviet Union, was agreeable to over-all elections in the country. They were, however, prepared for almost any other kind of negotiation between the two parts of Germany, for such negotiations would have further established the existence as a state of the German Democratic Republic. We shall return a little later to the attitude of West Germany toward such a possibility.

At the Vienna meeting in June 1961 between President Kennedy and Premier Khrushchev, the "most somber talks were on the subject of Germany and Berlin," to use President Kennedy's words.[3] On the subject of Germany, the Soviet Union presented an aide memoire dated June 4, 1961 on the question of a separate peace treaty between the Soviet Union and East Germany, and on negotiation between the two parts of Germany.

On June 11, 1961 Chancellor Adenauer twice brought up this matter in public speeches. Addressing a rally at Hanover, he ruled out negotiations between West and East Germany, as had been proposed in the Soviet aide memoire. He rejected this proposal again on the same day in a speech at Bamberg, during which he said that the Soviet memorandum showed Moscow's major interest to be the "perpetuation" of Soviet postwar conquest in Central Europe. On the same day, Mayor Willy Brandt of West Berlin supported Chancellor Adenauer's stand against negotiations with East Germany. His reason was that the East German regime was "supported by foreign bayonets [which] would represent Moscow's rather than Germany's interests in any negotiation." [4]

Chancellor Adenauer made fairly explicit the basic reason for his capacity to reject so firmly negotiations on any but his own terms. In his speech at Bamberg he said, "The West can decide on the next steps. President Kennedy put the West's case more clearly than ever at Vienna and the Soviet Union knows exactly what to expect." [5]

Clearly, Adenauer was relying heavily on the strength of the West, mainly of the United States. Without such strength his attitude toward the suggested negotiations might well have been different. Of course, as we have seen, East Germany too rejected negotiation except on its own terms, largely because of support from the Soviet Union.

It would be rash to conclude that if neither of the two German states could count on support from the outside, and if both states were effectively prevented from a resort to force, they would necessarily negotiate successfully. All we can say is that their present positions are extremely rigid and hardly conducive toward negotiation, and that events in each state have shown a continuance of dependence on outside support.

In a national foreign policy statement in November 29, 1962 before the Bundestag at Bonn, Chancellor Adenauer again rejected the idea of negotiation with East Germany, and strongly opposed the conclusion of a separate peace treaty between the Soviet Union and the German Democratic Republic. He said this would be "not a separate, but a separation treaty." [6] Chancellor Adenauer went on to say, ". . . my recent conversations with the President of the United States . . . have led to a unanimity of views on the essential problems." [7] Again, he was virtually telling his parliamentarians that there was strong backing for his position of rejection of feelers from the other side.

In the same important speech before the Bundestag on November 29, 1961, another very significant issue was raised by Chancellor Adenauer which indicated a new facet of rigidity in regard to possible negotiations. He was speaking on a subject which had periodically cropped up in regard to the European situation since 1955, that of regional security. In that year, 1955, at the Summit Conference at Geneva, Prime Minister Anthony Eden proposed a certain degree of disengagement in Central Europe. He said "if we could start on these lines we should have a chance of providing a constructive and encouraging plan to insure peace for Europe. These ideas would give real security: and it is for the lack of that security that Germany is kept divided today." [8] Later the proposal reappeared in various forms, including the Rapacki Plan, which was first put forward by the Polish Foreign Minister in his intervention in the general debate of the Twelfth Session of the United Nations General Assembly on October 2, 1957.

By the end of 1961, the Federal Republic of Germany had re-emerged as a military power of consequence and a major partner in the NATO alliance. Although now more confident of his strength, Chancellor Adenauer, in leading into his views on regional security arrangements, expressed deep apprehension regarding Premier Khrushchev's plans for a separate peace treaty with East Germany. In referring to Khrushchev's motives he said:

Khrushchev hopes that a recognition in any form of the Soviet zone [East Germany] will lead to a disintegration of the alliances between the Federal Republic and her partners and at the same time he tries to impose upon the Federal Republic an inferior status within the alliance as a means toward his aim of isolating the Federal Republic. [9]

While these words would appear to indicate that Adenauer was fearful lest the isolation of West Germany become a reality, he was well aware that his partners would not permit such isolation, for he went on to say: "The Federal government fully concurs in . . . President Kennedy's statement that there are three vital issues in Berlin which the United States is prepared to defend." [10]

Clearly, in these issues so vital to Berlin and to Germany, Adenauer was sure of the firm support of his major ally, the United States. It was this assurance which undoubtedly enabled him to state almost immediately thereafter, in his speech of November 29, 1962, that "we reject all regional security measures in Europe which are said to serve as stepping stones to an agreement on general disarmament." [11]

Here, then, is a striking rigidity which rules out negotiations on regional security measures in Europe such as disengagement, because the West Germans presumably feel that arrangements of this type would tend to isolate Germany from the West and thereby perhaps open the door to unforeseeable developments. The rigidity of East Germany is at least equally apparent. The behavior of both German states shows to what extent a junior partner in an alliance, sure of support from its allies, can be antipathetic toward the possibilities of negotiation.

The knowledge that the Soviet Union has supported India on the Kashmir issue has undoubtedly assisted India to maintain a certain position regarding possible negotiations to resolve the situation. Similarly, at any rate in India, the feeling is very strong that Pakistan has been recalcitrant and difficult over the Kashmir issue because of assurance of the support of the United States and other powerful Western countries. Indeed, Indian representatives at the United Nations have, on various occasions, been given to understand by Western representatives during discussions in the Security Council on Kashmir that the Western powers would have to vote with their ally, Pakistan. More recently, when Pakistan, although in a measure supported in its efforts at the United Nations by the West, felt the need for even greater support and strengthened its ties with China, its Foreign Minister, Zulfikar Ali Bhutto, stated on July 17, 1963 in the Pakistan National Assembly that an "attack from India on Pakistan today is no longer confined to the security and territorial integrity of Pakistan [but] involves the territorial integrity and security of the largest state in Asia." [12] In India it is felt that this alliance with China increases Pakistan's intransigence in regard to negotiations on Kashmir and other issues.

One might also point to the bolstering effect of the Soviet Union's support for Indonesia in the latter's policy vis-à-vis Malaysia. Referring to this support, a spokesman of the Foreign Ministry, Ganis Harsono, stated at Jakarta on September 18, 1964 that "the Indonesian people and Government are grateful for the sincere support rendered by the Soviet Union in the United Nations to oppose new colonial activities." [13]

Another instance is the case of Cambodia. That small country certainly exists in an enormously difficult context. Thailand has had longstanding disputes with Cambodia, and there have been raids over the Cambodian frontier line by armed groups from South Vietnam. To complicate the situation further, it is also contended that Cambodian territory is being used as "a passageway, a source of supply, and a sanctuary from counter-attack by the forces of South Vietnam." [14]

Prince Norodom Sihanouk has arranged to obtain military assistance from Peking. The Prince himself, speaking of this arrangement at Peking early in October 1964, referred to it as "new and most important." He added: "We [Cambodia and China], are indeed not only friends but brothers in arms." Sihanouk was also quoted as saying: "The solidarity between us is unbreakable. United States imperialism can never separate Cambodia from China. We firmly oppose United States imperialism." [15]

Here then we see Cambodia joining an important power center, and the almost inevitable concomitant of such a step seems to be a strong and somewhat bellicose attitude toward another power center, in this case the United States. A hardening of Cambodia's attitude toward negotiation was evident when Prince Sihanouk did not attend the Second Conference of Heads of State or Government of Non-Aligned Countries at Cairo in October 1964. There is little doubt that the promise of Chinese assistance will reinforce Cambodia's position in her dispute with South Vietnam and Thailand, and will probably make negotiation of those disputes less feasible. Indeed, Sihanouk's reluctance to join in a Geneva-type conference on Cambodia which he himself had advocated and asked for in April and May 1965 bears this out.

On the other side of the picture is the reluctance of South Vietnam to negotiate with Cambodia in 1963 and in the early part of 1964. The *London Economist* in its issue of February 23, 1963 made the following comment:

. . . Prince Sihanouk has been saying for months that his borders are under threat from the Siamese and Vietnamese. Since both are allied with the United States, the Cambodian head of state has tried, in his view unsuccessfully, to get the Americans to exercise a restraining hand on them. Last summer the British and Americans cold shouldered the Prince's proposal that the fourteen nations that had taken part in the Geneva conference on Laos should meet again and guarantee Cambodia's neutrality.

Cambodia continued to press for a conference to establish its neutrality. The *New York Times* reported from Saigon on December 4, 1963:

In an interview this morning, General Minh questioned the value of the proposed international conference on Cambodian neutrality and suggested that Cambodia's international problems could be better resolved through "neighbourly relations" with Thailand and South Vietnam.

It appeared that the South Vietnamese attitude was broadly in line with that of its powerful ally, the United States.

It is implicit in our argument that if a country involved in an international dispute or situation succeeds in obtaining the support of a powerful state or bloc of states, then that country feels less fearful that it might be overwhelmed in negotiations concerning the dispute. The case of Cyprus in 1964 is relevant.

The present status of Cyprus is determined by international treaty which gives Greece, Turkey, and the United Kingdom certain rights vis-à-vis Cyprus. Discussions were held in the summer of 1964 in which consideration was given by those countries, with the encouragement of their friends, to the possibility of a partition of Cyprus and the inclusion of the larger area of Cyprus in the Kingdom of Greece, the smaller area going to Turkey. Alternatively, consideration was given to making a small neighboring island available for the Turkish Cypriots, and letting all of Cyprus (excluding agreed military bases for the United Kingdom and perhaps Turkey) become part of Greece. Either of these two alternatives would have meant the end of Cyprus as a sovereign state. Consequently, the Foreign Minister of Cyprus, Spyros Kyprianou, accompanied by the Commerce Minister, visited Moscow at the end of September 1964 with a view to obtaining assurances of military aid from the Soviet Union in support of the stand of the Government of Cyprus, which was determined to maintain its separate statehood. The visit to the Soviet Union resulted in the issue of a joint Cyprus-Soviet communiqué at Moscow, which included the following statement:

Agreement was reached on practical measures of assistance that the Soviet Union will render to the Republic of Cyprus for safeguarding her freedom and territorial integrity.[16]

The communiqué also contained mention of Soviet support for the Cyprus government against "aggressive actions and intrigues of certain N.A.T.O. countries aimed at imposing upon Cyprus political solutions unacceptable to the people." [17]

The effect of this agreement between Cyprus and the Soviet Union is seen in a statement made by Foreign Minister Kyprianou on his return to Nicosia on October 1, 1964. He said that he believed "sincerely that the Soviet aid not only constitutes a major factor in the defense of Cyprus but also an important contribution to the cause of peace." [18] Speaking at the Second Conference of Heads of State or Government of Non-Aligned Countries at Cairo on October 9, 1964, President Myriarthefs Makarios urged self-determination for his country and stated:

In this spirit I appeal to all members of this conference for their understanding support for efforts to achieve a democratic solution in Cyprus in accordance with the principles of the United Nations Charter.[19]

It would appear that with the backing of a powerful state, the Soviet Union, Cyprus felt more secure in pushing negotiations in the sole direction that would be most satisfactory to itself, namely, its continuance as a sovereign state.

When in March 1965, and thereafter, the definite support from the Soviet Union on which the Greek Cypriots had counted seemed to falter, signs emerged of a renewed amenability of the Cyprus situation to negotiation. In a letter of mid-March 1965 to a Greek diplomat, Prime Minister Suat Hayri Urguplu of Turkey alluded to the Soviet Union's contradictory policies over Cyprus—on the one hand backing Turkey and on the other supplying arms to the Greek Cypriots.[20] The Soviet Union had shown a strong interest in mending its fences with Turkey, for it had sent a high-level mission to Ankara.

Shortly after this it was reported from London that on the eve of a NATO Ministerial Council meeting, the Greek and Turkish Foreign Ministers had met and as a result the two Governments had agreed to seek a peaceful solution of the Cyprus situation.[21] While these talks were in progress, Foreign Minister Andrei Gromyko visited Turkey, and a joint communiqué issued on May 22, 1965 stated that both the Soviet Union and Turkey wanted an independent Cyprus with the rights of the two communities protected.[22] This communiqué apparently made it so clear that Greece and the Greek Cypriots had lost the exclusive patronage of the Soviet Union for their stand, that Prime Minister George Papandreou reacted by postponing his planned trip to Moscow.[23] But this did not disrupt direct Turco-Greek negotiations on Cyprus. Indeed, if anything, it possibly decreased the intransigence of that side which had previously felt it could count on the unqualified support of one of the superpowers.

A much more inflexible attitude affecting the chances of negotiation comes into play when a state regards itself as moving forward on the advancing tide of history. The position of a number of such states was set out in the statement of the meeting of the representatives of 81 Communist and workers' parties which took place in November 1960 in Moscow. Section I of that statement contained the following remarks:

It is the principal characteristic of our time that the world socialist system is becoming the decisive factor in the development of society. . . .

Today it is the world socialist system and the forces fighting against imperialism, for a socialist transformation of society, that determine the main content, main trend and main features of the historical development of society. . . . The complete triumph of socialism is inevitable.[24]

The New China News Agency of Peking stated the position thus in its English text of a letter dated March 9, 1963, addressed by the Communist Party of China to the Communist Party of the Soviet Union:

The two great historical currents of our time, the forces of socialism and the forces of the national and democratic revolutions in Asia, Africa and Latin America, are battering the wall of the reactionary rule of imperialism, headed by the United States of America.[25]

Then, again, in its long epistle of June 14, 1963, the Central Committee of the Chinese Communist Party made the following statement:

The Chinese Communists firmly believe that the Marxist-Leninists, the proletariat and the revolutionary people everywhere will unite more closely, overcome all difficulties and obstacles and win still greater victories in the struggle against imperialism and for world peace, and in the fight for the revolutionary cause of the people of the world and the cause of international Communism.[26]

This absolute sureness of superiority, based on a belief in the ineluctable development of historical forces to a predetermined goal, inevitably affects the capacity of the Chinese Government to enter into negotiation and even to understand the meaning and significance of negotiations between other countries. In a strongly polemical out-

burst delivered on August 1, 1963, Liao Cheng-chih, an important
Chinese Communist Party Leader, stated:

Comrades and friends! We can now clearly see that the conclusion of
the treaty for a partial nuclear test ban represents a big conspiracy in
which the imperialists and their hangers-on are joining hands against the
socialist countries, against China and against the forces of peace of the
whole world.[27]

The volume from which the above citation is taken contains several
statements of this character. The statement is of relevance to our
present analysis in two respects. First, it is contemptuous about the
negotiation between the West and the strongest Communist power
which resulted in the partial test ban on August 1963. China was entirely unwilling to share in the results of that negotiation, because it
was convinced that the negotiation would not correspond to the
march of events dictated by the inevitable tide of history. Second, the
statement is even more remarkable in that it places in one single
clause of a sentence, with no punctuation to split the clause, the
phrase "against China and against the forces of peace of the whole
world." Here we see a complete and explicit identification of China
with the world forces for peace. In other words, what China decides
is right for peace is the precise way in which the world should look at
the requirements of peace. Since in international affairs negotiation is
a method of bringing about the peaceful evolution of international relations, this statement means that at the present time only those situations which China considers to be suitable for peaceful change can be
subject to negotiation. This is obviously a one-sided view of the
possibilities of negotiation, and not one which can be readily accepted
by other countries. Certainly it greatly restricts the deployment of
negotiation in international affairs, and illustrates forcefully the restrictive posture toward international negotiations of a state which
identifies its own policies with the advancing tide of history.

All national entities, of course, foster a belief in themselves, their
purposes, and their destinies. However, most modern states tacitly
assume that there is room for many beliefs to flourish peacefully, and
for a multiplicity of national entities to develop. Most states do not
identify belief in their own purposes and destiny with the inevitable
beliefs and destinies of the whole world. They respect the historical
fact that the political and social manifestations of even the most basic
ideas are destined to change. However, it is not an uncommon
phenomenon for a state gripped by a revolution of national re-

surgence to be carried away by its own fervor, excitement, and romanticism, and to identify its own desires and sense of movement forward as being necessary and equally applicable to the rest of the world.

We see something of this in Sukarno's doctrine of the New Emerging Forces as distinct from the Old Established Powers. He delivered a stirring and marathonic speech on August 17, 1964, in which he called upon his people to:

Return to the romanticism, dynamism, dialecticalism of the revolution! Return to the Mandate of the Suffering of the people! Return! Return! [28]

The President went on to say:

The Indonesian revolution proceeds towards the well-known three objectives. The Indonesian revolution proceeds towards socialism. The Indonesian revolution proceeds towards a new world without "exploitation de l'homme par l'homme" and "exploitation de nation par nation." . . . How could such a revolution be made to keep going without romanticism, without dynamism, without dialecticalism? [29]

Here we see President Sukarno identifying the Indonesian revolution with a new world throughout which there will be certain norms of behavior between man and man and nation and nation. Obviously, such a far-ranging concept must affect Indonesia's attitude in its relations with other countries. This explains why, as the speech continued and President Sukarno went into particular issues, he was able to say:

"Malaysia" is being "installed" in front of the door of the Republic of Indonesia; "Malaysia" is still spreading itself out as a watchdog of imperialism in front of the house of the Republic of Indonesia. . . . March forward, keep on pounding away, keep on crushing that "Malaysia" although it is helped and aided by ten imperialists at once! [30]

On the face of it, such an attitude is incompatible with the negotiation of the Malaysian problem. This is another case which fits in with our principle, that an overwhelming belief by a particular state that it is marching with the one and only tide of history creates in that state a rigid attitude toward most forms of international negotiation.

Recent moves in Cambodia would seem to suggest the development of a somewhat similar position. Indeed, President Sukarno, directly after the above words, went on to say:

In Cambodia I saw with my own eyes how a big imperialist country tried to intimidate the government of small Cambodia, and made every effort to subdue Cambodia. But truly this prince of ours [Prince Norodom Sihanouk was present while President Sukarno was speaking] is a Great Prince: he too like us accepts the imperialists' challenge, saying, "Here I am, where are you?" He too, like us, accepts the imperialists' challenge, saying "go to hell with your aid." [31]

Developments in Cambodia (including the later severing of diplomatic relations with the United States) might bring that country into the military struggle, perhaps more indirectly than directly, in Southeast Asia. If this should occur, Cambodia, which so far has been the most peaceful of the states of former Indochina, would be less in a position to do what it did in May 1964, namely bring to the Security Council a complaint against South Vietnam and state as did its representative, Voeunsai Sonn, that "Cambodia is neutral and intends to remain so."

The conviction of being on the advancing tide of history can grip nations and states in far-reaching ways. We have quoted certain statements emanating from Peking which would indicate that the Chinese Communist Government regards it as its duty actively to assist all revolutionary situations in other countries tending toward the development of Communist regimes. In other words, the conviction of being on the advancing tide of history extends to the conviction that other states must be assisted in moving with the same tide. This attitude is definitely restrictive in regard to negotiation. On the other hand, the position of the Soviet Union appears to be more ambivalent. In his interview given to United States publisher Gardner Cowles in Moscow in 1962, Premier Khrushchev explained that in an earlier era

Capitalism buried, interred, feudalism. . . . Capitalism, however, has engendered irreconcilable contradictions, and a new, progressive social system—communism, with entirely different social relations between people than under capitalism, has arisen to take its place. We are convinced that communism will win because it provides better conditions for the development of society's productive forces, makes possible the fullest and most harmonious development of society as a whole and of every individual. Capitalism fights against communism, but the process of mankind's development cannot be stemmed. Sooner or later, communism will win throughout the world and, consequently, communism will bury capitalism.[32]

Premier Khrushchev also stated that the Twentieth Congress of the Communist Party of the Soviet Union "made it perfectly clear and obvious that the allegations that the Soviet Union intends to overthrow capitalism in other countries by means of "exporting" revolutions are absolutely unfounded." [33]

These statements accord with the more relaxed attitude of the Soviet Union toward international negotiations in recent years, which contrasts with the narrower attitude of China. China does not directly oppose all negotiation, but it entertains a zealous belief that its terms alone are the right basis for any serious discussion, and apparently considers it entirely proper that negotiation must not interfere with its determination to spread the Communist revolution.

Leonid I. Brezhnev, the First Secretary of the Soviet Communist Party, speaking in Red Square in Moscow on October 19, 1964 (at the celebration of the first launching of three persons in a space ship) stated:

The general line of our party worked out by its 20th, 21st and 22nd congresses is a Leninist line. It was, is and will be the only immutable line in the entire domestic and foreign policy of the Communist party and the Soviet state.

Brezhnev went on to say that:

The foreign policy of the Soviet Union is predicated on the Leninist principles of the peaceful coexistence of states with different social systems, tireless struggle for the consolidation of peace, for friendship and cooperation among nations, for the further relaxation of international tension.

However, he added:

The Soviet People see their international duty in the support of the just struggle of the peoples against imperialism, colonialism, and neo-colonialism; for their social and national liberation; for peace, democracy, national independence and socialism.[34]

Much will depend on how the Soviet Union interprets the word "support" as it is used in Brezhnev's speech. Obviously, the Soviet Union will continue to support anticolonial national liberation and socialistic movements. This support can be evidenced at conferences, at the United Nations, in diplomatic activities in general, but it can also take other forms.

Countries experiencing a new surge of power sometimes espouse slogans and postures that affect their attitude in negotiation. For example, President Sukarno frequently refers to the "newly emerging forces," a description of those countries that are alleged to be asserting their full rights and in the process of so doing are throwing off previous inhibitions and attitudes. So strongly attached is President

Sukarno to this concept that at the Second Conference of Heads of State or Government of Non-Aligned Countries held at Cairo in October 1964, he wanted a special reference on the agenda to countries in the category of "newly emerging forces." However, it would appear that the concept was not regarded as precise enough for acceptance by some of the other participants, including Mongi Slim of Tunisia, a highly skilled and experienced international diplomat.

A special category of countries, such as the one sought to be created by President Sukarno, becomes like a club. Its members tend to develop sympathetic and friendly relationships with each other. This becomes a *parti pris* position which can cause complications in international affairs. What, for example, does a country sympathetic to the concept do if one of the "newly emerging forces" commits a flagrant aggression against its neighbor? Does it condone the aggression because nations of the "newly emerging forces" category are always "right" in their dealings with countries outside the club? Is a "newly emerging forces" country permitted to arrogate to itself the right to decide issues involving other countries by the use of its "newly emerging" military force? The implications are clear enough that some of the attitudes associated with such a concept make it difficult for a country to convince other states that it is seriously inclined to negotiate international issues and disputes.

The foregoing analysis, then, suggests the following principles:

When a country involved in an international dispute or situation can count on the tangible assistance or support of a powerful state or bloc of states, it will tend either to favor negotiation only on its own terms (assuming that its supporters back its negotiating positions) or to be antipathetic toward negotiated settlements.

The stronger the conviction of a country that it is riding the advancing tide of history, the more narrow and rigid its negotiating postures in regard to international disputes or situations in which it is involved.

CHAPTER EIGHTEEN

Effects of Previous Power Status

IN THE POST-World War II era, there have been striking readjustments of the power levels of certain countries. We have witnessed enormous accretions of power in the United States and in the Soviet Union, and something similar appears to be occurring now in China. These accretions are based largely on the internal resources and capacities of the countries and their people. There have also been special circumstances and conditions determining the diminution of power of other important states. The whole process of decolonialization has brought a reduction of power to a number of Western European states, involving the surrender of authority over some three-eighths of the world's people.[1]

Former colonial powers such as the United Kingdom, France, Belgium, Germany, and the Netherlands have experienced considerable decreases of influence, which have affected their postures in international relations. These decreases in power and influence are an inevitable concomitant of the upsurge of certain international forces. They have, generally speaking, made the countries concerned more amenable to negotiation in the settlement of international disputes and situations.

The most striking example of adjustment to a new power status in the post-World War II world is that of the United Kingdom. Before the War, Britain was still the master of the largest empire that any country had ever acquired. In the fifteen years following the end of World War II, much of the empire had been lost and the process of divestment of power over the remaining areas was continuing. In this process of loss or renunciation of empire and of adjustment to a relative reduction of its power status, there is little doubt that Britain has shown a remarkable capacity for international negotiation. The most important single event in this process was the withdrawal of British authority from the Indian subcontinent. The ability of the United Kingdom to deal with reemerging India and with Pakistan through negotiations was at once a demonstration of its political perspicacity and a most rigorous test of its political maturity and wisdom. That both newly independent states have remained members of the Commonwealth is in itself striking evidence of the success with which Britain deployed these qualities. In this process she agreed to a new concept of the Commonwealth, one which would accommodate the republic of India and later the several other republics among the independent ex-colonies in Africa and Asia.

Indian leaders have frequently acknowledged the skill and effectiveness of Britain's negotiating capacity during and after the period of divestment of that country's power. Prime Minister Nehru said at a banquet held in New Delhi on January 9, 1958 in honor of Harold Macmillan, then Prime Minister of the United Kingdom:

. . . above all, the chief thing which, I think, strikes people not only in India and the United Kingdom but in other parts of the world is the manner in which the change was brought about. The manner was not only unique, but, as I said, strangely dramatic, which after these long years of conflict, almost as if by magic wand, put an end to that spirit of conflict, and led to a desire to cooperate in spite of very considerable differences in opinion or in our reactions to events.[2]

Previously, when presenting to the Indian Parliament for ratification the declaration on the continued membership of India in the Commonwealth of Nations, Nehru had said:

I would like to pay a tribute to the Prime Minister of the United Kingdom and also to others there, because they also approached the problem in this spirit [of friendship and good will], not so much to score a debating point or to change a word here and there in this declaration.[3]

It is equally interesting to notice the attitude of the United Kingdom on some issues in which it was not directly involved and in which its power and prestige were not seriously at stake.

Although the Foreign Secretary of the United Kingdom was one of the two cochairmen of the Laos Conference of 1961 and 1962, the United Kingdom was not directly involved in the events which led to the Conference. It would have been perfectly possible for the United Kingdom to have taken a relaxed and somewhat detached view of its function. Its representatives could well have held that a conference chairman guides procedures but should not involve himself in substantive discussions. However, quite to the contrary, Malcolm MacDonald, the United Kingdom representative, played a leading role in the negotiations and was of special assistance in bringing about agreement on several occasions between the United States and the Peking Government. He assisted greatly in evolving a form of international conference negotiation which was at once more informal and more effective than the general procedures of such negotiation. He constantly took, or was open to, initiatives which he then developed in situations which were made as relaxed as possible by the provision of appropriate hospitality. (This writer makes these statements on the basis of his participation as the representative of India, and as one of the six inner-circle negotiators at the Conference.) The role of Malcolm MacDonald as cochairman was acknowledged by all the participants. When Andrei Gromyko referred to his cochairman from Britain in his last intervention at the Conference on July 21, 1962, he was in fact paying tribute to the work of Malcolm MacDonald. He said: "I should like to extend my appreciation to my colleague, the British Co-Chairman of the Conference, whose co-operation largely contributed to the removal of the obstacles that arose in the course of the Conference and to the attainment of the fruitful results." [4] On the same day, Maurice Couve de Murville, the Foreign Minister of France, paid "tribute to the wisdom and patience of Mr. MacDonald and Mr. Pushkin, the deputies of our two co-chairmen, which they have shown in conducting to a positive conclusion long and complicated discussions." [5]

In the complicated case of Rhodesia, the United Kingdom avers that its powers are extremely tenuous. However, in terms of General Assembly resolutions, Rhodesia is a non–self-governing territory for which responsibility vests in the administering power, the United Kingdom. As this is the international status of the territory, it has been the subject of detailed study by the United Nations Special Committee on the Situation with Regard to the Implementation of the Declaration on the Granting of Independence to Colonial Countries and Peoples.[6] The special Committee includes such staunchly anti-colonial countries as Cambodia, Ethiopia, India, Iraq, Mali, Syria, Tanzania, and Yugoslavia, as well as the United Kingdom, the United States, Australia, Italy, Venezuela, and other countries. There are natural ties between Rhodesia, with its 220,000 settlers largely of United Kingdom origin, and Britain. Moreover, Rhodesia is perhaps the world's largest producer of copper, a metal of particular importance to the highly developed industrial activities of Britain. Under these circumstances, one might expect Britain to play down its responsibility toward the 4,000,000 black inhabitants and act as the spokesman at the United Nations of the ruling group in Rhodesia. However, to do so would create complications for Britain with the African states at the United Nations and with the African and Asian member states of the Commonwealth. This has clearly been a most difficult situation for the United Kingdom in terms of its international relationships.

A study of the detailed United Nations documents relating to the work of the Special Committee indicates how skillfully the United Kingdom has acquitted itself in the negotiations. In March and April, 1964, the Special Committee adopted three resolutions calling upon the United Kingdom to take various measures in connection with the situation in Rhodesia. The United Kingdom did not vote against any of these resolutions, nor did it vote in favor. It took this course in order to be free to assist in negotiating a compromise solution. Furthermore, the United Kingdom frequently expressed its willingness to entertain at London delegations composed of members of the Special Committee, in order to explore with them the possibility of bringing about a peaceful solution. One such meeting took place from May 30 to June 5, 1964. The United Kingdom team of negotiators was headed by the Right Honorable Duncan Sandys, the Secretary of State for Commonwealth Relations and for the Colonies. In its report on these discussions, presented to the Special Committee in June 1964, the following observations were made by the subcommittee which went to London:

The Sub-Committee interpreted the willingness of the United Kingdom Government to discuss the question as an indication of its desire to find a solution to the problem. . . .

As to the threat of a unilateral declaration of independence, to which the sub-committee has alluded, the United Kingdom Government had explained to the Southern Rhodesia Government in no uncertain terms that it would be totally opposed to such a step. . . .

The Ministers reaffirmed the conviction that they had expressed in their discussions with the sub-Committee last year that only agreement and persuasion, not force, could lead to rapid progress in the solution of the problems of Southern Rhodesia. . . . In the belief of the Ministers, a compromise was not impossible. . . .

These discussions had revealed to the sub-Committee that so far as objectives were concerned, there was a wide measure of agreement.[7]

The above statements are a fair indication of the flexibility and aptitude for negotiations displayed by the British delegation in its meetings with the representatives of the Special Committee. So much were these factors in evidence that the subcommittee, which was composed of representatives of Mali, Sierra Leone, Ethiopia, and Yugoslavia, felt that it could make the following statement:

> . . . though in the view of the United Kingdom Government this situation did not constitute a serious threat to international peace and security, it appreciated that conditions of tension prevailed in the Territory. The Sub-Committee also noted the belief expressed by the United Kingdom Government that in order to prevent a deterioration of the situation, a compromise solution was not only desirable, but was not impossible.[8]

In the delicate and explosive context of the Rhodesian situation, the United Kingdom, for its part, managed to direct matters in such a manner that negotiation was at least kept alive. On May 6, 1965 the United Kingdom abstained on the resolution adopted by the Security Council [9] exhorting Britain to take action to prevent Rhodesia from declaring its independence. Lord Caradon explained that the reason for the abstention was that the United Kingdom questioned the technical competence of the United Nations in this matter, but that his Government favored negotiations and discussion.[10] Even though Britain did not succeed in diverting the Rhodesian white minority from formally declaring independence, one must in all fairness ask the question, "What would have been the attitude and the actions of the United Kingdom thirty years earlier?" to realize the great difference that exists in that country's political viewpoint today.

The new negotiating spirit of Britain in regard to international disputes and situations was virtually the subject of Prime Minister Alec Douglas-Home's important statement in the debate on foreign affairs in the British House of Commons on June 17, 1964. He said:

> All the speeches which have followed my right honourable friend's [referring to the speech of Foreign Secretary R. A. Butler who opened the Foreign Affairs debate] were consciously seeking ways of escaping the old confrontations of the cold war which have consumed so much of our resources in recent years and have threatened us from time to time with extinction since the end of the last war.[11]

In this striking statement, a Tory Prime Minister was observing that *all* the speeches in the debate—whether made by Tory, Labour, or Liberal members—were virtually seeking possibilities of peaceful negotiation instead of the "old confrontations of the cold war." In short, Douglas-Home was affirming the existence of a British upsurge in favor of negotiations.

Two further quotations from the same statement by Douglas-Home compel attention:

Far better . . . that China should be in the United Nations, and there should be increased contact between the West and China. . . .
. . . a fat Communist is to be preferred to a thin Communist. These arguments seem at long last to be making some impression on the United States of America. . . . We should increase trade with Russia, and try to take advantage of the fact that I have recorded that society in Russia is evolving very fast.[12]

Britain, however, is not the only country which has developed a strong penchant for negotiation in a situation of diminishing power. The Netherlands, with considerable skill at the United Nations, was able to obtain international endorsement of its plea that Surinam and the Antilles become a part of the Kingdom of the Netherlands. Barring the somewhat different case of Greenland, this was the unique instance when the United Nations agreed to a distant and transoceanic area's becoming part of a metropolitan country.

While it is true that at first the Netherlands put up strong opposition to the settlement through the United Nations of the issue regarding the status of West Irian (formerly West New Guinea), the Dutch rarely objected to the negotiation of that issue directly with Indonesia. Indeed, in his very first intervention on this subject at the United Nations, Foreign Minister J. M. A. H. Luns pointed out that soon after the transfer of sovereignty to the Indonesian Government of the old Dutch East Indies, two conferences were held by the Indonesian and the Netherlands Governments about the future status of West Irian.[13] The Dutch speeches on the subject at the United Nations, as those who were present through those years will recall, sought not so much to maintain unchanged the status of West Irian as to question the Indonesian view that sovereignty had already been transferred by the Linggadjati agreement signed on March 25, 1947.[14] Even when the issue was contested, the Dutch did not repudiate the need to negotiate. Eventually negotiations did take place, with the help of mediation, and by the agreement reached on August 15, 1962 between the Governments of Indonesia and Netherlands, the latter agreed to hand over the territory through the United Nations to Indonesia.[15]

When Foreign Minister Luns visited Indonesia in July 1964, the two countries laid the ground for an extensive trade agreement. I was later told by high officials of the Indonesian Government that relations had become extremely good with the Netherlands, and that the Dutch were cooperative and helpful in every way. The visit to Indonesia of Foreign Minister Luns, as it was described to me by Indonesian officials, was a climax in a sustained Dutch effort to improve relations through negotiation. It would appear that the Netherlands went further than had been expected by Indonesia in the extent of its initiative and in the resulting economic agreement.

Some of the warmth and generally constructive character of the visit of Foreign Minister Luns was expressed in the joint communiqué issued at Jakarta on August 1, 1964. Such communiqués usually suffer from the dryness and formality of official protocol language. The communiqué, however, read:

Dr. and Mrs. Luns felt especially honored by this invitation and highly appreciated the friendly reception accorded to them and their party. . . . The Netherlands is prepared to send experts, receive trainees and finance bilateral projects. . . . It was confirmed that as soon as possible still existing discriminations in the financial and economic relations between the two countries will be discontinued on both sides. This will also open the possibility for furthering economic cooperation.[16]

Another phenomenon that has resulted from the great political changes of the post-World War II era is that previously held and stated positions, when they militate against negotiation, often discourage other countries from negotiating with the country concerned even after the original statements have lost their force.

A primary example of such a situation is the case of the Soviet Union. The Government of that country is based upon the political ideology of Communism. It is often stated by prospective negotiators with the Soviet Union that Communism fosters and promotes militant activity with reference to and within other countries, and therefore renders any real negotiations with the Soviet Union extremely difficult. At the height of the Cold War period, a series of statements made by Dean Acheson, as Secretary of State, emphasized this difficulty. In an address delivered at the University of California at Berkeley on March 16, 1950, Acheson said:

They have always, at the same time, maintained the pretense that they are the interpreters of the aspirations of peoples far beyond their borders. In the light of that professed philosophy, they have conducted, as masters of the Russian state, a foreign policy which now is the center of the most difficult and troublesome problems of international affairs, problems designed to keep the peoples of the world in a state of deepest apprehension and doubt.[17]

Again, in an address on April 30, 1951 to the United States Chamber of Commerce in Washington, D.C., Dean Acheson stated:

In the five and one half years that have passed since the end of the war, the men who control the destinies of the Soviet Union have continued to press forward not only with the traditional territorial aspirations of Old Russia but also with the revolutionary aims for world rule of the Bolshevik conspiracy.[18]

This attitude was reflected in the speeches of other United States negotiators. On November 12, 1948, Frederick Osborn, speaking for the United States in the First Committee of the General Assembly, made the following remarks after referring to attitudes of the Soviet Government in regard to disarmament and Berlin:

These actions force us to believe that the Soviet Union is pursuing the aim of world revolution and of destroying the economic and political systems which other peoples have chosen for themselves. Thus the Soviet Union has created a spirit of inquietude in the rest of the world.[19]

On the subject of disarmament negotiations Osborn went on to say:

. . . it seems clear that we will not attain ". . . an atmosphere of real and lasting improvement in international relations," as a prerequisite to disarmament, as required by this resolution, until the Soviet Union, not only by its words but in its actions, ceases to threaten the world with Communist aggression.[20]

In a radio address to the nation on November 7, 1951, President Truman said, "The aggression in Korea has shown that Communist imperialism will resort to open warfare to gain its ends." [21]

A few years later, in a debate on disarmament in the First Committee of the General Assembly of the United Nations on October 12, 1954, United States Ambassador James J. Wadsworth told us the following:

If the Soviet Union has really abandoned its policy of disarming the free world without disarming the Soviet bloc, this is indeed a change in policy. The previous policy . . . was far older . . . than the United Nations. . . . We can find it in the writings of Lenin as early as 1916 when he said "Only after the proletariat has disarmed the bourgeoisie will it be able, without destroying its world historical mission, to 'throw all armament on the scrap heap.' The proletariat will undoubtedly do this, but only when this condition has been fulfilled, certainly not before." [22]

Ambassador Wadsworth virtually posed a question and a challenge to the Soviet Union. Had they or had they not abandoned a previous position which appeared to him to make true negotiations for disarmament virtually impossible? It is a matter of coincidence that the United States spokesman put the issue in this way at a time when Stalin's era was nearing its completion. Incidentally, it is the mark of a good negotiator, and this Ambassador Wadsworth is, that he framed the issue in the manner of part probe and part challenge.

Perhaps here we have a turning point, a willingness to question the Russian position and not to be completely arrested by previously expressed doctrinaire statements regarding the nature of the Communist movement. Of course, the turning point was by no means a sharp one; it was, indeed, the gentlest of curves. This was inevitable, if only because the general nature of the international situation did not lend encouragement to any more decided indication.

When President Eisenhower wrote to Nikolai Bulganin, then Premier of the Soviet Union, on August 4, 1956, his letter was again part probing and part the expression of grave doubts based on previous Russian positions. Referring to the agreement that Germany should be reunited by means of free elections, and to other matters discussed at the summit conference, he wrote:

I must confess that I am perplexed as to how we can work together constructively if agreements which are negotiated at the highest level after the most thorough exploration do not seem dependable.[23]

This was the President's expression of doubt. However, he ended his letter with a mixture of probing and hope. His concluding paragraph was:

We realize that efforts are being made in your country to eradicate some of the evils of an earlier period. This we welcome . . . . Those evils were also projected into the international field. . . . This situation needs also to be remedied by a new spirit for which I earnestly appeal.[24]

The period of the unmitigated Cold War was partly produced by the grave doubts which the Western world had about the application of certain tenets of Communism by the Soviet Union to its policies in international affairs. Those grave doubts continued even after the summit conference at Geneva in the summer of 1955, and made negotiations between the two sides not only difficult but largely unfructuous.

The agreement over Austria in 1955 was not so much an exception as a calculation by the leaders of the Soviet Union that there was a decided possibility of Austria's being united under a government friendly to them. This itself was seen as a prospective gain, considering that Austria was in a general sense a "Western" country. The Communists fared very badly at the hands of the Austrian electorate, but nevertheless Austria has remained unswervingly neutral and has to some extent justified the Russian calculation. I witnessed the very friendly relationship between Prime Minister Khrushchev and Austrian Federal Chancellor Julius Raab when Mr. Khrushchev paid a state visit to Austria in 1960.[25]

It was only after successive statements of the Communist Party of the Soviet Union had redefined its position, and similar efforts had been made at international meetings of Communist parties, particularly in 1960, that more meaningful negotiations became possible between East and West. There were, of course, other factors at work, including the personality of Mr. Khrushchev; the growing demand in the Soviet Union and other Communist countries for a better standard of living both materially and through some relaxation of restrictive regulations; the striking growth of nonalignment (although in a purely power sense the nonaligned countries have never been a significant factor); and the hazards created by an unchecked arms race which had reached the potential proportions not merely of massive destruction but of something approaching complete devastation. Nevertheless, in order to make worthwhile negotiation possible it has been necessary for the Soviet Union's leaders virtually to retrace or explain away previous ideological positions.

An important landmark in this process was an article by Nikita Khrushchev on peaceful coexistence in the United States publication *Foreign Affairs* of October 1959. Explaining the concept of peaceful coexistence, Khrushchev wrote:

Apart from the commitment to non-aggression, it also presupposes an obligation on the part of all states to desist from violating each other's territorial integrity and sovereignty in any form and under any pretext whatsoever. The principle of peaceful coexistence signifies a renunciation of interference in the internal affairs of other countries with the object of altering their system of government or mode of life or for any other motives.[26]

He was aware of the doubt which had come to exist in the Western world regarding the sincerity of the idea of peaceful coexistence. On this point his statement was:

It is often said in the West that peaceful coexistence is nothing else than a tactical method of the socialist states. There is not a grain of truth in such allegation. Our desire for peace and peaceful coexistence is not conditioned by any time-serving or tactical considerations.[27]

Later in the article he stated:

We Communists believe that the idea of Communism will ultimately be victorious throughout the world, just as it has been victorious in our country, in China and in many other states. Many readers of *Foreign Affairs* will probably disagree with us. Perhaps they think that the idea of capitalism will ultimately triumph. It is their right to think so. We may argue, we may disagree with one another. *The main thing is to keep to the positions of ideological struggle, without resorting to arms in order to prove that one is right.*[28]

The article in question cannot be regarded as being solely Khrushchev's handiwork. We must remember that it came several years after the important Soviet Communist Party meeting of 1956. He and his colleagues had been able by 1959, it would appear, to get general acceptance in the Soviet Communist Party of a restatement of Communist doctrine. Except in China and Albania, this trend gathered strength in other countries.

In November 1960 the representatives of 81 national Communist parties met in conference at Moscow, and they issued an agreed statement which included the following phrases:

The foreign policy of the socialist countries rests on the firm foundation of Leninist principles of peaceful co-existence and economic competition between the socialist and capitalist countries. . . .

Peaceful co-existence of countries with different systems or destructive war—this is the alternative today. There is no other choice. . . .

. . . the imperialist reactionaries who tried to arouse distrust for the Communist movement and its ideology, continue to intimidate the people by alleging that the Communists need wars between states to overthrow the capitalist system and establish a socialist system. The Communist Parties emphatically reject this slander. . . .

. . . The Communist Parties which guide themselves by the Marxist-Leninist doctrine, have always been against the exportation of revolution.[29]

Although the language cannot be described as charitable, the substantive meaning of the above statements, at any rate at face value, was somewhat more reassuring to the Western world than were previous impressions created by Communist leaders. Strengthened by the trend in most Communist parties in the world, Khrushchev could speak even more clearly about these issues by 1962. On July 10, he addressed a World Congress for General Disarmament and Peace at Moscow:

We believe that if either side works for the victory of its ideology and policies by augmenting its armed forces and its threats of war, we will surely move towards a world-wide nuclear war. We believe that this struggle [between the two systems] should not be developed into a war between States with different social systems, but that matters should be settled through peaceful competition.[30]

After about six years of repetition of such statements, we entered an era of somewhat more fruitful negotiation. The Laos Agreement was about to be signed. The Eighteen-Nation Committee on Disarmament had convened, and it was clear to all diplomats who had been engaged in international negotiation over the previous decade that there was a definite relaxation in the approach of the Communist states. Those developments made it possible for President Kennedy to respond with a restatement of American policy in relation to the Soviet Union. On June 19, 1963 he delivered his famous speech at the American University in Washington, D.C. In that speech he asked the United States to "reexamine our attitude toward the Soviet Union," and he went on to tell his audience that "no government or social system is so evil that its people must be considered lacking in virtue." Toward the end of the speech he said: "So let us not be blind to our differences, but let us also direct attention to our common interests and to the means by which these differences can be resolved." [31]

The year 1963 brought three agreements with the Soviet Union, and indicated that explanations, restatements, and disavowals by Khrushchev had played a role. Speaking immediately after the second of the agreements, that of the limited test ban,[32] President Kennedy said,

Nuclear test ban negotiations have long been a symbol of East-West disagreement. If this treaty can also be a symbol it can symbolize the end of one era and the beginning of another, if both sides can by this treaty gain confidence and experience in peaceful collaboration, then this short and simple treaty may well become an historic mark in man's age old pursuit of peace. Western policies have long been designed to persuade the Soviet Union to renounce aggression, direct or indirect, so that their people and all people may live and let live in peace . . . this treaty, if it can be followed by further progress, can clearly move in that direction.[33]

From the statements of President Kennedy we should take note of the following words of his address to the United Nations on September 20, 1963. At the beginning of that address he referred to the fact that "The clouds have lifted a little so that new rays of hope can break through." [34] He then referred to various improvements in the international situation, and stated:

The contest will continue—the contest between those who see a monolithic world and those who believe in diversity—but it should be a contest in leadership and responsibility instead of destruction, a contest in achievement instead of intimidation. . . . And in the contest for a better life, all the world can be a winner.[35]

These movements in the position of the Soviet Union, and the response from the United States, make it possible now for the two sides to negotiate without the almost total hesitation and apprehension fostered by the previous Stalinist approach. Nevertheless, there remains a great deal of continuing suspicion in the West as to the true objectives of the Soviet Union. Negotiation is still overshadowed by what occurred before previous positions were altered.

The Soviet Union's new postures, moreover, have not always been extended to positions in detail, as was evident in the Soviet stand on the manner of verification of arms reduction.

Premier Khrushchev proposed to the other countries which were to meet at the Eighteen-Nation Committee on Disarmament Conference that the Conference should initially convene at the summit. Communications were exchanged between President Kennedy and Premier Khrushchev. There was some mention in them of substantive positions relating to disarmament and verification. President Kennedy argued that Premier Khrushchev's letter had shown that there had, in effect, been no change in the Russian appreciation of the United States' position on verification, and that the Soviet Union was still maintaining its own previous positions in regard to this important issue. He stated: "For example, if, as we have proposed, there is an agreement to reduce the level of armed forces to a specified number, we must be able to insure through proper verification mechanisms that this level is not exceeded.[36]

At that time, February 1962, there appeared to have been no change in the Soviet position on verification measures. They maintained that although there should be effective verification of disarmament—that is, of actual reductions of armed forces, weapons, production facilities, missiles etc.—there should be no verification on the levels of retained weapons and forces. This point has continued to be part of the core debate on disarmament at the Eighteen-Nation Committee Geneva Conference.

There has been some movement on both sides regarding the verification of retained armament, but not enough to resolve differences. To a participant at the Conference who is of neither the Western nor the Eastern alliance, the present positions of the two sides seem to be less far apart than is alleged by the two sides themselves. For example, Soviet representatives continue to assert that the United States insists on a full and detailed verification of all retained armaments, and that this amounts to 100 percent inspection over the whole of the Soviet Union, even at the time of the initial disarmament measures which would decrease armaments by a small fraction of total weaponry. This assertion by the Soviet Union would appear to show how nearly indelible has been the effect of previous verification proposals (that is, previous positions) advanced by the Western side up to and including 1960. Although the United States has shifted ground and has proposed partial verification of retained arms (through a zonal inspection system which would progress *pari passu* with the implementation of agreed disarmament measures), and has declared its willingness to consider alternative verification proposals, its previous positions apparently continue to arouse suspicions on the Soviet side. Similarly, although the Soviet Union has made some movement in the direction of increased verification measures and has proposed verification *in situ* of retained missiles and their launching sites, the Western view seems still to be that the Soviet Union is not agreeable to verification of retained weaponry, and continues to maintain its old positions, which were regarded as being opposed to verification in general. It would seem that previously stated positions of the Soviet Union on verification, which were certainly very negative, are continuing to arouse suspicions on the Western side to a greater degree than the new positions would appear to justify.

It would assist in understanding this point if we were to follow excerpts from an actual session of negotiation relating to control and verification measures at the Eighteen-Nation Committee on Disarmament Conference. There was a considerable degree of probing of this issue on May 11, 1962. Arthur Dean, the United States negotiator, was the first speaker that day. He said:

There is a real problem, at least in Western minds, both about verifying the implementation of the obligation to cut down to agreed levels and about discovering possible clandestine stockpiles of armaments or clandestinely maintained troop units.

We have said that we want assurance against such dangers, and Mr. Zorin has chosen to interpret the word "assurance" to mean that we are demanding 100 per cent inspection in the first stage for a 30 per cent reduction. I must say again that this is not correct. "Assurance" to us means reasonable and adequate assurance, no foolproof assurance, which is never attainable anyway.[37]

After two other representatives spoke, General E. L. M. Burns of Canada, quoting Michael Wright, said:

"The question," said Sir Michael Wright, "therefore, is whether the 100 per cent inspection spoken of by Mr. Zorin [who had said that there could be 100 per cent inspection in the Soviet Union to verify a 100 per cent elimination of the means of delivery of nuclear warheads] would include verification that there are no weapons hidden "under the jacket." If it does include this, an important avenue of progress is opened up. If it does not include this, the problem remains with us both over conventional forces and arms levels and over nuclear delivery vehicles." [38]

Let us always keep in mind that what we are dealing with here are not tanks or fighter aircraft, or cannon, or any of those arms of which a few could escape detection without making any crucial difference, but with nuclear weapons and their means of delivery. . . . no responsible statesman would be willing to trust to the good faith of the other side that it was not hiding a few such weapons "under the jacket." [39]

What was the Soviet reply? Valerian Zorin, the Soviet representative, said:

We are no less decidedly in favor of such control as is possible and necessary [than you are], and our differences with you are not on this subject . . . on the principles of the approach to the question of control there are no serious differences between us, except for your desire to verify the remaining armaments. . . .

We say frankly and honestly that in the course of the disarmament process some armaments and armed forces not subject to reduction or elimination during a given stage will remain outside of control, but the main point is that these armed forces and armaments will be continually reduced until they are brought down to zero. . . . It is asserted that this involves a certain risk. . . . Nevertheless, we are prepared to take such a risk in order to achieve real disarmament, since no control—as, incidentally, Mr. Dean has also said today—can provide 100 per cent foolproof assurance.[40]

What emerged on that date was that the Soviets too agreed to a measure of control and verification. Doubtless Valerian Zorin was sincere in saying that he thought that in principle there was no great difference of approach. But he significantly added the highly important proviso, "except . . . to verify the remaining armaments." Precisely here the two schemes of verification differ. The difference is that the United States' scheme progresses into the area of retained weapons to check against clandestine stocks, whereas the Soviet Union's plan generally stops short of this area. Since May 1962 there has been some movement forward on the Soviet side—in that they have agreed to the inspection of certain retained arms—but just how far this goes is not clear.

By stopping short, the Soviet Union aroused suspicion in the minds of the Western countries as to its motives. This suspicion might or might not be fully justified. However, strong affirmations in favor of negotiations to resolve the issue of verification and control in regard to disarmament measures will not be sufficient to carry negotiations to a solution if one side maintains its previous positions regarding "no control over retained arms," while the other side insists on at least some degree of such control.

With all the doubts and hesitations that affect negotiation with the Soviet Union because of that country's former positions, its Government is markedly more amenable to negotiatory procedures than Peking, which has adamantly adhered to a more aggressive attitude. In 1960, while seeming to support Khrushchev's proposal for general and complete disarmament, one of the more important Chinese Communists, Ch'ang-Sheng Liu, said scornfully "There are people who believe that such a proposal can be realized while imperialism still exists and that the danger of war can be eliminated by relying on such a proposal. This is a unrealistic illusion." [41]

It appeared that there really had been no change in the Chinese Communist position since John Foster Dulles described it when he was Secretary of State:

A typical Chinese Communist pamphlet reads: "We Must Hate America, because She Is the Chinese People's Implacable Enemy"; "We Must Despise America because It is a Corrupt Imperialist Nation, the World Center of Reaction and Decadency"; "We Must Look down upon America because She is a Paper Tiger and Entirely Vulnerable to Defeat."

By print, by radio, by drama, by pictures, with all the propaganda skills which Communism has devised, such themes are propagated by Red rulers. They vent their hatred by barbarous acts, such as seizures and imprisonments of Americans.[42]

This is why the talks between the United States Ambassador at Warsaw and his Chinese counterpart have proved to be the longest infructuous dialogue in the world. This is, moreover, why the statements of the Chinese delegation at the Laos Conference of 1961 and 1962 were decidedly the most full of invective of all the statements by the leading countries; and this is why in the detailed process of negotiating at Geneva during that Conference the largest number of hours were spent in getting agreement with the Chinese representatives.[43]

The following excerpts are typical of the tone and substance of the statement made by Deputy Minister Chang Han Fu on August 23, 1961 at the Laos Conference:

The imperialist absurdity of so called "protection of sovereignty" has already gone bankrupt, and the development of this absurdity into the nonsense of so-called "supplement to sovereignty" [an idea mentioned by the U.S. delegate with reference to the International Control Commission in Laos] can only make this imperialist theory all the more stinking and repulsive.

. . . The U.S. has been continuously interfering in the international affairs of Laos and has gone so far as to . . . provoke a civil war there.

Why does the U.S. delegate ask for the dissolution of the Pathet Lao Fighting Units? Could it be that the U.S. delegate is another Laotian prince? Why should the United States interfere in the internal affairs of Laos? Who has bestowed this right on the United States? [44]

These are just a few of scores of similar remarks. The crucial negotiations at the Laos Conference took place in a long series of meetings of the heads of the six core delegations, of which no verbatim transcript was prepared. I represented India throughout those meetings, and can state that the bluntness and invective of the Chinese representative surpassed his recorded performances.

In one or two of his statements, Premier Khrushchev has sought to distinguish his policy from that of the Chinese Communists. Hinting strongly at the Chinese, Khrushchev said on April 1, 1964 at Budapest: "There are people in the world who call themselves Marxist-Leninists and at the same time say there is not need to strive for a better life. According to them only one thing is important—revolution." [45] At the same time, at an international meeting of lawyers at Budapest, Mrs. Han Yu-tang, Vice President of China's Supreme Court, delivered herself of equally critical innuendoes about the Soviet Union. "Certain people," she said, were pursuing an "erroneous line of not opposing imperialism, not supporting national independence movements and not relying on the people's mass struggle." [46] Here, clearly stated in juxtaposition, are the differences between the Soviet and Chinese positions.

It is, of course, not only among the great powers that negotiation is inhibited by previous statements. Between the Arab states and Israel, one inhibitory factor to negotiation (there are admittedly several others) is the effect of strong positions already taken. On the question of Arab refugees, the repeatedly stated position of the Arab states is that the refugees should be allowed to return to their homes in Palestine. This position is, moreover, in accordance with General Assembly Resolution 194 of December 11, 1948. It has become so strongly crystallized, and Arab public opinion has become so aroused by strong statements that the refugees must return to their homes, that other settlements seem impossible to consider. A study on the Middle East prepared for the use of the Committee on Foreign Relations of the United States Senate, dated June 9, 1960, stated the following with regard to the possibilities of refugee settlement in Iraq: "Iraq, which has no refugees, could accommodate an unlimited number. Yet here, too, public opinion would probably be opposed, certainly initially.[47]

Israel, on the other hand, has recently stated that it is unwilling to allow any substantial return of refugees, the General Assembly resolution notwithstanding. Thus, we have two totally incompatible positions strongly adhered to and—together with other factors—making negotiation on the refugee question virtually impossible.

From an observation of the effects on negotiation of previous power status and previously held positions, therefore, we may find support for the following principles:

> When international events cause a country to adjust itself quickly to a relative reduction in power status, it tends to develop a penchant for negotiation in the solution of international disputes and situations.
>
> When a country or a party to an international negotiation declares itself to be in favor of negotiations on a particular issue, but in so doing contradicts previously declared and often unabrogated positions, its motives usually appear suspect to its potential or actual negotiating partners.

CHAPTER NINETEEN

Pluralistic and Single Ideology Societies

THE POSTURES OF governments in international negotiation are necessarily related to the various important currents and forces which motivate the people of their countries. In a pluralistic society such forces and currents are clearly more numerous and imperative than they are in monolithic societies. However, even in pluralistic societies governments exercise varying degrees of authority over other forms of political, economic, or social associations and activities; and even in monolithic societies there is evidence that public opinion makes itself felt, and that certain groups have considerable influence.

In the Soviet Union the Writers' Association has long held a certain position which has given it a degree of real influence in various issues. The same has been true of the Soviet Academy of Sciences. In a non-Communist monolithic society such as Portugal, the Church undoubtedly has an important place of its own. In many pluralistic societies there are curbs, exercised directly or indirectly, on political parties with certain kinds of objectives. Some parliamentary governments have also enacted regulations curbing freedom of the press and of other public media of communication.

When we draw a distinction, therefore, between the two categories of "pluralistic" and "monolithic" societies, we must remember that some of our observations for one category might be applicable in some degree to the other.

It is obvious that in a pluralistic society, strong political, social, religious, economic, and other organizations may have an effect on the government's negotiating postures. When the people feel very strongly in a particular way, they can effectively express this feeling through their churches, political parties, trade unions, farmers' associations, and women's groups, and might push a government's position in a particular direction in an important international issue, through the voice of their representatives. Such forces sometimes tend to offer a large number of alternative suggestions or positions to a government in regard to an international issue; on the other hand, they sometimes tend to reduce the alternatives open to a government on a particular issue. For example, it has been said that after World War II, popular support in the United States for ratification of the Draft Charter of the United Nations was so overwhelming that the Senate had no alternative but to ratify it. This important international document has had a profound effect on the international postures of the United States. Of course, the Charter has greatly affected the international habits of all its member states, and will continue to do so.

In a monolithic society, a thoroughgoing rejection, often contemptuous and generally ill-informed, is inculcated in regard to ideas, practices, and modes of social, political, and economic thought other than those sanctioned by the espoused code of life. This characteristic tends to give such countries strong and united urges in certain directions. In the Communist countries there is a strongly antagonistic feeling toward all such manifestations as are designated, in international forums and meetings, as imperialism and colonialism. There is in such countries a strong rejection of "capitalism."

However, there has also been a tendency in certain nonsocialist countries for a complex of forces, including those under state direction, to inculcate in the people an antagonistic reaction to Communism and to social and political manifestations which may be attributable or related to Communist influences. Whenever such strong feelings, whatever their direction, have been injected into a community, the people naturally tend to react against conciliatory negotiating postures toward a state in which the "enemy" ideology is espoused and practiced.

Both because of its constitutional guarantees and because of a form of government in which power is diffused rather than centralized, the United States offers a good example of a pluralistic society and the effects of such a society on negotiating postures. The pressure of Congress on the Administration, for example, often affects the negotiating position of the United States Government.

When Hubert Humphrey was a Senator from Minnesota, he made a detailed survey of the United States policy in the field of disarmament and arms control. He presented his findings on the floor of the Senate on February 4, 1958. For a couple of years prior to the time of his speech, the United States had pursued the policy of offering to the Soviet Union, as the basis of disarmament negotiation, a package proposal which put together various items such as a nuclear test ban, a cutoff of production of fissionable materials for weapons purposes, the reduction of stocks of nuclear weapons through the transfer of agreed quantities of fissionable material from weapons uses to non-weapons uses, and so on. Indeed, on December 14, 1957, this package approach had been ratified by a General Assembly resolution.[1] However, the Soviet Union and its allies had voted against the resolution and fifteen countries, mostly nonaligned states, had abstained, expressing the view that the resolution could not establish an acceptable basis for disarmament negotiations. In his speech, Senator Humphrey proposed that the United States break up its disarmament package and offer the various points in it as separate proposals. First among those proposals he mentioned the suspension of nuclear weapons tests.

This important statement by the Democratic Senator [2] initiated moves in the Republican Administration to break up the disarmament package. The first result was that the United States was able to discuss with the Soviet Union, through an expert committee which met at Geneva in the summer of 1958, the technical aspects of the single issue of a possible cessation of nuclear weapons testing. The pressure exercised in and through the Senate apparently helped to bring about a change in the negotiating posture of the United States Government.

In the steps toward formulating a full-scale nuclear test ban treaty, the exchange of letters between President Kennedy and Chairman Khrushchev in the wake of the Caribbean crisis initiated a new phase of negotiations on the question of inspection regarding underground nuclear testing. In a significant departure from its immediately prior positions—a departure which had been urged by the nonaligned countries at Geneva—Mr. Khrushchev had informed Mr. Kennedy that the Soviet Union would agree to two or three on-site inspections per year in their territory. However, the United States' position continued to be that there should be eight to ten inspections per year.[3]

In order to get the negotiations going again, the Soviet Union followed up preliminary talks that had been held in New York, by sending Vasily Kuznetsov, its First Deputy Foreign Minister, to the Geneva Disarmament Conference. The United States, too, was represented at the Conference at an equivalently high negotiating level by William C. Foster. During this period, I had frequent talks with both these negotiators.[4] The United States negotiator would insist that it was impossible for his Government's Administration to accept the Soviet proposal for three on-site inspections per year, as this figure was inadequate and would never be accepted by the United States Senate. Kuznetsov said that the understanding of the Soviets had been that all the Administration needed to gain Senate acquiescence was agreement on a small token figure of on-site inspections. The United States and the Soviet negotiators were both profoundly aware of the influence of the United States Congress on their negotiations. As events turned out, no agreement was reached by Foster and Kuznetsov, and no comprehensive test ban treaty has been signed.

In the hearing before the Senate Committee on Armed Services in February 1963, Defense Secretary Robert McNamara made a statement about the removal of Jupiter missiles from Italy and Turkey. He spoke of a report of the Joint Committee on Atomic Energy of February 11, 1961, which took an adverse view of the Jupiter missile. He stated that this report initiated consideration in the Administration of discontinuing the deployment of the missile. He was pointedly questioned by the Chairman of the Committee, Senator Richard Russell:

Senator Russell: So that is one place where Congress did play an important role?

Secretary McNamara: It did indeed, Mr. Chairman. . . . Through a series of investigations and hearings it brought to the attention of the Executive branch action that had not been taken that was required.[5]

The retention or removal of Jupiter missiles in Turkey and Italy is a matter which had entered into negotiations between the United States and the Soviet Union. The work of a Congressional Committee enabled the United States Government to move in a certain direction in its negotiations with the Soviet Union in regard to these missiles.

Important opinion-makers represent another of the concentric circles of public pressure on the United States Government. In the final stages before the endorsement by the Senate of the limited test ban treaty, the report of the Committee on Foreign Relations to the Senate [6] contained numerous citations of the views of the many scientists questioned by the Committee. Senator J. William Fulbright, the Chairman of the Committee, in his statement to Congress on September 9, 1963 referred to the question of the possible development by the

Soviet Union or the United States of an anti-ballistic missile system. He argued that the proposed limited nuclear test ban would not affect such developments if they were otherwise technically feasible, and stated that this judgment was supported by "such eminent nuclear weapons scientists, among others as . . ." He then named six scientists. This is a clear case of the influence of eminent persons on a position of Congress, and indirectly on the Administration, in a most important international negotiation.

Of course, it is not only eminent individuals who bring pressure to bear on the United States Congress or on the Administration. Much of this work is done by organizations, although to strengthen their position such organizations often choose persons who have acquired standing in Washington, D.C. For example, the National Council of the Churches of Christ wished to be heard by the Senate Foreign Relations Committee in the hearings on the partial test ban treaty held in the summer of 1963. This religious organization, with a total constituency of more than forty million members, chose as its representative Francis O. Wilcox, who for many years had been the staff director of the Committee and had then served as Assistant Secretary in the Department of State. His testimony did not primarily express a "Christian" point of view, but that of a highly informed ex-official of the Government, who is a political scientist and is now Dean of the School of Advanced International Studies at Johns Hopkins University. He was asked to give his views on the wording of the proposed treaty, on the use of nuclear weapons in war, and on legal issues relating to certain clauses of the treaty. It is not possible to say to what extent an individual witness affected the report of the Committee, but because of the size of the constituency of this witness, and his own expert knowledge, it is reasonable to assume that his deposition carried weight.

There have been and are a number of strong pressure groups which influence United States policy in its international trade negotiations. Such groups have been especially active in the trade in such commodities as beef, cheese, chickens, and chemicals. There have been special tariffs on the import of foreign chemicals into the United States as a result of the potent activities of a chemical industry lobby. Similarly, a quota on cheese imports was established in 1952 because of the pressure of farm groups, mainly from the Midwest.

The pressure in trade issues on Congress and the Administration are not always restrictive. Several important organizations have kept up pressures for liberal policies, with varying degrees of success, which have affected the United States position in its negotiations with other countries. In the postwar period the League of Women Voters has submitted testimony to Congress almost annually since 1945 in favor of extending the Reciprocal Trade Agreements Program. It has acted on several occasions to prevent additional tariff restrictions on the import of certain commodities. In 1947 the League joined with the Garden Clubs of America, and successfully stopped a bill to increase the tariff on tulip bulbs. In the late 1940s the League fought with some success against a bill to raise high duties on wool imports. It has shown its liberality by going beyond the interests of its own sex in opposing the raising of import duty on briar pipes! The League was among the first organizations to register support for the International Trade Organization and United States membership in it. This was a proposed United Nations Specialized Agency which almost became a reality in 1948.

The League has particularly tried to strengthen the United Nations in such ways as suggesting greater use of the United Nations' resources for settling international disputes. It made an effort to urge the Government to use the United Nations as the main vehicle in furnishing economic and military assistance to Greece and Turkey in 1947, and for administering the European Recovery Program, which commenced in 1948.

All these instances involve efforts to secure adoption by the Administration of more flexible positions in relation to other countries and the United Nations. Such flexibility, of course, affects the negotiating posture of the United States.

People tend to make use of the opportunity which society provides to express themselves on issues, whether national or international. For many obvious reasons there is an increasing interest in international matters. In a many-faceted society such as that of the United States, this has led to a constant and continuing activity by individuals and groups to impress their views on the course and conduct of foreign relations.

Among the monolithic societies, we have seen some loosening in the postwar period of the tight bans which sought to preserve the closed character of the Soviet Union. Almost simultaneously, however, we have seen strong and forthright regimentation of an even larger society of people, the Chinese. While one can never predict the future course of developments in any country, the odds are very high that in China as in the Soviet Union rigid monolithic discipline will break down simply because the people will not stand for its endless continuation.

Premier Khrushchev, speaking in Budapest on April 1, 1964, said, "Communism would achieve little if it could not give the people what they wanted." He added:

The important thing is that we should have more to eat—good goulash—schools, housing, and ballet. How much more do these things give to the enlargement of man's life. It's worth fighting and working for these things.[7]

To take another aspect of Soviet life, it would appear that discussion is taking place in the Soviet Union to introduce the profit motive in the country's economy. Dr. Lev A. Leontyev, a Soviet economist, said recently that efforts should be made to "combine planned, centralized management of the national economy with maximum scope for initiative and independence at the local level and in enterprise." [8] This suggestion was published in *Pravda,* and thus was given wide currency in the Soviet Union and became a potential influence on the views of the Russian people.

Even more interesting was a statement by Khrushchev when he was Premier, publicly opposing excessive secrecy in certain affairs of the Communist Party. His own words at Moscow on August 10, 1964 were: "Why should we make a secret out of the fact that the Party's Presidium has decided to convene a meeting of the Central Committee?" [9] In September 1964, Mr. Khrushchev told a group of visiting Japanese parliamentarians that Mao Tse-tung was espousing the general theories of Hitler.[10]

It is not surprising that these and other indications of loosened controls in the Soviet Union, and a consequent breakdown of the original monolithic pattern, should have led to some review of the image of the Soviet Union in Western countries. At an international conference at Stanford University in October 1964 to study the history of Communism, Professor Merle Fainsod of Harvard said that Khrushchev had contributed to the disintegration of the Communist empire by opposing militant world revolution and by concentrating on raising the living standards of the Soviet people. He added—and this is another dimension of the breakdown of monolithic tendencies —that the Sino-Soviet split had given Eastern European countries an opportunity to assert independent policies. On the other hand, at the same conference Boris Souervien, now of France and until 1924 a

Communist and an official of the Third International, said that the Soviet Union had not completely renounced the harsh theories and practices of Stalin. This statement itself implies that a degree of renunciation of such practices has taken place.

Those who have followed both the enunciation and the implementation of Soviet policy over the past fifteen years cannot but be aware of a considerable change in attitude. The vitriolic and completely unyielding statements of Andrei Vishinsky at the United Nations in the early 1950s have been succeeded by more flexible positions. The changes in the Soviet disarmament plan on the important issue of vehicles for delivery of nuclear weapons announced by Foreign Minister Gromyko at the Seventeenth and Eighteenth Sessions of the General Assembly in 1962 and 1963 have been in marked contrast to the rigidity of previous positions.

When monolithic tendencies are present in a society, however, the rigid positions assumed by some of that society's representatives are directly felt in international negotiation. I can well remember, for example, a private meeting which V. K. Krishna Menon and I had in 1955 with Foreign Minister Vyacheslav Molotov and several of his aides at San Francisco at the Tenth Anniversary Session of the General Assembly. We were met with complete stonewalling when we tried to probe Mr. Molotov on issues relating to disarmament. There was no disposition whatever on his part to respond to any suggestions or even to offer some elucidation of the Soviet position. The circumstances were not such that Mr. Molotov had any reason to avoid being communicative, at least on the facts of the Soviet position. The meeting took place at the Soviet villa, and no one was present but members of his delegation and the two of us from India.[11]

On the other hand, at frequent meetings which I have had with Andrei Gromyko and with his deputies Vasily Kuznetsov and Valerian Zorin about disarmament matters, we have spent many hours discussing possibilities, elucidating positions, and trying to find solutions. The contrast between the old rigid monolithic position of the Soviet Union and the new, more relaxed, somewhat less secretive ebullience of Premier Khrushchev and his colleagues was demonstrated on a June morning in 1961 when Premier Khrushchev arrived in Vienna for his meeting with President Kennedy. Mr. Molotov, at that time stationed at Vienna, went to the train to receive him. I was among those present. The meeting between the new and the old was icy cold. Mr. Khrushchev strode past the old regime with the determination of a man who had decided to go his own way.

When we come to the Chinese Communist Government we discern the continuing effect of a monolithic state structure. Mao Tse-tung laid down his position clearly in 1949 in his article, "On People's Democratic Dictatorships." On June 30 of that year he stated:

To sit on the fence is impossible. A third road does not exist. Not only in China but also in the world, without exception, one either leans to the side of imperialism or to the side of socialism. . . .

In an era when imperialism still exists, it is impossible for a genuine people's revolution in any country to win victory without various forms of help from the international revolutionary forces.[12]

It is true that since Mao Tse-tung made the above pronouncements the Chinese Government has attended conferences in 1954 and 1961–1962 at which efforts were made to establish the independence and neutrality of some of the states of former Indochina. However, the Chinese approach to neutrality in those countries is one that must be seen as subject to the Chinese axiom—consistent with its monolithic position—that such countries should be encouraged to progress in the direction of a Communist revolution.

The continuing and lengthy ideological discussion between the Communist parties of the Soviet Union and China has clarified for the outside world the ideological positions of the two countries. One of the most important documents on the Chinese side has been a very long letter dated June 14, 1963 from the Central Committee to the Soviet Communist Party. The full text of the letter in its 25 sections was printed in English in the Chinese weekly, *Peking Review*. In Section 3 of this letter we find the following:

If the general line of the International Communist movement is one-sidely reduced to "peaceful coexistence," "peaceful competition" and "peaceful transition," this is to violate the revolutionary principles of the 1957 declaration and the 1960 statement, to discard the historical mission of proletarian world revolution, and to depart from the revolutionary teachings of Marxism-Leninism.[13]

In Section 6 the letter sets out what all the Communist and workers' parties in the socialist camp should do. One of these "shoulds" is: "help the revolutionary struggles of the oppressed classes and nations of the world." [14] In Section 12 we find a statement which appears to be of direct relevance to China's role in such conferences as those of 1954 and 1961–1962. The text of the letter reads:

The proletarian party must be flexible as well as highly principled, and on occasion it must make such compromises as are necessary in the interest of the revolution. But it must never abandon principled policies and the goal of revolution on the pretext of flexibility and of necessary compromise.[15]

Section 14 of the letter developed the Chinese view relating to wars, and it carried the previous parts of the letter—including the dogmatisms just cited—to their logical conclusion. Nuclear weaponry notwithstanding, the Chinese Communists went back to the old Klauswitzian notion and stated:

. . . as Marxist-Leninists see it, war is the continuation of policies by other means, and every war is inseparable from the political struggle which gave rise to it. . . . Lumping just wars and unjust wars together and opposing all of them indiscriminately is a bourgeois pacifist and not a Marxist-Leninist approach.[16]

War, according to the Chinese Communists, may be necessary in order to end imperialism and colonialism or to achieve the Communist revolution. Premier Khrushchev, on the other hand, had already made a statement on the decay of colonialism when the colonialists would be deprived of their weapons (as would the colonized) under a regime of international disarmament. In his address of July 10, 1962 to the World Congress for General and Complete Disarmament at Moscow, he stated:

There is a close inter-connection between the struggle for national liberation and the struggle for disarmament and peace. The struggle for general disarmament facilitates the struggle for national independence. The achievements of the national liberation movement, in their turn, promote peace and contribute to the struggle for disarmament.

The colonialists have always established and maintained their rule by force of arms. Naturally, to deprive them of arms would mean drawing the teeth of the colonialist sharks.[17]

But the Chinese view is to scorn this approach. Here is Peking's answer to the new Russian position:

However, certain persons [the euphemism for Mr. Khrushchev and his party throughout the Chinese letter] now actually hold that it is possible to bring about "a world without weapons, without armed forces and without wars" through "general and complete disarmament" while the system of imperialism and of the exploitation of man by man still exists. This is sheer illusion.[18]

Mr. Khrushchev has often said that those who talk about war in our nuclear age are foolish. The same Chinese letter, however, went on to express the view that it is the people who make history; the role of technology does not change this, and the emergence of nuclear weapons has not altered the necessity for the proletarian revolution. These postures make it extremely difficult for the Chinese to engage meaningfully in international negotiation. While the Chinese Government has repeatedly stated its willingness to negotiate its border dispute with India, it has not been able to accept as a basis of negotiation the entirety of the proposals advanced unanimously by the six Colombo powers, which include states extremely friendly to China, namely, Burma, Cambodia, Ceylon, Ghana, and Indonesia. The sixth state is the United Arab Republic, which has also maintained friendly relations with China. To negotiate exclusively on one's own terms is hardly negotiation.

The Chinese Delegation at the Laos Conference of 1961–1962 was not unconstructive, but it was undoubtedly working within the kind of framework later made explicit to the outside world in the Chinese Communist Party's letter of June 14, 1963. It is difficult to see how any other explanation can be given of the Chinese willingness to accept, as the letter indeed states, "such compromises as are necessary in the interest of the revolution." The statements of the Chinese Delegation at the Laos Conference were consistent with the monolithic attitude expressed by the Chinese Communist Party. Marshal Chen Yi stated at Geneva that regarding foreign forces in Laos, the problem simply was to get rid of the forces introduced by the United States,[19] and once this was achieved all would be well in the future. This did not prevent some twenty battalions (the figure attributed to Prince Souvanna Phouma) of soldiers from North Vietnam from entering Laos in 1964, undoubtedly with the knowledge and probably with the blessing of China. Presumably the Chinese view would be that the introduction of certain foreign troops is just, whereas the introduction of other foreign troops is unjust.

At the Laos Conference the tone of the Chinese statements was set by an unbreakable sense of self-righteous assurance. In international affairs, an unbreakable sense of assurance is generally evidence of intransigence, and intransigence is a quality which is attributable to monoliths, whether material or ideological. At the Laos Conference, in referring to and making his own interpretation of statements from the Western side, Marshal Chen Yi said on June 12, 1961:

The Chinese delegation will never be a party to the dirty business of preying upon the Laotian people and enforcing an international condominium over Laos in the name of international control over its neutrality.[20]

The Marshal, on another occasion, accused the United States of wanting to "obtain all the national defense secrets of Laos through

the International Commission." He added "the United States has
indeed made this preposterous demand." [21] Later in the same statement Chen Yi, when comparing the French-American draft proposal
with the proposals of the Soviet Union, made a most interesting statement which is completely in line with the total assurance bestowed on
a speaker by a position based on a single doctrine or ideology. He
stated:

The French-American draft protocol cannot be the basis for our discussion, nor can it be compared and reconciled with the Soviet proposals.
How can we lump together right and wrong and then strike a mean between them? [22]

In the same statement, the Marshal tells us that the primary need
was "to make the United States and its followers" undertake not to
interfere in any manner in the internal affairs of Laos. In referring to
the scope of SEATO he said, "If the United States persists in this attitude, what is the meaning of our sitting here and discussing respect
for Laotian neutrality?" [23]

These remarks serve to bring out the strong resistance of the Chinese Delegation toward any point of view other than their own. It
may well be that their attitude has been accentuated, at least in part,
by the isolation of China from the normal intercourse of countries in
international organizations. But its source, judging from Chinese
Communist Party documents, is the ideological rigidity of the doctrine which China has espoused.

It does not, of course, follow that even in the case of single
ideology governments there are not occasions and circumstances in
which other considerations play a role and come to dominate approaches toward negotiation.[24] Whether a government is based on one
ideology or a plurality of thinking, it must still confront problems of
national interest and survival. Even the Peking Government appears
to have freed itself completely from ideological restrictions in some of
the close alliances which it has recently developed. Ideology is of no
consequence when an alliance appears to subserve Chinese border interests and other ambitions, as we shall see in the context of Chapter
Twenty-five.

Regardless of these inconsistent actions, however, the Chinese
keep coming back to a strongly monolithic ideological position. Early
in February 1964, the Chinese Communist Party's daily newspaper,
the *Chinese People's Daily,* republished an editorial from *Hung Chi,*
the ideological journal of the Communist Party's Central Committee,

condemning certain policies of the Soviet Communist Party. This document included the following statement:

The leaders of the C.P.S.U. are bent on seeking Soviet-United States cooperation for the domination of the world. They regard United States imperialism, the most ferocious enemy of the people of the world, as their most reliable friend and they treat their fraternal partners and countries adhering to Marxism-Leninism as their enemy. . . .

The leaders of the C.P.S.U. seek United States-Soviet cooperation and tirelessly fawn upon United States imperialism, and have thus disgraced the great Soviet Union. What is this if not anti-Soviet? [25]

Finally, it reiterated Chinese support for Communist revolutions wherever they may occur:

The leaders of the C.P.S.U. describe our support for Marxist-Leninists in other countries as a divisive act. In our opinion it is simply a proletarian internationalist obligation which it is our duty to discharge.[26]

The attitude of obligation to instigate and maintain a Communist revolutionary tendency in all regions of the world dominates Chinese approaches to negotiation. This does not mean that China is opposed to negotiation. It does mean that China's unswerving adherence to an ideology restricts its scope for genuine, lasting compromise.

The ideology adopted by the Chinese distorts their vision and makes them see prospects of Communist revolution where they do not exist. In an interview given to Dr. Hugo Portisch, Editor of *Der Kurier* of Vienna, on July 24, 1964, a Chinese official (believed to be Marshal Chen Yi) stated:

If I were an American I would vote for Goldwater. He would be good for the United States and he would be good for the world. He would, namely, push the internal situation in the United States to the extreme.[27]

China, in looking at the world through the narrow angle lens of its single ideology, is restricting the possibilities of understanding other countries and of reaching viable settlements with them. Fortunately for the world, there are other tangible realities which sometimes act as a brake on the single-track ideological urges of peoples and countries.

From the foregoing analysis we may conclude that ideology has a very direct effect on the process of international negotiation, in the following ways:

In pluralistic societies—assuming a considerable degree of dissemination of and receptivity to public information and views—opinion makers and pressure groups are able to contribute to enlarging or restricting the range of positions open to a government in formulating its posture for the negotiation of an international dispute or situation.

In a single ideology country, to the extent that the government reflects the tenets of that ideology in its approaches to the negotiation of an international dispute or situation, it restricts its own flexibility and capacity for reaching agreements.

CHAPTER TWENTY

Single Ideologies at the Negotiating Table

IN THE preceding chapter we considered the effect of a vigorous single ideology on the approach of a government to international negotiation. But when an international issue passes from the stage of declaration or indication of position to the stage of actual negotiation, how does a single ideology country then tend to behave? Do the country's representatives direct themselves entirely in terms of ideology, for example an ideology which might have declared its solidarity with the "have-not" countries or with those considered to be emerging from a period of domination by other countries? Or will ideological considerations play no part in the detailed positions taken up by such a government? Or will we find that the ideology merely adds another dimension alongside such generally operative factors as the vital interests of the country concerned? These are some of the questions which arise in considering how a single ideology country behaves when it is sitting at the negotiating table.

We have seen how in negotiation all countries will protect and promote their vital interests, primarily those interests bearing on such tangible realities as national security and national prosperity. In practice, "vital interests" are wider than those tangibles and include the fluctuating factor of a desired level of national power, and the elusive element of national prestige. To put the matter in everyday language, a country will pursue its own best interests throughout negotiation. In this regard a single ideology country cannot be distinguished from others.

Until a few years ago the analysis of this issue would have been directed almost entirely to the attitudes of the Soviet Union. We could have reminded ourselves of and explored in some depth, for example, the negotiations between Churchill and Stalin about the Balkan countries. We would have observed that both men quickly reached agreement regarding the composition of the Allied occupation forces in those states as the Axis forces retreated. Indeed, as Churchill tells us, he wrote out on a half sheet of paper:

Rumania	
Russian	90%
The Others	10%
Greece	
Great Britain	
(in accord with the USA)	90%
Russia	10%
Yugoslavia	50–50%
Hungary	50–50%
Bulgaria	
Russia	75%
The Others	25%

He goes on to say:

I pushed this across to Stalin, who had by then heard the translation. There was a slight pause. Then he took his blue pencil and made a large tick upon it, and passed it back to us. It was all settled in no more time than it takes to set down.[1]

Later, when he wanted to protest against the development of events in the Balkans, where the principles agreed upon at Yalta were not being observed, Churchill made the following remark:

We were hampered in our protests because Eden and I during our October visit to Moscow had recognized that Russia should have a largely predominant voice in Rumania and Bulgaria while we took the lead in Greece. Stalin had kept very strictly to this understanding during the six weeks' fighting against the Communists and E.L.A.S. in the city of Athens, in spite of the fact that all this was most disagreeable to him and those around him.[2]

In the next paragraph of his work Churchill goes on to state that if he had pressed Stalin, the latter "might say, 'I did not interfere with your action in Greece; why do you not give me the same latitude in Rumania?' " ³

In these exchanges over the Balkans, we observe two highly realistic leaders, one the Prime Minister of one of the oldest and greatest democracies in the West, the other the leader of a great single ideology country, reaching an important understanding through a negotiation which took into account one another's national interests, without much regard to ideological considerations. Stalin let the Communists of Athens be decimated and defeated, and Churchill felt that he should let Stalin have a more or less free hand in Rumania. Ideology played a very small part in these negotiations, and in the events that followed them.

In the negotiations of the Eighteen-Nation Committee on Disarmament, a third party can readily detect that the proposals advanced by the two sides—the Western countries led by the United States and the Communists led by the Soviet Union—are generally dictated by the assessment of either side of its own best interests, including the maintenance of a security edge in its favor.

Keeping in mind the theoretical basis on which China approaches negotiation, discussed in the preceding chapter, let us now look at various aspects of the actual negotiations regarding Laos in 1961 and 1962. The preliminaries started at the beginning of 1961. The representatives of the fourteen countries constituting the conference gathered at the negotiating table in May of that year, and the agreements were not signed until the end of July 1962. There was thus a period of almost a year and a quarter during which Chinese attitudes toward and in negotiation became apparent.

Shortly before the Fourteen-Nation Conference on Laos was convened at Geneva, there was a big rally in Peking in its support, addressed by Marshal Chen Yi. The obvious reason for the vociferous support of the proposed conference was that the Chinese were keen to see United States forces and influence removed from a state which borders on China. It is understandable from the Chinese point of view that they should not want to see the "enemy" powerfully entrenched on their doorstep. It would be in keeping with the protection of the vital interests of China for her to seek to exclude the United States from Laos. China's strong support for the Conference was perfectly reasonable in terms of hard-headed self-interest, and it does not seem necessary to bring in ideological considerations, although, of course, we cannot exclude the possibility that they were operative in some degree.

At the Peking rally Marshal Chen Yi made the following statement, after praising the material support which had been given by the Soviets to the Souvanna Phouma Government: "If the lawful government headed by Prince Phouma requests support from the Chinese government the Chinese government, too, will certainly give it." [4] This quotation is important because it shows how ready China is to shift from negotiation to the use of force in pursuit of its own interests, which in Laos was the exclusion of the United States. This is a factor which tends to make Chinese positions at the negotiating table truculent, and rather unstable.

When the Laos Conference met in May 1961, it was immediately striking that China seemed to regard as important a display of massive strength. About a sixth of the seats in the large Council Chamber at the Palais des Nations at Geneva were occupied by members of the Chinese delegation. China appeared to be giving notice that it would negotiate from strength.

China immediately showed that it had its own independent line at the conference. On the very first day of substantive speeches, Marshal Chen Yi made a comprehensive statement of the Chinese position, which was largely an attack on the United States and SEATO activities in Southeast Asia. In addition, he offered the general lines of a solution for the Laotian problem. What was remarkable about this first Chinese statement was that it set a pattern entirely different from the general sequence of Communist interventions at other international conferences. Each year at the sessions of the General Assembly the Soviet Union is among the first few speakers in the opening general debate. In a full statement the Soviet Union lays down the position which the other Communist countries then broadly follow. The same is true of other conferences, such as the annual general conference of the International Atomic Energy Agency and of the meetings of its Board of Governors. However, at the Laos Conference China did not wait for Soviet leadership to point the way. It stated its own requirements and did so in terms of its own national interests. Indeed, it did this even without waiting for the Laotian delegates to state their own case. Marshal Chen Yi said:

The Laotian peoples' right to settle their problems themselves should be guaranteed; no foreign power should be permitted to use force or the threat of force against Laos; and no country should be permitted to use aid as a means to violate the neutrality of Laos and interfere in its internal affairs. The military personnel of the United States and of the other countries which are interfering in Laos with United States support must

be withdrawn and the remnant Kuomintang troops in Laos must be disarmed and sent out of Laos.[5]

The first part of this formulation is unexceptional, but we then observe that the exclusion of foreign forces from Laos was interpreted
by Chen Yi to be the exclusion solely of the United States personnel
and other countries supported by the United States. There was no
mention of excluding the forces and personnel which were supporting
and fighting beside the Neo-Lao Haksat. Incidentally, Chen Yi said
nothing in this statement about the two French military bases in
Laos. It is true that the Chinese, much later in informal sessions of
the heads of the six main delegations, did ask for the removal also of
those bases, but it was an indication of their basic policy in regard to
Laos that they called for the exclusion specifically of the United
States and United States supported personnel. The Chinese attitude
would seem (especially when we remember the omission of France)
to have been dictated solely by the desire to exclude "the enemy"
from a neighboring state. This is a classical move in the direction of
the protection of vital interests, and has no connection with ideology.

This did not, of course, mean that the Chinese would not have preferred Laos to be dominated by the Neo-Lao Haksat party, which is
more pro-Chinese than the centrist party of Souvanna Phouma; and
needless to say they made no demand for the exclusion of the North
Vietnamese from Laos.

In fairness it should be stated that China, in its statements at the
Conference, strongly supported the centrist government of Souvanna
Phouma. Whether we regard their basic motives to be the strengthening of a truly neutral Laos under a centrist government, or the easing
of the way for the installation of a left-wing government under the
Neo-Lao Haksat (the more likely objective), the main immediate
purpose of the Chinese was to exclude the Americans, and they
seemed to be willing to achieve this without asking for any special
influence for themselves in Laos. It was admitted at the Conference
that no Chinese elements were in Laos supporting the Neo-Lao
Haksat. This was an interesting fact, especially when we take into
account the common border between Laos and China and the ease
with which Chinese elements could have entered the country.

It would appear that the Chinese felt that they could secure their
main objective best without physically entering Laos. Indeed, they
undoubtedly realized that if they were to introduce armed Chinese
elements into Laos there would be practically no chance of getting
the United States to agree to leave that country. They decided it was

best to have Laos run by its own political factions, but without any United States presence.

If China's main objective and urge in regard to Laos had been ideological, some attempt would have been made to introduce into the country highly trained Communist cadres which would have engaged in the task of spreading the Chinese brand of Marxism-Leninism.

That China places national interests above ideological considerations in international negotiation and relations is again borne out by the ambivalence which China has shown in regard to SEATO. At the Laos Conference a major effort of the Chinese delegation was to liquidate SEATO. The correspondent of the *Peking Review* at Geneva, referring to these Chinese efforts, stated: "The struggle to liquidate SEATO and the 'protection' it imposes on Laos has only reached the end of a stage." [6] In an editorial of July 24, 1962, one day after the signing of the Laos Agreements at Geneva, the *Chinese People's Daily* had announced triumphantly that:

The United States now once again has to agree, together with the other countries concerned, to respect the sovereignty, independence, and neutrality of Laos and to remove the "protection" imposed by SEATO on Laos.[7]

In connection with another negotiation—that which resulted in a Treaty of Friendship and Mutual Non-Aggression with Burma—the *Chinese People's Daily* said in an editorial of February 1, 1960:

The treaty also affirms that each Contracting Party undertakes . . . not to take part in any military alliances directed against the other Contracting Party. . . . Since United States imperialism is now doing its utmost to expand its aggressive military blocs, this article deals a stunning blow against the United States plot.[8]

Obviously, in international negotiations China strongly opposed Western military alliances. There was nothing ideological in this opposition. It was directed simply at getting the Western countries to withdraw from Southeast Asia. The attacks which China made on members of the alliances as such were not because they were anti-Communist states. This is borne out by the fact that it has been possible for China to make a close alliance, which would appear to cover defense, with Pakistan, a state which is an original member of SEATO and of other anti-Communist alliances. If China were a country strongly actuated by ideological sentiments it could not enter into alliances with countries which had proclaimed their staunch opposition to Communism and were close allies of the United States. However, since China and Pakistan are both inimical toward India, it is in their mutual interest to form an alliance. This step is understandable in terms of conventional diplomacy and is in keeping with the promotion of national interests, which take priority over ideological postures even in the case of China.

In the problem of disarmament, to what extent is China's attitude based on ideological considerations, and to what extent is it directed by patent and tangible self-interest? In 1959 Premier Khrushchev made the first Soviet pitch at the United Nations General Assembly for general and complete disarmament. Although as early as those days there were elements of friction in Sino-Soviet relations, China seemed to be confident that the Soviet Union would safeguard its interests, including assistance to develop nuclear weapons. For that reason China immediately came out strongly in support of the Soviet plan for general and complete disarmament. Marshal Chen Yi addressed the Standing Committee of the National People's Congress of China on June 21, 1960 and said:

On October 14, 1959, the Standing Committee of the National People's Congress adopted a special resolution supporting the proposal of the Soviet government for general and complete disarmament. . . . our government and people will, along with our great ally the Soviet Union, and all other peace-loving countries and peoples, spare no effort in our unswerving struggle for universal disarmament.[9]

On the same day the Standing Committee of the National People's Congress adopted a resolution which repeated, word for word, much of Marshal Chen Yi's speech and added, in the same strain: "The Chinese people will carry on an unswerving struggle for the realization of general and complete disarmament and lasting peace." [10]

Thereafter, Chinese relations with the Soviet Union deteriorated fairly steadily. On June 14, 1963, the Chinese Communist Party stated its position on most aspects of its dispute with the Russian party in its letter to the Soviet Communist Party.[11]

In this letter we see a complete reversal of the earlier Chinese position on general and complete disarmament. Since the Soviet Union was no longer assisting China in the nuclear field, China was no longer interested in the Russian version of general and complete disarmament. In fact, it sneered at the idea. This turnabout in China's policy led to a reversal in its negotiating posture, and was dictated entirely by China's desire to be a first-rate military power; in other words, by political considerations relating to its own interests, rather than by any ideological considerations.

True, if pressed the Chinese could claim that if they became a first-class military power this would be in the interests of world revolution, that is, their main ideological objective would be achieved. But even this argument has been subverted by current Chinese doctrine. On October 11, 1965, the *Chinese People's Daily* wrote, "Communism can be finally realized in China only when a world-wide victory is won for the proletarian revolution." [12] This statement makes it clear that the purpose of the international dissemination of their ideology is mainly to subserve Chinese national interests.

The change in Peking's negotiating posture in regard to disarmament became apparent when the partial test ban agreement was reached in August 1963. China's reaction was one of outrage. It ridiculed the agreement, because if it were to sign it its determination to develop nuclear weapons would have to be abandoned. In those circumstances China was not willing to talk of general and complete disarmament, but was willing to try to get the great nuclear powers to give up their nuclear weapons and called for a conference for that purpose. Obviously a conference which would decide to eliminate nuclear weapons would be one in which China would lose nothing; on the contrary, it would immediately step into a dominating military place with its very large army, reserves of manpower, and growing arsenal of conventional weapons.

Premier Chou En-lai in his note to all governments on October 16, 1964 repeated the terms of the official statement of that date on the detonation of China's atomic bomb.[13] Significantly, in the note and statement China does not ask for general and complete disarmament. Such a radical step would deprive that country of its superiority in conventional arms. All it seeks is to deprive other countries of their nuclear superiority. By the substance of its latest proposals, China makes it very clear that its negotiating posture in regard to the general problem of disarmament has shifted from its earlier (1959–1960) support for general and complete disarmament—which goes back to the time when it felt it could obtain nuclear weapons from the Soviet Union—to purely nuclear disarmament which would safeguard its own military strength.

In China's negotiation with Burma on the question of their common border, China changed its position when it decided that it might be prudent to equip itself with two peepholes over the mountain ranges into Burma. In its negotiations there was no trace of ideological considerations, but simply the decision of China to obtain first one advantage and then another, presumably in the interests of its own security.[14]

If China—undoubtedly the most ideologically oriented country in our era—acts almost entirely in accordance with the promotion and protection of its own interests when it comes to the details of negotiation, it can be justifiably stated that a country which is imbued with a strong ideological belief does not let those beliefs dominate its representatives in negotiations with other countries. From a consideration of this evidence, we would suggest that the following principle seems to operate:

At the negotiating table, or in informal negotiations or exchanges, the ideological beliefs of a country tend to have little influence on its demands and attitudes regarding matters of substance. Its assessment of its own best advantage in terms of material gain or military power, and the general protection and promotion of its other vital interests, will predominantly determine its conduct.

CHAPTER TWENTY-ONE

Some Minimal Requirements

SOME MOVEMENT from original positions is necessary if there is to be even a measure of success in negotiation. If a party will not move at all, or conversely if one party accepts the position of the other, then there is hardly need or scope for negotiation. Although the move which a party may be willing to make is sometimes more apparent than real, even an apparent move may be of value. It may save face; again it may give time for both parties to explain the situation further to wider international bodies such as the United Nations, or to their own people.

Where the states in confrontation cannot move from their positions, or where the moves are insufficient in relation to the fundamental issues involved, there is no immediate possibility of real negotiation. In the case of Berlin, although both sides have made certain suggestions, those suggestions have not altered basically incompatible positions which have continued to frustrate the possibilities of negotiation on the main issues involved. Similarly, Chinese reluctance to move sufficiently to accept fully the basis of negotiation suggested by the six Colombo powers has obstructed negotiation with India on resolving the border dispute.

While the parties must be willing to move, or give adequate appearance of so doing, it must not be expected that in this process any party will subject itself to a significant diminution of its international status. Negotiation is not a method for imposing radical "solutions." It might be possible for a series of negotiations over a considerable period of time to move an issue to a significantly different position from that which obtained before the commencement of the series of negotiations. But revolutionary change through negotiation is a rarity indeed.

Perhaps the most radical changes through negotiation have been those involving the emergence into independence of the African states in the last few years. However, those changes, for the most part, have been tempered by the process of negotiation. Most of the African countries which have merged from a British colonial past desire to continue to be associated with the United Kingdom as members of the Commonwealth of Nations. This association may appear to be largely formal, but it has substantive advantages, such as the encouragement of the maintenance of commercial and industrial connections, which are clearly of considerable material significance. Furthermore, in times of crisis the Commonwealth tends to become much more than a mere formality. When armed revolt suddenly broke out in Tanganyika in 1963, President Julius Nyerere appealed to the United Kingdom for immediate military aid, and although there was no defense treaty between the two countries the aid was immediately forthcoming. Again, at the time of conflict between India and Pakistan over the Rann of Cutch, the United Kingdom initiated negotiations through its mediatory efforts. Malaysia has been assisted not only by the United Kingdom, with which it has a defense treaty, but by other Commonwealth countries in meeting the Indonesian confrontation.

The disruption that might have resulted from the recent radical changes in the international status of the United Kingdom, achieved through negotiation, has been significantly offset by the new kind of relationship which has emerged between that country and most of its former dependent territories. This new relationship has helped to maintain the international position of the United Kingdom.

Most of the former African colonial possessions of France have remained tied to the metropolitan country in a close and often crucially loyal association. When the General Assembly voted on the question of Algerian independence, the "French" African states joined with the close allies of France, such as the United States and Belgium, in abstaining on the relevant resolutions of December 19, 1960 and December 20, 1961.[1] Indeed on the former occasion, the Republics of Cameroun, Chad, Gabon, the Ivory Coast. Malagasy, and Upper Volta joined Portugal and the Union of South Africa to constitute the only eight states which voted against the resolution. The resolutions merely called upon the parties to negotiate, and reiterated recognition of the right of the Algerian people to self-determination and independence—all of which had already been conceded by President de Gaulle. France has aided her ex-colonial

African friends liberally. French prestige in the world has not diminished as a result of the relinquishment of empire. Many observers hold that the contrary has been the case.

The retention of close ties with metropolitan countries indicates a significant movement on the part of the ex-colonial territories. Most of them had adopted platforms of complete independence and an ending of previous ties. The Indian National Congress Party as long ago as its annual meeting in 1929, under the presidency of Jawaharlal Nehru, adopted a deliberate change of policy for its goal. This goal would no longer be statehood within the Commonwealth as a self-governing dominion, but complete independence. From then on complete independence was the constant watchword of the Indian movement. However, the process of successful negotiation in its final stages generated enough good will for this adamant and clear-cut position to be altered, and for a new relationship to be devised. India became a republic within the Commonwealth. Such movements by ex-colonial territories indicate that even where the success in negotiation appears to be one-sided, the detailed positions show a yielding on both sides of the negotiating table.

In the post-World War II era, the only phase of disarmament negotiation which has recorded some success, however slight, is that which commenced on March 14, 1962, when the Eighteen-Nation Committee on Disarmament first convened. It will be recalled that the immediate background of the Committee commenced in 1959 with the adoption by the General Assembly of the resolution of November 20, 1959 which prescribed the goal to be general and complete disarmament.[2] Thereafter, the two sides agreed to meet in a Ten-Nation Committee consisting of five Western powers and five Communist states. The Ten-Nation Committee met from March to June 1960, but ended abruptly on June 27 when the Soviet delegation and its Communist allies walked out of a meeting and never returned. Although the basis of the 1960 meeting had been the unequivocal mutual acceptance of a comprehensive goal for disarmament (and this itself indicated some movement by both sides), and although a slight degree of flexibility was displayed at the 1960 negotiations, significant further movements had to be made before the United States and the Soviet Union could reach agreement on a Joint Statement of Agreed Principles. In the 1960 meetings, both the United States and the Soviet Union produced outlines of disarmament plans and statements of principles. Furthermore, on the very day that the conference foundered, June 27, 1961, the Western powers introduced a new version of their disarmament plan.

The Joint Statement of Agreed Principles formulated on September 20, 1961, which is the basis of the Eighteen-Nation Committee meetings, shows the following important movements forward by both sides from their 1960 positions: (1) It was the first agreed statement drawn up and subscribed to by both the United States and the Soviet Union on clear-cut comprehensive principles to govern disarmament negotiations. (2) The 6th Agreed Principle states: "This International Disarmament Organization and its inspectors should be assured unrestricted access without veto to all places as necessary for the purpose of effective verification." [3] In the above formulation the words "without veto" had not appeared in the previous statements of principle advanced severally by the United States and the Soviet Union in April 1960 during the Ten-Nation Committee on Disarmament Conference.[4] (3) The 7th Agreed Principle deals with the settlement of international disputes by peaceful means and the peacekeeping functions of the United Nations. Although the United States had frequently stressed the importance of these functions, its previous formulation of principles just referred to, and the two sets of disarmament plans which it presented in 1960 to the Ten-Nation Committee, did not contain as clear a statement on peacekeeping operations as did the 7th of the Agreed Principles of September 20, 1961. Similar observations are even more applicable to previous Soviet statements on the subject when compared with the Agreed Principles of 1961. The relevant part of the agreed document reads:

During and after . . . general and complete disarmament there should be taken, in accordance with the principles of the United Nations Charter, the necessary measures to maintain international peace and security, including the obligation of States to place at the disposal of the United Nations agreed man-power necessary for an international peace force to be equipped with agreed types of armaments. Arrangements for the use of this force should insure that the United Nations can effectively deter or suppress any threat or use of arms in violation of the purposes and principles of the United Nations.[5]

In addition to the foregoing movements from both sides, the Joint Statement of Agreed Principles registered other significant movements severally by the United States and the Soviet Union.

For the United States the important words in the 1st Agreed Principle dealing with the goal of disarmament negotiations, "war is no longer an instrument for settling of international problems," constituted a new formulation in the program of disarmament. The agreement of the United States to the 3rd Principle, the abolishing of the "organization and institutions designed to organize the military effort of states, cessation of military training, and closing of all military training institutions," [6] was new. In the 4th Principle, dealing with the timetable, the United States agreed for the first time that each "stage [should be] carried out within specified time-limits." As to the task of the negotiators, the United States agreed that "efforts should continue without interruption until agreement upon a total program has been achieved." [7]

Similarly, the Soviet Union made a number of movements from previous positions so as to enable a joint formulation to be written. In the timetable the Soviet Union agreed that:

. . . transition to a subsequent stage in the process of disarmament should take place upon a review of the implementation of measures included in the preceding stage and upon a decision that all such measures have been implemented and verified and that any additional verification arrangements required for measures in the next stage are, when appropriate, ready to operate. (Principle 4) [8]

Then again the Soviet Union agreed to the balancing of all disarmament measures as set forth in the 5th Principle:

All measures of general and complete disarmament should be balanced so that at no stage of the implementation of the treaty could any State or group of States gain military advantage and that security is insured equally for all.[9]

On the crucial subject of verification, the Soviets agreed to the important phrase in the 6th principle that there would be "effective international control as would provide firm assurance that all parties are honoring their obligations." [10] Regarding the maintenance of peace, the Soviet Union took a step by agreeing to the 7th Principle, that "progress in disarmament should be accompanied by measures to strengthen institutions for maintaining peace and the settlement of international disputes by peaceful means." [11]

There have been other cases in which the most powerful states have moved from their original positions. We have noted how both the United States and the Soviet Union made significant moves in the Caribbean crisis in October 1962.

Small as well as large powers have demonstrated the necessity for movement at the conference table. We might recall the efforts of the United Nations between 1955 and 1958 to deal with the problem of Cyprus at a time when the island was still a British colony. The issue was brought to the United Nations by the Government of Greece, and their demand then was for enosis, that is, the union of Greece and Cyprus. The Turkish position was that Cyprus had been wrested from

Turkey by the British, and that if the British were to leave the island should be returned to them. In any event, they strongly opposed enosis. Typical of the handling of the situation then was the long debate at the Eleventh Session of the General Assembly in 1956, when four draft resolutions were introduced in the First Committee. Two were introduced by Greece—one seeking to gain Assembly recognition of the right of self-determination for the people of Cyprus, and the second asking for the appointment of a fact-finding committee.[12] The United Kingdom, as the country then in authority on Cyprus, introduced a draft resolution noting that states should refrain from intervention in the internal affairs of other states and asking Greece to cease its support for terrorist activities on the island.[13] The fourth draft was introduced by Panama, and sought to set up a committee to make an on-site study of the situation which would be followed by recommendations to the Twelfth Session of the General Assembly.[14]

However, these draft resolutions seemed to many states to require one side to move much more in the direction of the other side than was feasible. For example, adoption of the Greek texts would probably have established their own case for enosis. The British text would have resulted in leaving things as they were, namely, in the hands of the colonial power. The Panamanian text was in a sense too ambitious and sought to take the question out of the hands of those directly involved and vest it in a United Nations committee. This text did not refer to arbitration, but that is what it might in practice have amounted to, and arbitration, as we have observed at the beginning of this study, is not part of the process of negotiation and must generally be regarded as a more radical measure.

Under these circumstances, after close consultation with the foreign ministers of Greece (Avengelos Averoff-Tossizza), Turkey (Fotin Zorlu), and the United Kingdom (Selwyn Lloyd), the Indian delegation evolved a formula which appeared to sustain and urge the possibility of some movement on all sides. The operative paragraph of this text, almost each word of which had to be informally checked and rechecked with the representatives of the countries concerned, read:

[The General Assembly] expresses the earnest desire that a peaceful, democratic and just solution will be found in accord with the purposes and principles of the Charter of the United Nations, and the hope that negotiations will be resumed and continued to this end.[15]

This formulation put the issue back where it belonged, namely in the realm of negotiation. The Assembly adopted it without a single vote in opposition.[16] Ultimately it was this approach which led to the talks at Zurich between the Greek and Turkish Governments and which produced the agreements for an independent Cyprus in 1959. The agreements, although they broke down a few years later, were based on movement at the time by all sides. Cyprus did not become part of Greece as the latter had demanded; the British remained in possession of important bases on the island; and the Turkish minority obtained a veto in the Government of Cyprus on a number of important issues. That the success of the 1959 negotiations turned out to be temporary does not invalidate the genuine character of the negotiations. As a general rule in international affairs, progress toward solutions comes in stages, and those efforts which make a contribution by eliminating some causes of conflict for a period of time need not be regarded as failures. The process of adjustment which is advanced by negotiation is a delicate and intricate one, and must often proceed on a trial and error basis.

A recent example of movement on the part of two countries is furnished by the issues which followed the emergence of Yemen as a republic in 1962. Saudi Arabia, as we have mentioned in an earlier context, became involved in the situation because it appeared to favor the regime of the ousted Imam. The new Republic of Yemen received military assistance from the United Arab Republic, and in the debate on credentials at the Seventeenth Session of the General Assembly the representative of the United Arab Republic contended that the forces of his country had been requested by the Yemen republic and were at the disposal of the Supreme Command of the Yemeni Army with the sole purpose of insuring that Yemen could practice its inherent right of self-defense. The General Assembly, by its vote on the report of the Credentials Committee, took the view that Yemen had become a republic.

However, Saudi Arabian forces and those of the United Arab Republic continued to be virtually at war in Yemen. Indeed the dimensions of the conflict grew. The Secretary-General of the United Nations stepped in. He reported to the Security Council in June 1963 that Saudi Arabia and the United Arab Republic were willing to have the United Nations observe a progressive process of disengagement of their forces in Yemen. The Security Council adopted a resolution approving the United Nations observation.[17]

This observation remained in force for over a year, but the military confrontation continued because the political issues underlying it had not been resolved. However, shortly before the convening in September 1964 of a summit meeting of the Arab states at Alexandria, efforts were put in train with the help of friendly governments to find a compromise which would be satisfactory to Yemen and to the governments of Saudi Arabia and the United Arab Republic. These efforts succeeded in a measure, but only after some movement had been made by both Saudi Arabia and the United Arab Republic. On September 14, 1964, the two Governments announced their agreement. The movements of these two interested powers apparently provided that the leaders of the opposing factions in Yemen would be changed and that a new government would be set up which would include some royalists.[18] On September 25 Abdel Hakim Amer, the First Vice President of the United Arab Republic, addressed a group of tribal leaders in Yemen and reportedly stated: "The monarchy in Yemen is gone forever. The revolution will remain until Yemen takes her rightful place in freedom and civilization." [19] This was apparently intended to reassure the Yemeni Republican leaders, who were reported to have felt that the movement made by the United Arab Republic in order to arrive at the compromise arrangement with Saudi Arabia amounted to an abandonment of their cause.

The several instances which we have just examined deal with cases of real movement by all the parties directly involved in international situations which came to be the subject of negotiation. However, there are occasions when the movement is more apparent than real, although even in such cases the terms of the settlement may reflect a mutual movement. In this category a good illustration is provided by the issue of West Irian. We have dealt with aspects of this issue, but the point to be noted here is that the preponderant movement was made by the Netherlands. West Irian is now in the hands of Indonesia. However, an important element in the position of the Netherlands throughout the negotiations has been preserved in the terms of the final agreement, which provides for the participation of the population of West Irian in an act of free choice to determine the ultimate status of the territory.[20] Although it is generally assumed that the free choice which is to be exercised by the population of West Irian will not result in any change in the new arrangement by which the territory has become part of Indonesia, in conceding that this provision be included in the agreement the Government of Indonesia appeared to have moved from its original position, which was that Indonesia was to comprise the entire territory of the Netherlands Indies.[21]

The foregoing illustrations also support the general rule that each party to an international negotiation must emerge from it without having suffered a complete defeat. Broadly speaking, particularly in the past, states have often felt that if they were to be defeated anyway they might as well struggle to the last so as to try to exact the least unfavorable terms for a settlement. Although armed conflict is less possible today in view both of commitments to the Charter of the United Nations and of the nature of the weapons at the disposal of the major military alliances, the determination to struggle to the end rather than accept complete defeat is generally a continuing aspect of the character of the nation state.

Where negotiation is frustrated and cannot succeed, the root causes will often include the apprehension on one side that the results of negotiation would entail an eclipse of its international position or status. In the matter of German unification, the implementation of proposals based on elections covering the whole territory of the Federal Republic and the Democratic Republic would probably result in a severe diminution of the status of one side, the German Democratic Republic, and by extension the Soviet Union. Similarly, the intractable attitude of the Government of the Union of South Africa stems partly from its apprehension that to negotiate on the basis of equal rights for all its inhabitants would result in the eclipse of the power of the present minority Government. That this attitude does not appear to be morally justifiable because it brushes aside the rights of a vast majority does not alter the fact that it seriously blocks the possibilities of negotiation. Somewhat similar positions prevail in Rhodesia and South-West Africa.

In the case of the Portuguese possessions, particularly Mozambique and Angola, the situation is more complex. However, Portugal is certainly apprehensive that it would suffer a considerable diminution of its status in international affairs if it had to divest itself of its colonial possessions. The fact that other countries have given up larger colonial empires and have done so without an ultimate significant loss of status does not appear to move the Portuguese Government, because it sets undue store by outmoded and discarded criteria of national status. But, as we have stated, the position is more complex, and other factors are involved. Furthermore, apparently Portugal feels that it still has enough support for its general position to enable it to continue to hold its colonial possessions. Whatever the factors involved, genuine negotiation has to be realistic. It has to take the positions of the parties into account; where it cannot take them into account, or when one party continues adamant in spite of the movement of the other, the issue passes beyond the realm of negotiation, and conflict becomes a likely alternative. On the side of the African suppressed majorities, the attitude is equally—and inevitably—adamant. It was expressed in the words of President Kenneth Kaunda of Zambia in his address to the Nineteenth General Assembly on December 4, 1964:

Yet I warn you that we in Africa cannot hold our people back forever and prevent their burning indignation and shame from breaking out into action which might set the whole world alight.[22]

From our consideration of the necessity that states engaged in international negotiation be capable of movement from a fixed position, two principles seem to follow:

The parties to a dispute or situation which becomes the subject of international negotiation must give evidence at some stage of the negotiations of a degree of willingness to make some movement, either apparent or real, from their original or starting positions.

The minimal requirements of a party to an international negotiation tend to include the implicit condition that it should emerge from the negotiation, irrespective of the final results achieved, without appearing to have suffered total eclipse or significant diminution of its international status.

CHAPTER TWENTY-TWO

Movements from Original Positions

EACH STATE involved in negotiation dislikes having to move from its own position toward that of the "opponent," because any such movement involves a degree of concession. This reluctance tends to express itself in evasiveness, even after there has been indication that a state is willing to move from its original position.

There have been striking examples of this kind of evasiveness in recent negotiations, but perhaps in none more than in those on the cessation of nuclear testing. The most complete change of position in reversal of previous movements was the withdrawal by the Soviets in 1961 of their acceptance of a system of international control posts, which would have covered all countries including the Soviet Union, to monitor the carrying out of the terms of an agreement to end nuclear testing. Equally striking was the fact that although Premier Khrushchev, in a letter dated December 19, 1962 addressed to President Kennedy,[1] accepted a small number of on-site inspections in connection with the monitoring of a ban on nuclear tests, that offer was withdrawn by the Soviet Union in the late spring of 1963.

There were shifts in position on the other side also. For example, on September 3, 1961, President Kennedy and Prime Minister Macmillan made a proposal to Premier Khrushchev that the three Governments of the United Kingdom, the Soviet Union, and the United States should agree not to conduct nuclear tests in the atmosphere. The two Western heads of government stated in their proposal that they were prepared "to rely upon existing means of detection, which they believe to be adequate. . . ."[2] However, this offer to rely on the existing means of detection was later withdrawn. When the Eighteen-Nation Committee on Disarmament met in March 1962, the

Western representatives reverted to a demand for control arrangements to insure detection of nuclear tests in all media. This remained the Western position until August 27, 1962, when two draft treaties were introduced at the Eighteen-Nation Committee Conference, the first for a comprehensive test ban and the second for a ban on nuclear weapons tests in the atmosphere, in outer space, and under water. For the latter [3] the Western powers reverted to the position that no control measures were necessary.

These movements and reversals of positions were expressions of attempts by the two sides to maximize the response of the other side. Such tactics are of the essence of negotiation. Doubtless they create difficulties. They lead to accusations of bad faith, and in the minds of third parties not connected directly with the negotiations they promote cynicism about the sincerity of the negotiating states. In regard to disarmament and arms control, such cynicism has been publicly and privately expressed by delegates of countries other than the superpowers and their close allies. However, when one understands that both negotiating tactics and the realities of the situation might impose some of these seemingly meaningless movements and retractions on the parties, then one must also see that cynicism on the part of others is out of place.

In order to understand the processes and principles which underlie the movements of parties, we must take into account the obvious tendency to maintain original positions as firmly as possible. Broadly speaking, the more powerful side will be less willing to move; nevertheless, all parties to an international negotiation would appear to be subject to certain principles in the movements they make.

Certain aspects of the long negotiation connected with what was originally the concept of SUNFED illustrate the tactic of chaffering. Those negotiations came to a crisis in 1957. Until that time there had been pious genuflection to the idea of SUNFED, partly because the idea was remote enough to be divorced from the realm of practicability. However, the pressure on the part of the less developed countries was mounting strongly, and it became incumbent upon those states which could not agree to the establishment of SUNFED to state their position clearly. In their explanations they drew attention to what they had done to assist the less developed countries; they pointed to common interests, and they made compromise proposals which they stated were significant and of great value.

Congressman Walter H. Judd of the United States is recorded as saying in the discussions of SUNFED at the Twelfth Session of the

General Assembly: "In the matter of economic development, the basic interests of the developed and underdeveloped countries were the same." [4] He then went on to say that the United States had already made over $11 billion available directly to underdeveloped countries as economic aid, and "it had established a Development Loan Fund . . . [with] . . . an initial capital of 300 million dollars in the form of a revolving loan fund." Furthermore, the United States Congress had authorized the appropriation of an additional $625 million for the Development Loan Fund for the fiscal year 1959. The Fund was also authorized to guarantee loans from private sources for purposes of economic development in the less developed countries.[5] In view of these important steps taken by his country, he inquired if it was necessary or realistic to set up SUNFED. Indeed, explained Mr. Judd:

> . . . at the risk of causing keen disappointment . . . the United States would not only vote against any resolution . . . that contemplated the immediate establishment of such a Fund but would also refuse to participate in the work of any preparatory committee which might be appointed to draft the regulations of the Fund.[6]

Under the circumstances, the United States proposed to enlarge the existing program of technical assistance in the United Nations. While admitting that his proposal was not equivalent to SUNFED, Mr. Judd gave full play to its advantages, thus maximizing the step which his Government was willing to take. He stated that the proposed

> . . . increase in technical assistance obviously would not be sufficient to provide a complete substitute for SUNFED as far as the financing of basic projects was concerned, but it would help the recipient countries to train their man-power and use their resources more productively.[7]

Mr. Judd's reference to his proposal as not providing a complete substitute for SUNFED was, of course, an understatement which few have outdone at the United Nations!

But on the side of the less developed countries, there was an equal underplaying of the proposed United States step. Ambassador Joza Brilej, speaking for Yugoslavia, stated that "the adoption of the United States proposal was . . . inconceivable unless it was linked to a decision to establish SUNFED." [8] The representative of Indonesia, Ambassador Zairin Zain, expressed the same thought in the most diplomatic language:

The United States proposal seemed admirable in itself; there was ample scope for technical assistance in the fields mentioned by the United States representative, and his delegation would wholeheartedly support it if it could be sure that it was not intended to compete with the 11-Power proposal [to set up SUNFED]." [9]

These were typical efforts to maximize the steps which the less developed countries were willing to take. However, Congressman Judd was supported by R. D. J. Scott-Fox of the United Kingdom, who said bluntly that his Government felt that an "effective SUNFED was impracticable in the foreseeable future." [10] His statement was stronger than that of the United States representative, partly because of its timing in the debate. It was made after a large number of the less developed countries had sought to maximize their concession of willingness to adopt the United States proposal, but only *if* the United States and its friends would in turn respond by adopting the proposal of the less developed countries to establish SUNFED. It was this suggested bargain that the British were rejecting. Mr. Scott-Fox stated, "It would be unrealistic and even prejudicial to the whole future of economic development to indulge in ambitious general plans while ignoring the views of major potential contributors." [11] At the same meeting, Congressman Judd tried to soften the blow. He is recorded as stating:

Inasmuch as the United States Government found it impossible to support the establishment of a capital development fund at the present time, his delegation was proposing the Special Projects Fund in the belief that it at least afforded a reasonable hope of making an effective contribution to economic development.[12]

The United States representative was again maximizing the step which his Government was willing to take. But the less developed countries continued to minimize the concession offered to them and to press their own proposal. D. W. Rajapatirana of Ceylon pointed out that the Eleven-Power Draft Resolution to set up SUNFED was the natural outcome of past work in which the United States and other countries had joined. He added, "It was very disappointing, therefore, to find that the United States was not now prepared to support the establishment of a Capital Finance Fund." [13] The next day, Brija Kanta Thaker of Nepal stated that "his delegation accordingly, supported the immediate establishment of SUNFED . . . the decision to establish SUNFED would demonstrate that the United Nations realized that prosperity, like peace, was indivisible." [14]

The debate did not end with the argument of the Nepalese delegate. Many speakers followed him, but the major effort was always the same. The developed countries maximized their concession, and the less developed countries minimized it and sought acceptance of their proposal. Mrs. Ellen Louk Fairclough, the delegate of Canada, had practically the last word at that session, and it was a realistic word. She said that "United States participation in any new program was essential." [15]

The victory in that phase went to the developed countries. The realism expressed by Mrs. Fairclough triumphed, but not without enormous efforts on the part of each side to maximize its own movements and to minimize those of the other side.

The issue of SUNFED involved an economic negotiation, but the same process is at least equally in evidence in most political negotiations. Disarmament negotiations, which have been on again and off again for even longer than negotiations for SUNFED, have constantly involved this interplay of maximizing and counterpart minimizing. When Soviet Premier Bulganin wrote to President Eisenhower on September 19, 1955 and reverted to the proposals which the Soviet Union had made on May 10, 1955 in the disarmament subcommittee meetings at London, he stated:

I think you will agree that the proposal introduced by us concerning levels of armed forces, the dates for coming into effect of the prohibition of nuclear weapons and for the establishment of control posts can promote the reduction of tension in international relations and strengthening of peace. I do not see, therefore, any reasons why we could not arrange to reach agreement on these questions.[16]

Premier Bulganin tried to enhance the reasonableness of his own step by stating that he could not see any reason why agreement could not be reached. Later, Foreign Minister Molotov, speaking for the Soviet Union at the Geneva meeting of foreign ministers, again stated the case for the Soviet proposals, in as conciliatory a way as was compatible with the policy of his Government at that time. He maximized the element of concession in the Soviet proposal by working into it a seeming acceptance of President Eisenhower's "Open Skies" proposal. He stated:

Does it mean that we are against the proposal of President Eisenhower under any circumstances? No, it does not mean that. Our attitude towards this proposal could be different if the measures proposed by him were considered in direct connection with the solution of the problem of reduction of armaments and of prohibition of atomic weapons. With this proviso the Soviet Government is prepared to consider the above-mentioned proposal favourably, . . ." [17]

A further effort of the Soviet Union to maximize its own steps and to downgrade or minimize the difficulties raised by the Western delegation was made at the United Nations General Assembly by Vasily Kuznetsov, perhaps the most nonpolemical of Soviet delegates to recent international political gatherings. Directing attention to the technological difficulties relating to the detection of nuclear warheads, he said:

We do not deny the existence of technical difficulties connected with the establishment of control over the execution of measures for the prohibition of atomic weapons. . . . The Soviet Union, desiring to remove the threat of a devastating atomic war, proposes that, pending the conclusion of an international convention on the reduction of armaments and the prohibition of atomic weapons, the Soviet Union, the United States, the United Kingdom and France should each undertake not to be the first to use atomic and hydrogen weapons against any country, and should call upon all other States to do the same. If the nations were to assume such obligations, that would constitute a major step toward the removal of the threat of atomic war.[18]

However, Henry Cabot Lodge minimized the Soviet step. He first agreed with the Belgian delegate, who had said:

How can we rely on the undertaking that this aggressor would have assumed not to use the atomic weapons if that same aggressor was capable of violating the fundamental undertaking of the United Nations Charter not to resort to aggression by any weapon whatsoever? [19]

He went on to disagree with Kuznetsov's other arguments:

Mr. Kuznetsov tries to reinforce his proposed ban on atomic weapons by citing the supposed effectiveness of international conventions prohibiting the use of chemical and bacteriological weapons. . . .

If chemical warfare could have been employed with the versatility of the atomic weapons on any battlefield in a manner so decisive as to prevent retaliation on the aggressor, does anyone believe that the Nazi War machine would not have used it in World War II? [20]

The minimizing of the Soviet proposal was so successful that the proposal was virtually abandoned. Indeed, it has not since then been seriously raised in disarmament and arms control negotiations by its Soviet authors.

As the long process of disarmament discussions has continued, the tactic of inflating one's own concessions and deflating the importance of those of the other side has been repeatedly manifest. It was evident in the first protracted round of discussions at the Conference of the Eighteen-Nation Committee on Disarmament, when Valerian Zorin summed up the Soviet position exactly three months after the start of the Conference (June 14, 1962) by minimizing a move of the United States. That move had taken place about a month after the opening of the Conference, in the presentation by the United States delegation on April 18, 1962 of an Outline of Basic Provisions of a Treaty on General and Complete Disarmament in a Peaceful World.[21]

After maximizing the virtues of the Soviet draft treaty on general and complete disarmament, Zorin stated that in contrast "The United States outline does not solve the problem of eliminating the threat of nuclear war either in the first or in subsequent stages." [22] The last four words in this citation were not in entire accordance with the facts, but were part of the tactics of minimizing the movements of positions of the other side. Zorin continued in the above strain:

Nor does the United States envisage overmuch even in the reduction of conventional arms. On the contrary, it proposes a considerably smaller reduction in armed forces and conventional arms (to 2.1 million men) than does the Soviet Union (to 1.7 million men).[23]

Here, again, he was coloring the situation by mentioning the figures only for the first stage of the disarmament process, without revealing that for the second stage the figures in the two plans were practically at the same level—1,050,000 in the United States plan and 1,000,-000 in the Soviet plan. Moreover, he did not mention that at the end of the third stage of the disarmament process both plans appeared to achieve, in principle, equivalent levels of armed forces. In this context the somewhat higher figure proposed by the United States for the first stage of disarmament does not have the significance which Zorin's minimizing remarks tended to convey. He went on to state that the United States' plan was directed at undermining the security of states which were not members of the United States system of military alliances. He said: "This is graphically illustrated by the open unwillingness of the United States to accept any obligations on the liquidation of military bases abroad." [24] What is not mentioned here is that the United States plan, as it develops, could progressively denude bases of their armament until they are, in fact, abolished at the end of the plan.

The same tactics were used by Zorin in regard to other positions of the United States, such as those on verification and control over disarmament measures. This approach appeared to the other delegates present to be designed to stir the United States into making further movements which would, perhaps, be more acceptable to the Soviet Union. It is precisely this that the tactic of minimizing the other side's movements seeks to achieve. It does not, of course, follow that such a tactic is particularly effective. My own reaction made this clear when, speaking after Arthur Dean, Valerian Zorin, and some other delegates, I pointedly ignored the major portion of Zorin's speech and stated:

I . . . welcome the last few remarks made by our Soviet colleague in which he has said that we must all reflect on everything that has gone on in these last three months with a view to insuring the success of this Committee in addressing itself to its main task.[25]

At the end of the next round of discussion at the Disarmament Conference, First Deputy Foreign Minister Kuznetsov was much more urbane in his persuasiveness about the developments of the Soviet position. He stated:

Showing goodwill and readiness to seek for mutually acceptable solutions, the Soviet Government agreed to accept the procedure proposed by the United States for the reduction of conventional armaments, put forward a compromise proposal on the level of the armed forces of the USSR and the United States by the end of the first stage, and declared its readiness to carry out in the first stage measures to reduce the risk of war, and to extend the over-all period for the completion of all disarmament measures and, in particular, the measures of the first stage.[26]

He then went on to minimize the United States proposals:

The United States plan does not provide for the prohibition of nuclear weapons; and during the negotiations the Western Powers have made no secret of the fact that they intend to preserve these weapons of mass destruction, under the pretext of equipping with these weapons the international armed force which it is proposed to establish in connection with the implementation of general and complete disarmament.[27]

At the end of his statement he lightened the tone of his criticism:

Evidently we have not been sufficiently experienced propagandists [protagonists might have been a more accurate rendering into English] of the Soviet Union's position, since we have been unable to convince Mr. Dean of the soundness of our position.[28]

At the same closing meeting of the second phase of the Conference, there was also some maximizing on the Western side of its own movements. Arthur Dean, the United States delegate, asserted that the United Kingdom and the United States have "made major moves during this period" [29] to solve the problem of reaching agreement on a nuclear test ban. Francesco Cavalletti, the representative of Italy, also sought on the same day to maximize the move of the Western states (which indeed was a return to the basic position taken by President Kennedy and Prime Minister Macmillan in their communication to Premier Khrushchev of September 3, 1961) in offering the Soviet Union a partial ban on nuclear weapons tests, covering those which yield radioactive fallout. Francesco Cavalletti, in his eloquent mood of maximizing, stated:

Several appeals have been addressed to the nuclear Powers to stop these tests which threaten the very being of the human race and of future generations, and the seriousness of the danger has been impressively stated. I recall the moving speech, a little while ago, of the Indian representative, Mr. Lall, who spoke of the millions of deformed beings who might be born as a result of atmospheric testing.[30]

When we speak of maximizing a move, we do not pass judgment on the nature of the move. It might be a very good move or a very bad one. In this particular case of test ban negotiations, the move on the Western side was a very useful one as it paved the way for the partial test ban treaty of August 1963.

There have been recent efforts on the part of the People's Republic of China to promote negotiations to ban the use of nuclear weapons. On October 16, 1964 the Chinese news agency Hsinhua released the following English text of the Peking Government's statement on its first nuclear explosion:

The Chinese Government hereby formally proposes to the governments of the world that a summit conference of all the countries of the world be convened to discuss the question of the complete prohibition and thorough destruction of nuclear weapons, and that, as a first step, the summit conference should reach an agreement to the effect that the nuclear powers and those countries which will soon become nuclear powers undertake not to use nuclear weapons, neither to use them against non-nuclear countries and nuclear-free zones, nor against each other.[31]

Peking tried to make out that it was offering a big concession, namely, a willingness to surrender its nuclear weapons capacity. President Johnson's reply came in the text of his address on October 18, 1964:

It fools no one when it [China] offers to trade away its first small accumulation of nuclear power against the mighty arsenals of those who limit Communist Chinese ambitions.[32]

President Johnson tried to persuade China to move toward the position of most other countries, by suggesting that it sign the limited test ban treaty.

This incident is a rare case of negotiation, by open means of communication, between two states one of which does not recognize the other. In the brief course of the negotiation, the tactic of maximizing a concession was practiced by the Chinese with the expected result.

Many other negotiations could be cited which would illustrate the tactic of maximizing moves or concessions (by the party making them) and of minimizing such steps (by the party to which they are directed). Such moves have taken place in the relations between India and Pakistan, particularly in the long discussions, assisted by the mediatory efforts of the International Bank, which eventually led to the solution of the difficult problem of apportioning the waters of the Indus and the other rivers of the Punjab between the two countries.

The second aspect of movements in negotiations to be considered here is that when a country decides to accept a movement made by the other side, even if it is a small movement, the accepting country tends to exaggerate the extent of the movement, generally for propagandistic reasons. Meanwhile, of course, it continues to press the other party to move further in its own direction. On July 16, 1962 the Eighteen-Nation Committee on Disarmament reconvened after about a month's recess. In his opening statement to the Conference, Valerian Zorin announced that the Soviet Union, "striving to do everything in its power for the speediest possible settlement of the problem of general and complete disarmament," had decided to "accommodate the United States" by making a number of amendments to its own disarmament proposal, taking into account Western positions.[33]

He went on to say: "We are prepared to meet the United States of America and adopt its proposal for reduction of conventional arms." [34] He then announced adoption of various other, on the whole minor, points in the draft outline of the United States for a treaty on general and complete disarmament. These he described as follows, and, as in his introductory words, the language is most significant:

In going half way to meet the Western Powers' position on a number of important issues, and in introducing additions . . . the Soviet Government expects that the United States and the other Western Powers will suitably appreciate this act of goodwill by the Soviet Union and will, for their part, make efforts to reach the earliest possible agreement on the draft treaty.[35]

In describing the Soviet Union as having come half-way, and in inviting the West to move the remaining half of the way, Zorin was greatly overstating the movement made on his side, welcome and real though it was. At the same time, although acting otherwise, he was asking a great deal of the Western powers in expecting them to do the rest that was necessary to insure agreement.

Naturally the Western powers tended to minimize the Soviet movement. Arthur Dean, although welcoming the Soviet suggestions, drew attention to the global defense responsibilities of the United States. He then stated "I believe that, despite the very interesting suggestions from our Soviet colleague, we are going to be faced with these rather basic problems." [36]

A little later in the year, at the Seventeenth Session of the United Nations General Assembly, Foreign Minister Gromyko was even more expansive in his description of Soviet acceptance of Western moves. He stated:

We accepted the ideas of the Western Powers in regard to the reduction of conventional armed forces and armaments, and we met them half way in regard to force levels, even though we believed a more radical reduction of armaments and armed forces would be more in keeping with the interests of prompt disarmament.[37]

The convening of the Eighteen-Nation Committee on Disarmament coincided with a move of considerable significance by the United States in regard to arms control measures. Up to that time, and including the brief infructuous disarmament negotiation of 1960 in the Ten-Nation Committee on Disarmament (composed of five Western and five Communist powers), the United States had maintained that it would be necessary to undertake a complete verification of all the arms contained in the lists of armaments provided by countries which were signatories to a disarmament treaty.

On the other hand, the Soviet Union insisted that verification measures should cover only the armaments being eliminated. If in a particular stage of the disarmament process x tanks and y plants for the production of small arms were to be eliminated, this elimination should take place under the supervision of the agreed control authorities. There was, however, to be no verification of the quantity of retained tanks and plants for the manufacture of arms to insure that there was no rearmament to make up for or surpass what had been eliminated.

However, when the United States introduced its outline of basic provisions at the Eighteen-Nation Committee on Disarmament Conference on April 18, 1962, it departed from its previous position and proposed, in addition to destruction of armaments under international supervision, only partial verification of retained armaments. This was to be done through a series of surprise spot-checks in gradually increasing areas of each country. The system proposed has been described as a zonal inspection system which was first mooted at one of the Pugwash conferences.

It would be fair to describe this change from complete verification of retained armaments to partial verification as a considerable movement in fact toward compromise or toward the Soviet position on the question of verification of armaments.

Although this is so, the United States negotiator at Geneva did not maximize this move as a concession to the Soviet Union. Arthur Dean, in his statement of June 14, 1962, described the move of the United States as follows:

We think we have made a reasonable effort to meet the legitimate concerns, the honest doubts, that States might have in connection with verification of these agreed levels of armaments during the disarmament process.[38]

This was a cautious but an accurate description. It was not the kind of tendentious statement which would characterize the negotiating tactic we are discussing. Why did the United States not adopt that tactic? Is this a case of a departure from a general rule? The reply to these questions can be found by examining the course of events that occurred some months prior to the statement of Arthur Dean.

In September 1961, a most important development took place in the history of disarmament negotiations. That was the formulation of a joint statement of agreed principles by the United States and the Soviet Union. On the question of verification in connection with an agreed program of disarmament, the agreed statement of principles said:

All disarmament measures should be implemented from beginning to end under such strict and effective international control as would provide firm assurance that all parties are honoring their obligations. During and after the implementation of general and complete disarmament, the most thorough control should be exercised, the nature and extent of such control depending on the requirements for verification of the disarmament measures being carried out in each stage.[39]

These words were susceptible to the interpretation that verification measures were to be related to the actual disarmament measures and not to weaponry which would not at a given time fall within the scope of disarmament measures. In this interpretation, the agreed statement of principles would seem to take the Soviet rather than the Western position. In order to correct such an impression, John J. McCloy, the leader of the United States negotiating team, wrote to Valerian Zorin, the leader of the Soviet team, and expressed the view that although the United States had not pressed for the retention of a sentence on verification of retained armed forces and armaments, it had endorsed the agreed statement:

. . . upon the express understanding that the substantive position of the United States government as outlined in the above quoted sentence and in our memorandum of 14 September 1961 remains unchanged, and is in no sense prejudiced by the exclusion of this sentence from the joint statement of agreed principles.

The quoted sentence to which the statement referred was:

Such verification should ensure that not only agreed limitations or reductions take place but also that retained armed forces and armaments do not exceed agreed levels at any stage.[40]

It was on this basis that the United States went to the Eighteen-Nation Committee on Disarmament Conference. When it proposed a compromise regarding the verification of retained arms, it did not retract from the position as set out by John J. McCloy. If it had introduced its compromise with a fanfare of words, it would have run the serious risk of creating the impression that it had abandoned the principle upon which the McCloy letter laid such clear emphasis. However, the compromise proposal *was* maximized by the allies and partners in negotiation of the United States, who were less inhibited in their presentation. Joseph Godber, then British Minister of State for Foreign Affairs, upbraided Valerian Zorin at Geneva for describing the position of the United States on verification as a "maintaining [of] its old attitude on control." [41] Godber added "but when the United States put forward its draft outline of a treaty, it moved forward very materially from that position [the old position] when it advanced the idea of zonal inspection.[42]

This statement of Godber's is in line with our point. He describes the United States move as a very material one in a forward direction, and when his statement was made to the Russian representative it tended to give the impression that a great advance had been made on the Western side toward meeting the Soviet side halfway.

Our analysis of what happens when the parties engaged in international negotiation move from their original positions would, therefore, suggest the following principles:

> Each party to an international negotiation tends to maximize any new position it takes up, any movement from a previous position, or any concession which it offers, and to minimize similar steps by the other party or parties to the negotiation, and thereby attempts to stimulate movement toward its own position or in directions acceptable to it.
>
> When a party to a negotiation decides to move toward the position of the other side, and in so doing accepts a concession or movement by the other side, it tends to maximize the movement or concession to which it is responding; but its objective remains as stated in the immediately preceding principle, namely, to induce the other side to move toward its own position.

CHAPTER TWENTY-THREE

Degrees of Interest in Negotiation

WE HAVE DEALT with some of the problems deriving from the relative levels of power of the parties involved in a dispute or situation, and the effects of power on vital interests and thereby on negotiation. However, irrespective of the power levels of countries, the degree of interest in a situation or dispute has a bearing on an international negotiation. There have been cases in the post-World War II era when the demand for negotiations were pressed so strongly by the country whose interests were primarily concerned, that the great powers, which cannot remain uninvolved in any delicate international issue, have been drawn into the negotiations. Both of the conferences on the states of former Indochina that took place in 1954 and 1961–1962 are good examples of this tendency.

There was at first a decided reluctance on the part of some of the Western powers to be drawn into the conference of 1954. John Foster Dulles, in his address of March 29, 1954 to the Overseas Press Club of New York, said:

The United States position [not to exchange United States performance for Communist promises] was made clear at the recent Berlin Conference. There, by standing firm, I finally obtained the reluctant agreement by Mr. Molotov that the Geneva Conference would not be a "Big Five Conference" and that the invitation to Geneva would itself specify that neither the invitation to, nor the holding of, that conference should be deemed to imply diplomatic recognition where it had not already been accorded.[1]

Eventually, indeed, although the United States participated in the Geneva Conference, it did not become a signatory to the agreements.

The conference was held because of the strong pressures of the

Indochinese themselves. The French and the Chinese, with the Soviet Union and the United Kingdom, were also in favor of the conference. The degree of interest of those states which were centrally involved created, as it were, a negotiating vortex into which the other states were drawn.

Again in 1961, there was a marked reluctance on the part of some countries to confer over Laos. Until the last moment it was not known whether Thailand and South Vietnam would attend, and the United States, too, felt that unless there was an effective cease-fire in Laos there would be no point in discussing the political issues. Indeed, the views of those countries delayed the opening of the Conference beyond the announced date. But once again there was a strong force at work. That was the pressing desire of the centrist Laotians for a conference to end the fighting in their country. They had mustered the backing of such neighboring countries as China, India, Burma, Cambodia, and North Vietnam. For the most part those countries were apprehensive of the possible spread of the conflict in their region. Their views prevailed and the conference was held. The very strong and importunate interest in negotiation by those primarily concerned had its way.

It does not follow that the negotiating posture adapted by the countries that are vitally interested in setting up a negotiation are necessarily the most conducive to the smoothest development of the process of negotiation. On the contrary, countries that are directly concerned tend to have very fixed views as to what is to be done. In certain cases these views are obviously the only ones which will succeed, for example, where a country is negotiating for its independence. The wearer knows where the shoe pinches. A country which is subjected to the pressure of a situation or dispute knows where the remedy must be applied, and broadly what that remedy should be. But this is not to say that circumstances always make it possible to devise or apply the best remedy.

When there is an armed conflict between two countries because of aggression or domination, the concern of the country which is the victim is obviously greater than that of the other country or than that of third countries. A third country might, of course, have a vital interest in the region in which conflict has broken out, but those countries which are directly involved are concerned in a manner which is absent in the concern or interest of other countries. Obviously, if China and India are involved in a border dispute, their concern about this matter exceeds that of the friends and allies of either country.

When Christian Herter, as Secretary of State of the United States, was asked at a press conference about the attitude of the United States toward the China-India border dispute, he said, in effect, that the United States had not taken a position on the matter.[2] This was in the earlier stages of the dispute, but it illustrates very well the tertiary degree of concern even of a very great power in regard to a situation involving the two most populous countries in the world.

When Afghanistan and the Soviet Union met to settle the issue of the disputed sovereignty over the islands in the River Oxus, the meeting was a matter of considerable concern to Afghanistan and of direct concern to the Soviet Union, but it created hardly a ripple of interest in the Atlantic and Far Eastern countries.

The question of the seating of the People's Republic of China in the United Nations is obviously of multilateral concern in the international community, yet there are various degrees of interest, which are reflected in the presentation and discussion of the issue. Certain countries have felt themselves very closely concerned. India, for example, with its long common border with China, took the initiative for many years in bringing the issue to the United Nations. However, when the border situation became more tense and it seemed to the Indians that China was imposing its way by the stealthy use of force, India in 1960 departed from its practice and handed over the initiative in raising the issue of representation before the General Assembly to any other country which would take it up. In 1960, the Soviet Union took the initiative. What dictated this change in Indian policy? India was still interested in the question of the representation of China at the United Nations. However, in deciding not to present the question in 1960 and thereafter, India was indicating that its interest had become subordinate to other aspects of its relationship with China. In short, India was more concerned over the border situation and its settlement than with the question of Chinese representation in the United Nations, but it was still in favor of the Peking Government's being seated in the United Nations. On this basic issue there was no shift of position. It has voted in favor of all proposals at the United Nations, and in the Specialized Agencies and other United Nations bodies, to bring in the Peking Government.

While the attitude of India toward the representation of China has shifted slightly, the negotiating attitude of the United Kingdom in regard to this matter reflects the greater shifts of a country less closely involved. The United Kingdom was among the first few countries to recognize the Peking Government. However, up to and including the Fifteenth Session of the General Assembly, in 1960, the United Kingdom voted against the discussion of the item in the General Assembly. From 1961 on, the United Kingdom has voted in favor of discussion, but it has been opposed to the immediate seating of the representatives of the Peking Government. Presumably its attitude could again alter, especially as long as a Labour Government is in office. These fluctuations show the uncertain character of the interest of an important country which is not directly concerned in a particular issue.

On the other hand, certain countries have been so directly concerned in this issue that their positions have been steady and consistent. The United States has firmly and consistently opposed any alteration in the representation of China at the United Nations. Vitally interested in this question, the United States strives to affect the course of negotiation and its outcome year after year. Similarly, the Republic of China on Taiwan is obviously directly involved and it too has maintained a steady and consistent posture of strong opposition to the seating of the Peking Government.

One would expect the Soviet Union, as a close ally and the leader of the Communist world, to maintain a steady pressure at the highest peak in favor of China. But in a sense the Soviet Union is not as involved in this issue as are the Taiwan Government and the United States, and its position has shown a degree of fluctuation. Although in 1960, 1961, and 1962 the Soviet Union took the initiative in raising the question before the General Assembly, in 1963, 1964, and 1965 it decided not to do so. By now China had raised border claims against the Soviet Union, and the governing parties in the two countries were engaged in fierce doctrinal conflict. It fell to Albania to raise the issue in 1963, and to Cambodia and others to do so in 1964 and 1965.

Take the question of the payment of expenses for the peacekeeping operations of the United Nations. Clearly the Soviet Union is heavily involved. So heavy is its involvement that on October 9, 1964, when the Security Council met to consider only the question posed in a letter from the Minister of External Affairs of Malawi (formerly Nyasaland), namely, that of the admission of his country to the United Nations, Ambassador Nikolai T. Fedorenko, the representative of the Soviet Union, took this occasion to deliver a statement on the position of his Government regarding the payment for the peacekeeping operations undertaken by the United Nations in the Gaza Strip and in the Congo. Mr. Fedorenko stated:

I would like to make it perfectly clear that the position and the attitude of the Soviet Government on this matter remains absolutely unchanged, and that the Soviet Union is not prepared to pay one single kopek, one single cent, for the illegal operations of the United Nations in the Middle East and the Congo. This, of course, does not apply to our contributions to the regular budget of the Organization.[3]

The degree of interest displayed by the United States on the question of Soviet payment is equivalent to that of the Soviet Union. The United States, too, has adopted the in-season and out-of-season approach characteristic of the Soviet Union's statements on the issue, but it has been firm in its stand. Apart from its submissions to the Twenty-One Member United Nations Working Group on the Examination of the Administrative and Budgetary Procedures of the United Nations, and its statements at other United Nations forums, United States officials have been active elsewhere on this issue. For example, Under Secretary of State George W. Ball referred to the matter on October 4, 1964 on the radio program, "Washington Reports to the People," sponsored by labor groups. Referring to the loss of voting privileges in the General Assembly if a country is more than two years in arrears with its dues, Under Secretary Ball said, "We are going to insist on the full carrying-out of these provisions." [4] The United States Congress, too, has displayed its strong interest in this issue. By a 351–0 vote on October 17, 1964, the House of Representatives urged President Johnson to start action designed to deprive the Soviet Union and other countries of their General Assembly votes unless they paid their United Nations debts.[5] From this action we can see how the countries which regard themselves as most centrally involved make a variety of efforts to impress their views on the process of negotiation and on the results of negotiation.

Another example of international activity of countries which regard themselves as closely involved in an issue was the Security Council debate of October 9, 1964 on the admission of Malawi. All eleven members of the Security Council voted for admission—a welcome unanimity. Two of the countries on the Council were from Africa—the Republic of the Ivory Coast and the Kingdom of Morocco. Their representatives took the occasion to express their views regarding the ending of colonialism in certain parts of Africa. Referring to the part played by the United Kingdom, the former Administering Power in Malawi, Ambassador Arsène Assouan Usher of the Ivory Coast stated:

There can be no doubt that, if the African majority of Malawi and that of Northern Rhodesia can govern the destiny of their country, that of Southern Rhodesia can do so as well. Therefore, we reserve the privilege of applauding the work of decolonization in Africa by the United Kingdom pending the solution of the problem of Southern Rhodesia . . .[6]

Ambassador Usher was followed by Ambassador Dey Ould Sidi Baba of Morocco:

. . . this country [Malawi]—as the whole of Africa trusts—will not fail to make a great contribution to the achievement of the objectives that the States of that continent have set themselves. Thus we shall be able to go ahead in the inexorable march of history and further the phenomenon of decolonization which peoples such as those in Southern Rhodesia, Mozambique and South Africa, . . .[7]

These statements, reflecting the closeness of concern felt by African countries, were directed to increasing the negotiating pressures on other countries.

We have mentioned the issue of the islets in the River Oxus, which are of interest both to the Soviet Union and Afghanistan. To Afghanistan, the much smaller of the two countries, the major islets were of considerable importance. When the two countries met in 1948 to negotiate the question, the Afghans were apprehensive that they might be asked to surrender the major islands to the Soviet Union. However, their delegation, headed by General Abdul Kayeum, pressed the Afghan view so strongly and persuasively that the Soviet Union agreed that the largest and only really major islet, Karkad, which is almost ten miles long, should remain with Afghanistan. Of course there were other factors involved. The islets were of much greater agricultural importance to Afghanistan with its relatively small percentage of cultivable land than to the Soviet Union. But these factors also explain the persistence of the Afghans and reinforce the point we are making.

A persistent attitude arising out of a preponderant interest in an issue may have the result of gaining, even for the relatively weak, a considerable degree of acceptance of its point of view in international negotiation.

What happens in those rare cases when the degree of interest between the two sides is in equilibrium? A good case is the question of disarmament. Particularly after about 1960, as we have observed, the two major sides came to realize the importance of progress in the field of disarmament measures. Both of them are vitally interested in this question. For both of them the issue goes to the root of their national security and the protection of the ways of life which they have chosen. Each of them apprehends that any advantage to the other in an agreed plan of disarmament might result in its destruction or humiliation. For all these reasons, each of the superpowers has striven to its utmost to press its own point of view on the other members at disarmament conferences. The eight nonaligned members of the Eighteen-Nation Committee have come to be treated by the two sides virtually as if they were a body of assessors or jurors. Not that the two superpowers would, or could, be expected to accept any given findings of the eight nonaligned states on their disarmament proposals; nevertheless, both of them are concerned that their proposals should be regarded by this "third group" as reasonable. At the close of the 1964 meetings of the Conference, both William C. Foster speaking for the United States, and Semyon K. Tsarapkin speaking for the Soviet Union, while concentrating on the attitude of each side to the other, also wove in their appreciation for positions taken by the eight nonaligned states. Tsarapkin, who was the first speaker on the last day of the session, September 17, 1964, said:

We note with satisfaction that the representatives of the non-aligned States have raised their voices in the Committee in favor of the destruction of all nuclear weapons as quickly as possible. . . .

The representatives of the non-aligned States . . . insisted upon the conclusion of an all-embracing agreement on non-proliferation . . . speaking frankly such a declaration is constructive and timely . . .[8]

William C. Foster, who was the last major speaker at the final meeting, referred to a joint memorandum prepared by the eight nonaligned countries on the need for steps toward a treaty to ban all nuclear weapons tests. He said:

The joint memorandum reflects the sincere desire of the eight nations to hasten the achievement of a comprehensive test ban. That desire is shared by my nation and, I believe, by most of the nations of the world. We believe the memorandum to be a most useful contribution to this Conference, another among the significant contributions made by the eight nations.[9]

Where the interest of both the major parties to a negotiation is virtually equal, and particularly when the issue involved is as crucial a one as disarmament, we must expect the international negotiation to be arduous in the extreme and long-drawn-out. Such cases of approximately equal concern and interest are more the exception than the rule, yet they illustrate that when the degree of interest of each side is great, then each side will maintain great pressure in negotiation.

Another effect of extreme concern over the outcome of an issue under negotiation is that the side with the larger interest tends to be extremely rigid in its postures.

In a case that is not very well known in the Western world, involving a large Asian country and a small one, the latter successfully held to a very rigid position. The case arises out of the presence of persons of Indian origin in Ceylon. The valuable tea and rubber plantations of Ceylon have been developed virtually by the labor of Indian immigrants. There were rules governing such immigration, but the rules were not very strictly enforced, partly because both territories were under British authority and partly because geographical proximity made it difficult to enforce them to the letter. The result was that when Ceylon regained its independence, almost a million persons of Indian origin in Ceylon—a sizeable portion of the island's population—found themselves without citizenship. The Government of Ceylon proposed to the Government of India that the whole group should be repatriated, as they were not citizens of Ceylon. The broad view of the Government of India in regard to Indians who migrate to Africa, Latin America, Fiji, and elsewhere, is that they have a choice of becoming citizens of the country to which they migrate or of returning to India, but that the Government of India will not assist them in pressing claims to any special status. This seems a reasonable view based on general practice in most parts of the world.

However, small Ceylon held firmly to its position. At various times the Prime Ministers of Ceylon and India met. Indeed, they met on an average of every two years for some sixteen years, but the issue remained unresolved. During the interim all illegal Indian immigration to Ceylon had ceased, and in that way the Government of India had taken steps to protect Ceylon from an influx of external population. However, Ceylon remained adamant. It was not until Madame Sirimavo Bandaranaike, the Prime Minister of Ceylon, visited Delhi in October 1964 that agreement was reached with respect to the major part of the problem. Of the approximately one million persons involved, Ceylon agreed to grant citizenship to less than one-third. The Government of India undertook to accept repatriation of 525,-000 over a period of fifteen years. The status of the remaining 150,000 to 175,000 persons remained to be discussed later. Regarding those remaining persons, Madame Bandaranaike said on October 30, 1964 as she was leaving Delhi, "I have every confidence that a satisfactory solution will be reached even in regard to that residue and within a very short time." [10]

This is a case of negotiation in which a small country, tenaciously adhering to its own point of view, was able to gain much of the substance of its contention at the expense of over a half million people whose families have lived in Ceylon for as long as three or four generations. Whatever the rights or wrongs of this negotiation, it remains a striking example of how the strong concern of a Government can affect the results of international negotiations. Ceylon is small and densely populated. It has a large group of Ceylonese citizens of Indian origin, and their presence poses a problem of national language and cultural homogeneity. For these reasons as well as for directly economic ones, the Government of Ceylon was determined to exclude a large number of Indian workers and their families. On the other hand, India is a much larger country. Its economy is developing fairly rapidly and the absorption of a half million persons over a fifteen-year period should not create a significant national problem. Under these circumstances, and given the fact that both countries were resolved to settle the issue peacefully, Ceylon was almost bound to win in the end.

Several potential disputes in Europe, too, might be traced to the rigid or firm positions of governments on issues which concern their national security. The question of the creation of a multilateral nuclear force for NATO illustrates this. Two different concepts of the protection of national security are involved. On the one hand there is the French concept of de Gaulle that it is dangerous for Europe to continue to base its regional security largely on trans-Atlantic decisions. On the other hand there is the official view of the Federal Republic of Germany that an Atlantic partnership is essential to the defense of Europe. Both these views appear to be firm, and both create thrusts in their own directions. These thrusts in their turn strongly affect the course of negotiations. In the case of France, the thrust is so strong that the Government has more than once threatened withdrawal from NATO. In the case of Germany, repeated statements are made by that country's leaders that its army cannot afford to be equipped with weaponry less powerful than that of the potential enemy. This view creates a strong drive for the possession, or at any rate the copossession within the NATO framework, of nuclear weaponry. Unless one of these two concepts of national security gains dominance on the Continent, it would seem that the rigid positions which are evolving will wreck negotiations for West European unity, and will create new international alliances or ententes.

In another part of the world we have recently witnessed a confrontation of the adamant positions on the one hand of the Rhodesian (minority) Government, and on the other of the British Labour Government, the United Nations, and the leaders of the African majority in the territory. As a result of these adamant positions Prime Minister Ian Smith of Rhodesia has evaded negotiations with the British Labour Government and has, of course, not been willing to extend the field of negotiation to leaders freely chosen by the African majority. Here again we witness adamant positions based on the close concern of the parties in the protection of their most central interests. Negotiation is unlikely to become possible, unless there is a change in the posture of one of the major parties, for example, the substitution of another leader for Ian Smith.

In the light of the examination and analyses we have made in this chapter, we would suggest the following principles of negotiation:

> The degrees of interest of the parties to an international negotiation are rarely precisely equal, and the party with the greater degree of interest or concern tends to strive the harder to bring the issue to negotiation and to impress firmly its point of view on the outcome of the negotiations.
>
> The greater the degrees of interest of the parties to a given situation or dispute, the more firm or rigid will the negotiating postures of each tend to be, with consequent difficulties and sometimes stalemates in the attainment of compromise solutions.

CHAPTER TWENTY-FOUR

The Personal Factor

THERE ARE two opposing forces at work in the post-World War II era which have a strong bearing on the effectiveness of any individual negotiator. These two forces are largely beyond the control of the negotiator, and yet between them they constitute the major determinants of his actions in negotiation. In the first place, negotiators can now be in virtually instantaneous communication with their governments, with the result that on all important issues the governments direct and instruct them down to the smallest detail. It follows that negotiators, particularly when the subject of negotiation is of significance to their countries, can take little or no initiative. But this is only one aspect of the modern situation in which negotiators find themselves.

The second major determinant is that, in spite of the availability of instantaneous communication, the negotiator might not be able effectively and rapidly to reach the source of his instructions. If the negotiator, when he transmits the views of other negotiators and their governments to his government and seeks instructions, finds that his communications slip into the lower levels of his foreign office and that position papers are then put up at those levels, which gradually seep upward to the decision-making echelons, then he may be greatly handicapped as an effective negotiator on behalf of his government. This is the fate of many negotiators.

All foreign offices are structured hierarchically, and each subject or issue under negotiation falls within one of the many substructures. This arrangement often creates a paralytic dichotomy, in that while a negotiator at the appropriate level—and it might be a very high level —is working at the negotiating table with his opposite numbers from other countries, the subject under discussion at the negotiating table will also be analyzed in the appropriate hierarchical substructure in his foreign office. Out of the maws of such analyses the negotiator is apt to be sent instructions which are out of date, irrelevant, or unconstructive. It is rare for foreign office analyses to have the quality of immediate and constructive applicability at the negotiating table. This situation, of course, applies only to those analyses which purport to be the basis of instructions to a negotiator. Analyses of a factual character, particularly of the background of an issue, or of analogous cases, or of the views of other governments whether involved in the negotiation or not, are all of great value to a negotiator. They help to equip him with the material which enables him to operate in depth in his interchanges with other negotiators.

If the negotiator is able to tap the source of authority in his government and can largely ignore the dilatory instructions from the foreign office, then quick communications can insure that the nuances of the position of his government are much better represented than in previous eras. This factor often gives flexibility and potential movement to a negotiation. Moreover, since it soon becomes apparent when a particular negotiator is in close touch with the source of instructions, he wins the esteem and reliance of his colleagues. However, in spite of instantaneous communication and a good rapport with the government, a negotiator will find from time to time that communication falters and he is left on his own.

The personal characteristics and qualities of a negotiator are of importance, provided it is assumed that he is in close contact with the sources of power and authority in his government. If he is not, then no matter how brilliant, deeply understanding, and responsive he is, his good qualities will serve practically no purpose. Assuming, however, that the relationship of the negotiator to the sources of authority is direct, and one of mutual confidence, then his personal capacities —his hospitality and charm, as well as his mental incisiveness, capacity for hard work, determination, and even his importunity—will be among the factors that assist him and his government in pursuing the negotiation to a successful conclusion.

Most well-informed persons, including scholars and national columnists, would agree that a foreign minister or secretary of state is a very high level negotiator. It is not surprising, for example, that President Kennedy, in disagreeing with Premier Khrushchev that the Eighteen-Nation Committee on Disarmament Conference should be initiated at the summit, stated in his letter dated February 25, 1962,

"I can assure you that the Secretary of State would present my views with complete authority." [1] The previous President of the United States, Dwight D. Eisenhower, often praised Secretary of State John Foster Dulles and relied upon him as his highest level negotiator.

However, it must not be assumed that because a foreign minister is usually a high level negotiator he can always be regarded as such. Indeed, in the communication to which President Kennedy was replying, Premier Khrushchev had made certain statements which expressed a somewhat different view. In his letter of February 10, 1962 to President Kennedy and Prime Minister Macmillan he had said, "But why should we confine ourselves to half-measures and merely be represented by our Ministers for Foreign Affairs at the beginning of the Disarmament Committee's work?" [2]

Then again, in his letter of February 21 Premier Khrushchev, further arguing in favor of a summit meeting and the need to break the deadlock over disarmament, wrote:

Therefore neither ministers, no matter how highly they may be respected by the Governments and peoples of their countries, nor other representatives, no matter what their rank, can achieve anything unless the Heads of Government place the negotiations on a solid foundation.[3]

In spite of these greatly varying views, on the whole foreign ministers are regarded as very high level negotiators. Indeed, the fact that Prime Minister Nehru should have held the portfolio of foreign affairs throughout his seventeen years in office is in itself an indication of the level of importance which has come to be attached to the person who holds the rank of foreign minister. In the United States the Secretary of State ranks as the senior member of the Cabinet. Even in the Soviet Union there have been times when the foreign minister has been a man very close to the sources of power in his Government. Vyacheslav M. Molotov, who had been Prime Minister and who was a most important member of the Presidium for many years, was certainly a very high level negotiator. This fact is strikingly illustrated by the strong desire expressed in the closing stages of the war by Winston Churchill and others, that Molotov rather than another Soviet diplomat should lead the Soviet delegation to the United Nations Conference on International Organization at San Francisco. Prime Minister Churchill, in a communication dated April 1, 1945 to Joseph Stalin, expressed his misgivings about the possibilities of Molotov's absence from San Francisco:

We had hoped the presence there of the three Foreign Ministers might have led to a clearance of many of the difficulties which have descended upon us in the storm since our happy and hopeful union at Yalta.[4]

Anthony Eden, who was then the United Kingdom Secretary of State for Foreign Affairs, wrote to Churchill on April 15, 1945, saying:

Stettinius said that both Stalin and Molotov had shown signs of being deeply moved by the President's death. Stalin had asked Harriman whether there was any contribution he could make at a moment like this to assist to promote the unity of the great Allies. Stettinius said that fortunately Harriman had not at once replied "Poland," but instead had suggested that it would be a good thing if Molotov could come to San Francisco for the Conference. Stettinius had seized on this, and telegraphed urging not only that Molotov should come to San Francisco, but that he should come to Washington first for conversations.[5]

The Charter of the United Nations contains a provision, regrettably fallen into abeyance, the intention of which is to institute regular periodic meetings at foreign minister level. Article 28.2 reads:

The Security Council shall hold periodic meetings at which each of its members may, if it so desires, be represented by a member of the government or by some other specially designated representative.

This was a flexible formulation, but the intention and the hope were clear enough. I recall Dag Hammarskjöld's telling me of his efforts to resuscitate the substance of this article. He had visited London in 1955 as Secretary-General of the United Nations. In his official capacity he had been given the honors and general treatment normally accorded by the Government of the United Kingdom to a visiting foreign minister. This had naturally pleased Hammarskjöld, and had to some extent inspired him to think in terms of periodic gatherings of foreign ministers at the Headquarters of the United Nations. Such gatherings would have provided a recurring high level negotiating forum at which current issues could be discussed, clarified, and perhaps resolved. His idea was an excellent one, in full conformity with Article 28.2. However, I learned later from Dag Hammarskjöld that there had been some reluctance, particularly on the part of John Foster Dulles, to agree to fall in with his suggestion to activate the provision of the Charter. The United States was able to argue that its permanent representative at the Headquarters of the United Nations was himself of Cabinet rank.[6]

During the Suez crisis in 1956, Hammarskjöld did succeed in persuading most members of the Security Council to send their foreign ministers to New York. That was the occasion on which, as we have observed, the Security Council held its only private negotiating sessions. In spite of promising developments at those sessions, an armed clash in the Suez area took place in which two permanent members of the Security Council were directly involved. This unfortunate outcome did not encourage further periodic meetings of the Security Council at foreign minister level.

However, it has become the practice for each United Nations General Assembly session to open at least at the level of foreign minister. The result is that the first few weeks of each session offer opportunities for negotiation or discussion of many kinds of issues. Discussions such as those which led to the establishment of the United Nations Emergency Force in 1956, the resolution which promoted the withdrawal of the United States Marines from Lebanon, and the declaration on the ending of colonialism, were all taken at the United Nations when most of the important governments were represented by their foreign ministers or heads of government. This whole movement was greatly stimulated by the fact that Dag Hammarskjöld possessed in an extraordinary degree the personal qualities which were conducive to the development of the organs and venue of the United Nations for the purposes of international negotiation. He developed a new concept of the office of Secretary-General, by virtue of which he was able to make clear to the great and to the smaller powers that he stood vigilant and ready personally to enter any situation which needed sensitive and high level negotiation. He created a new high level center of diplomatic activity. It was a tribute to this fact that in 1958, when Khrushchev as Prime Minister proposed to meet at the summit with the President of the United States and the Prime Ministers of France, the United Kingdom, and India, he invited a sixth person to the proposed conference—Dag Hammarskjöld.

U Thant has magnificently preserved the high level role for the Secretary-General which his predecessor fashioned. U Thant's decisive and crucial action in regard to the Cuban crisis of 1962 and his handling of the West Irian situation are examples of the work he has done, and it is doubtful whether anyone but the Secretary-General of the United Nations could have registered these achievements. U Thant spoke modestly about these functions in his address at the University of Denver on April 3, 1964:

The Office of the Secretary-General, in particular, has been found to be a useful place for the mediation and conciliation of disputes and for informal diplomacy and exchanges of views, while at times the Secretary-General has been called upon to assume executive functions, especially in relation to peace-keeping operations, which have necessarily put upon him responsibilities far greater than those envisaged in the Charter.[7]

It is, of course, essential for the Secretary-General to be sensitive to the tangible realities of the political world which he neither holds in his hands nor creates. That is why U Thant, and Dag Hammarskjöld before him, have been insistent that the mandates given to them by the organs of the United Nations should be as clear and precise as possible. This has been particularly necessary, because the organs of the United Nations are quite capable of deliberate imprecision for the purpose of leaving the difficult steps to the Secretary-General. He is then expected to report to the relevant organ on his efforts to take those steps, and the organ in its turn either gives some precision to the next phase of the task at hand or again urges the Secretary-General to develop it himself. This type of activity on the part of the General Assembly and Security Council is a recognition of the high level of negotiating capacity which circumstances and exceptional personalities have come to engender in the office of the Secretary-General.

The type of high level negotiation required of the Secretary-General touches the extreme limits of political difficulties. It was in the course of probing some of these limits—his attempt to negotiate a cease-fire and otherwise obtain a settlement in the Congo—that Dag Hammarskjöld died.

A rare instance of high level negotiation, yielding rapid results, occurred in the first week of November 1956 at the First Emergency Session of the General Assembly. Recognizing the importance of the occasion created by the military action undertaken by France, Israel, and the United Kingdom on the territory of Egypt, John Foster Dulles and Lester B. Pearson attended the session. The United States immediately introduced a resolution.[8] It called for a cease-fire, cessation of the movement of military stores in the area, and the withdrawal of the parties (Egypt and Israel) to the existing armistice lines. It further asked the Secretary-General to report on compliance, but it did not provide any mechanism to assist and observe compliance. A mechanism had to be found. On behalf of India, I introduced a draft resolution, which was cosponsored by eighteen other states, to suggest a possible mechanism. Our proposals asked the Secretary-General to use the existing United Nations Truce Supervision Organization to obtain compliance with the proposed withdrawal of all forces behind the armistice line.[9]

It was at this stage of the proceedings that Lester Pearson, in amplification of my suggestion to use the existing mechanism, proposed that the Secretary-General should submit a plan within forty-eight hours for setting up an emergency international United Nations force "to secure and supervise cessation of hostilities." Mr. Dulles immediately accepted this suggestion. Lester Pearson then drafted a resolution on his proposal. Before it was introduced, I informally suggested a few amendments, including a clause to the effect that the Secretary-General's plan should have the consent of the nations concerned. These changes were accepted by Mr. Pearson, and his draft resolution was adopted in the small hours of the morning of November 4, 1956.[10] So, too, was the draft resolution I had introduced, but France, Israel, and the United Kingdom voted against this resolution whereas they abstained on the resolution proposed by Mr. Pearson. It was thus that the quick rapport between John Foster Dulles and Lester Pearson achieved results, assisted somewhat by the fact that the nineteen countries which had sponsored the resolution introduced by me also voted for the Canadian text.

There are occasions of important negotiation in which the plenipotentiary does not possess a formal high level designation, but instead is placed in a position of direct approach to the source of relevant power of authority in his government. To give a well-known example, when Aleksei I. Adzhubei went to see Chancellor Ludwig Erhard in 1964 on the matter of a visit to Bonn by Premier Khrushchev, he was undertaking a delicate diplomatic and negotiating mission not on the basis of his formal position (which in a diplomatic sense was non-existent), but merely because of his close connection with the source of power in the Soviet Union.

A negotiator with a close connection with the source of power—provided of course that he has within himself the skill, resourcefulness, and ingenuity to initiate constructive proposals—may prove to be as effective a negotiator as one at the highest diplomatic level. When V. K. Krishna Menon developed and introduced at the Seventh Session of the General Assembly the resolution on the Korean situation containing substantive proposals relating to the then unsolved problem of prisoners of war, he held no position in the Indian Cabinet; yet he formulated a delicate negotiating arrangement which eventually came to be adopted,[11] and made possible a cease-fire in Korea. He did this without specific instructions on matters of detail from the Government of India. He was able to act as he did because he understood and was attuned to the thinking of Prime Minister Nehru on such matters. Numerous situations occurred in the Conference on Laos and in the current disarmament conference when, as the representative of India, I was able to make substantive suggestions of some importance because I knew that I would be backed by Prime Minister Nehru and Krishna Menon, even though there might be some reluctance regarding the adoption of my proposals at the top permanent official level of the Indian Foreign Office. A case in point is the drafting of the important eight-nation memorandum on the cessation of nuclear tests of April 16, 1962. This document,[12] which became the focus of the negotiations on the cessation of nuclear tests for the better part of a year, contained a number of carefully balanced suggestions. These suggestions were worked out by my colleagues from some of the other nonaligned nations and myself at Geneva. It was only my direct approach to those in ultimate authority in India which gave me the confidence to insist on certain formulations in this important document.

Very often a government or other authority will formally endow a negotiator with the title of personal representative of the head of state or other authority, or will make him a special envoy so as to increase his effectiveness as a trusted negotiator. For example, Ambassador Ellsworth Bunker was the representative of U Thant in the negotiations relating to the solution of the problem of West Irian. Averell Harriman came into the Kennedy Government with the designation of Ambassador-at-Large, which really meant that he was a high level special envoy in close touch with the sources of power in the United States. Dean Rusk, soon after the commencement of the International Conference on the Question of Laos, announced to the Conference that he would return to his post and that he would be succeeded by Harriman as the leader of the delegation. He added, "Our delegation will be led by Ambassador-at-Large Harriman, one of our most distinguished public servants, and most experienced diplomats." It will not, I believe, be a betrayal of confidence to give an example of how Averell Harriman's special relationship with the source of power worked beneficially in the Laos Conference. He and I were engaged in a most crucial discussion on the functions of the International Control Commission in Laos in regard to investigations of breaches of the agreement on the neutrality of Laos. Our discussions went on longer than expected, the issue concerned being an intricate one. At a certain point Averell Harriman looked at his watch and said, in effect, "Let us try and reach agreement on this matter in the next hour or so, because I am expecting a call from President Kennedy at noon and I want to tell him that this issue has been cleared up." As I recall, we did reach agreement. Eventually, apparently with the approval of President Kennedy, a clause on that particular aspect of the functions of the International Control Commission was agreed upon with the other countries, including the Soviet Union and the People's Republic of China.

The personal qualities of a negotiator are of little value unless he has an effective relationship with his government, whether on account of his high formal position in that government or for other reasons. At the same time, if he has such a relationship with his own government, his personal capacities and the way he conducts himself will be of the utmost importance. An impatient and only moderately intelligent negotiator, or a negotiator whose timing is poor and who will be sitting at home or playing golf when the sequence of developments requires that he should be visiting his opposite numbers or refining his draft proposals, or doing both, will not help the cause of the negotiation. Of course, all negotiators must take time off and all of them have their human limitations. Yet again and again I have witnessed the effectiveness of constantly applied and alert diligence. Certainly Hammarskjöld would not have been able to achieve what he did had it not been for the fact that he could work fifteen to eighteen hours a day without respite over long periods of time—and not only work long hours but be as alert at the end of his day as at the beginning.

I have been involved in numerous negotiations in which I have paid as many as thirty separate visits in one day to other delegates in the process of refining proposals with a view to getting agreement. In the late 1950s a leading magazine in this country planned to do an article on the most effective delegation to the General Assembly of the United Nations. There were many delegations larger than the Indian delegation, but the magazine chose the delegation of India because the handful of men who were my colleagues (V. K. Krishna Menon, Ali Yavar Jung, G. S. Pathak, among the representatives, and a group of brilliant advisers including Balachandra Rajan, M. A. Vellodi, M. E. Chacko, and Avtar Singh), exerted themselves to their fullest capacity, and thereby greatly increased the effectiveness of the delegation. Part of the effort of the delegation was to create and maintain good working relations with Henry Cabot Lodge and his team, Arkadi Sobolev and his mission, Omar Loutfi and his colleagues of the United Arab Republic, U Thant (then the representative of Burma), A. R. Pazhwak of Afghanistan, Gunnar Jarring of Sweden, Hervé Alphand of France, Pierson Dixon of the United Kingdom, and the numerous other delegates; and, of course, with Dag Hammarskjöld and his team of advisers.

At an important international conference, the American representative once exclaimed to his sizeable delegation that the representative of a certain other country involved in the negotiation seemed to be more effective singly than the whole of the United States delegation!

In any negotiation, more may go on outside the formal meetings than in them. Whether this happens depends largely upon the qualities and caliber of the individual negotiators. At the Conference on Laos, informal discussion became almost institutionalized. Although the Conference operated on the basis of agreement on issues by all the fourteen countries at the conference table, and although on this basis all of them had to be persuaded to agree, some countries were represented by negotiators who were in a position to contribute to the process of advancing and exploring creative proposals more effectively than others. Moreover, the realities of power and influence tended to make the agreement of some countries more important to obtain than that of the others. For these reasons, even private formal meetings with full records were discontinued for some time so as to create opportunities for informal meetings of groups of heads of delegations. At those meetings the delegates were in intimate informal contact. Together they probed the various issues involved, to uncover the basic or irreducible positions. In this process, the skill of individual negotiators was an important factor.

At the Eighteen-Nation Committee on Disarmament Conference, the Canadian and Indian delegations (because of their experience at the Laos Conference) pressed strongly for and obtained agreement to the idea of a cochairmanship, that of the United States and Soviet delegates. Our purpose in pressing for their close association was to create continuing opportunities for informal contact between the superpowers. There is little doubt that the continuing informal contacts made possible by this arrangement have helped to keep the disarmament conference going and to achieve the few positive results so far obtained. So effective have these arrangements been that at times they turned into formal negotiations. This occurred early in 1963 when agreement was reached between the United States and Soviet cochairmen on the establishment of a direct communications link between Washington and Moscow.[13]

At other times the delegates to the Conference have received, as I did in the years 1962 and 1963, information from one or both of the cochairmen on significant issues discussed by them in their informal meetings. It goes without saying that some of the cochairmen have been more effective than others. This has resulted in a fairly consistent overtone of pressure by the fifteen delegations at the Conference (other than those of the United States and the Soviet Union) for a most careful selection in Washington and Moscow of the leaders of the two nations' delegations. This selection is not just a matter of rank. I can think of top-ranking persons who might be in those positions and whose performance could conceivably be disastrous. And I can think of others whose performance would be fully as constructive as the work of those appointed.

We may recall the outstanding instance of diplomatic skill in the effective and constructive cochairmanship at the Laos Conference by Malcolm MacDonald of the United Kingdom and Giorgy Pushkin of the Soviet Union. Malcolm MacDonald held no position in the British Government, but he had the rank of Ambassador in his capacity as leader of the United Kingdom's delegation. Giorgy Pushkin was a Deputy Foreign Minister. The personal qualities of these men were of great help in the work of the Conference, and enabled it to keep at its task even when the situation looked most gloomy.

We have all seen cases in the post-World War II era in which negotiating skill and capacity have been unequal to the task. The atrophying of personal qualities can contribute to unfortunate developments. Negotiation can become too much of a personal or domestic game if a leader allows himself the fallacy of complete identification of his personality with the political entity of his state. It seems that many important Soviet officials felt that the process of identification had gone too far in the case of Prime Minister Khrushchev. This may have been one of the reasons for his replacement as Prime Minister and First Secretary of the Communist Party of the Soviet Union. We have referred to the ailing leadership of the United Kingdom throughout the Suez crisis, and to Prime Minister Nehru's personal attributes and their consequences on possibilities of negotiation between China and India.[14]

I have of necessity treated the subject matter of this chapter with restraint, since we are dealing with the post-World War II era and many of the important figures involved in the cases discussed are still politically active. The examples and events explored, however, give us sufficient evidence to suggest these interrelated principles:

The extent to which a negotiator is in direct touch with or can approach the sources of authority in his government—rather than the formal level of his position in the governmental hierarchy—has a significant bearing on his effectiveness in negotiation and, therefore, on the results he obtains.

Assuming that a good working relationship exists between a negotiator and the sources of authority in his government, the personal qualities of the negotiator—his tact, energy, understanding, and sensitivity, as well as his capacity to engage in informal discussion— are of direct relevance to the success or failure of a negotiation.

CHAPTER TWENTY-FIVE

Maneuverability and Flexibility

WE HAVE SEEN that certain kinds of ideological positions, and, even more, the relative levels of power of states, have profound effects on negotiating postures. However, governments do not function as unregulated agglomerations of power or ideologies. They work within structures, most of them designed on the basis of written constitutions.

In some governmental structures power is virtually centralized in the leader of the majority party, which forms the executive and controls the legislature, the two active arms of most constitutions, as distinct from the judiciary with its interpretative function.

In other governments, power is shared in varying ways. Under the United States presidential form, not only are executive and legislative powers separated, but the legislature, particularly the Senate, exercises significant authority even in the executive field. Important executive appointments have to be confirmed by the Senate, and the assent of that body is required before a treaty can be brought into effect. In the French presidential system, under the 1958 Constitution of the Fifth Republic the president is vested with full authority to enter into treaties

The treaty-making function, the exercise of which depends upon and frequently varies with the form of government, has a considerable bearing upon maneuverability in international negotiation. When the purpose of the negotiation is to enter into an international agreement in the form of a treaty, and when ratification is dependent upon the vote of the legislature or on the will of a president who stands outside and above the government (as at present in France), the maneuverability and flexibility of that country's representatives at the negotiating table are significantly reduced.

Most international negotiators have, at one time or another, known United States representatives to assert, generally in private or informal discussion, that a certain suggestion is not worth pursuing because "the Senate would never agree to it." It has been suggested that this is a tactic sometimes used when certain United States negotiators are unwilling to consider a particular proposition. Even when this is so, the fact remains that the structure of the Government either directly restricts maneuverability or furnishes a reason for restricted maneuverability during the course of negotiations. It is common knowledge that early in 1963, when the Soviet Union had said it would agree to up to three on-site inspections per year in the terms of the treaty to ban all nuclear weapons tests, United States negotiators felt that this number would not be acceptable to the Senate. President Kennedy referred to this matter, at least by implication, in his news conference of March 21, 1963, when he said:

. . . we are now talking, the Soviet Union and the United States, about whether we have seven or three [inspections]. We have come this far, and I think we ought to stay at it. . . . The fact of the matter is when the treaty is signed, if it ever is signed, and I hope it is, it must go to the Senate and it must be approved by two-thirds of the Senate.[1]

This statement made it clear the the President was taking into account the fact that the number of inspections would have to be approved by the Senate.

Since the Constitution of the United States requires that treaty agreements be approved by the Senate, and since any substantive disarmament agreement is likely to be in the form of an international treaty, the argument of Senate approval invariably applies in disarmament discussions. In all crucial aspects of such discussions, those negotiating with the United States are likely to hear their American colleagues say that one proposal or another would not commend itself to the United States Senate.

This attitude of the United States negotiators is realistic. For example, in June 1963 when the Senate was discussing the Authorization Bill in respect to the United States Arms Control and Disarmament Agency, Senator Frank J. Lausche proposed an amendment to insure that the Government would not enter into international obligations in arms control and disarmament through the back door of executive agreements authorized by legislative resolutions passed by both Houses. Senator J. William Fulbright accepted this amendment and the Senate adopted it.[2] The effect of the amendment in the Authorization Bill is that no disarmament agreement can be adopted by the executive without Senate approval.

This example shows how the form of governmental structure has a direct bearing on maneuverability in the conduct of negotiations. On the other hand, where governmental power has only one center there are no formal or structural restrictions on maneuverability. This would appear to have been the case in President Nasser's position in regard to Yemen. When it came to the negotiation with Prince Faisal of Saudi Arabia at the Summit Conference of Arab States, President Nasser was able to arrive at an accord in September 1964 which appeared to depart significantly from the previous position of his Government. The accord did not exclude the followers and supporters of the Imam of Yemen from a share of power in Yemen. On the contrary, it sought to bring them into the Government and, therefore, to diminish the power of the group which had hitherto received the unqualified support of the United Arab Republic. In the negotiation with Prince Faisal, President Nasser did not suffer from any lack of maneuverability. Article 125 of the Constitution of March 25, 1964 reads, "The President of the Republic concludes treaties and communicates them to the National Assembly accompanied with suitable comments." [3] It is true that certain treaties are to be approved by the National Assembly, but since the president of the republic has wide powers which extend to the right to dissolve the National Assembly (Article 91 of the Constitution of March 25, 1964) it may be presumed, at least at the present time, that ratification by the National Assembly is not so difficult a task as the mustering of a two-thirds majority in the United States Senate.

Another example where the apex of government seems to enjoy considerable maneuverability in negotiation is that of the Soviet Union. In recent years there has been an almost constant pressure from the heads of the Soviet Government for summit conferences. On the Western side there has generally been a fair amount of receptiveness to such ideas by the British Government and sometimes by the French, both countries in which power is highly centralized. However, in the United States the general approach appears to be that a summit conference should be resorted to only in very exceptional circumstances and after preparatory work has been done at the level of foreign ministers or at lower levels. At least one important reason for the difference in attitudes toward summitry is that the President of the United States, powerful executive though he is, cannot commit his country to major agreements with a foreign state. The process of ratification of agreements is much easier for a Prime Minister of the

United Kingdom to fulfill. As far as the Soviet Union is concerned, the head of government, if he has the backing of the Presidium on a particular issue, is in a position to gain the acceptance of the Central Committee of the Soviet Communist Party and of the appropriate governmental bodies without any difficulty.

When the eight nonaligned countries had agreed on a draft proposal to break the deadlock in the long negotiations for the cessation of nuclear testing, before presenting the proposal to the Eighteen-Nation Committee on Disarmament in April 1962 I informally showed it, as a matter of courtesy, to the United States Government representatives and to those of the Soviet Union. Valerian Zorin strongly attacked the proposal. With all his ability in dialectical discussion, he sought to persuade me not to have the eight nonaligned countries present it. His opposition was vehement and forthright. However, I remained convinced that the proposal could, perhaps, be useful and should be presented. Three days after presentation, which was on April 16, 1962, the Soviet Government issued a statement welcoming the proposal, praising the nonaligned governments for having prepared it, and accepting it as the basis for negotiation on the cessation of nuclear testing. It would seem clear that as far as the head of the Soviet delegation was concerned, the proposal was outside the scope of the governmental instructions within which he was operating. However, no sooner had the proposals appeared than the Soviet Government altered its position, in a manner which Zorin was apparently unable to anticipate. Such a quick and considerable modification of position could take place only within a governmental structure which would not feel its maneuverability was restricted by such considerations as difficult and elaborate procedures of ratification of agreements.

Before presentation, the United States delegation opposed the proposals of the representatives of the nonaligned states, but not as strongly as did the Soviet delegation. However, once the proposals had been presented, the United States acceptance of them as a possible basis of negotiation was more limited and circumspect than that of the Soviet Union. The reason stated was that our proposals did not come out unambiguously for a stated number of obligatory on-site inspections in order to police a test ban.[4]

The United States representatives, having to take into account what they could get their Government to adopt, made a much smaller movement—from qualified opposition to qualified acceptance of the proposals—than that of the Soviet Union.

When a country has a parliamentary form of government with ex-

ecutive and legislative powers controlled by the party in power and in
particular by its leaders—as is the case in the United Kingdom and
India—the maneuverability in negotiation is theoretically very great,
but not as great as when the form of government is of the Soviet
type.

A leader may be removed at any time by his parliamentary colleagues; and he and his colleagues are elected by secret ballot
against competing candidates of other parties. This whole structure
makes it incumbent on the leader of the parliamentary party in
power, or the prime minister, to be vigilant in regard to public opinion. He owes his power to the support of public opinion. Throughout
the Chinese-Indian border dispute, the Indian Government has found
its maneuverability restricted by the fact that the Indian system of
parliamentary democracy makes the Government constitutionally dependent upon the will of the people.

In a general sense, great power might give a country great maneuverability in negotiation, provided of course the form of government does not restrict the requisite degree of maneuverability demanded by the situation and circumstances involved. But maneuver-
ing in a negotiation must be distinguished from maintaining basic
flexibility. The latter facility is not usually displayed by powerful
states in the course of negotiation. As long as a state considers that it
is sufficiently powerful to determine the course of events in a manner
acceptable to itself, it tends to be deaf to other possibilities of settlement, either those advanced by the states directly involved in the negotiation or by third parties. Power tends to rigidity in international
negotiations, and total power tends to total rigidity. Fortunately, a
state of total power is, of course, never attained in international
affairs, since all countries are vulnerable to comprehensive alliances
against them.

A prime example of the inflexibility of more powerful states is the
former attitude of the colonial powers toward their possessions. The
British in the post-World War I era, when their power seemed adequate to the situation, showed no real desire to give up their hold on
India. Even during World War II, at the point when Germany had
subdued France and the rest of the Western European Continent, the
British showed no willingness to relinquish power in India. The near-
est they came to it was the Stafford Cripps mission in 1942, when
they asked the Indian leaders to join in supporting the war effort
fully, in return for a promise of steps toward dominion status after
the conclusion of the war. The Indian leaders were not able to accept

this offer, on the grounds of principle and for practical considerations. The principle involved was that for the country to be able to join enthusiastically in the struggle against Hitlerism, it must first be free. The practical consideration was that a promise of deferred action in international affairs does not give cause for confidence in eventual performance. Looking back, one might criticize this attitude, but given the history of British power in India it was to be expected at the time. As long as Britain was sure of its power, it continued to hold India and to offer terms in its negotiation with the Indian leaders which did not exhibit any real flexibility.

When it came to their smaller possessions, the colonial powers were far more inflexible and went so far as to make negotiation nearly impossible. In July 1954, the British Minister of State for Colonial Affairs, Henry Hopkinson, in announcing that the British Government had decided to take a fresh initiative in regard to Cyprus, stated:

They [Her Majesty's Government] wish to make it clear once again that they cannot contemplate a change of sovereignty in Cyprus.[5]

In stressing his point, Mr. Hopkinson said:

It has always been understood and agreed that there are certain territories in the Commonwealth which owing to their particular circumstances can never expect to be fully independent.[6]

Here the British clearly stated, as late as 1954, their attitude of complete inflexibility in regard to the ending of colonialism in Cyprus. However, the violent upheaval in Cyprus became more widespread and difficult to control, and the pressure of world opinion expressed in the United Nations threw itself against the maintenance of colonial power in opposition to the wishes of the Cypriot people. It was not until Britain found that the task of maintaining its power in Cyprus was almost impossibly complicated that the Zurich negotiations between the Greeks and Turks in 1959 could take place.

The attitude of total rigidity was sustained as long as power seemed adequate to the situation and as long as other forces (in this case, organized world opinion at the United Nations) did not pit themselves against colonial power.

France's position in Algeria was comparable to that of Britain in Cyprus. With 400,000 men deployed in Algeria in the early stages of the struggle against the National Liberation Front, France felt it had adequate power to maintain its position, and during that period it remained completely inflexible. Even so liberal a Prime Minister as Pierre Mendès-France stated in the French National Assembly on November 12, 1954:

One does not compromise when it comes to defending peace at home and the unity and integrity of the Republic. The Algerian departments are part of the French Republic. They have been French for a long time, and they are irrevocably French.[7]

Although it was this attitude which Mendès-France took to the problem of negotiation with Algeria, in a subsequent speech to the National Assembly on February 3, 1955 he said:

We choose either a policy of agreement, or else one of repression and force, with all its horrible consequences. I ask you with all my strength and conviction to choose the first.[8]

But to Mendès-France the policy of agreement, that is, of negotiation to reach agreement, had to be worked out in the context of Algeria's remaining irrevocably French. At the negotiating table there was to be no departure from this basic inflexibility. As we all know, this remained broadly the position until General de Gaulle was able to alter it in 1959, when it had become clear that by superior power alone France could not hold Algeria. What is more, it could not stop the Algerian nationalists from obtaining arms and other supplies from sympathetic states; and it could not silence the growing support for the Algerian cause at the United Nations.

It might be argued that the fact that so many areas have been decolonialized by the Western powers in recent years establishes the latter's flexibility. But two countervailing arguments seem to validate the opposite view. First, this change came only when those states lost their status as top powers as a result of the emergence in the post-World War II period of the United States and the Soviet Union as the leading powers. As long as the Western European states had been powers of the first order they remained inflexible. Second, the very suddenness of the change of position of the Western European powers has been an indication of brittleness rather than flexibility. Because colonialism had been established and maintained along inflexible lines, the change of power balances in the world caused the sudden crumbling of the colonial position.

Another case of inflexibility as an expression of power is the recent crisis over the payment of financial dues assessed by the General Assembly to meet the cost of United Nations peace-keeping operations in the Middle East and the Congo. As the critical hour approached, namely, the Nineteenth Session of the General Assembly, the weaker of those countries which were in arrears to the extent of two years of their total annual assessment toward the costs of the United Nations paid up. Those states included Nationalist China and six Latin American countries, Argentina, Bolivia, Guatemala, Haiti, Paraguay, and Uruguay. The Soviet Union and the Eastern European countries closely allied with it, along with France, refused to pay. The attitude of both the Soviet Union and France as expressed privately was that if the General Assembly saw fit to adopt a resolution depriving them of the vote, so much the worse for the General Assembly. They would leave the General Assembly, and this, they felt, would grievously impair, if not virtually destroy, the capacity of the General Assembly to discuss issues and to arrive at reasonable recommendations. Certainly, discussions on such issues as disarmament, Korea, the peaceful uses of outer space, International Cooperation Year, and so on, would become almost meaningless if the Soviet Union and France were absent from the General Assembly. Whatever may be the rights or wrongs of their position, it is clear that the basic power of the Soviet Union and France had much to do with their inflexibility in this situation. It might equally be argued that in the attempts to negotiate this issue, the other side (headed by the United States and the United Kingdom), had equally great if not greater power, and that this aggregation of power was also displaying its inflexibility. It is true that when two great powers or combinations of powers are poised against each other, flexibility tends to be absent from their negotiating postures. Each side holds out hoping that the other will make the first move.

In recent negotiations in the European Economic Community, France, in spite of its treaty of friendship and cooperation with Germany, has stood firmly against the Federal Republic of Germany in the matter of prices for agricultural commodities. This was a case of inflexibility by two powerful states. The confrontation was such that France held the trump cards. It had become a nuclear power, and its leader had shown enough independence to reject various possibilities of cooperation even with the United States. France's attitude became high-handed; so much so that in its editorial of November 10, 1964, *Le Monde* wrote that Franco-German relations had suffered, and added: "Without doubt the responsibility for the rapid deterioration falls in great part on the French Government." [9]

However, France had stuck to its position on agricultural prices until Germany indicated that it would yield. *Le Monde* reported that the relative optimism in Western diplomatic circles was founded essentially on two elements, one of which was the impression that "little by little under the double pressure of France and the United States, for once acting together, the German leaders were ready to show themselves as conciliatory on the question of agricultural prices." [10] We see here how superior power can play a determining role by maintaining its own rigidity of position until the other side relents.

In its attitudes toward the Multilateral Force, and toward NATO in general, France is in a key position and undoubtedly knows it. NATO would lose a great deal of its significance without France, not because France supplies a very large proportion of NATO armed forces but because NATO is, after all, symbolic of the unity of the Western powers against the Communist world. The defection of so powerful a country as France, whose prestige in the world is increasing, would be a most serious blow to the expression of Western unity. France, in its insistence on maintaining its opposition to the United States-backed proposal for the MLF, is again conscious of its power in the European complex. The purpose of MLF is to prepare the way for a European nuclear deterrent. By remaining out of the MLF, France will possess a counter-deterrent to the MLF and thus make virtual nonsense of the idea of an integrated European nuclear deterrent.

France is in a position of special significance and great power, and it appears to be using those factors to maintain an almost defiant position in regard to the issues involved. On the other side is the much greater power combination of the United States and the Federal Republic of Germany, reinforced by an unexpectedly sympathetic attitude on the part of the Labour Government in the United Kingdom toward some version of the MLF. As might be expected, this group of states is also exhibiting a great deal of inflexibility in regard to the MLF project. Whether this inflexibility derives from the desire of the Christian Democratic Party in Germany for an MLF agreement so as to retain power, or whether other reasons are involved, is not necessarily relevant to our argument. The point is best stated in a *New York Times* report from Bonn dated November 18, 1964:

The United States and West Germany have agreed to press to completion the project for an allied nuclear fleet even if France acts on her threat to quit the North Atlantic Treaty Organization in protest.[11]

No reasons were given by the *Times* correspondent for this attitude. According to the *Times,* this powerful group of countries intended to go ahead with the MLF even if the result should turn out to be an important defection from NATO, and even if there should be further consequences of relevance to the unity and integrity of the Western alliance. In the final event, one side or the other may alter its position, but this would only happen after a display of great inflexibility by both sides.

Other examples of inflexibility as an expression of great power can be cited. The attitude of the Soviet Union over the Hungarian issue in 1956 was, generally speaking, one that rejected all negotiation through the organs of the United Nations. This attitude was backed by the almost impenetrable power of the Soviet Union. On the other hand, where power was not so great in relation to the forces ranged on the other side it was not possible for the United Kingdom and France to reject negotiations in the United Nations for the withdrawal of their forces from the Suez area.

In his reply of October 29, 1964 to Chou En-lai's message of October 16 on the convening of a world-wide summit conference on disarmament, General de Gaulle displayed the inflexibility related to a position of power. The General has for some years insisted that disarmament start with the elimination of the vehicles for the delivery of nuclear warheads; in other words, with a conference of the nuclear powers rather than a world-wide conference. In his correspondence of February 1962 with Khrushchev, he stated that: "In order to have a chance to succeed, it is, in my opinion, necessary that negotiation take place between the powers that possess nuclear weapons or that will possess them in the near future." [12] Again, in his reply to Chou En-lai more than two and a half years later, General de Gaulle rejected the Chinese suggestion of a world conference and maintained his adamant position from strength, namely that he would participate "in all serious negotiations which could be organized between the competent and responsible powers to discuss on a constructive and practical base the problems of disarmament." [13] In his reply General de Gaulle also maintained his previous position that disarmament should direct itself first to the elimination of the vehicles for delivering nuclear weapons. Indeed, General de Gaulle accurately stated his position when he included in his reply to China the sentence: "The position of the Government of France remains the same." [14]

Without making a judgment as to whether his position is or is not the most constructive, one can see that General de Gaulle's inflexibility in regard to disarmament negotiations is closely related to the growing power and prestige of France.

Although a consciousness of power gives inflexibility to the position of a country in international negotiations, the consciousness of power varies from one situation to another. For example, Britain felt very conscious of its power in Cyprus in the mid-1950s, but in the developments in the Suez area in the same time span, relatively Britain was not powerful and was forced into a position of flexibility. The most significant indications of shifts of power in our era have taken place in regard to colonial possessions. Both the British and the French, after having made downright assertions of continuing sovereignty in regard to their colonial possessions, maneuvered themselves out of colonial power when it became apparent that the total complement of world forces was highly unfavorable to them. This movement away from colonialism is an indication of the maneuverability which a great power has in certain international situations. The creation of a multiracial Commonwealth [15] has been one of the striking results of the capacity of the United Kingdom for successful maneuverability. Much the same can be said of France, which retained close ties with a number of its previous colonies, especially those in Africa, after the end of its colonial domination.

From our consideration of the effects of the forms of government and the extent of power on flexibility and maneuverability in international negotiation, the following principles now appear to emerge:

> The forms and conventions of the constitutional structures of states have a direct bearing on the maneuverability of governments in the course of a negotiation.
>
> In an international negotiation, a powerful state tends to be inflexible whatever its form of government; it may, nevertheless, show considerable maneuverability.

CHAPTER TWENTY-SIX

Negotiation and International Law

WHAT IS the effect of international law on the negotiating postures of countries? Has the growing corpus of international law in the post-World War II era made countries more inclined to seek peaceful settlements of international situations and disputes through negotiation rather than to resort to force? On the face of it, it would seem that the answer to this question must be in the affirmative. One hundred and seventeen countries had adhered to the Charter of the United Nations by the end of 1965, under the terms of which they solemnly undertook "to settle their international disputes by peaceful means" and to "refrain in their international relations from the threat or use of force" in any manner inconsistent with the purposes of the United Nations. In addition to the Charter of the United Nations there are several hundred international agreements in force on the pacific settlement of disputes, although it should be borne in mind that most of them were negotiated in the late nineteenth and early twentieth centuries when the international community consisted of a circumscribed part of the world centered in Western Europe.

Those agreements, conventions, and treaties of the pre-World War II era still constitute a considerable body of the international law which flows from the four sources stated in Article 38 of the Statute of the International Court of Justice.[1] The four sources of law which the ICJ applies in deciding disputes submitted to it are considered by many nations to be weighted in favor of the old group of Western European nations which for centuries regarded themselves as the core of the civilized world.

As international conventions and treaties increasingly come to be negotiated on a broad base, and thereby include the views of states with different backgrounds, customs, legal systems, and traditions, the greater will be the impact of international law on the behavior of states. Even though the number of broad-based international conventions is growing, however, it is possible to cite cases from the recent past where a narrow approach has been preferred to a broad-based one in the making of international law.

Two cases which came within or near the orbit of the United Nations show the opposing trends of our era. One is the matter of the neutralization of Antarctica. This issue was initially mooted by the delegation of India to the United Nations. It fell to me to draw up a memorandum explaining the reasons for which it was thought best that Antarctica should not become part of the battle for positions in the Cold War. The matter seemed clearly one of general interest. For example, the Indian Ocean mingles with the waters of Antarctica, and military bases on Antarctica could create security problems for the states on the farther littoral of that ocean. The delegation of India hoped to have the General Assembly discuss this issue at its Eleventh Session and make a recommendation on the basis of which a convention of neutrality would be drawn up, to be adhered to by all states. However, for reasons which were not wholly clear, the Western powers and several of the Latin American states opposed discussion of this issue at the General Assembly. Instead, a conference was called at Washington and a handful of states, including the great powers, but excluding entirely the countries of Asia—except Japan —and all African states, drew up an agreement on the neutralization of Antarctica. The agreement in itself appears to be working, but it has tended to foster the idea that general international agreements can best be negotiated by a small group of countries, and in this respect the manner in which it was made is somewhat out of step with the requirements of an interdependent and shrinking world.

Another type of development is exemplified in the steps which preceded the negotiation of a statute for the International Atomic Energy Agency. In this case, too, a narrow basis was at first selected for the negotiation of the statute. In 1955 the United States announced at the Tenth Session of the General Assembly that, together with a group of seven other states—all Western—it was drafting a statute for a proposed International Atomic Energy Agency. It also stated that the draft statute would be circulated to all other governments for their comments before adoption. A number of countries at the United Nations, including most nations of Asia and Africa and some from South America, questioned this approach. We have noted that the

United States eventually responded to their misgivings and enlarged the negotiating body by including one state from Latin America (Brazil), one state from Asia (India), and two Communist states (Czechoslovakia and the Soviet Union). Furthermore, it was agreed that the draft produced by those countries would be submitted to a world conference before it was finally adopted.[2]

How important it is that the basis of negotiation should be widened is indicated by the events which followed the foregoing decisions. At the negotiation among the twelve countries which were named to constitute the drafting body for the statute of the IAEA, the major issues were explored in great depth, particularly by the United States, along with the Soviet Union and India, two countries which were not in the original group of eight. It is true that as a result of the inclusion of such states as India and the Soviet Union, the negotiations in Washington took perhaps two months longer than would otherwise have been the case, but this detailed consideration produced a draft statute which was later adopted by the world conference without any significant modification. As a result of the drafting of the statute on a broad basis, the IAEA has been directed from the beginning by a Board of Governors on which all areas of the world are represented. While most Asian and African countries still feel that their representation is inadequate, it has at any rate been large enough to insure that the decisions of the Board of Governors have been, generally speaking, acceptable to all the member states of the Agency. It is most doubtful that this would have been the case had the agency been set up on a narrower base, as originally contemplated, and with a more restrictively constituted Board of Governors.

As more and more international conventions and treaties come to be developed on the basis of a wide participation of countries from all the regions of the world, a genuine and universal respect for international law will develop, which will in itself tend to make countries more amenable to the peaceful settlement—through negotiation and other processes—of disputes and situations in which they are concerned.

The fact that we have in our era such important instruments as the Charter of the United Nations, which was negotiated by fifty states, does tend to influence countries toward the peaceful settlement of disputes and situations. One cannot quarrel with history, but it is unfortunate that the process of decolonialization had not gone further in 1945 than was actually the case. It would have been in many ways preferable for our present era if the Charter of the United Nations had been negotiated not by fifty nations but by at least twice as many countries. It would then have gained something from the increased emphasis which the less developed countries would have placed on economic issues, and it might have stimulated consideration of a clearer demarcation of functions between the General Assembly and the Security Council.

The United States in its Outline of Basic Provisions of a Treaty on General and Complete Disarmament in a Peaceful World, introduced to the Eighteen-Nation Committee on Disarmament in April 1962, included the thought that in the maintenance of international peace and security the International Court of Justice should be much more fully involved than hitherto in the settlement of disputes.[3] At the Conference, in commenting on this proposal, which I favored in principle, I felt it necessary to bring into the open certain relevant considerations. First, I pointed out that a very small number of states—at that time 38—had accepted the jurisdiction of the Court. Although the membership of the United Nations has gone up by almost 100 percent since 1955, no state had accepted the jurisdiction of the Court in 1961 or 1962. I also noted that only one contentious case a year, on the average, had been taken to the Court. Most of those contentious cases, indeed virtually all of them, have dealt with relatively minor international issues rather than with questions connected with significant international disputes. The one exception, potentially, is the dual case brought by Ethiopia and Liberia against South Africa concerning South Africa's mandate in South-West Africa. These twin cases were referred to the Court on November 4, 1960, but the rejoinder of South Africa was not to be filed before the Court until November 20, 1964, a delay of over four years.[4] At the Geneva Disarmament Conference, I pointed out that before increased responsibilities could be effectively assigned to the International Court, thought would have to be given to the reasons which make states reluctant to accept the jurisdiction of the Court.

First I drew attention to the fact that owing to its relatively recent origin, the indefinite character and scarcity of its rules, and the constitutional difficulties of amending obsolete rules and creating new ones, international law exhibits considerable gaps and anachronisms in its total corpus. Indeed, a decision in accordance with international law is frequently impossible to arrive at. I recalled the following statement of Clarence Wilfred Jenks:

It is not the primary function of international law in the latter half of the 20th century to protect vested interests arising out of an international distribution of political and economic power which has irrevocably changed, but to adjust conflicting interests on a basis which contemporary opinion regards as sufficiently reasonable to be entitled to the organized support of a universal community.[5]

The above citation brings out a very important reason for the lack of respect which many countries have had for international law as it has been administered even in our era. The rectification of this situation will be necessary if an atmosphere is to be created in which the rule of law can truly flourish in international relations and promote peaceful settlements through negotiation or through judicial processes.

The newly independent states in general favor greater international cooperation in the peaceful settlement of disputes in accordance with concepts of law and justice which they can accept as valid. The process of creating widely acceptable international law is one which the Charter of the United Nations recognizes. The General Assembly is categorically instructed to initiate studies and make recommendations for the purpose of "the progressive development of international law and its codification." [6] The General Assembly has created the International Law Commission for this purpose, and the Commission has achieved some noteworthy results. Such international instruments as the Convention on the High Seas (which came into effect on September 20, 1962); the Vienna Convention on Diplomatic Relations (April 24, 1964); and the Convention on the Continental Shelf (June 10, 1964), are some of the final results of work largely initiated or explored in its early stages by the International Law Commission.

The process of revising antiquated instruments of international law is likely to be both arduous and slow. Meanwhile, the germane political and international factors grow apace. The membership of the United Nations is approaching 120, and as many as 119 countries attended the United Nations Conference on Trade and Development held in the first half of 1964. The political fact of the enfranchisement of all countries of the world means that the process of bringing up to date and universalizing international law must go beyond its present initial stage.

At the Geneva Disarmament Conference I referred to the fact that (perhaps for insufficient reasons) the judgments of the International Court have not come to command the respect which will be necessary if its jurisdiction is to become more widely acceptable. Without criticizing any of the learned judges, or in any way objecting to the

Court's composition, I pointed out that the vast majority of the world, in Asia and Africa, was represented at the time by only one-fifth of the judges.[7] It is not often that the judges differ from the national political positions of the countries from which they come. A jurist, no matter how eminent, is nevertheless a product of his background and is influenced by it. For this reason, the International Court of Justice should reflect adequately the points of view which exist in the various regions of the world.

It may have been purely accidental that when the Court tendered its advisory opinion on the obligations of member states under the Charter of the United Nations with regard to the financing of the United Nations Emergency Force and the organization's operations in the Congo, the judges took positions which corresponded with those of the governments of their countries on this burning political issue.[8] When a judge expresses a view which is not that of the government of the country from which he comes, this fact attracts attention. In referring to the views of Lord McNair on the Anglo-Iranian Oil Case, Professor Jimenez de Arechaga of Uruguay, a past-president of the International Law Commission, said:

Lord McNair in his historic opinion in the Anglo-Iranian Oil Case, an important instance of a judge voting against the contention of his own state, described the system as follows: [9]

In spite of the gaps in international law, its narrow basis, the inevitably slow processes of its development on a wider basis, and a considerable degree of existing caution regarding the judgments of the International Court of Justice, it might be argued that the growing cognizance of international law accompanied by a growing respect for it tends to dispose countries toward peaceful settlements. It might also be argued that the strong nations of today are inhibited to some extent by these facts and considerations, and that relative strength alone does not determine their attitudes toward international negotiation.

Sir Gerald Fitzmaurice, who has had long practical experience in the problems of international law both as legal adviser to the Foreign Office of the United Kingdom and as judge in the International Court, has suggested that certain elements in the post-World War II formulations of international law—such as the interdiction of the use of force contained in the Charter of the United Nations—"have had the ironic effect of weakening general respect for international law." We would not, for our part, find it possible to accept this view. For one thing, Sir Gerald formulated the argument after the United Nations had frustrated the Franco-British attack on the Suez area; and it is difficult to see how that attack could, even by implication, be regarded as a valid expression of the processes of law.

In the present formative stages of a new international law based on the ideas and practices of the entire world community instead of a part of it, there are cross-currents which inevitably will add to the complexities of the situation. In the line of descent of the old international law, the emperors of the West were regarded by medieval lawyers as "law-givers not for the Occident alone, but for the *Universus Orbis*." [10] It was only relatively recently that theoreticians in the field of international law came to see that an international legal system "is valid only as international law conforms to the actual practice of States and other organizations which enjoy juridical personality." [11] Although the theoreticians have reached this position in contemporary thinking, it is natural that in the process of the redrafting of international law states with an older tradition in these matters should often find themselves resistant to change.

In the colonial issue, at least in the initial stages of the confrontation between the colonies and the administering powers, there was no doubt as to where the relatively greater strength lay. But with the passage of time and the development of the idea that sovereignty is vested in the people, colonialism became less in keeping with the evolving concepts of international behavior and the direction in which international law was groping—such as the emphasis in the Charter of the United Nations on self-determination, a formulation which was not contained in the Covenant of the League of Nations. Those developments influenced some of the relationships between the colonial rulers and non–self-governing peoples. Although there had been violence and the use of force by the United Kingdom in the past, at the close of World War II events on the Indian subcontinent, Burma, Ceylon, and elsewhere in the old British Empire might be cited as evidence of the new influences at work.

Certain other colonial powers did everything possible to hold their possessions by force. France did this in Indochina and again in Algeria. Portugal has continued to do so in respect to all her colonies, and the exit of Belgium from the Congo was so sudden that it conformed neither to the use of force nor to negotiation, but rather to an expression of sudden realization of incapacity. Taken all together, the interaction between the colonial powers and their possessions in our era has not shown a consistent trend in favor of respect for the new corpus and tendencies of international law.

The United Kingdom and France, together much more powerful

than Egypt, were not restrained in 1956 from using force over the Suez issue. For the most part, the crisis over that issue was the result of an atavistic attitude on the part of certain powers toward a perfectly understandable development, and subsequent events showed how unnecessary was that attitude. Atavistic tendencies are seldom in accordance with developing international rules.

The Soviet Union, although acting at the request of the President of Hungary, was not restrained in the use of force in that country in 1956, in spite of the formulations in the Charter of the United Nations and of the resolutions of the General Assembly. India and China were not—and this is true of both of them—acting fully in accordance with the new spirit of international law as expressed in the Charter of the United Nations in increasing the military confrontation on their common border. And, when China finally attacked India in October 1962, it was departing violently from the new precepts of international law. Indonesia was not restrained by its membership in the United Nations from attacking a small neighboring state which is also a member of the United Nations; it showed its unilateral disregard for the norms of international conduct by withdrawing from the United Nations and the Specialized Agencies.

The recent and present events in the Caribbean, Southeast Asia, Africa, and the India-Pakistan border, show that if there is an increasing respect for international law it is not having the effect of completely restraining states from using force.

However, it can be argued that when the Asian-African states year after year brought the issue of Algeria to the General Assembly and asked for a peaceful settlement, they were trying to create conditions for negotiations and were doing so because international law now provided them with the opportunity of using the forum of the General Assembly for their purpose. In this sense, it may be said that they were showing a certain respect for international law, but it would be a mistake to ignore the fact that they were using a method that was in their national interests, as they conceived them.

It might be said that those countries which are asking for international conferences on Southeast Asia are expressing themselves in favor of peaceful settlements through means which are in conformity with Chapter VI of the Charter of the United Nations. Again, it might be argued that the effort of the six Colombo powers to find a basis for negotiation between China and India for the settlement of the border dispute is an effort wholly in keeping with the Charter of the United Nations and other formulations of international law. Other instances of this type can be cited, and in some degree they do point in the direction of an increasing respect for international law. However, on closer examination it is often found that the states concerned were not being totally restrained in the use of force. In spite of the efforts of the Colombo powers, China and India seem to be continuing military preparations. Force is being used in Southeast Asia and elsewhere, and even when the case of Algeria was being brought to the United Nations it could be said that this was due to the fact that the National Liberation Front wanted time to reequip itself and reach a position of greater military strength.

What of the relationship of power to international law? Are the great powers more responsive to the trends of international law?

We can point to the case of the landing of the United States Marines in Lebanon and observe that the immediately succeeding events at the United Nations showed how a superpower was able to retreat gracefully because its action had not been in keeping with the current trends of international relations and law. In this case it might be said that the relative strength alone of the United States did not determine its behavior.

On the other hand, in August 1964, when Turkey decided that its airplanes should strafe the small island of Cyprus, the relatively greater power was not restrained by current theoretical developments in international relations and law.

Although the United States acted in accordance with Article 51 of the Charter of the United Nations in reporting to the Security Council the measures it took to quarantine Cuba in 1962, its action in instituting the quarantine and taking other measures against Cuba were hardly in full conformity with international law. It is also difficult to give the approval of international law to the United States actions in the Dominican Republic in 1965.

Whatever the reasons—and there were such good reasons as the absolute refusal of Portugal to negotiate, the United Nations resolutions on the termination of colonialism, and indications that Portugal might enter into a deal regarding the territory concerned with a third power inimical to India—India did not act in accordance with current developments of international law in its manner of taking over Goa, and its actions were a display of its relatively greater strength rather than its respect for international law.

South Africa's flouting of the long series of annual resolutions is a clear case of disregard of the findings of the overwhelming majority of the membership of the United Nations with respect to the obligations of South Africa under international law, in terms of the Charter to which that country has subscribed. Certainly South Africa as a signatory is disregarding its solemn obligation to uphold human rights without racial distinction.

At present, power, rather than respect for international law, continues to be a dominating factor in international relationships. At the same time, there are certain slight indications of the opposite tendency.

Our conclusion must therefore be that the time has not yet come when we can formulate principles which express accurately the influence of international law on the conduct of states, particularly as a factor which predisposes them toward or influences them in negotiation. We do, however, see certain incipient trends which can be stated as hypotheses. Those hypotheses might, in the foreseeable future, develop into principles which will significantly affect international relations. This is likely to happen provided that continuing steps are taken, through such organs as the International Law Commission and through the accumulation of precedents in the other organs of the United Nations, to insure the operation of the process of the development and codification of international law on a universal or near-universal basis. Another step in this direction would be an amendment of Article 3 of the Statute of the International Court of Justice so as to secure an expansion of the present number (fifteen) of judges, to reflect the recent very considerable increase in United Nations membership.

From an over-all view of the present status of international law, the hypotheses we would suggest are:

The growing respect for, or commitment to, international law among the members of the world community tends to restrain a state in the use of force and predisposes it toward peaceful settlement through negotiation.

When a negotiation concerns a matter in which the position of a relatively strong party is not in keeping with current trends in international relations and law, its relative strength alone does not determine its postures in negotiation.

Notes

Chapter 1. The Era of Negotiation

1. *New York Times,* December 30, 1964.

Chapter 2. Defining International Negotiation

1. Eighteen-Nation Committee on Disarmament Conference document ENDC/30, April 18, 1962, pp. 17–18. For the story of the formation of the Committee, and its relationship to the United Nations General Assembly and the Disarmament Commission, see *Infra,* Chapter 8.

2. In the author's own experience as a district officer and magistrate in what is now West Pakistan, the inhabitants of whole villages were bound over to keep the peace because decisions of the civil and criminal courts had not stopped a continuing exchange of murders between two factions.

3. See International Court of Justice, Advisory Opinions of June 7, 1955 (on voting procedure on questions relating to reports and petitions concerning South-West Africa), and June 1, 1956 (on admissibility of hearings of petitioners by the Committee on South-West Africa). See also *Ethiopia v. South Africa* and *Liberia v. South Africa:* Preliminary Objections, Judgment of December 21, 1962. International Court of Justice Reports, 1962, p. 319.

4. It should be noted that the comprehensive tenor of Article 94.1 of the United Nations Charter may be derogated from by the nature of the declaration which a state makes regarding recognition of the jurisdiction of the International Court of Justice under Article 36 of the Court's Statute. By the terms of its declaration a state can seriously diminish the number and kinds of cases to which it will be a party, and thereby restrict the applicability of the scope of Article 94.1.

5. League of Nations Covenant, Articles 12, 13, 14.

6. *Ibid.,* Articles 12, 15.

7. United Nations Charter, Articles 33, 34, 36.

8. *Ibid.,* Article 36.3.

9. From the same root the French derive *negocier* (to trade or traffic)—another aspect of the meaning of the word "negotiate" in current diplomatic usage.

10. *Yearbook of the United Nations, 1958* (New York, Columbia University Press in association with the United Nations, 1960), p. 50.

11. General Assembly Resolution 1004 (ES-II), November 4, 1956.

12. *Yearbook of the United Nations, 1956* (New York, Columbia University Press in association with the United Nations, 1957), p. 74.

13. Annual Report of the Secretary-General on the Work of the Organization, 1962–63. General Assembly Official Records, 18th Session, Supp. No. 1 (A/5501), p. 35.

14. Introduction to the Annual Report of the Secretary-General on the Work of the Organization, 1956–57. See also Dag Hammarskjöld, *Servant of Peace: a Selection of the Speeches and Statements of Dag Hammarskjöld,* ed. by Wilder Foote (New York, Harper and Row, 1963), pp. 144–45.

15. General Assembly Resolution 268 (III), April 28, 1949.

16. United States Treaty Series, No. 780.

17. United Nations Charter, Article 33.   18. *Ibid.,* Article 37.

19. *Ibid.,* Articles 36, 37.

20. The Conference was convened on March 14, 1962, and has since continued in session except for brief recesses, United Nations General Assembly sessions, and a session of the United Nations Disarmament Commission from April to June 1965.

21. For text see United States Arms Control and Disarmament Agency (USACDA), *Documents on Disarmament, 1963,* pp. 236–38.

22. The partial test ban prohibiting nuclear weapons testing in the atmosphere, in outer space, and under water.

23. Security Council document S/PV.1117, May 18, 1964, pp. 2–6.

24. Even after the military clash of 1965, one of the main efforts both inside and outside the Security Council was to get the leaders of India and Pakistan together to explore the possibilities of a settlement.

25. Convention for the Peaceful Settlement of International Disputes, agreed at The Hague, October 18, 1907, Articles 2–8.

26. This call was made by a number of representatives, including the author, in August 1955.

27. United Nations Press Conference, August 25, 1955, Note No. 1158 (mimeographed), pp. 10–11.

28. General Assembly Resolution 938 (X), December 3, 1955, paragraph 3.

29. For another statement of differences between mediation and good offices, see L. Oppenheim, *Disputes, War and Neutrality,* Vol. II of *Inter-*

national Law, ed. by H. Lauterpacht (New York, McKay, 1952), § 9.

30. *"Expresses* the wish that in a spirit of effective cooperation, pourparlers will be entered into and other appropriate means utilized, with a view to a solution in conformity with the purposes and principles of the Charter of the United Nations." General Assembly Resolution 1184 (XII).

31. Report of the Rapporteur to Commission II, to the Plenary Session, United Nations Conference on International Organization, San Francisco, 1945, document 1180, June 24, 1945.

32. The French view was countered by Henri Rolin, the delegate of Belgium. See Verbatim Minutes of the Fourth Meeting of Commission II, June 21, 1945, United Nations Conference on International Organization, San Francisco, documents 1151 and 1207.

33. General Assembly Resolution 268 (III) A.

34. Verbatim Minutes of the Fourth Meeting of Commission II, June 21, 1945, United Nations Conference on International Organization, San Francisco, document 1207.

35. Verbatim Minutes of the Third Meeting of Commission II, June 18, 1945, United Nations Conference on International Organization, San Francisco, document 1088.

36. United Nations Charter, Article 97. 37. *Ibid.,* Article 26.

Chapter 3. The Primary Bases

1. Annex to General Assembly Resolution 1890 (XVIII), November 11, 1963, para. 5.

2. General Assembly Resolution 1785 (XVII), December 8, 1962, para. 5(b).

3. Security Council document Annex 16 (S/203), p. 170.

4. Security Council document S(360/Rev 1).

5. *Yearbook of the United Nations, 1946–47* (Lake Success, New York, United Nations Department of Public Information, 1947), p. 336.

6. Security Council document S/3287, letter dated September 8, 1956.

7. Security Council Report of 730th Meeting (11th Year), paragraph 85.

8. Article 25 reads: "The Members of the United Nations agree to accept and carry out the decisions of the Security Council in accordance with the present Charter." One view is that the decisions referred to are exclusively decisions taken under Chapter VII of the Charter.

9. For a general survey of the facts of the case see pp. 23-25 of the Secretary-General's Report on the Work of the Organization, 1954–55. General Assembly Official Records, 10th Session, Supp. No. 1 (A/2911).

10. The two resolutions will be found respectively in Security Council documents S/3378 and S/3538.

11. These two resolutions will be found respectively in Security Council documents S/3575 and S/3605.

12. Letter of President de Gaulle of February 18, 1962, and French Foreign Ministry Statement of March 5, 1962 in *New York Times,* February 20, 1962, and *Le Monde,* March 7, 1962, respectively.

13. For a treatment of the facts of this Conference see *infra,* Chapter Five.

14. Quadripartite Communiqué of the Berlin Conference, February 18, 1954.

15. *Ibid.*

16. See statements of Prime Minister Nehru in the Indian Parliament, August 19, 1963. (Indiagram No. 159, August 20, 1963, issued by the Information Service of India, Embassy of India, Washington, D.C.)

17. Article 99 reads as follows: "The Secretary-General may bring to the attention of the Security Council any matter which in his opinion may threaten the maintenance of international peace and security."

18. From the Introduction to the Annual Report of the Secretary-General on the Work of the Organization, 1958–59.

19. Dag Hammarskjöld, *Servant of Peace,* p. 335.

20. "The Secretary-General shall . . . perform such other functions as are entrusted to him by [the General Assembly, the Security Council, the Economic and Social Council, and the Trusteeship Council]."

21. United Nations Press Services, O.P.I. Note No. 2951, pp. 6–10.

22. United Nations Press Services, O.P.I. Note No. 3075.

23. "Essential Principles for a Disarmament Program," in Disarmament Commission document DC/C.1/1; also in U.S. Department of State, *Documents on Disarmament, 1945–59,* pp. 357–58.

24. *Ibid.,* para. 3.

25. General Assembly 434th Plenary Meeting Records. (Italics added)

26. General Assembly Resolution 715 (VIII), November 28, 1953, Operational Paragraph 6.

27. Quoted by Philip Noel-Baker in *The Arms Race* (New York, Oceana Publications, 1958), p. 19.

28. *Ibid.,* p. 24. The stalemate continued virtually until the Eighteen-Nation Committee on Disarmament convened at Geneva in 1962.

29. For further comments on the question of Goa see *infra,* Chapter Nine.

30. U.S. Department of State, *Documents on Disarmament, 1945–59,* pp. 408–13.

31. *Ibid.,* p. 462.

Chapter 4. Acceptance of Peaceful Methods

1. North Atlantic Treaty, April 4, 1949, Article 5.

2. Treaty of Friendship, Cooperation, and Mutual Assistance, May 14, 1955, Article 4.

3. Security Council document S/5181, letter dated October 22, 1962

from the Permanent Representative of the United States to the President of the Security Council.

4. Security Council document S/PV.1022, October 23, 1962, p. 17.

5. *Ibid.,* pp. 26–27.

6. Security Council document S/PV.1204, October 24, 1962, p. 10.

7. *Ibid.,* p. 14.   8. *Ibid.,* p. 20.

9. Security Council document S/PV.1023, October 24, 1962, p. 19.

10. Security Council document S/5182, October 22, 1962.

11. Security Council document S/5187, October 23, 1962.

12. Security Council document S/5182, October 22, 1962.

13. Security Council document S/5187, October 23, 1962.

14. Security Council document S/PV.1022, October 23, 1963, p. 15.

15. *Ibid.,* p. 37.

16. Treaty of Guarantee, Article 1; and Constitution of the Republic of Cyprus, Article 49.

17.   Security Council document S/5575, March 4, 1964.

18. *New York Times,* June 29, 1964.

19. Transcript of Prime Minister Inonu's Press Conference of June 25, 1964, Southern District Court Reporters, U.S. Court House, Foley Square 7, New York.

20. Security Council document S/5625, March 26, 1964.

21. *New York Times,* June 29, 1964; and Prime Minister Papandreou's press conference at Washington, D.C., June 25, 1964.

22. *New York Times,* July 1, 1964.

23. *Ibid.,* July 5, 1964.

24. After a meeting of the NATO Foreign Ministers in May 1965 at London, Greece showed some disposition toward direct negotiation.

25. *Prime Minister on Sino-Indian Relations,* (Indian Parliament, Part II, External Publicity Division: New Delhi, Government of India, Ministry of External Affairs, 1962), Vol. I, p. 98.

26. *Ibid.,* p. 115.

27. *Ibid.,* p. 116. On the Indian side, the other person present was the author.

28. *Ibid.,* p. 394.   29. *Ibid.,* p. 98.   30. *Ibid.,* p. 105

31. *Ibid.,* p. 210.   32. *Ibid.,* p. 99.

Chapter 5. Agreement on Objectives

1. Eighteen-Nation Committee on Disarmament Document ENDC/7, March 16, 1962.

2. *Ibid.*

3. Eighteen-Nation Committee on Disarmament document ENDC/8, March 19, 1962.

4. Text contained in the United States delegation unpublished verbatim records of the Conference.

5. Second Plenary Session of the International Conference on Laos, May 17, 1961, from the unprinted verbatim text of Conference prepared by the United States Delegation to that Conference.

6. After his strong attack on United States policies in Southeast Asia, Marshal Chen Yi said on May 16, 1961 in his opening statement to the Conference: "Even the United States has now expressed favor for the peace, neutrality, and independence of Laos, and has sent delegates to take part in the present Conference. This is anyhow to be welcomed. It is our hope that the United States delegates will seriously work jointly with all of us to seek avenues to a peaceful settlement of the Laotian question." (From unpublished Conference Record)

7. The opening was delayed (the Conference assembled on May 12 but did not convene until May 16) mainly because the United States and certain other countries thought the Conference could not meet for meaningful discussion until the warring factions in Laos had entered into an effective cease-fire. It took a few days for the cochairmen of the Conference, Lord Home (as he then was) and Andrei Gromyko, to convince delegations that reports from Laos indicated that a cease-fire was substantially in effect.

8. Article I of the Presidential Decree on the Nationalization of the Suez Canal, Egyptian Government's Official Gazette No. 60, July 26, 1956. (Translation in *The Suez Canal Problem, July 26–Sept. 22, 1956.* Washington, D.C., U.S. Department of State publication 6392.)

9. *Ibid.*   10. *The Suez Canal Problem,* pp. 72–78.

11. *Ibid.,* p. 92.   12. *Ibid.,* p. 158.

13. Although the Security Council adopted a resolution (S/2298 Rev. 1) on September 1, 1951 calling upon Egypt to terminate restrictions on the passage of international shipping and goods through the Suez Canal, wherever bound, there was a further discussion on this issue in the Security Council in October 1954 on a complaint by Israel against Egypt (S/3300 dated October 4, 1954) which was inconclusive. Egypt maintained that its attitude was conditioned by the fact that a state of belligerence continued to exist between Egypt and Israel, adding that it was not possible to afford free passage through the Canal to enemy ships which might threaten its security and that of the Canal. Other members of the Council expressed the view that while Egypt could take steps to protect the security of the Canal in accordance with Article X of the Constantinople Convention of 1888 concerning the defense of its own territory, and in accordance with Article 51 of the Charter, it could do so only while taking into account the spirit of the Constantinople Convention and the relevant recommendations made in Security Council resolutions. However, no additional resolution was adopted to clarify the matter further.

14. *The Suez Canal Problem,* pp. 174–77.   15. *Ibid.,* pp. 180–81.

16. *Yearbook of the United Nations, 1957* (New York, Columbia

University Press in cooperation with the United Nations, 1958), p. 47.

17. Resolution No. 44 (I), Treatment of Indians in the Union of South Africa, December 8, 1946.

Chapter 6. Procedures

1. For text see U.S. Department of State, *Documents on Disarmament, 1945–59*, pp. 393–400.

2. Agreement has been reached to enlarge the Security Council to 15 members and the Economic and Social Council to 27, but these are obviously quantitative rather than qualitative changes.

3. For text, see *Yearbook of the United Nations, 1946–47*, pp. 4–9.

4. *United Nations Conference on International Organization, San Francisco, 1945* (Berkeley, University of California Press, 1945), Vol. I, pp. 112–13.

5. *Ibid.*, pp. 137–38.   6. *Ibid.*, p. 181.

7. *Ibid.*, pp. 137–38.   8. *Ibid.*, p. 181.   9. *Ibid.*, p. 191.

10. *Ibid.*, p. 234.   11. *Ibid.*, p. 245.

12. General Assembly Resolution 180 (IX), December 4, 1954.

13. General Assembly Official Records, 10th Session, Agenda Item 18: First Committee, October 7, 1955, p. 6.

14. *Ibid.*, October 10, 1955, p. 10.

15. *Ibid.*, October 11, 1955, p. 15.

16. *Ibid.*, October 14, 1955, p. 32.   17. *Ibid.*, p. 33.

18. *Ibid.*, October 17, 1955, p. 37.

19. *Ibid.*, October 18, 1955, p. 39.

20. General Assembly documents A/C.1/L.131 and Add. 1 and 2.

21. General Assembly Official Records, 10th Session, Agenda Item 18: First Committee, October 25, 1955, p. 65.

22. *Ibid.*, p. 67.

23. *Yearbook of the United Nations, 1956*, p. 104.   24. *Ibid.*

25. Joint Communiqué of December 12, 1954, issued on the occasion of Prime Minister U Nu's visit to Peking.

26. Prime Minister U Nu's Statement to the Burmese Chamber of Deputies, April 28, 1960 (published by the Director of Information, Union of Burma, 1960), p. 2.

27. *Ibid.*, p. 5.   28. *Ibid.*, p. 7.   29. *Ibid.*, p. 9.

30. *Ibid.*, p. 9.   31. *Ibid.*, p. 14.   32. *Ibid.*, p. 16.

33. *Ibid.*, p. 25.

34. For the Chinese version, see the *Peking Review* of the relevant dates.

35. William R. Willoughby, *The St. Lawrence Waterway* (Madison, University of Wisconsin Press, 1961), p. 161.

36. For text see R. R. Baxter, *Documents on the St. Lawrence Seaway* (New York, Praeger, 1961), pp. 11–17.

37. *Ibid.*, pp. 17–18.   38. *Ibid.*, pp. 54–57.

39. For text see U.S. Department of State Bulletin, August 16, 1941, p. 125.

40. *New York Times,* June 24, 1964.

41. An amusing sidelight on these discussions between the scientists of the two sides is that by a slip of the tongue "desalinization" was frequently referred to as "destalinization." This became so frequent a slip, that the scientists decided that it was safer to use the word "de-salting"!

42. *New York Times,* July 7, 1964.   43. *Ibid.,* July 17, 1964.

44. "Water Desalination in Developing Countries."

45. *New York Times,* February 20, 1962.

46. The proposal is contained in a statement dated July 31, 1963. It was then addressed to all governments in a letter from Prime Minister Chou En-lai dated August 2, 1963. For text see the *New York Times.* August 5, 1963. The proposal was repeated by China following its first and second nuclear explosions, in October 1964 and May 1965 respectively.

47. Transcript of a press conference by Chancellor Adenauer at the National Press Club, Washington, D.C., November 15, 1962.

48. See excerpts in the *Christian Science Monitor,* November 21, 1962.

49. This declaration was signed by both de Gaulle and Adenauer.

50. Address of Maurice Couve de Murville to the French National Assembly, January 24, 1962.

51. Dr. Ludwig Erhard's statement to the Bundestag of the Federal Republic of Germany, Bonn, October 18, 1963.

52. U.S. Department of State publication 6046, pp. 67–78.

53. This aphoristic and somewhat cryptic resolution (the shortest ever to be adopted in the Political Committee of the General Assembly) read: "The General Assembly decides not to consider further the item entitled 'The question of Algeria' and is, therefore, no longer seized of this item on the agenda of its tenth session" (Resolution 909 [X] dated November 25, 1955). France accepted this as a removal of the offensive item; and the Afro-Asian countries maintained their position of principle by the fact that the resolution did not impugn the competence of the United Nations and was moreover to be effective for only the current session of the General Assembly.

54. The General Assembly adopted Resolution 1012 (XI) on February 15, 1956 by a vote of 75 in favor, with none against and 1 abstention; on December 10, 1956 it adopted Resolution 1184 (XII) by 80 votes in favor and 0 against.

55. General Assembly Resolution 1573 (XV), December 19, 1960.

56. General Assembly Resolution 296 J (IV).

57. *International Court of Justice Reports of Judgments, Advisory Opinions, and Orders, 1950* (New York, Columbia University Press, 1953), p. 10.

58. General Assembly Resolution 718 (VIII).

59. The last resolution prior to admission was 918 (X), which was adopted by 52 to 2 with 5 abstentions on December 8, 1955.

60. For India's amendment to the proposal of Canada, see U.S. Department of State, *Documents on Disarmament, 1960,* p. 366.

61. General Assembly Resolutions 1617 (XV), April 21, 1961; and 1720 (XVI), December 20, 1961.

62. General Assembly document A/PV.733, August 13, 1958.

63. *Ibid.*   64. General Assembly document A/3878.

65. General Assembly document A/3893/Rev. 1.

66. General Assembly document A/PV.746, August 21, 1958.

67. *Ibid.*

68. General Assembly Resolution 1237 (ES–III), August 21, 1958.

69. Security Council document S/PV.1024, October 24, 1962, p. 20.

70. *Ibid.,* p. 21.

71. Security Council document S/PV.1025, October 25, 1962.

Chapter 7. Mediation, Conciliation, and Good Offices

1. I have in mind the Commonwealth which is by now (1966) probably the most international "club" yet established. It is a club in the British sense; shop is rarely talked. The idea is to develop a common feeling through friendly association. It is presumed that, in the long run, this process facilitates the amelioration of situations in which the club members might be involved.

2. Security Council document S/3793. Resolution adopted by the Council on February 21, 1957.

3. Security Council document S/3821, April 29, 1957.

4. Security Council document S/5575, March 4, 1964.

5. Security Council document S/5625, March 26, 1964; after the death of Tuomioja, Galo Plaza was designated mediator.

6. *New York Times,* July 4, 1964.   7. *Ibid.,* July 31, 1964.

8. Report on the Cyprus Question by Prime Minister George A. Papandreou. Debate in Greek Parliament, July 3, 1964 (Athens, Press and Information Department, 1964), p. 2.

9. *Ibid.,* p. 3.   10. *New York Times,* July 31, 1964.

11. *Ibid.*

12. Report on the Cyprus Question by Prime Minister George A. Papandreou. Debate in Greek Parliament, July 3, 1964, p. 5.

13. General Assembly, First Committee document A/C.1/SR.726, November 23, 1954, p. 394.

14. General Assembly Plenary Meeting document A/PV.477, September 24, 1954.

15. General Assembly Resolution 915 (X), December 16, 1955.

16. General Assembly document A/C.1/SR.905, p. 200.

17. General Assembly document A/C.1/SR.909, p. 228.

18. General Assembly document A/4915, October 7, 1961.

19. General Assembly document A/4944, October 27, 1961.

20. Indonesia's withdrawal from the United Nations does not nullify the provisions of the Treaty, but it creates an interesting practical situation regarding the implementation of this provision.

21. Australian Command Paper: West New Guinea. Indonesian-Netherlands Agreement, August 21, 1962, p. 5. The text of the agreement of August 13, 1962 on the transfer of the admission of West Irian to the United Nations and Indonesia is printed as Annex I to this command paper.

22. Information Release of Permanent Mission of Morocco, to the United Nations, New York, October 23, 1963.

23. *Ibid.*, p. 4. 24. *New York Times*, October 12, 1963.

25. *Ibid.*, October 13, 1963. 26. *Ibid.*, October 16, 1963.

27. Security Council document S/3666.

28. Security Council document S/PV.735, October 5, 1956, p. 25.

29. Security Council document S/PV.742, p. 7.

30. Security Council document S/3671.

31. *Ibid.*, p. 6. 32. *Ibid.*, p. 7. 33. *Ibid.*, p. 9.

34. *Ibid.*, p. 12. 35. Security Council document S/PV.743, p. 1.

36. *Ibid.*, p. 18–19.

37. Security Council document S/3728. See also *Yearbook of the United Nations, 1956*, pp. 23–24.

Chapter 8. The Wider Forums

1. In the 744th meeting of the Security Council, February 21, 1957, V. K. Krishna Menon, speaking for India on the India-Pakistan question, said: "So far as member states which are not members of the Security Council are concerned, when proceedings under Chapter VI are being pursued, its relevance to them is based only upon consent." (S/PV.744.) See also statement of the Permanent Representative of France at the 28th meeting of the Working Group on the Examination of the Administrative and Budgetary Procedures of the United Nations (General Assembly document A/AC.113/47, October 16, 1964, p. 4): "The United Nations operations in the Middle East and the Congo were not undertaken in pursuance of binding decisions under Chapter VII of the Charter. Hence, the recommendations of the Council and the Assembly in these matters bind only those States which have accepted them."

2. United Nations Charter, Article 35.2.

3. Article 25 reads as follows: "The Members of the United Nations agree to accept and carry out the decisions of the Security Council in accordance with the present Charter."

4. Regarding Security Council decisions which might be recommendations, see United Nations Charter, Articles 36, 37, 38.

5. South Africa and the General Assembly's consideration of aparthied.

6. At the United Nations Conference on Trade and Development in 1964, "the 75" became the appellation of the collectivity of less developed countries which tended to work together. My choice of the figure 75 in the text is an allusion to this development at the Conference. The number later rose to 77.

7. United Nations Charter, Article 28.1.

8. The great powers seem about to readjust the negotiating balance in the major United Nations organs by turning increasingly to the Security Council—which was busier in 1964 than in any one of the preceding 15 years. There appears to be some apprehension that at times the "seventy-seven" could lead the General Assembly to adopt unrealistic positions. Inherent in the issue of United Nations finances is also the important question of the appropriate roles of the Security Council and the General Assembly.

9. All the items mentioned in this sentence are taken from the agenda of the 18th Session of the General Assembly, and are cited illustratively.

10. On this occasion I jokingly said to Dag Hammarskjöld that he had elevated the Secretary-Generalship of the United Nations to the category of the world's six leading powers!

11. Security Council document S/4078, August 5, 1958. Actually, the Council adopted a United States resolution calling for an Assembly session.

12. Resolution 1237 (ES-III), adopted unanimously by the Third Emergency Special Session of the General Assembly on August 21, 1958.

13. General Assembly Resolution 1632 (XVI), October 27, 1961.

14. General Assembly Resolution 1762 (XVIII), adopted on November 6, 1962 by a vote of 75 in favor, none against, and 21 abstentions.

15. United Nations Charter, Article 26.   16. *Ibid.,* Article 11.

17. General Assembly Resolution 1 (I), January 24, 1946.

18. General Assembly Resolution 41 (I), December 14, 1964.

19. General Assembly Resolution 191 (III), November 4, 1948.

20. General Assembly Resolution 192 (III), November 19, 1948.

21. General Assembly Resolution 300 (IV), December, 5, 1949.

22. General Assembly Resolution 496 (V), December 13, 1950.

23. General Assembly Resolution 808 (IX), November 4, 1954.

24. *Ibid.,* conclusion of Operative Paragraph 1.

25. India, Australia, and the Philippines.

26. Note Verbale of June 13, 1956 from the Indian Representative (the author) to the Chairman of the Disarmament Commission. Document DC/95 in Disarmament Commission Official Records: Supplement for January to December 1956, p. 51.

27. General Assembly Resolution 1150 (XII), November 19, 1957.

28. General Assembly Resolution 1252 (XIII), November 4, 1958, Part D. The first time that this greatly enlarged Disarmament Commission met to debate the substance of disarmament was in April 1965. This meeting

was, in a limited sense, a substitute for the 19th Session of the General Assembly which had proved to be abortive.

29. General Assembly Resolution 1722 (XVI), December 20, 1961.

30. United Nations Charter, Article 24.1.

31. General Assembly document A/2694, and statement of Foreign Minister Luns to the General Assembly on September 24, 1954, A/PV.477.

32. Agreement between the Republic of Indonesia and the Kingdom of the Netherlands concerning West New Guinea (West Irian).

33. *Ibid.*   34. United Nations Charter, Article 1.4.

35. Security Council Resolution 106 (1955), March 29, 1955. On the very next day the Council adopted another unanimous resolution requesting the Chief of Staff of the United Nations Truce Supervision Organization to consult with the parties concerned.

36. Security Council Resolution 108 (1955), September 8, 1955.

37. Security Council document S/3538, January 19, 1956.

38. Security Council document S/3575, April 4, 1956.

39. Security Council document S/3605, June 4, 1956.

40. Security Council Official Records, 688th Meeting, paragraph 99, January 13, 1955.

41. Security Council document S/2298, Rev. 1.

42. Security Council document S/5575, March 4, 1964.

43. Security Council document S/5603, March 13, 1964.

44. Security Council document S/5866, Rev. 1.

45. Verbatim report of Conference prepared by the United States delegation, USVR/1, May 16, 1961, pp. 14–15.

46. *Ibid.,* May 16, 1961, p. 36. (Italics added)

47. *Ibid.,* July 21, 1962, p. 1.

48. United Kingdom delegation verbatim record, July 21, 1962, p. 37.

49. *Ibid.,* July 21, 1962, p. 8.

50. Statement of Ambassador João Carlos Muniz of Brazil at the First Plenary Meeting of the Conference on the Statute. International Atomic Energy Agency document IAEA/CS/OR.1, September 20, 1956, p. 96.

51. Document IAEA/CS/OR.4, p. 8.

52. Document IAEA/CS/OR.5, September 25, 1956, p. 21.

53. Document IAEA/CS/OR.3, September 24, 1956, p. 6.

54. Document IAEA/CS/OR.1, September 28, 1956, p. 2.

55. At Oxford, when S. H. Beer and I were being tutored in political theory by A. D. Lindsay, then Master of Balliol, he gave us an illustration which also throws some light on the developments to which I have just been referring. Lindsay told us that at that time (1933) he had been a member of the Hebdomadal Council of Oxford University for seventeen years. He went on to say that the Council's rules of procedure prescribed that decisions would be taken by a majority vote. Lindsay then said that in the seventeen years of his membership many issues of significance to the University had arisen and had been fully debated,

but in not a single case had a vote been taken. Without exception, in all cases, a consensus had emerged and the general agreement had made it unnecessary to take a vote. A council consisting of selected Heads of the Oxford colleges might be expected to be able to arrive at a common viewpoint as one of the most intellectually elite bodies in the world; moreover, the problems considered, in spite of the proudly guarded privileges and jurisdictions of the individual foundations, which are the colleges at Oxford, are not as tension-creating as international issues! Nevertheless, the point comes through that when a small group of persons make an effort to be reasonable, even stubborn difficulties tend to become tractable and unanimity emerges.

56. *New York Times,* July 27, 1964.   57. *Ibid.,* August 12, 1964.

58. Text of Agreement is in Iraq Ministry of Foreign Affairs Publications on Kuwait. *The Truth about Kuwait,* July 1961, No. 1, p. 8.

59. *Ibid.,* p. 14.   60. *Ibid.,* p. 22

Chapter 9. The Optimum Scope

1. United Nations Charter, Article 2.3.   2. *Ibid.,* Article 2.4.

3. *New York Times,* August 10, 1964.   4. *Ibid.*   5. *Ibid.*

6. Security Council document S/5866/Rev. 1, August 9, 1964.

7. Security Council document S/PV.1143, August 11, 1964, p. 121.

8. *Ibid.,* pp. 121–22.   9. *New York Times,* August 13, 1964.

10. United Nations Charter, Article 35.2.

11. The Presdent's request will be found in Security Council document S/PV.1141, August 7, 1964, pp. 18–20.

12. Security Council document S/5849. This was a brief letter from Ambassador Adlai Stevenson requesting the President of the Security Council to consider urgently "the serious situation created by deliberate attacks of the Hanoi Regime on the United States naval vessels in international waters."

13. Countries which were represented at the 1954 Geneva Conference were: Cambodia, the Democratic Republic of Vietnam, France, Laos, the People's Republic of China, the State of Vietnam, the U.S.S.R., the United Kingdom, and the United States (in all, nine countries). However, at the Laos Conference in 1961–62, five additional countries were invited: Burma, Canada, India, Poland, and Thailand.

14. *New York Times,* August 12, 1964.

15. Report in Security Council document S/5832, July 27, 1964.

16. Ambassade de France, Service de Presse et d'Information, New York. Speeches and Press Conferences, No. 208, July 23, 1964.

17. *New York Times* transcript of President's news conference, July 25, 1964.

18. United Nations Security Council document S/PV.1141, August 7, 1964, pp. 47–50.

19. *Ibid.,* p. 57.

20. United Nations Press Service Note to Correspondents. No. 2951, July 8, 1964, pp. 5–6.

21. General Assembly Official Records, 10th Session, General Committee, 103rd meeting, September 22, 1955.

22. General Assembly Official Records, 10th Session, 530th Plenary Meeting, September 30, 1955, A/PV.530, p. 194.

23. Security Council Official Records, 120th Meeting, October 4, 1962, S/PV.1020, pp. 15–17.

24. Security Council document S/PV.117, May 18, 1964, p. 6.

25. These clashes have taken place in spite of the presence of a United Nations group to try to lessen the chances of violation of the ceasefire.

26. *New York Times,* August 11, 1962, p. 2.

27. A short, sharp war in fact resulted in August and September, 1965.

Chapter 10. Three Factors Which Impede Negotiation

1. Ambassade de France, Service de Presse et d'Information, New York. Speeches and Press Conferences, No. 208, July 23, 1964.

2. *New York Times,* July 6, 1964.   3. *Ibid.,* July 7, 1964.

4. *Ibid.,* July 11, 1964.   5. *Ibid.,* July 22, 1964.   6. *Ibid.*

7. *Ibid.,* July 23, 1964.

8. Security Council document S/PV.1118, May 19, 1964, pp. 19–20.

9. United Nations document S/PV.1118, May 17, 1964, p. 26.

10. *Ibid.,* p. 27.

11. Indiagram No. 199, November 24, 1964, Embassy of India, Washington, D.C.

12. Jawaharlal Nehru, *India's Foreign Policy: Selected Speeches, September 1946–April 1961* (New Delhi, Government of India Publications Division, 1961), pp. 373–74.

13. USACDA, *Documents on Disarmament, 1962,* p. 969.

14. Security Council document S/PV.1022, October 23, 1962, p. 13.

15. USACDA, *Documents on Disarmament, 1962,* p. 1239. (Italics added)

16. USACDA, *Documents on Disarmament, 1962,* p. 971. (Italics added)

17. Security Council document S/PV.1142, August 8, 1964, pp. 39–40.

18. *Ibid.,* p. 41.   19. *New York Times,* June 24, 1964.

20. *Ibid.,* August 7, 1964. (They did not say which state constitutes the teeth!)

21. *Ibid.,* August 18, 1964.   22. *Ibid.,* August 7, 1964.

23. I say this on the basis of several conversations with the Marshal— a genial and yet blustering person, sensitive to the arts (a writer of Chinese verse) but ruthless. I also have in mind the brief but intensive

negotiation which Krishna Menon and I had with him and Chang Han Fu in July 1962 on the Sino-Indian border situation, during which there was in evidence an alarming readiness to substitute for discussion a resort to force. Apparently this characteristic persists—at least in words—when the Marshal talks of an infinitely more powerful antagonist than India.

24. Winston Churchill, *The Hinge of Fate* (Boston, Houghton Mifflin, 1950; New York, Bantam Books, 1962), Bantam edition p. 593.

25. *Ibid.*

26. Winston Churchill, *Closing the Ring* (Boston, Houghton Mifflin, 1951; New York, Bantam Books, 1962), Bantam edition p. 151. (Quoted by permission of Houghton Mifflin Company)

27. *Ibid.*, p. 541.   28. *New York Times,* June 13, 1964.

29. Tenth Press Conference of General de Gaulle as President of the French Republic, July 23, 1964. Ambassade de France, Service de Presse et d'Information, New York, Issue No. 208.

30. *Ibid.*

31. See *supra,* page 77, regarding John Foster Dulles' effort to get me to withdraw India's opposition to the first draft resolution.

32. Jawaharlal Nehru, *India's Foreign Policy, Selected Speeches, September 1946–April 1961,* pp. 441–43.

Chapter 11. Vital Interests

1. Harold Nicolson, *Diplomacy* (New York and London, Oxford University Press, 1964), 3rd edition, Chapter 2.

2. Quotations from United Nations Security Council Official Record Supplement for November 1948, document S-1100, Interim Report of the United Nations Commission for India and Pakistan.

3. Security Council document S/PV.763, January 23, 1959, p. 22.

4. Department of State, *Documents on Disarmament, 1945–59,* p. 685.

5. *Ibid.*, p. 686.   6. *New York Times,* July 13, 1962.

7. *New York Times,* January 12, 1962.

8. *The Soviet Stand on Disarmament* (Documents on Current History, No. 21. New York, Crosscurrents Press, 1961). pp. 7–8.

9. *New York Times,* August 1, 1964.

10. USACDA, *Documents on Disarmament, 1961,* p. 652.

11. USACDA, *Documents on Disarmament, 1962,* p. 972.

12. USACDA, *Documents on Disarmament, 1962,* p. 646. As is common knowledge, the sucessors in power of Khrushchev have repeatedly maintained that they will continue to follow policies of coexistence and peaceful competition with the non-Communist world.

13. United Nations General Assembly Official Records, 12th Session, First Committee, 928th Meeting, December 9, 1957, A/C.L/S.R.928, pp. 353–54.

14. *Ibid.*, paragraph 17, p. 356. The mention of the Aaland Islands takes up a previous remark of Selim Sarper, in which he stated that in spite of an overwhelming vote in a plebescite among the inhabitants to join Sweden, the League of Nations had decided that the Islands should form part of Finland because of historical, geographical, and strategic reasons.

15. *New York Times,* August 15, 1964.

16. General Assembly document A/PV.733, August 13, 1958, p. 8.

17. General Assembly Resolution 1237 (ES-III), August 28, 1958.

18. And of quickly arresting conflict when it did occur in 1965.

Chapter 12. Third-Party Intrusions

1. For example, Malaysia's negotiating position in regard to Indonesia has undoubtedly been strengthened by the support it has received from the United Kingdom, Australia, New Zealand, and some other Commonwealth members.

2. Permanent Mission of the Republic of Indonesia to the United Nations, Release No. 80, June 26, 1964.

3. Her Majesty's Stationery Office, London, Command Paper 263, p. 2.

4. Permanent Mission of Indonesia to the United Nations, Release No. 80, June 26. 1964, p. 3.

5. *New York Times,* May 24, 1965.   6. *Ibid.*

7. Her Majesty's Stationery Office, London, Command Paper 1518.

8. *Christian Science Monitor,* June 26, 1961.

9. *Manchester Guardian,* June 30, 1961.

10. London *Times,* July 3, 1961.

11. British Information Service Reference and Library Division, New York. T. 16, July 6, 1961.

12. *Manchester Guardian,* August 18, 1961.

13. *Yearbook of the United Nations, 1961* (New York, Columbia University Press in cooperation with the United Nations, 1963), p. 149.

14. Security Council, 1034th Meeting.

15. This conclusion is also borne out by the events of the Lebanese crisis of 1958, when Lebanon regained its standing in the region by moving toward the other Arab states. This stabilized its international (and internal) position more than any external support.

16. *Yearbook of the United Nations, 1957,* pp. 56–58.

17. *Yearbook of the United Nations, 1960,* pp. 194–95.

18. *Yearbook of the United Nations, 1961,* pp. 148–52.

19. Resolution 1948 (XVIII) of December 11, 1963. The United Kingdom alone voted against this resolution. Seven countries, including the United States, abstained. However, little further information has been collected, and since the 19th Session of the Assembly proved to be abortive the issue was not considered in 1964–65.

20. Security Council document S/5298, April 29, 1963.

21. *Ibid.*, p. 2. 22. *Ibid.*, p. 3.

23. Security Council document S/5325, June 7, 1963.

24. Security Council document, S/5331, June 11, 1963.

25. See *Le Monde,* August 19, 1964.

26. *Public Papers of the Presidents of the United States: Dwight D. Eisenhower, 1954* (Washington, D.C., Office of the Federal Registrar, National Archives and Records Service, 1961), pp. 382–83.

27. Foreign Minister Chen Yi's statement to the International Conference on Laos, May 16, 1961, taken from the United States delegation's transcript of the meeting.

Chapter 13. Alliances of Powerful States

1. Arnold J. Toynbee, *A Study of History,* abridgment by D. C. Somervell (New York, Oxford University Press, 1957), Vol. II, p. 7.

2. *New York Times,* June 9, 1959. 3. *Ibid.*, March 26, 1959.

4. *Ibid.*, June 18, 1959. 5. *Ibid.*, June 28, 1962.

6. *Ibid.*, January 14, 1963.

7. Tenth Press Conference held by General de Gaulle, July 23, 1964. Text from Ambassade de France, Service de Presse et d'Information, New York. Release No. 208, July 23, 1964.

8. In *Foreign Affairs,* July 1960 (p. 555) President Ayub Khan stated: "Moreover in the context of present day world politics Pakistan has openly and unequivocally cast its lot with the West, and unlike several other countries around us, we have shut ourselves off almost completely from the possibility of any major assistance from the Communist bloc. We do not believe in hunting with the hound and running with the hare. We wish to follow, and are following, a clear and unambiguous path."

9. *New York Times,* May 11, 1962. 10. *Ibid.*

11. *Ibid.*, July 18, 1963. 12. London *Times,* July 18, 1963.

13. *New York Times,* April 27, 1964.

14. *Ibid.*, March 25, 1962. 15. *Ibid.*, March 26, 1962.

16. *Ibid.*, April 21, 1962.

17. *Ibid.*, November 2, 1962. 18. *Ibid.*

19. *Ibid.*, September 30, 1963.

Chapter 14. Deterrent Force

1. This does not mean that circumstances could not arise in which hostilities would necessarily be precluded. Some diplomats who saw the Caribbean crisis of 1962 at close quarters thought that at the height of the crisis the world was near catastrophe.

2. See *supra,* page 183.

3. Jawaharlal Nehru, *India's Foreign Policy: Selected Speeches, September 1946–April 1961,* p. 65.

4. Protocol No. III, Annex I. See Committee on Foreign Relations, U. S. Senate, *Documents on Germany, 1944–59,* May 8, 1959, p. 132.

5. *Ibid.,* p. 211.   6. *New York Times,* March 12, 1960.

7. Eighteen-Nation Committee on Disarmament document ENDC/PV.207, August 13, 1964.

8. Text as published by Reuters News Agency on August 4, 1962.

9. Text distributed by Ambassade de France, Service de Presse et d'Information, New York.

10. *Ibid.*

11. USACDA, *Documents on Disarmament, 1962,* p. 1276.

12. U.S. Department of State, *Documents of Disarmament, 1960,* p. 51.

13. USACDA, *Documents on Disarmament, 1961,* p. 18.

14. *Ibid.,* p. 41.   15. *Ibid.,* p. 66.

16. *New York Times,* May 10, 1964.

17. U.S. Department of State, *Documents on Disarmament, 1960,* pp. 13–14.

18. *Ibid.,* p. 19.   19. *Ibid.,* p. 67.

20. USACDA, *Documents on Disarmament, 1961,* pp. 532–34.

21. *New York Times,* April 4, 1964. After the change in Soviet leadership there has been much less criticism of Chinese nuclear policy. The Chinese tests have not been condemned. However, in responding to the Chinese proposal for a world conference on disarmament (the proposal was made on October 17, 1964, but the Soviet reply did not issue till December 28, 1964), the Soviets while supporting the Chinese proposal stated that they also favored steps to "limit" or "slow down" the nuclear arms race. This could have been directed partly against the Chinese nuclear effort.

22. USACDA, *Documents on Disarmament, 1961,* p. 237.

23. *Ibid.,* p. 16.   24. *New York Times,* September 23, 1963.

25. "Our Armed Forces Combat Laws and Ordnances are Products of Mao Tse-tung's Thinking," *Bulletin of Activities* (*Kung Tso T'ung Hsun*), Peking August 1, 1961.

26. *Chinese People's Daily* (*Jen-min Jih-pao*), Peking, July 29, 1963.

27. *Chinese People's Daily,* July 26, 1963.

28. U.S. Department of State, *Documents on Disarmament, 1960,* pp. 14–15.

Chapter 15. Economic Weakness

1. A comparison between the aid figures for India, which has remained nonaligned, and the aid figures for Pakistan, which is aligned with the West, will show this difference. The total commitments of economic aid for development programs plus agricultural commodity aid and technical assist-

ance during the period 1960–65 amounted to $3 per capita for India and $8 per capita for Pakistan. (Figures based on releases from the International Bank for Reconstruction and Development)

2. Communiqué of the Conference of Afro-Asian Countries, issued at Bandung, April 24, 1955. Text in *American Foreign Policy, 1950–55, Basic Documents* (Washington, D.C., Department of State Publication 6446), Vol. II, pp. 2344–52.

3. *Ibid.* (Italics added)   4. *Ibid.* (Italics added)

5. General Assembly Resolution 400 (V), November 20, 1950.

6. General Assembly Resolution 520 (VI), January 12, 1952.

7. *Ibid.*   8. *Ibid.*   9. *Ibid.*

10. General Assembly Resolution 724 (VIII), December 7, 1953.

11. General Assembly Official Records, 10th Session, Supp. No. 17 (A/2906).

12. General Assembly Resolution 923 (X), December 9, 1955.

13. *Yearbook of the United Nations, 1956,* p. 166.

14. General Assembly Second Committee Records, 408th Meeting, January 2, 1957, A/C.2/SR.408.

15. *Ibid.,* 409th Meeting, January 4, 1957, A/C.2/SR.409.

16. *Yearbook of the United Nations, 1956,* p. 166.

17. General Assembly Resolution 1030 (XI), February 26, 1957.

18. *Yearbook of the United Nations, 1957,* p. 141.

19. General Assembly Resolution 1219 (XII), December 14, 1957.

20. *Ibid.*

21. For these facts see United Nations publication entitled *Target: an Expanding World Economy,* a United Nations Special Fund Report, 1963.

22. *Yearbook of the United Nations, 1962,* p. 247.

23. For text of Declaration see USCDA, *Documents on Disarmament, 1961,* pp. 375–83.

24. Jawaharlal Nehru, *India's Foreign Policy,* p. 257.

25. *New York Times,* June 25, 1961.

26. *Manchester Guardian,* June 26, 1961.

27. *New York Times,* July 20, 1963.

28. For text see Boutros Boutros-Ghali, *The Addis Ababa Charter,* International Conciliation publication 546, January 1964 (New York, Carnegie Endowment for International Peace), pp. 53–62. (Especially Article II, paragraph 2b)

29. Report of the United Nation's Conference on the Application of Science and Technology for the Benefit of the Less Developed Areas, Vol. I—*World of Opportunity* (New York, United Nations, 1963), p. 117.

30. *Ibid.,* p. 217.

31. Economic and Social Council document E/Conf. 46/C.4/SR.4, p. 9.

32. *Ibid.,* p. 7.

33. Economic and Social Council document E/Conf.46/C.4/SR.7, May 8, 1964, p. 3.

34. Economic and Social Council document E/Conf.46/C.4/SR.8, May 14, 1964, p. 14.

35. *New York Times,* September 17, 1955.   36. *Ibid.*

37. In describing them as such, I am adhering to the provisions of General Asembly Resolution 1542 (XV) of December 15, 1960, which considered that these territories were Non–Self-Governing within the meaning of Chapter XI of the Charter. However, in the Constitution of Portugal of 1951 these territories, which till then had been listed as colonies, were redesignated as provinces in Overseas Portugal.

38. General Assembly document A/5446/Add.1, July 17, 1963, p. 27.

39. General Assembly, 17th Session Annexes, document A/5238, October 8, 1962, p. 134.

40. *Ibid.,* p. 141.

41. James Duffy, "Portugal in Africa," *Foreign Affairs,* April 1961, p. 481.

42. James Duffy, "Portugal's Colonies in Africa," *Foreign Policy Bulletin* (New York, World Affairs Center, Foreign Policy Association), Vol. XL, No. 12, March 1, 1961.

43. P. J. Honey, ed., *North Vietnam Today* (New York, Praeger, 1962), pp. 132–33.

44. *New York Times,* September 29, 1963.

45. Reuters dispatch, Singapore, October 13, 1963.

46. *New York Times,* October 1, 1963.

Chapter 16. Economic Development and International Trade

1. General Assembly Resolution 724A (VIII), December 7, 1953.

2. ECOSOC Resolution 982 (XXXVI), August 2, 1963.

3. General Assembly Resolution 1837 (XVII) of December 18, 1962 and Resolution 1931 (XVIII) of December 11, 1963. Both these resolutions are entitled "Conversion to Peaceful Needs of the Resources Released by Disarmament."

4. General Assembly Resolution 1931 (XVIII), December 11, 1963, para. 3.

5. General Assembly Resolution 1838 (XVII), December 18, 1962.

6. *Ibid.,* paragraph 8.   7. *Ibid.,* paragraph 1.

8. Jawaharlal Nehru, *India's Foreign Policy,* p. 598.

9. *The Charter* (Cairo, U.A.R. Information Department), pp. 101, 103.

10. Jawaharlal Nehru, *India's Foreign Policy,* pp. 568–69.

11. *New York Times,* April 25, 1955.

12. USACDA, *Documents on Disarmament, 1961,* p. 381.

13. Eighteen-Nation Disarmament Committee document ENDC/PV.2, March 15, 1962.

14. *Ibid.*

15. USACDA, *Documents on Disarmament, 1962,* pp. 28–29.

16. *Ibid.,* p. 156.

17. Winston S. Churchill, *The Grand Alliance* (Boston, Houghton Mifflin, 1950; New York, Bantam Books, 1962), Bantam edition pp. 366–68.

18. Anthony Eden, *Full Circle* (Boston, Houghton Mifflin, 1960), pp. 586–87.

19. *Ibid.,* p. 592.   20. *Ibid.,* pp. 593–94.

21. General Assembly Official Records, 11th Session, A/PV.590, p. 232.

22. General Assembly Official Records, 11th Session, A/PV.593, p. 281.

23. General Assembly Official Records, 11th Session, A/PV.594, November 24, 1956, p. 296.

24. *Ibid.*

25. General Assembly Official Records, 11the Session, A/PV.601, November 29, 1956, p. 412.

26. Resolution 1785 (XVII) regarding the United Nations Conference on Trade and Development, December 8, 1962.

27. *Ibid.*   28. Resolution 1897 (XVIII), November 11, 1963.

29. Paragraph 7 of the Annex attached to Resolution 1897 (XVIII), November 11, 1963.

30. Economic and Social Council document E/CONF. 46/C.2/SR.5, April 23, 1964, p. 2.

31. Final Act, Part I, Section III, paragraphs 17 and 21.

32. *Public Papers of the Presidents of the United States: Dwight D. Eisenhower, 1954.*

33. House of Commons Official Report (London, HMSO, June 17, 1964), Vol. DCXCVI, No. 123, Column 1322.

34. See Drew Middleton in the *New York Times,* September 16, 1964.

35. *New York Times,* September 8, 1964.   36. *Ibid.*

37. New York *Daily News,* September 9, 1964.   38. *Ibid.*

39. *New York Times,* September 16, 1964.

40. *Ibid.,* January 1, 1964.   41. *Ibid.* September 16, 1964.

42. *Ibid.,* March 8, 1963.   43. *Ibid.,* November 11, 1963.

Chapter 17. Two Underlying Inhibitory Factors

1. U.S. Department of State, *Documents on Disarmament, 1945–59,* p. 481.

2. *Ibid.,* p. 493.

3. President Kennedy's radio and television address, June 6, 1961; see USACDA, *Documents on Disarmament, 1961,* p. 170.

4. *New York Times,* June 12, 1961.   5. *Ibid.*

6. *Deadline Data on World Affairs,* Deadline Data, Inc., New York, 1962.

7. *Ibid.*

8. U.S. Senate Committee on Foreign Relations, *Documents on Germany 1944–59*, p. 149.

9. *Deadline Data on World Affairs*, Deadline Data, Inc., New York, 1962.

10. *Ibid.*	11. *Ibid.*

12. Quoted in the Parliament of India on August 13, 1963 by the late Prime Minister Nehru. See Indiagram No. 155, August 13, 1963, Embassy of India, Washington, D.C.

13. *News and Views*, issued by the Permanent Mission of Indonesia to the United Nations, New York, September 22, 1964, No. 115, p. 7.

14. Statement of Adlai Stevenson in the Security Council on May 21, 1964, document S/PV.1119, pp. 23–25. Mr. Stevenson was stating the charge made, but, of course, not admitting its correctness.

15. *New York Times*, October 7, 1964.

16. *New York Times*, October 2, 1964.	17. *Ibid.*	18. *Ibid.*

19. *New York Times*, October 10, 1964.

20. *New York Times*, March 20, 1965.	21. *Ibid.*, May 11, 1965.

22. *Ibid.*, May 24, 1965.	23. *Ibid.*, May 25, 1965.

24. Documents Supplement to *New Times*, No. 50, 1960, p. 2.

25. For text of Chinese letter see the *Washington Post*, March 15, 1963.

26. *New York Times*, International Edition, July 5, 1963.

27. *Peoples of the World Unite, for the Complete, Thorough, Total and Resolute Prohibition and Destruction of Nuclear Weapons* (Peking, Foreign Languages Press, 1963), p. 73.

28. *News and Views*, issued by the Permanent Mission of Indonesia to the United Nations, New York, September 24, 1964, No. 118, p. 7.

29. *Ibid.*, p. 9.	30. *Ibid.*, October 6, 1964, No. 124.

31. *Ibid.*, pp. 7–8.

32. N. S. Khrushchev, *The Revolutionary Working-Class and Communist Movement* (Moscow, Foreign Languages Publishing House, 1963), p. 11.

33. *Foreign Affairs*, October 1959, p. 5.

34. For text see *New York Times*, October 20, 1964.

Chapter 18. Effects of Previous Power Status

1. This calculation excludes, of course, areas which were not colonies but over which a considerable degree of influence was exercised by the colonial powers. Such spheres of influence included large parts of China.

2. Jawaharlal Nehru, *India's Foreign Policy*, p. 571.

3. *Ibid.*, p. 143.

4. Verbatim record as prepared by the United Kingdom delegation to the International Conference on Laos, July 21, 1962, p. 7.

5. *Ibid.*

6. The Committee was originally established by United Nations General Assembly Resolution 1654 (XVI) dated November 27, 1961.

7. United Nations General Assembly document A/AC.109/L.128, June 17, 1964, pp. 7, 9, 16.

8. *Ibid.*, p. 17.   9. Security Council Resolution 202.

10. Security Council document S/PV.1202, May 6, 1955, pp. 52–53.

11. House of Commons Official Report (London, HMSO, June 17, 1964), Vol. DCXCVI, No. 123, Column 1305.

12. *Ibid.*, Columns 1308, 1312.

13. General Assembly document A/PV.477, September 24, 1956, p. 43.

14. See statement of Ambassador Sudjarwo of Indonesia in the First Committee of the General Assembly on November 23, 1954, A/C.1/SR.726, p. 390.

15. This agreement was taken note of by the General Assembly in its Resolution 1752 (XVII) on September 21, 1962, the draft resolution having been sponsored jointly by Indonesia and the Netherlands.

16. Text supplied by the Permanent Mission of the Netherlands to the United Nations, New York.

17. U.S. Department of State, *American Foreign Policy, 1950–55, Basic Documents,* Vol. II, p. 1929.

18. *Ibid.*, p. 1945.

19. U.S. Department of State, *Documents on Disarmament 1945–59,* p. 181.

20. *Ibid.*, p. 182.   21. *Ibid.*, p. 276.   22. *Ibid.*, p. 441.

23. *Ibid.*, p. 686.   24. *Ibid.*, p. 687.

25. As Ambassador of India to Austria I was privileged to be present at several of the Austrian Government functions for Prime Minister Khrushchev and his party.

26. *Foreign Affairs,* October 1959, p. 3.   27. *Ibid.*

28. *Ibid.*, p. 5.

29. Supplement to *New Times,* No. 50, 1960, pp. 8, 9, and 14.

30. USACDA, *Documents on Disarmament, 1962,* p. 646.

31. Quotations from text in John F. Kennedy, *The Burden and the Glory,* edited by Allan Nevins (New York, Harper & Row, 1964), pp. 55–57. It is interesting and relevant that Allan Nevins refers in a footnote on p. 53 to the relaxed and amiable meeting between Khrushchev, Harriman, and Lord Halisham (Quentin Hogg), on July 15, 1963 in Moscow. Allan Nevins' comment is, "It seemed evident that Russia was taking a new attitude."

32. The first agreement was the direct communications line between Washington and Moscow.

33. John F. Kennedy, *The Burden and the Glory,* p. 61.

34. *Ibid.*, p. 68.   35. *Ibid.*, p. 72.

36. Letter from President Kennedy to Premier Khrushchev, February 5, 1962, in Committee on Foreign Relations, U.S. Senate, *United States Foreign Policy Compilation of Studies,* Vol. I, pp. 61–63.

37. Eighteen-Nation Committee on Disarmament document ENDC/ PV.35, May 11, 1962, p. 15.

38. Cited from Eighteen-Nation Committee on Disarmament document ENDC/PV.33, May 8, 1962, p. 29.

39. Eighteen-Nation Committee on Disarmament document ENDC-PV.35, May 11, 1962, p. 40.

40. *Ibid.*, pp. 60–62.

41. U.S. Department of State, *Documents on Disarmament, 1960,* p. 120: Address of the Vice President of All-China Federation of Trade Unions (Ch'ang-Sheng Liu), June 8, 1960.

42. U.S. Department of State, *American Foreign Policy, 1950–55, Basic Documents,* Vol. II, p. 2377.

43. I make this remark not to disparage the Chinese delegation. Perhaps the isolation of China contributes to its inflexibility in negotiation. However, my statement is a sober appraisal of China's position at the Conference. I do not think its objectiveness is affected in any extent by events between China and India or by my personal friendship with Deputy Foreign Minister Chang Han Fu and his colleagues, with whom I negotiated for almost 14 months at the Conference.

44. From the United States delegation's verbatim record of the Conference, USVR/25, pp. 21–23.

45. *New York Times,* April 2, 1964.   46. *Ibid.*

47. Committee on Foreign Relations, U.S. Senate, *United States Foreign Policy, Compilation of Studies,* p. 1309.

Chapter 19. Pluralistic and Single Ideology Societies

1. General Assembly Resolution 1148 (XII), November 14. 1957.

2. U.S. Congressional Record, February 4, 1958.

3. A little later at the Geneva Conference, Delegate William C. Foster of USACDA announced that the United States would reduce its demand to seven inspections per year.

4. In my capacity as the delegate of India to the Disarmament Conference.

5. Hearings Before the Committee on Armed Services, United States Senate, 88th Congress, 1963. p. 8.

6. U.S. 88th Congress, First Session, Executive Report No. 3, September 3, 1963.

7. *New York Times,* April 4, 1964.   8. *Ibid.,* September 8, 1964.

9. *Ibid.,* August 11, 1964.   10. *Le Monde,* September 17, 1964.

11. Many years later, when Molotov came to Vienna as the Deputy Governor of the Soviet Union on the Board of the International Atomic Energy Agency, I was the Governor on the Board for India. Quite frequently, Mr. Molotov called to see me. On one of these occasions I mentioned the above incident to him. Seemingly much more relaxed in his less exalted position, Mr. Molotov at least greeted my recollection with a pleasant smile—but with no elucidation.

12. John Wilson Lewis, *Major Doctrines of Communist China* (New York, Norton, 1964), pp. 228–29.

13. *New York Times,* International Edition, July 5, 1963.

14. *Ibid.*   15. *Ibid.*   16. *Ibid.*

17. USACDA, *Documents on Disarmament, 1962,* p. 653.

18. *New York Times,* International Edition, July 5, 1963.

19. His first statement at the Laos Conference, dated May 16, 1961: "The military personnel of the United States and of the other countries which are interfering in Laos with United States support must be withdrawn, and the remnant Kuomintang troops in Laos must be disarmed and sent out of Laos."

20. From translation of text of Chinese speech included in the verbatim record prepared by the United States delegation.

21. *Ibid.,* June 26, 1961.   22. *Ibid.*   23. *Ibid.*

24. See, in regard to Laos, *infra,* pp. 283–84.

25. *New York Times,* February 7, 1964.   26. *Ibid.*

27. *New York Times,* August 7, 1964.

Chapter 20. Single Ideologies at the Negotiating Table

1. Winston S. Churchill, *Triumph and Tragedy* (Boston, Houghton Mifflin, 1953; New York, Bantam Books, 1962), Bantam edition p. 197. (Quoted by permission of Houghton Mifflin Company)

2. *Ibid.,* pp. 361–62.   3. *Ibid.,* p. 362.

4. *Peking Review,* February 10, 1961.

5. From the unpublished record of the Conference as kept by the United States delegation.

6. *Peking Review,* October 4, 1961.

7. *Peking Review,* July 27, 1962.

8. *Chinese People's Daily,* February 1, 1960.

9. *Peking Review,* January 26, 1960.   10. *Ibid.*

11. See *supra,* pp. 273–74.

12. *Peking Review,* October 22, 1965, p. 29.

13. *New York Times,* October 17 and 19, 1964.

14. See *supra,* pp. 63–64.

Chapter 21. Some Minimal Requirements

1. General Assembly Resolutions 1573 (XV), December 19, 1960; and 1724 (XVI), December 20, 1961.

2. General Assembly Resolution 1378 (XIV), November 20, 1959.

3. USACDA, *Documents on Disarmament, 1961,* p. 441.

4. See U.S. Department of State, *Documents on Disarmament, 1960,* pp. 79–80, 80–81.

5. USACDA, *Documents on Disarmament, 1961,* p. 441.

6. *Ibid.,* p. 440.   7. *Ibid.,* p. 441.   8. *Ibid.*   9. *Ibid.*

10. *Ibid.*   11. *Ibid.*

12. General Assembly documents A/C.1/L.168 and A/C.1/L.170.

13. General Assembly document A/C.1/L.169.

14. General Assembly document A/C.1/L.171.

15. General Assembly document A/C.1/L.172.

16. General Assembly Resolution 1013 (XI) February 26, 1957; the vote was 57 in favor, none against, and 1 abstention.

17. Draft Resolution presented by Ghana and Morocco, Security Council document S/5330, June 11, 1963.

18. *New York Times,* September 15, 1964.

19. *Ibid.,* September 27, 1964.

20. See document S/5169: Letter of the Secretary-General to the President of the Security Council dated September 21, 1962, transmitting among other documents the Agreement between the Republic of Indonesia and the Kingdom of the Netherlands concerning West New Guinea (West Irian). However, President Sukarno was reported to have stated on May 24, 1965 that a plebiscite in West Irian was no longer necessary (*New York Times,* May 25, 1965).

21. See statement of Ambassador Sudjarwo of Indonesia in the First Committee of the 9th Session of the General Assembly, November 23, 1954. Document A/C.1/SR.726, p. 390.

22. *New York Times,* December 5, 1964.

Chapter 22. Movements from Original Positions

1. USACDA, *Documents on Disarmament, 1962,* pp. 1239–42.

2. USACDA, *Documents on Disarmament, 1961,* p. 351.

3. USACDA, *Documents on Disarmament, 1962,* pp. 804–7.

4. General Assembly document A/C.2/SR.492, November 18, 1957.

5. *Ibid.,* p. 214.   6. *Ibid.,* p. 215.   7. *Ibid.*

8. General Assembly document A/C.2/SR.493, November 19, 1957, p. 219.

9. General Assembly document A/C.2/SR.495, November 25, 1957, p. 229.

10. General Assembly document A/C.2/SR.496, November 27, 1957.

11. *Ibid.,* p. 234.   12. *Ibid.,* p. 236.

13. General Assembly document A/C.2/SR.497, November 28, 1957, p. 241.

14. General Assembly document A/C.2/SR.498, November 29, 1957, p. 244.

15. General Assembly document A/C.2/SR.500, December 3, 1957.

16. U.S. Department of State, *Documents on Disarmament, 1945–59,* p. 521.

17. *Ibid.,* pp. 544–45.

18. *Ibid.,* p. 570.   19. *Ibid.,* p. 580.   20. *Ibid.*

21. Eighteen-Nation Committee on Disarmament document ENDC/56, April 18, 1962, Corr. 1, April 25, 1962, p. 30. See also USACDA, *Documents on Disarmament, 1962,* pp. 351–82.

22. Eighteen-Nation Committee on Disarmament document ENDC/ PV.56, June 14, 1962, p. 26.

23. *Ibid.,* p. 30.   24. *Ibid.*   25. *Ibid.,* p. 45.

26. Eighteen-Nation Committee on Disarmament document ENDC/ PV.82, September 7, 1962, p. 27.

27. *Ibid.,* p. 28.   28. *Ibid.,* p. 32.   29. *Ibid.,* p. 21.

30. *Ibid.,* p. 15.   31. *New York Times,* October 17, 1964.

32. *Ibid.,* October 19, 1964.

33. Eighteen-Nation Committee on Disarmament document ENDC/ PV.57, July 16, 1962, p. 21.

34. *Ibid.,* pp. 21–22.   35. *Ibid.,* pp. 25–26.   36. *Ibid.,* p. 34.

37. USACDA, *Documents on Disarmament, 1962,* p. 903.

38. Eighteen-Nation Committee on Disarmament document ENDC/ PV.56, June 14, 1962, p. 14.

39. For text of the joint statement, see USACDA, *Documents on Disarmament, 1961,* pp. 439–42.

40. *Ibid.,* p. 442.

41. Eighteen-Nation Committee on Disarmament document ENDC/ PV.55, June 13, 1962, p. 48.

42. Eighteen-Nation Committee on Disarmament document ENDC/ PV.56, June 14, 1962, p. 19.

Chapter 23. Degrees of Interest in Negotiation

1. U.S. Department of State, *American Foreign Policy, 1950–55, Basic Documents,* Vol. II, pp. 2379–80.

2. *New York Times,* November 13, 1959.

3. Security Council document S/PV.1160, October 9, 1964, p. 47.

4. *New York Times,* October 5, 1964.   5. *Ibid.,* October 18, 1964.

6. Security Council document S/PV.1160, October 9, 1964, pp. 18–20.

7. *Ibid.,* pp. 21–25.

8. Eighteen-Nation Committee on Disarmament document ENDC/ PV.217, September 17, 1964 (provl.), pp. 18–20.

9. *Ibid.,* p. 72.   10. Embassy of India, Indiagram, October 30, 1964.

Chapter 24. The Personal Factor

1. USACDA, *Documents on Disarmament, 1962,* p. 62.

2. *Ibid.,* p. 35.   3. *Ibid.,* p. 52.

4. Winston S. Churchill, *Triumph and Tragedy,* Bantam edition p. 375. (Quoted by permission of Houghton Mifflin Company)

5. *Ibid.,* p. 413.

6. This was true of Henry Cabot Lodge and of his successors, Adlai Stevenson and Arthur J. Goldberg, both members of the National Security Council.

7. *United Nations Monthly Chronicle,* May 1954, Vol. 1, No. 1, p. 83.

8. General Assembly Resolution 997 (ES-I), November 2, 1956.

9. General Assembly Resolution 999 (ES-I), November 4, 1956.

10. General Assembly Resolution 998 (ES-I), November 4, 1956.

11. General Assembly Resolution 610 (VII), December 3, 1952.

12. Eighteen-Nation Committee on Disarmament document ENDC/28, April 16, 1962. See also USACDA, *Documents on Disarmament, 1962,* pp. 334–36.

13. For text of Memorandum of Understanding Between the United States and the Soviet Union Regarding the Establishment of a Direct Communications Link, June 20, 1963, see USACDA, *Documents on Disarmament, 1963,* pp. 236–38.

14. There were other reasons, too, which militated against negotiation.

Chapter 25. Maneuverability and Flexibility

1. USACDA, *Documents on Disarmament, 1963,* p. 113.

2. U.S. Congressional Record, Vol. 109, p. 10,343.

3. *The Constitution, March 25, 1964,* U.A.R. Information Department, Cairo, p. 34.

4. I will not go into the substance of the proposals, but in my view they insured an unstated number of inspections as and when warranted, and possibly a larger number than the handful of obligatory inspections on which the United States was insistent. For the proposals themselves see Eighteen-Nation Committee on Disarmament document ENDC/28, April 16, 1962.

5. United Kingdom Parliamentary Debates, Hansard (Debate of July 28, 1954), Vol. DXXXI, Col. 504.

6. *Ibid.,* Col. 508.

7. Quoted in Dorothy Pickles, *Algeria and France* (New York, Praeger, 1963), p. 33.

8. *Ibid.,* p. 36.   9. *Le Monde,* November 10, 1964.

10. *Ibid.,* November 13, 1964.

11. *New York Times,* November 19, 1964.

12. *Ibid.,* February 20, 1962.   13. *Le Monde,* November 2, 1964.

14. *Ibid.*

15. Consisting, as of May 1965, of 21 states spread out over all the continents.

Chapter 26. Negotiation and International Law

1. The four sources are:

a. International conventions, whether general or particular, establishing rules expressly recognized by the contesting states;

b. international custom, as evidence of a general practice accepted as law;

c. the general principles of law recognized by civilized nations;

d. . . . judicial decisions and teachings of the most highly qualified publicists of the various nations, as subsidiary means for the determination of rules of law.

2. General Assembly Resolution 912 (X) II, December 3, 1955.

3. See Stage I of United States Outline, paragraph 3b under heading H, USACDA, *Documents on Disarmament, 1962,* p. 367; and Stage II, paragraph 1b under heading G, *Ibid.,* p. 374.

4. Annual Report of the Secretary-General on the Work of the Organization, 1963–64, p. 125.

5. Clarence Wilfred Jenks, *The Common Law of Mankind* (New York, Praeger, 1958).

6. United Nations Charter, Article 13.1(a).

7. For a fuller treatment of some of these issues, see my statement in Eighteen-Nation Committee on Disarmament document ENDC/PV.55, June 13, 1962, pp. 16–28.

8. See "Certain Expenses of the United Nations (Article 17, Paragraph 2 of the Charter)," Advisory Opinion of July 20, 1962: *International Court of Justice Reports of Judgments, Advisory Opinions and Orders, 1962,* p. 151.

9. Clarence Wilfred Jenks, et al., *International Law in a Changing World* (New York, Oceana Publications in cooperation with the United Nations, 1963), p. 56.

10. Paul Guggenheim, "The Birth of Autonomous International Law," in *International Law in a Changing World,* pp. 83–84.

11. *Ibid.,* p. 87.

Index